A CORNUCOPIA OF PRAIS
INSATIABLE

"Exuberant . . . hilarious . . . Greene dishes about life—and lust."
—*Entertainment Weekly*

"A steamy, bodice-ripping, lusciously lewd romp through the boudoirs and dining rooms of several continents."
—*Toronto Star*

"Serves as a reminder of how fresh and clever Ms. Greene can be."
—*Washington Post*

"An orgasmic good read. Gael Greene demonstrates her insatiable appetite for not just food, but for life in general."
—Tim Zagat, CEO, Zagat Survey

"It's subtitled Tales from a Life of Delicious Excess. And does it ever live up to that . . . Makes a reader see how far we've come in appreciation of fine food."
—*Providence Journal*

"A delicious writer . . . Greene writes wonderfully of the sensuous passions of eating and drinking."
—*Forbes*

"She offers the panoramic, important, ever-changing restaurant picture of NYC since the Fifties until now."
—*Buffalo News*

"Outrageously fun . . . provocative . . . Lively and large-spirited, this account sizzles."
—*Kirkus Reviews* (starred review)

"Passionate prose . . . Greene is a lovely writer with keen finesse."
—*Chicago Sun-Times*

more...

"I predict a runaway hit for INSATIABLE, which has all the sex (plus food) that the law will allow. I simply couldn't resist it."
—Liz Smith

"Her breathless prose is a good match for the ripening culinary revolution and the sexual tumult of 1960s and 1970s New York."
—*New Jersey Star-Ledger*

"When a book features recipes like 'Infidelity Soup' and 'Chocolate Wickedness,' you know you're in for some fun."
—*St. Petersburg Times* (FL)

"Delivers the goods on a life spent in pursuit of love and lust and foie gras . . . A priceless, invaluable history lesson, a step-by-step accounting of how we (but New York in particular) went from a nation enamored of Velveeta cheese and mushroom soup in a can to one that now treats chefs like rock stars and eating as a sensualist indulgence on par with a sticky one-night stand with a beautiful stranger."
—Jason Sheehan, *Denver Westword*

"Should whet your appetite."
—*Newsweek*

"A delicious read . . . brims with vivid and gluttonously gossipy prose."
—*Publishers Weekly*

"Gael Greene knows more about restaurants than most restaurateurs and chefs. At times I wanted to kill her. Now I'm laughing about it. I must admit this is a great book."
—Sirio Maccioni, owner, Le Cirque

"Grab your knife and fork and put on your seatbelt. Get ready for Gael Greene's real-life wild ride from tender steaks to silky sheets."
—Bobby Flay, chef/owner, Mesa Grill and Bar Americain

"Gael's life and career coincide with two notable transformations in American life, the sexual and the gastronomic revolutions. She had the inclination, talent, and sensual gifts to take an active part in both and, through her candid memoir, we become the spellbound witnesses of her achievements in the first ranks of both fronts. A significant social document, a fascinating tale told with the wit and passion that are purely Gael's."
—Marcella and Victor Hazan, coauthors of *Marcella Says . . . : Italian Cooking Wisdom from the Legendary Teacher's Master Classes, with 120 of Her Irresistible New Recipes*

"What an irreverent, Rabelaisian life my friend Gael Greene has led as a seminal American food critic. As to her sex life, I thought I was her confidante, but I had to cover my eyes!"
—Barbara Goldsmith, author of *Obsessive Genius*

INSATIABLE

TALES *from a* LIFE *of* DELICIOUS EXCESS

Gael Greene

WARNER BOOKS

NEW YORK   BOSTON

To Clay Felker for his inspired casting and unswerving faith in provocation

To Don Forst, after all these years, still buffer and champion

To Steven Richter, my bemused and game Road Food Warrior

And to the memory of delicious times with Craig Claiborne

———————————

Some of the material in the book has previously appeared elsewhere in slightly different form.

Copyright © 2006 by Gael Greene
Reading Group Guide copyright © 2007 by Hachette Book Group USA

Warner Books
Hachette Book Group USA
237 Park Avenue
New York, NY 10169
Visit our Web site at www.HachetteBookGroupUSA.com

Book design by H. Roberts Design

Printed in the United States of America

Originally published in hardcover by Warner Books.

First Trade Edition: April 2007
10   9   8   7   6   5   4   3   2   1

Warner Books and the "W" logo are trademarks of Time Warner Inc. or an affiliated company. Used under license by Hachette Book Group USA, which is not affiliated with Time Warner Inc.

The Library of Congress has cataloged the hardcover edition as follows:
Greene, Gael.
    Insatiable : tales from a life of delicious excess / Gael Greene. — 1st ed.
       p. cm.
    ISBN-13: 978-0-446-57699-4
    ISBN-10: 0-446-57699-9
  1. Greene, Gael. 2. Food writers—United States—Biography. 3. Gastronomy. I. Title.
    TX649.G74A3 2006
    641.092—dc22   2005034429

ISBN-13: 978-0-446-69510-7 (pbk.)
ISBN-10: 0-446-69510-6 (pbk.)

CONTENTS

ACKNOWLEDGMENTS

Most of *Insatiable* was written in the sanctuary of the little blue bedroom in East Hampton in the tight family embrace of the Schusters, Fran and Howard. In the lakeside cottage near Brewster with my loving friend Vicki Polon cheering me on (and bringing fruit and snacks hourly). And in an East Hampton guestroom with my longtime confidante Barbara Goldsmith closeted in her own writing room alongside. The gift from Lili Lynton of her bright and airy Parisian pied-à-terre overlooking the garden of the Picasso museum and the luxurious haven of Randy Mickelson's San Polo apartment in Venice freed me two winters in a row to write far from hometown distractions. Maurie and Hermine Nessin twice gave us August in their Aspen home.

Brilliant *New York* editors along the way—Deborah Harkins, Quita McMath, Phoebe Eaton, Robert Ickes among them—cajoled, provoked, and even tortured me into being better, funnier, tartly nastier than the first-draft me. I owe them far more even than I owe *Roget's Thesaurus*. Editors and publishers after Clay—Joe Armstrong, James Brady, Ed Kosner, Caroline Miller—stoically bore the burden of staggering expense accounts. In my earliest writing days, when I channeled that Cosmo Girl for Helen Gurley Brown, Jeanette Sarkisian (now Wagner) guarded my words with intelligence and empathy. I'm grateful to Arthur Kretchmer at *Playboy* for excerpting *Blue Skies, No Candy* when no other magazine would dare.

Don Congdon, my dapper, wise, and widely respected old-world agent, took me in when I was an ingenue and guided my growth with unflagging enthusiasm for thirty years.

My new agent Jane Dystel believed in this book even more than I did and brilliantly plotted its path to Warner Books, where I owe a special debt to strong publisher Jamie Raab for shepherding this memoir, and for creating a contagion in-house. Harvey-Jane Kowal and Carol Edwards devoted hours to documenting research, inserting proper French accents, and tidying a sloppy manuscript. Thanks to Jimmy Franco for promotional strategy and to Ben Greenberg, patient and unflappable liaison. Special thanks to Larry Kirshbaum, who was also there for Warner's dazzling launch of the paperback of *Blue Skies, No Candy* and promised me the moon again.

A pride of fine and opinionated cooks, bakers, and cookbook writers devoted precious time to testing my recipes: Rozanne Gold, Andrew Dornenburg, Eddie Schoenfeld, Adrienne Zausner, Vicki Polon, Mitch Weinstein, and Joan Harper (she flatly refused to use Crisco in my retro blueberry pie). And I'm grateful to Arthur Schwartz for finding a macaroni recipe so close to Mom's. Karen Page and Suvie Saran have shared their priceless network and connections with a generosity beyond simple friendship.

I owe the remarkable definition of my arms and the neatness of my thighs to Che Florio and Karen Munson.

An instinctive, uninformed notion led James Beard, Barbara Kafka, Joe Baum, Donald Tober, Roger Yaseen, Ed Gifford, Harley Baldwin, and me that Sunday in 1981 to feel that we who were so richly fed must bring food to the city's frail, aging shut-ins. That whimsy became serious and professional thanks to the dedication and tenacity of Citymeals-on-Wheels executive director, Marcia Stein, the princes of New York's grand families who lent weight to our board, and all the mayors beginning with Ed Koch, who cheered us on. To the relays of bright young staffers who toiled in the cubicles making Citymeals' board members' wild dreams into fund-raising triumphs and social policy and contracts fulfilled, I'm sorry I abused you.

I learned from so many—and stole from a few. Confessions follow.

All of us: my friends, my far-flung family, everyone I work with, my guy, and I myself must acknowledge a debt to the late, loving Mildred Newman—the unique and wise therapist with the green tea and the glamorous shoes—for the veneer of sanity that tempers my narcissism in this life of unbounded cravings.

INSATIABLE

PRELUDE: THE CRAVING

I could embellish the story and write that I was just pulling a crusty pair of homemade baguettes out of the oven the fall afternoon of the momentous phone call. I like that image. But then how could you trust me? The unadorned truth is that I was more likely mashing an excess of Hellmann's mayonnaise and a jot of Dijon mustard into some canned tuna (I won't pretend I made my own mayonnaise, either). It was Clay Felker, asking me to be the restaurant critic for his infant *New York* magazine, just launched a few months earlier, in April 1968, and already provoking major buzz.

Me as a restaurant critic. I was taken by surprise . . . and, for a rare moment, didn't know quite what to say. (I almost always have something to say, even if I haven't a clue what I'm talking about. Not an admirable habit but apparently incurable.) Of course I planned to write for *New York*. It was new and brash, with an impressive stable of contributing editors that included Tom Wolfe, Jimmy Breslin, Gloria Steinem, Peter Maas, Harold Clurman, Barbara Goldsmith, Nicholas Pileggi, Jill Krementz, Albert Goldman, and Dick Schaap. There was no magazine anywhere like it. It was the talk of the town.

"I'd love to write for you," I told Clay. "Once you start paying reasonable fees." I was earning major money freelancing for *Ladies' Home*

Journal, McCall's, and *Cosmopolitan.* "How the World's Great Beauties Stay Beautiful," "How America Lives: The Woman with Seven Houses" (Marylou Whitney, of course . . . how America lives indeed). The word was that everyone at *New York,* star writers and unknowns alike, would be paid the same puny three hundred dollars an article till the magazine began to make money.

Eventually, I thought, I might want to write about food and restaurants, or almost anything. I'd written a long, juicy play-by-play for Clay Felker on Henri Soulé reopening La Côte Basque a few years earlier, when *New York* was the Sunday magazine of the ill-fated *Herald Tribune.* It was full of dish, like Soulé's despair when fate gave Pat Nixon a luscious-looking fillet of striped bass that had apparently gasped its last breath in a gasoline wake. So, clearly that's where Clay's inspiration was coming from.

But to be *the* restaurant critic . . . in direct competition with the Great God Craig Claiborne. How reckless of Clay to nominate me as a candidate to brandish my fork in that world.

"What would you tell people my credentials are?" I asked.

"Well, aren't you a food person?"

James Beard was a food person. Julia Child, my friend Paula Wolfert. I'm not normally one to sell myself short, but this would be serious exposure. I was just someone who followed Craig Claiborne's trail in search of gastronomic epiphany. I was a cook. I'd taken a cooking class and learned to make pasta from scratch. "Well, I've eaten around," I conceded. "But I can't afford to write more than two or three times a year for a three-hundred-dollar fee."

"That's ridiculous," said Clay. "Dozens of people are begging to be *New York*'s restaurant critic so they can charge all their meals to us."

Blinding lightbulbs exploded. Suddenly, it was all so clear. I could order from the right side of the menu instead of from the left as I'd always done (the dutiful daughter, the compassionate date, the penny-pinching wife). So I said "Yes" quickly, before my doubts could erode his confidence.

"We have to do it like Craig Claiborne does at the *Times,*" I said. "Anonymously. I'll have to eat a minimum of three times before judging a restaurant—with friends—like he does. And pay the check."

"Of course," said Clay. "Of course."

My husband, then an editor at the *New York Times,* was thrilled for me—and for our budget. Don Forst and I were a folie à deux of passionate foodies. We'd been saving our money to eat in all the great restaurants, skipping dessert, sharing an appetizer, braving the haughty maître d's and the withering sommeliers as we thriftily ordered half a bottle of wine. We'd taken a ridiculously circuitous detour to France from Italy to be buttered up and become deliciously sloshed at the fabled La Pyramide—the Michelin three-star sacred to the late, great Fernand Point—because Don's best friend said it was worth any detour. What did I know? I'd read *Blue Trout and Black Truffles,* by Joseph Wechsberg, and found myself inhabited by exotic cravings. And we'd gone back to France the next year, having died and then risen to heaven in a small two-star inn off the autoroute near Lyon, where a chef named Alain Chapel was cooking his heart out to win that third Michelin boutonniere. I'd bravely ordered the famous *gâteau de foies blonds,* the gossamer blond livers, and the challenging calf's ear. Indeed, now that I thought about it from the perspective of Clay's vision, my whole life had been leading up to this unforeseen, unimaginable moment.

Where should I start? I wondered. What restaurant would I celebrate or riddle with ridicule first? Would anyone trust me? What horrible arrows of innuendo were my betters going to shoot behind my back? I could almost hear Craig's soft drawl of derision: "I took her to lunch once and now she thinks she's a restaurant critic."

In the days before professional gossipists multiplied like gerbils, *Women's Wear Daily's* "Eye" saw all and spilled all. Publisher John Fairchild's irreverent focus on social X rays—designers on dawn disco patrol, working-class beauties who married up, and their hangouts—had transformed the Fairchild family's dowdy little garment-business rag. He skewered the designers who displeased him, put slashing black lines through anyone he deemed a fashion victim, and documented the in and out of Manhattan dining mercilessly.

Having grown up in a fashion world—Daddy would sometimes take me to New York on buying trips for his women's specialty shop, Nat Greene's, on Livernois and Seven Mile Road in Detroit—I was already spoiled at thirteen, with half a dozen dresses by the great American original Claire McCardell hanging in my closet. I was tall. Skirts were long. And only the more expensive, more generously cut dresses were long enough for me.

Thus in 1957, I was already obsessed with fashion when I arrived in New York, having quit my wire-service job for the promise of a one-week tryout on the city desk at the *New York Post* (a job I got). I read *WWD* religiously so I could decide which Yves Saint Laurent or Givenchy designs to look for when authorized $69.95 copies arrived at Ohrbach's, the late, lamented discount temple on Thirty-fourth Street.

Maybe I didn't have the nerve to leap on the scene, criticizing veteran French chefs and fabled restaurateurs. But I was a reporter after all. I could write the who, where, what, and why. And I knew the sociology of Manhattan dining because I read *Women's Wear*. It was my bible, my *Almanach de Gotha*. John Fairchild's "Eye" was my muse. I owed everything I knew about what I thought of as "Toot New York" to *Women's Wear*. I certainly knew enough not to wear my brown knit faux Saint Laurent pantsuit to La Côte Basque, because Madame Henriette Spalter, the late Henri Soulé's ex–cashier/mistress, who now ran the place, considered the new mode unforgivably déclassé. Lynda Bird Johnson Robb had been required to strip off her taboo pants and eat lunch at La Côte Basque in her tunic.

I never dreamed I'd ever get close to dishing with *WWD*'s deliciously bitchy Fairchild at his favorite frog pond, La Grenouille. But thanks to his all-seeing "Eye," I knew that William Paley had been fussing over every tiny detail of the Ground Floor, the new restaurant in Black Rock, his Eero Saarinen–designed CBS Building on Sixth Avenue. That sounded just right for a soft landing at *New York* magazine that fall of 1968.

It was a year of drama and upheaval. Columbia University was an armed camp just two miles north of where I hung my navy blue linen "Givenchy." The city was deeply divided, the Establishment press aghast and disapproving of the student sit-ins at Columbia. "Are we the Establishment?" I asked Don, who was often exasperated with the rulings of his bosses at the *Times*. How embarrassing. The mantra was "Never trust anyone over thirty." Of course I had to lie and silently subtract a few years so I could echo the rallying cry. There was mayhem at the Democratic National Convention, terrifying images of cops beating back the crowds, starving babies in Biafra. And I would be nervously focused on what famous faces were planted in Mr. Paley's custom-order chairs. That was my mission. At times, the reality of the staring eyes and distended bellies of the hungry did pepper my view of our town's budding gourmand excess with guilt. Yet everything I wrote would be feeding the fever of foodism, ultimately turning on susceptible taste buds to what would become a contagion, a cultural delirium.

After all, this was the mind-bending sixties, a time of unbridled experimentation and flaunting the rules. Not that I was inclined to be that thoughtful. I was too nervous. No one could have predicted how obsessed with food Americans would become. Certainly not me. All I knew was that this first critique, my exposure to the magazine's demanding and savvy readership, would be a challenge. I knew I could so easily sound naïve and get laughed off the masthead.

I invited a friend to join me for lunch and went off to teach myself how to be a restaurant critic. I tried to think of it as just another journalistic assignment. It didn't occur to me, as it does now, that I was a not-quite-innocent Alice tumbling down that rabbit hole. That in this upside-down world of the sixties (which didn't really end till sometime in the mid-seventies), I would stumble into an astonishing new world as a person I scarcely recognized and never planned to be.

1

The Fried Egg and I

Lvis Presley was coming to town to do two shows at Olympia Stadium. At twenty-one, I was one of the hormone-raging millions with a crush on Elvis—the young, beautiful, seemingly unspoiled Elvis. He was the bad-boy Adonis of high school, who drove the principal (or in his case, Ed Sullivan) wild with the swivel and grind that made nymphets squeal. And I was not immune. No New York newspaper would hire me fresh from college in 1956—I had applied everywhere and sent countless résumés—so I was languishing at home in Detroit, Michigan, the most junior staffer at United Press International. I wrote a letter to Colonel Parker, asking if I could spend the day with Elvis and write about it for the powerful wire service, UPI. I got back a mimeographed invitation to Presley's official press conference. I was insulted and frustrated but not discouraged. The bureau chief said I could cover Elvis anyway, as long as it was on my day off.

I wore a simple body-skimming black shantung dress (my most slenderizing) with white stitching along the neck and cap sleeves, shiny black patent-leather pumps, and little white kid gloves. I knew Olympia Stadium from childhood, from Barnum & Bailey circus days, from falling in love with hockey and Gordie Howe in my uncle's Red Wing hockey seats, from seeing Sonja Henie—so doll-like—and thinking I could skate, too, if I weren't quite so tall and clumsy, but would anyone ever be able to lift me?

I arrived backstage early to study security and find its most vulnerable link. Lamar was his name. He was in charge of guarding the door and a pair of twenty-four-karat-gold pants with a sequined stripe, which he carried in a padlocked garment bag. Not for nothing had I spent all those double-bill Saturdays in the movies. I had Ida Lupino and Joan Crawford down pat. I could do Bette Davis eyes. I squared my shoulders, channeling Roz Russell in *His Gal Friday,* and flirted with the chubby guardian. From his rolling drawl, I figured he must be one of Elvis's Memphis mafia.

"Do you sing, too?" I asked, tickling his tweed elbow. Lamar was examining my ring finger through the white leather and seemed cheered to confirm that I was not married.

At that moment, a slim figure in a red suede cloth jacket was slipped into the room by a phalanx of uniformed security guards. Elvis curled his lip, smiled, and flicked back his shiny black cowlick with a toss of his head, then seated himself on the edge of a table, sizing up the gathering with an "I'm all yours" wink. He was looking right at me. I felt weak, and I blushed all over. The massed journalists—two police reporters, one yawning rewrite man, a drama critic, and a farm-news columnist (few newspapers had pop-music columnists at the time)—struggled to meet the challenge. I was too feverish to speak. I just stood there, pulse pounding, mesmerized, wondering if my heart could survive it. Then, after gamely responding to their lame and predictable queries, too quickly Elvis was gone.

Lamar took my hand. "If you want to stand close by, you can watch the show from the nearest aisle and slip back here before the crush at the end. Then you can go to the hotel with us to hang out and have a Coke between shows," he offered.

I stood on the rise of the aisle, trying for a journalist's cool, part of me observing the hysteria, part of me trembling and aching to jump up and down, too. I watched the fans, mostly teenage girls with bobbing ponytails, leaping out of the seats, reaching out to him, screaming and weeping, tearing at their hair as he curled a lip or a hip, collapsing in petit mal seizures. His handlers had to carry Elvis offstage midway through the last song to get him out alive before the mob realized that it was over and charged after their idol.

Lamar grabbed my hand—still sheathed in its little white glove—
and the bag containing the twenty-four-karat-gold pants and tucked me
into a limo with an assortment of silent young louts, the full Memphis
crew. We pulled out of the underground bay.

"But where is Elvis?" I cried.

"He's behind us in a taxi," Lamar promised.

At the Book-Cadillac Hotel, there were clots of fans waiting to catch
a glimpse of Elvis. As we piled out of the limo, they surged toward us and
then drew back with shrugs of disappointment and rejection.

Upstairs in a twenty-fourth-floor suite, the Memphis cronies sipped
their cola—in those days, Coke was something that came in a bottle with
a waistline. They divvied up the comics from the Sunday papers. Lamar
seemed resigned to my indifference, as if maybe he'd been through this
drill before. Nobody looked at me. I was too familiar, an offering for the
King.

Oh dear heaven. I stopped breathing. Elvis. He stood in the door,
smaller than life—small in life, I mean, pompadored hair slick. He sized
up the room and astutely realized I was the only female in it. He slunk
directly toward me, slender in shiny black faille trousers and a sheer blue
short-sleeved eyelet organdy shirt, till one leg was brushing my thigh.

"And who are you?"

I babbled something about press and UPI and Colonel Parker.

He didn't seem to be listening. Silently, he took my hand—yes, still
gloved—and led me to a bedroom. I was thinking, Oh my God . . . this
is Elvis. . . . I am going to do it with Elvis. I am not going to be coy. I
will not make him talk me into it. He didn't ask. I didn't answer. He
closed the door, dropped his pants, and lay on the bed—very pale, soft,
young—watching me take off my clothes and, yes, at last, my little white
gloves. All the way up on the twenty-fourth floor, I could hear the girls
chanting on the street below: "We want Elvis. We want Elvis."

And look who has him, I was thinking. As . . . it . . . happened. In a
feverish heat. Skin on skin. I think it was good. I don't remember the essential details. It was certainly good enough. I know the reality of it was
thrilling beyond anything I might have imagined.

"I need to sleep now," he said when it was over.

I grabbed my clothes and fled into the bathroom to dress. As I picked
up my purse, wondering if a good-bye kiss would be appropriate, Elvis

opened his eyes, blinked, as if he wasn't sure for a moment what I was doing there.

He twitched a shoulder toward the phone. "Would you mind calling room service and ordering me a fried egg sandwich?" The fried egg sandwich—that part I remember. I can't remember how big It was, how long the sex lasted, or even who was on top (probably me). But I have never forgotten the fried egg sandwich.

Yes, the totemic fried egg sandwich. At that moment, it might have been clear I was born to be a food writer. I just didn't know it yet.

2

A Peanut Butter Kid
in a Velveeta Wasteland

I AM CERTAIN I WAS BORN HUNGRY. I COULD NEVER GET ENOUGH ATTEN-tion, enough love, or enough peanut butter. I was the focus of my parents' adoration for only three years before my sister, Margie, butted into our lives.

"Your mother is bringing home a little monkey from the hospital," my grandmother said, which was her way of observing that my sister, unlike blue-eyed, platinum-ringleted princess me, was golden-skinned, with shaggy black hair and big brown eyes. A monkey? I took that literally. The three of us were fine. I didn't need a sister and I didn't need a monkey. I feel I can remember fierce anger even as an infant when my mother left me out on the porch, zipped up in a baby bunting (because fresh air was supposed to be good for babies). I screamed, she said, and kicked, desperate to get a foot free, and to this day I sleep with one foot outside the covers no matter how cold it is.

There is a photograph of me that says it all, a flaxen-haired toddler pushing a doll buggy with such force and fierce determination, I wonder if my mother wasn't terrified.

My mom asked my dad to shower me with his attention so I wouldn't be jealous of my little sister, Margie. That was the beginning of Daddy's girl. A Daddy's girl stands on Daddy's shoes and dances to Frank Sinatra on the record player. A Daddy's girl is precocious and flirtatious. A Daddy's girl goes to his office on Saturdays and pastes up ads like Daddy does. At the age of seven, I wrote some little stories based on family gossip, and my father pasted them into a tabloid page called "Chit Chat of This and That" and had it printed. I charged a nickel each for tear sheets that I passed out at the next holiday dinner, when a long table and all its extensions stretched across Grandma's dining room into the living room to accommodate all the aunts and uncles (half of whom were not speaking to the other half, at least half the time), with a bridge table at the end for the youngest cousins. A Daddy's girl can do anything, and whatever she does in life, she will be a star. At least that's the message I got from my dad. Always. I was gifted, brilliant. I would excel in whatever field I chose to exercise my multiple talents—art, writing, theater, film. This may sound like your typical pathological narcissism, and maybe it was. But I would swear it wasn't really anything my ego dreamed up; it was the message I got from him.

Some of my close friends grew up in dysfunctional families, or so they say. The stories they tell are shocking and hard for me to imagine. One of my most intimate friends insists I must be in denial, making it up that my family was not dysfunctional, too. But the truth is, for better or worse, my family was fully functional. My father, Nathaniel Robert, known as Nate and later Nat, a Clark Gable type with a mustache but not the dimples, worked in advertising in that early decade. I thought he was handsome and, later, so did my teenage friends and most of the women in his orbit when he moved into the retail fashion world. His professional scene in the forties was nothing like the hypercreative ad world of the Man in the Gray Flannel Suit. He had a one-man office and bound volumes with numbers and drawings that he cut out and pasted into layouts that would become newspaper ads for supermarkets. My mother, Saralee, shopped, kept Daddy sane, took his side on every issue, thawed and overcooked dinner, and played mah-jongg with the girls. Two crack. Three bam. I did my homework to the click of the Bakelite tiles.

There was always a maid. When the big freezer first arrived on the domestic scene—a huge white coffin in the basement that would revolutionize a housewife's world—it seemed like Mom loved it more than she loved any of us. Our dinners were almost incidental. She cooked to feed the freezer, lovingly labeling and dating containers of pea soup and chili, goodies that got carried home from parties but were never eaten, and later the top tier of her daughters' wedding cakes. I think the loving couple was supposed to thaw the thing and share it at some appropriate wedding anniversary. But one by one, my mother's children tortured her by divorcing—yes, even my brother, Jim (who arrived a few weeks after Pearl Harbor). Perhaps we all had exaggerated romantic expectations. I'm not sure what Saralee did with these sweet iceberg hunks, if she was ever able to bring herself to the finalty of tossing them in the garbage.

Saralee and Nat were very lovey-dovey. I see them when young, Daddy hugging her from behind as she stands at the sink . . . laughing because we are watching. She turns her lips toward him and they kiss. It was a wonderful way to grow up—not quite *Leave It to Beaver*, but definitely not *A Long Day's Journey into Night*. So I am not sure if anyone in my family is to blame for the fact that my Rorschach test made my first psychotherapist so nervous.

Unlike many of the legendary food-world greats, I did not grow up in a country kitchen steamy with the fragrant smells of muffins and pies just out of the oven or glorious stews simmering on a back burner. My grandma's cook did not sneak me cookies or spoil me with last summer's peach conserve piled on freshly baked bread. My grandmother's cook was my grandmother. Jam was Smucker's. My aunt Eve did cook—she was famous for her chocolate cake and her caramelized baked ham draped with rings of pineapple and maraschino cherries (we didn't know red dye number four was toxic, but she didn't do ham that often, so nobody died). I never got to watch her cook. Cooking wasn't on my agenda. I didn't see my future self finding intellectual fulfillment confined to the kitchen with a can of Crisco and a flour sifter. But then, neither did Julia, I am sure, or Martha. My vision was pretty much formed by Hollywood career gals like Rosalind Russell and Kate Hepburn.

Indeed, I was born on the frozen steppes of a vast culinary wasteland. Saralee was never at her best in the kitchen. She made macaroni and cheese from the recipe on the box. It became my template for great macaroni and cheese. True, her layered Jell-O molds were much appreciated at weddings and showers and her pea soup was world-class (amazing, considering she did it without a ham bone and without an onion). Mom cooked meat until carbonized because that's the way Daddy liked it. There was one lone cookbook in our kitchen, *The Settlement Cookbook,* violated and bruised, rudely grease-stained, its spine long ago broken.

There was a certain aura of terror and paranoia about food in our house, disguised, of course, as innocent fussiness, as in "The guy's a finicky eater." No garlic ever darkened our kitchen because Daddy had an aversion to garlic, which, for some reason, he was unable to detect in its unbridled abundance at his favorite Italian restaurant, Lalli's. This is not something my mother would have called to his attention—he had a temper when provoked, and I remember my mother as dedicated to smoothing ruffled feathers and rearranging reality to protect Daddy from blowing his stack.

So I didn't grow up primed and stuffed from birth to emerge a passionate foodie. Still, it must have been in my DNA. Deprivation and hunger unleashed it. In a family of finicky eaters, I was the only adventurer. On the maid's days off—Thursdays and Sundays—when we ate out, often at the Atlantic Garden, Mom ordered egg fu yung, sauce on the side, while Dad and my sister, Margie, got breaded veal cutlet. I begged Mom to taste my fabulous wor shu oop, but she begged off, as if breaded duck were some alien Chinese conspiracy that might prove to be a by-product of opium. My affection for chicken livers and my cracking the bones of fried frog's legs with my teeth were considered adolescent affectations . . . or a sadistic plot to make my sister lose her appetite.

"Whose child is she?" my mother would ask. "Frog, crab. Next it will be snails." She'd read that the French ate snails. Mom had a good point there. I couldn't possibly be the child of these parents. I liked to imagine I was the illegitimate child of royalty, left on their bourgeois doorstep, except that, if you discounted my blue eyes and blond hair, I did look a lot like a mix of the two of them.

At camp, my first time away from home, when I was seven, I was tall, so my folks put me in a bunk with the eight-year-olds. I hated every minute. Being hopelessly unathletic, the only activities I was willing to sign up for were art and raiding the icebox. Each cabin took turns hijacking the fridge. We carried flashlights and tiptoed, but even at seven, I was suspicious. Surely someone knew what we were up to. That giant tub of peanut butter on a low shelf and the saltines alongside seemed too obvious. You'd think I might have gotten cozy in a camp with such large jars of peanut butter. But no. Every time my parents called, I cried, beg-

ging them to take me home. Finally, unable to stand the pitiful sobs and
my litany of trauma, they drove up and took me home. I am sure this is
why I never learned to play well with others. All my life, people have assumed I am an only child. No, I am not an only child. I just act as if I were
the only child. I am left-handed. That's enough to overcome.

Midway through my sophomore year in the College of Architecture
and Design at the University of Michigan—I'd skipped three times in
grade school and arrived at sixteen—I was paralyzed by the despair of
unrequited love for an ambivalent upperclassman I'd found at the *Michigan Daily* and by the discovery that my precocious artistic talent as a child
was utterly inadequate for a career in design. I was in the wrong college.
I was in the wrong body. I was in the wrong century. Voluptuous had not
been fashionable for years.

I needed to change my major and stop eating dormitory food, but I
was anxious about admitting defeat. I would be entering the College of
Literature, Science, and the Arts, three semesters late, after everyone
else had already waded through the Great Books and my only hope of
catching up were Classic Comics. I don't think Classic Comics did
Aristophanes or Dostoyevsky. The Count of Monte Cristo, yes. This ed-
ucational gap may have affected my writing. It certainly has affected my
abilty to do crossword puzzles. Somehow, I managed to convince my parents a year in Paris would cure my romantic malaise (about which I was
convincingly vague). I am sure neither I nor they had any idea what a year
in Paris could mean for a seventeen-year-old girl on her own. It was
1952. No one we knew had been to Paris. One of my aunts knew a
woman who knew a woman who would rent me a room in her Right
Bank apartment. That sounded safe enough to Nat and Saralee.

Freed from the Velveeta cocoon, I leaped into the richness of a world
I could not have imagined. Who wouldn't be impressed by the vast range
of mysterious vegetables unknown in Detroit, a whole universe of cheese
and unheard-of innards. Even on my allowance, I could afford *boeuf à la
mode,* juicy *navarin* of lamb, couscous, and sweetbreads smothered in
cream in the little mom-and-pop bistros in the student quarter.
(I quickly found my way to the Left Bank when madame with the room
to let asked me to move out because I took too many baths and was such
a pig that I'd used her precious perfumed soap to wash my bobby socks.)

Every morning, I ran down five flights from my ancient studio with its warped wooden floor on the rue Dauphine to collect my breakfast in the markets of the rue de Buci—a crusty baguette, a bottle of milk, and, every morning, one hundred grams of a different cheese. Great dining was hardly primary on my list of desired sensory awakenings when I fled Detroit, but my innocent palate was ripe for seduction. One morning, I woke up covered with red spots. I accused my landlady of harboring bedbugs. She accused my curly-haired Algerian boyfriend of something worse. No, no, not my adorable Albert. He might have been an incurable male chauvinist, but he was scrupulously clean, even though it cost twenty-five cents to take a bath.

"You have an allergy to le Petit Suisse," the doctor said, blaming my favorite cream cheese. I wanted to have faith in his prescription, a powder to be dissolved in red wine and sipped slowly twice a day, since it was so un-Detroit, so French. My first gastrointestinal disease. My first alcohol-based cure. What could Detroit possibly offer me after moments like these?

Abandoning Paris for a month in Italy, I was offered a haven in Rome by the regal Principessa Katya, who had seemed amused by my energy when we met a week earlier on the beach in Positano. At first, she seemed rather indifferent to the kitchen and left me to make do nutritionally on my own.

One day, La Principessa came home bursting with exuberance and spilled a bag of walnuts on the counter. "Green walnuts," she said. "It's the season." It seems that green walnuts were to her as the madeleine to Proust as peanut butter was to me. Peeling the pesky nuts was tedious, and I watched in horror as her silken white fingers stained purple and brown. She didn't seem to care. Happily sautéing rice and bits of lamb for a nutty risotto, La Principessa (then in the throws of annulling a White Russian husband) salved the fears of impending poverty that consumed her. "Watch me. Learn," she cried. "All it takes is a bit of rice and ten cents' worth of lamb. . . . You need never go hungry." How wonderful not to be a virgin in Rome. It was there I discovered cunnilingus. And, on a lesser plain, linguine. In Latin, they seemed to be related.

Back in Paris that fall, I dabbled in journalism, mostly using my *Michigan Daily* press card to get into couturier launches and fabulous publicity lunches. It was embarrassing trying to explain to my self-styled intellectual friends how Americans could be so naïve as to elect Dwight

Eisenhower president or why the U.S. press was so tough on Charlie
Chaplin, the genius of *Limelight,* or why we were determined to execute
Ethel and Julius Rosenberg. None of these were my idea. From the perspective of Les Deux Magots, America seemed as boring as warm oatmeal. But I was homesick after almost a year away and decided to go
home for Christmas in December 1952.

When the University of Michigan dropout dropped back in, that
lamb risotto trick worked very well for me. With the dean of women's
permission, I lived off campus in Ann Arbor, in a basement flat with a
small kitchen, and I could feed any number of friends for a dollar or two.
That meant lamb bones, meaty but gristly, too. Still, I was quite popular
to a wide range of suitors and loyal pals. No one else cooked. I guess I
was quite a package on a basically conservative campus: free-range, no
curfew, sensuous and choosy, but bedable. The bonny young Brit who
slipped in the window at 2:00 AM, so eager for intimacy that he wore no
underwear inside his rough corduroy pants, struck me as irresistibly gal-
lant. I'm not sure how much his gift of chocolates figured in my warmth.
They *were* imported. Sex and food, inextricably linked. (His charm
served him well, because the next time we met, twenty-five years later,
he was a member of Parliament.)

One evening just before my senior year, picnicking in front of a
warming fire on a fluff of Greek flokati, all this vague gastronomic fum-
bling suddenly took on meaning over a casserole of baked ham layered
with cheddar, green peppers, and canned tomato sauce. I'd gone off for
a week in the autumn wilds on an island in Michigan's Upper Peninsula
with a married man. I seemed to have developed a weakness for married
men, possibly because they had a weakness for me. Not to be flip. In fact,
I was mad about this man who sat next to me on the rewrite desk at the
Detroit Free Press during the summer break of 1954. He seemed to me
vulnerable and needy. But maybe that was me, vulnerable and needy.
Perhaps it was just transient lust. Stolen sex was incredibly hot.

About that Rorschach test: The therapist reported that he'd never
tested a subject who'd found more sexual content than I in those standard ink blots. What did this mean? Who could predict? Obviously, I had
potential yet to explore. The referring physician shaded the therapist's
report a bit to shield my parents. They were already concerned about my
moping and unexplained tears, and probably about what Mom caught

me doing one night in the dark on the carpet in the library, a scene that caused her to retreat silently back up the stairs in her nightgown. That's how the therapist got summoned. I think I told him—or maybe he told me—married men were a pleasant procrastination, a way to avoid commitment while one was growing up and figuring out who one might become. Clearly, I was borderline sane, not so neurotic after all.

And this is the food part. My borrowed guy and I were off the radar that chilling early-fall day, far from reality in a borrowed cabin on an isolated wind-whipped lake. I'd brought four recipes clipped from *Ladies' Home Journal*—pork chops baked in buttermilk, hamburger in a biscuit wrap, cherry crisp, and that revelatory baked ham casserole.

Time has mercifully misted the taste memories. But I do know that everything I cooked was brilliant and extravagantly appreciated. Another point in favor of married men. No matter how pitiful your effort, it's more dazzling than Hers. This man who looked a little like a blond Dick Tracy . . . of course he broke my heart. He went back to Her, who didn't know how to layer ham and cheddar and green peppers, much less stuff canned cherries into Bisquick dough. (It was long before America fell in love with eating, but I suspect he would have said good-bye to me anyway.)

On Drummond Island, love and food became inextricably linked for me. It became a mantra: A woman does well to be beautiful, mysterious, haunting, witty, rich, and exotic in bed . . . but it never hurts to cook good. As in finger-lickin' good. I became a cook, graduating eventually from tuna casserole to Craig Claiborne's coq au vin and Julia's apple charlotte. This passion for cooking as well as eating would turn out to be a powerful edge for me when I went public as *New York* magazine's amateur restaurant critic.

Almost Like Mom's Macaroni and Cheese

This is a recipe food-writer friends have been passing around—I got it from Arthur Schwartz (a passionate New Yorker), who got it from Suzanne Hamlin (an ultimate southerner). I am using it because it's close to my memory of my Detroit-born mom's baked macaroni. The goal is crisp, not creamy. Use half-and-half instead of milk if you like it creamier.

Olive oil spray or 1½ tbsp. mild-flavored olive oil, plus 1 tbsp. for tossing later.
½ lb. small elbow macaroni
1 tbsp. salt
2½ cups shredded or chopped firm cheese (Needless to say, my mother used
    Velveeta, but I make this with sharp cheddar and Emmentaler, half and half.
    Once I threw in some leftover Brie, a triple crème from France, and a half
    cup of crème fraîche and the result was celestial.)
Optional: ½ cup chopped baked ham or snipped crisp bacon
1 cup whole milk
1½ tsp. salt
1 tsp. freshly ground pepper
4 tbsp. fine dry bread crumbs
¼ cup grated Parmigiano-Reggiano

Preheat oven to 350° F.

Spray the bottom and sides of a shallow 6-cup metal baking dish with olive oil spray. Bring several quarts of water to a rolling boil. Add tablespoon salt. Boil macaroni until just tender. Drain well. Immediately turn the macaroni into the baking dish (a flat baking pan gives more crispiness than a loaf pan). Use a pan that can go under the broiler later. Toss macaroni with tablespoon of olive oil. Then add cheese, optional ham or bacon, milk, salt, and freshly ground pepper and mix well.

Bake in the oven for 10 minutes, then remove from oven, close oven door, and stir. Taste for seasoning. Sprinkle fresh bread crumbs and grated Parmigiano on top. Bake another 15 minutes. If there is still some milk in the bottom, return to the oven for another 5 to 10 minutes. If topping has not browned and crisped like Mom's used to, stick it under the broiler (three or four inches away from heat) and brown, watching so it doesn't burn.

Serves 2 as a main course, 4 as a side dish.

3

~

ABOUT SEX AND ME

THE BEST LOVER TURNS INTO A PIZZA AT 3:00 AM. WHO SAID THAT? WAS it Woody Allen? For me, the best pizza would turn into a lover. I have read restaurant critics who claimed to have tasted chocolate ice cream that was better than sex. I have never eaten anything that was better than sex; *almost* as good as great sex perhaps, but never better. Though I am sure I was born hungry, I am less certain I began life as a sensualist. Really, who knows? I was allergic to wool. That may mean something.

I can't remember exactly when it began, how I got in touch with my sexual self. I do remember the terror and joy of discovering masturbation. I shared a bedroom with my sister after my brother, Jim, was born. Our room was beautiful, with matching bleached-wood dressers, quilted and flowered peach bedspreads my mother had had custom-made, and tuffets at the end of each bed with our names embroidered on them. The design effort did not lessen my annoyance at the loss of privacy.

At night after lights-out, I would get my sister to sing along with me so she wouldn't hear the sound of the bed creaking as my body rubbed against my wadded-up pajama bottoms. I did my heartrending Judy Garland vibrato as we sang "Somewhere Over the Rainbow" and then segued into a popular wartime anthem, "The White Cliffs of Dover," and its reassuring images of bluebirds flying free in a near tomorrow. Till, exhausted and satisfied, I fell asleep.

My parents were readers. I read, too, with a flashlight under the covers. At eight and nine, I read *Forever Amber; The Vixens* by Frank Yerby; and *Gone With the Wind*—again and again the sexy parts, skipping the war and politics. I used my mom's library card to defy the symbol that meant "not for anyone under eighteen" and to check out *The Razor's Edge* and *The Bad Seed*. I'm not sure how much I understood, but I read Hemingway and wanted to go to France as soon as I was old enough and sit in a café and feel the earth move.

Having breasts at ten, when every other girl in class was ironing board flat, didn't help. At ten and a half, I needed a bra. The boy at the desk in front of me seemed fascinated by this early budding and shoved a pile of books into me—to see if my bosom would bounce, I suppose. For quite a while, I felt my breasts as foreign objects, unwelcome intruders camping out on my chest, drawing everyone's stares. At the age of eleven, I was five seven. Truck drivers and sailors whistled. I thought how stupid they would feel if they knew I was just eleven. I had beautiful blue gabardine jumper pants with an empire midriff embroidered just like the pants Katharine Hepburn wore in *The Philadelphia Story*. By the time a few other girls got cute little perky breasts at last, mine were huge. I refused to get undressed for swimming in high school gym class, so my mother got a note from the doctor, saying that I was allergic to dust. To this day, I cannot swim, but I love sailing and I always sit as close as possible to the life preservers.

I was determined to be a virgin when I got married. As a freshman, I was deeply committed to preserving my virginity. I knew that nice girls did not go all the way. As a fifteen-year-old, my hormones were raging and I made out like crazy with the lifeguard at the Fontainebleau during Christmas vacation in Miami Beach, my best friend's hometown ex in Bay City, Michigan, and the twenty-one-year-old college boy next door. Both of us were naked in my mom's car behind the high school when the cops found us with their flashlights. Even the cops were embarrassed by the size of my tits. It's not that I didn't study, make good grades, write sensitive essays, work for the high school newspaper. I was not a full-fledged juvenile delinquent. In between hormonal flashes and frenzied "everything but," I tied for first in my high school graduation class with straight *A*'s, and delivered my valedictorian address in free verse.

Though I was not yet sixteen when I moved into Stockwell Hall at the University of Michigan, I was sure, with my height and wardrobe, no one would guess. In its roommate-matching wisdom, the dean of women's office had paired me with a freshman from the South whose father was also in the women's retail clothing business. Our wardrobes devoured every inch of the tiny room. I was choking on her crinolines. My high school pals headed for the College of Literature, Science, and the Arts. No one I knew drifted into the College of Architecture and Design. Well, I did have arty notions. I'd always taken life-drawing classes and studied painting. But I was also counting on no term papers to write and little homework, leaving more time for men. My mother had promised boys would be taller once I got to Ann Arbor.

I was curiouser and curiouser. And I guess I knew that nice girls probably didn't do what I was doing—on the floor of the darkroom at the *Michigan Daily*. I marvel at how many obsessed and aroused young men spared the thin sliver of membrane that kept me officially a virgin in the skilled acrobatics of everything but. Then, in early fall of my sophomore year, I managed to put my virginity into an indefensible position in the backseat of a Studebaker in the woods one rainy night—pleading, begging, crying. He wouldn't take no for an answer. I was furious and indignant, storming into the dorm just as the lights blinked curfew. I stewed and fumed in the shower. Then I climbed under the crinolines and got into bed. Well, that's that, I thought. I'm not going to be a virgin when I get married. I'll just have fun from now on. And I never looked back.

It may not sound like it in this condensed version, but actually I was very choosy. Perhaps my self-devised sexual etiquette was a bit eccentric, but even at seventeen and a half, during that liberating year abroad, I had my rules. I would never pick up a man at a bar, but somehow the handsome actor wearing his jacket on his shoulders Italian-style seemed safe in the mail line at the American Express office in Rome.

"Are you following me?" I asked.

"I thought you might be following me," he said.

That led to a wildly romantic three days of hitchhiking and walking to Positano and the fierce intensity of the long-delayed bedding.

And I am sure I was drawn to the architect in his unheated room on the rue de Fleurus, who warmed my underwear under his ass each morning, because he lived in the same building as Alice B. Toklas. I'd read that the owner of a major Left Bank art gallery had come by her collection of Modiglianis because she was the artist's mistress. Just my luck that the next artist to cross my path was not quite Modigliani. He was not getting enough to eat. He was so thin, his bony pelvis bruised mine. I accepted a painting, a self-portrait, and parked it in my folks' cellar, where mildew from a small flood actually improved it.

4

SLOW DEATH BY
MAYONNAISE

As CLAY FELKER HAD SUSPECTED AND CONFIRMED WITH HIS INSPIRED gift for casting in the fall of 1968, I was a foodie, a full-blown gourmand, long before New York and America fell in love with dining out . . . obsessed ahead of the times. Indeed, *foodie* wasn't even in the dictionary yet. When I did truly fall in love and he wasn't married, only elusive and uncertain for a while, I found a game dining coconspirator across the rewrite desk at the *New York Post*.

Don Forst had grown up in Brooklyn and his attorney father invested in restaurants. Don could handle the gruff maître d' at Lindy's, near Broadway, where we had strawberry shortcake after seeing Robert Preston and Barbara Cook in *The Music Man*. Don knew how to score three helpings of shrimp in pink Louis sauce at Mamma Leone's (where "LOTS" was the motto and we prepped at eating Italian). He was trained by his folks at how to scope out a table about to be vacated in vast, raucous Lundy's, the seafood gymnasium in Sheepshead Bay. Easy. You found people eating dessert and stood close, boring hate rays into the back of their necks, till they couldn't sit still another minute and decided to skip coffee. Then you elbowed all claimants away and swiftly ordered two shore dinners, double coleslaw, and blueberry pie à la mode. This was

New York City–honed sophistication that meshed perfectly with my Paris veneer.

Don worked nights and I worked days on the *Post* rewrite desk at the tail end of the fifties. He'd prepped at the *Houston Press* and the Newark *Star-Ledger*. I had been determined to escape Detroit the minute I could, but no news outlet in New York would hire me fresh out of college. I was stuck. When my United Press job in Detroit gave me weekdays off, I would fly to New York with scrapbooks and clippings, scrounging for an opening. Then a *Post* editor, barely looking up from his typewriter, offered me a one-week tryout during the summer. (That was how the *Post* filled out the city room during summer vacations.) But my boss in Detroit wouldn't give me a week off—I hadn't worked long enough to earn it. So I quit. The one-week tryout led to two, led to a month, finally led to a job.

A reporter I was dating introduced Don and me as we passed in the morning at breakfast in the *Post* luncheonette. Don was engaged to a Danish woman, he confided, a brunette with the most amazing full lips. Did he have to mention those lips? (Now that I think of it, "being engaged" was close enough to being married that I could feel safe.) I don't remember if he told me this before or after we moved from sunbathing on my terrace to my bedroom, both of us warmed and scented with that sweet smell of sun on skin, in a tangle of fierce and uninhibited lovemaking. I was already falling in love with his profile, his straight, thin nose and dark, sad eyes, the slight boyish body with one very muscular arm from playing squash. (Squash? In Detroit, we didn't eat squash, much less play squash, in my crowd.) I found him pleasingly urbane, funny and smart, endlessly profane. All the men at the *Post* used the *F* word at least once in each sentence as noun, verb, adjective, or adverb. He was also brashly cynical, like all romantics.

Don took me to dinner at his favorite place for impressing first dates (he later confessed), the Little Old Mansion, a southern restaurant in midtown with the cranky grande dame owner southern restaurants seemed to demand. On the way to dinner, he bought me a bikini— shocking pink on one side, reversing to black on the other. It was a tribute, I felt, to how juicy I'd looked on my terrace in a pink-and-white-checked gingham bikini. The slight qualms I felt, being an inch or two taller than he in heels, were quickly melting. On the banquette beside me, he sat tall. I had the lobster with black walnuts in a saffron rice ring.

Rather quickly, it began to feel like love to me. Before Don, there had been many men—wild crushes, consuming dalliances, fleeting affairs, one-night stands and one-week stands. But this was love at another level, not just lust and an electric sexual connection but also a joy in the amazing intimacy we shared and the way his need freed me to reveal my own.

It's easy to see now that all that traffic in and out of my bed before Don was due not just to my uninhibited appetite for sex but a way to get close and make somebody love me. I was rarely cool. I thought getting a man was like getting the story. You had to be smart and aggressive, tie up the phone, park on the doorstep, and shove interlopers out of the way when necessary.

I was a wreck when Don went off to Denmark to see why his fiancée, the brunette with the bee-stung lips, had not yet come back to New York. He didn't tell me all the details on his return, only that it was finished. I determined to show him how lucky he was—what a perfect mate he had in me. Collagen injections didn't exist then, so I couldn't do much to fatten my lips beyond cheating with lipstick beyond my lip line and pouting a lot. I comforted him with matzo ball soup and chocolate mousse.

It took a year to convince him that we should live together. His dark ground-floor studio, shades pulled to keep out the stares of passersby, was too tiny and grim. But there was a small one-bedroom walk-up with dormer ceilings and funny little windows on the top floor we could rent for very little money. Before he could change his mind, he had signed the lease. And we dragged our stuff upstairs and moved in. Of course, when my folks came to New York, we flipped the bell plate around so it said Greene and not Forst/Greene. That way, my parents could pretend they didn't know we were living together. We took them for dinner at the American Pavilion during the 1964 World's Fair, where Don, with great bravura, ordered a Richebourg, one of the greatest red Burgundies, expensive even then, and my mom threw in two ice cubes to chill it. I loved that he never held that against me.

Soon we were pooling our savings to explore all the great restaurants, Craig's favorites, whatever Silas Spitzer recommended in *Holiday* magazine, and *Gourmet*'s monthly picks.

Once I was with Don, other men became simply male humans, not possible conquests. I didn't see them as men I needed to seduce. I didn't have to prove anything anymore, because Don seemed to adore me. He was smart and funny and brooding, with a deep melancholy streak. Sometimes he would be telling a story so sad that he would cry. I was moved by his tears, his deep sadness. I would be his woman, his mistress, his muse, his good mother.

Don and I would lie in bed after making love, trading bedroom stories, tales of a thousand and one nights. He'd slept with hundreds of women. And it didn't matter how many men I'd been with. "Whatever you've done is what makes you what you are," he said. "And that's the you I love."

Blueberry Pie with Orange-Nut Crust

I believe this came from the Times in the sixties, and I made it into my own summer pie. The vintage recipe called for shortening, but I've substituted butter for twenty-first-century tastes.

Crust:
2 cups flour
¼ tsp. salt
2 tsp. sugar
8 oz. unsalted butter
2 tsp. grated orange rind
⅓ cup finely chopped almonds or pecans
5 tbsp. ice water (approximately)

Filling:
4 cups blueberries
½ cup sugar
2 tbsp. cornstarch

Preheat oven to 375° F. If you have a pizza stone, place it on the bottom rack.

Mix flour, salt, and sugar in the bowl of an electric mixer. Cut butter into eight pieces. Using the paddle attachment, add one piece at a time. Continue processing until pieces of butter are no larger than a pea. Add orange rind and nuts and process briefly. Remove bowl from mixer.

Sprinkle 3 tablespoons of the water over the mixture and mix in with a fork. Pinch the dough together. If it holds and doesn't feel dry, you do not need to add the remaining water. If it's dry and does not hold, add remaining water, 1 tablespoon at a time, as needed, to make the dough come together. Roll into two balls, flatten, and wrap separately in plastic. Refrigerate for approximately one hour.

Remove one pastry disk from the refrigerator 20 minutes before rolling. Roll the pastry and line a nine-inch pie plate with it. Refrigerate the pastry-lined plate and remove remaining disk from fridge while preparing the berries.

Pick over the berries, then gently toss with granulated sugar and cornstarch. Pour into pastry-lined pie plate.

Roll out remaining pastry. If you have a lattice-top form to punch out a checkerboard top, use it. Otherwise, cut 3 to 4 slits in the top layer of pastry once you have laid it over the blueberries. Moisten the edges and crimp to seal.

Place on the bottom rack of the oven, ideally on the pizza stone. Bake for 20 minutes. Reduce temperature to 350° and move the pie to the middle rack and bake for another 20 minutes. The pie is done when the juices start to bubble and the crust is nicely browned on the edges.

Serves 8.

5

SOMETHING BORROWED, SOMETHING BLUE

AGING HIPPIES LIKE TO SAY, "IF YOU REMEMBER THE SIXTIES, YOU WEREN'T there." I remember the sixties because food and sex were drugs that did not destroy memory cells. I still had a hangover of fifties' sensibility. I was curious about LSD, but it was supposed to bring out the real you from within. Forget about that. I could see from my friends who loved smoking marijuana that it was an escape from reality and brought on the munchies, a symptom I couldn't afford in my trade. Caught up in work, paying bills . . . and playing house, I still wore my panty girdle and white gloves. The counterculture was a sideshow. I covered it for the *New York Post* and for *Ladies' Home Journal*. Unlike Al Aronowitz, a middle-class New Jersey boy who went beat covering the Beats for the *Post* and claimed to have given the Beatles their first grass, I liked shoes and bags that matched, and clean sheets, preferably ironed. The chocolate velvet cake at the Four Seasons was about as druggy as I cared to go.

Looking back from the media-saturated world of today, where I suppose even prepubescents know what Bill Clinton did to flavor his cigar, it is difficult to believe how innocent we were. My article "Are You Man Enough to Take a Mistress?" must have seemed a provocative challenge to readers of *Nugget* when the men's monthly ran it in December 1962.

Mistress still had a slightly back-street connotation. *Mistress* had an aura of glamorous wickedness, so unlike today's everyday, socially acknowledged *live-in companion* or *domestic partner.*

Probably I'd sold the story before Don and I surprised ourselves by getting married on Labor Day weekend in 1961. I liked the idea of being his mistress (although, in fact, we shared the bills). We had watched our friends pairing off, having babies, moving to the suburbs because it was better for the children. Neither of us was eager to marry. I had actually convinced myself marriage was too big a commitment, since Don made it clear marriage was not his immediate goal. Don was not my dream man. His deep melancholy sometimes felt like more than I could carry.

"We'll just live together as long as it's wonderful," I said. He agreed. And it was wonderful.

When I traveled for a *Post* story, I never felt the smallest flicker of lust for anyone. I thrived on that as evidence of how much I loved Don, how much I felt loved. Most of my out-of-town assignments for the *Post* were brief, but an investigation of illegal baby adoptions involving New York couples took me to Las Vegas and Los Angeles for almost a month. Back in New York, I found Don gloomy and annoyed by the long separation.

"I want to get married," he said. "If you don't want to marry, then we should end this and one of us should move out."

I was caught by surprise. He had convinced me he would never marry, and I was cozy and comfortable just as we were, no legal tie. "But darling, we don't need to be married," I said. "We're great together. . . . We're better than being married. What made you suddenly decide you want to do this?"

"I think we should do it for your parents," he said.

That stopped me for a minute or two. I didn't laugh. "Are you sure?" I asked. "You're upset about my parents?"

"I hate the subterfuge . . . the pretense." He was lying facedown on the hated gold coverlet of our bed, bought to match the twenty-five-dollar gold-and-red cotton fake Persian rug from the Salvation Army that I also hated—all my least favorite colors, but I believed everything should match.

I got someone to recommend a crisis therapist. I went four times and I heard myself talk. "I'm too tall. He's too short. I can't live without him.

Marriage should be forever. I don't ever want a divorce. How do I know if he's really the one? He gets depressed and he hates his mother. That's not a good sign. But I love how emotional he is. . . . I love that he cries. I don't think I want to live without him."

What did the therapist say? I'm sure he had something to say. Crisis therapists, unlike strict Freudians, are allowed to, expected to, talk. But I listened to myself and decided I would marry Don, invoking the same mantra that had protected me so far—for as long as it was wonderful. What a relief! I wasn't signing on forever. It was in the back of my mind, unspoken, freeing me to marry. Once I said yes, I was really excited and committed. I was going to be married. How amazing. And my parents would be happy, too. They were convinced I'd never find a man who would marry anyone who'd slept around as much as I had (and they didn't know the half of it).

"Who would buy a cow if you've already got the milk?" Daddy had said. Well, now we would have crème fraîche and mountains of whipped cream.

We went to Detroit to get married.

My mom's friends gave me a shower. "You must have a shower," Mother said, "because I've been buying shower gifts for everyone else's daughters and nieces for twenty-five years and now it's my turn." Her canasta pals brought me nightgowns, very sexy nighties, red satin with spaghetti straps, black with a see-through lace midriff, off-the-shoulder baby-doll pajamas. Did they know?

Daddy gave us the choice of a fancy wedding or five thousand dollars. I negotiated a small wedding in my sister's backyard, facing a ragtag forest, and four thousand dollars. Mom's friend the florist had promised me a Gothic arch or Corinthian columns. My heart dropped and I found myself snarling when I saw the four stumpy poles stuck in the dirt. "What are those cigarette butts?" I cried.

"They are not Greek columns?" my mother asked.

"I should have known no one in Detroit could produce a Gothic arch." I stormed around in my shorts and rubber curlers, trying not to cry and destroy my eyes.

Don looked terror-stricken but handsome, deeply tanned (working nights will do that) in a dark gray pinstripe suit from Brooks Brothers, his first new suit since his high school graduation. I had no ring for him.

I was very sensitive about wedding rings for men. I had seen too many men slipping their wedding bands in their pockets or flipping them on the dresser before jumping into bed with me. I didn't want to imagine Don ever taking off our wedding ring for a few hours.

Probably we should have taken the whole five thousand dollars Daddy offered, but I wanted Detroit to know I wasn't making it up—I really was getting married. I felt disoriented: The cigarette-butt debacle. Anxiety about Don meeting my eccentric family in one fell swoop. His mother as sweet as treacle (of course we had to invite her). It was all so unnerving that afterward, when we arrived in our honeymoon suite at the St. Clair Inn just for the night—we'd take a real honeymoon in Italy later that fall—we immediately called room service and ordered six desserts, all of them bordering on inedible, and ate every one.

This was just a small hiccup before the glorious food revolution that was coming.

My Ex-Sister-in-Law's Orange Pour Cake

I baked this moist tea cake for Christmas gifts in the sixties. I placed each cake on a vintage carved breadboard that cost five dollars back then and wrapped it in cellophane. Imagine having the time for such domestic arts. I am deeply envious.

Cake:
2 cups flour, plus 2 tbsp.
½ cup butter, softened
2 eggs
⅔ cup sugar
1 tsp. baking soda
2 tbsp. grated orange zest
½ cup chopped nuts (walnuts or pecans)
¾ cup sour cream

Topping:
½ cup sugar
¼ cup orange juice
1 tbsp. grated orange rind

Preheat oven to 375° F.

Cream 2 tablespoons of the flour into softened butter in a large bowl. Beat eggs in small bowl. Add sugar and combine with flour and butter mixture.

Sift remaining flour with baking soda and add slowly into the egg-butter-sugar mix until combined. Add grated orange rind, nuts, and sour cream. Pour or spoon into greased metal loaf pan.

Bake 30 minutes.

For the topping, combine sugar, orange juice, and 1 tbsp. grated orange rind.

Remove cake from the oven when done and pour topping on cake while cake is still hot.

6

INNOCENTS ABROAD

IN *BLUE TROUT AND BLACK TRUFFLES*, JOSEPH WECHSBERG, MY MODEL OF A peregrinating epicure, had written, "All epicurian roads lead to Vienne." Not Vienna, but Vienne, a small outpost dating back to Roman times, south of Lyon. Don's best friend, Jules, was just back from army service in France with the newly converted's galloping obsession for gastronomic adventure. He could see we were smitten with food. He was properly impressed by my adaptation of Café Chauveron's mussels in Chardonnay cream, glazed under the broiler. "Not exactly the same," we all agreed. "But really close." Don poured a $1.89 bottle of Chablis. We told Jules our plans for a belated honeymoon in Italy. Jules urged us to make time to discover France. We revised our itinerary. Of course we would go to Vienne. Not sensibly by train from Paris, as more seasoned gourmands would have, but naïvely, determinedly, from Rome—by two trains, an autobus, and a taxi, about the most obtuse detour one might contrive.

Never having known the glories of La Pyramide—famously "Chez Point," when the legendary Fernand Point was alive—I can only detail the glories committed in his memory as they fertilized our budding gluttonous sensibilities. La Pyramide was dramatically spruced up years later. But back in 1962, it was still the same modest *maison* Point had

ruled, with Madame Point sitting on a tall chair at the entrance, checking out arrivals, and, I felt, writing us off as innocents abroad. Well, we
had our doubts about La Pyramide, too. The tacky little dining room
with its funereal gladioli seemed ominously bourgeois, without promise.
Maybe we had found our obsession too late.

But then came a molded pyramid of sweet butter to marvel at, huge,
enough to butter toast for a family of four for a week, and a rich, gamy
terrine framed in the tenderest pastry crust. A fresh knife and fork heralded a round of truffle-studded foie gras set into a square of brioche—
exactly the yellow cakelike texture of the richest challah. I had never
tasted fresh foie gras before—so pink and delicate and buttery. It filled
my mouth with silk and demanded attention. I knew at once this could
become an addiction. Then a ritual change of silver and the waiter arrived with a small pastry boat filled with a ratatouille of autumn vegetables, each distinctly itself yet happily married. By then, we were getting
a little tipsy and congratulating ourselves for our brilliance in being alive
and at the kitchen's mercy.

The *truite saumonée* was stuffed with a poem of mushrooms and vegetables and was painted with a potion blending butter, cream, and port.
We drank a wine we'd never heard of called Condrieu, icy golden *vin du
pays* in an unlabeled bottle. It cost one dollar and was so fragile that it
could not be exported, we were told (though now it is widely exported
and you can't get half a thimbleful for one dollar). With the crusty
mustard-slicked and crumbed duck and its accompanying sauceboat of
béarnaise, we shared a half bottle of heady and imperious Hermitage.
The miraculous duck . . . how did they do it?

The elderly maître d', Vincent, invited me to the kitchen to see the
cooking of the duck.

"Us?" asked Don, who did not speak French.

"*Non, moi,*" I said, rising dizzily. In the soot-blackened alcove, a Boy
Scout troop of teenage cooks paused to stare, one of them tossing coals
from a wheelbarrow into the oven where the bird had been grilled. I
muttered what compliments I could muster in French, given my inebri-
ated state.

Back at the table, there was a challenging confrontation with creamy
Saint Marcellin cheese and something goaty in a leaf, then ice cream and
the house's mythic eight-layered Gâteau Marjolaine. Just at the point I

knew another bite was impossible, a platter of the pastry chef's frivolities appeared—diminutive cream puffs, itsy napoleons, mini-tartlets.
Between groans of pain and ecstasy, we devoured them one by one.
Everyone was giggling—Vincent, the waiters, a few lingering clients.
Flushed faces all around us were giggling. Somehow we got the check
and somehow we paid, dispensing francs equal to the twenty-seven-
dollar tab and a tip or two. Someone aimed us out the door and in the
direction of La Résidence—two triumphant pilgrims, leaning into each
other for support . . . totally, blissfully, wondrously sauced.

Raw Tomato Sauce
for Pasta

*Don and I loved a pasta with an uncooked tomato sauce that we ate at a shack
on the beach in Ischia during our belated honeymoon. I gave the idea to Craig
once. He said it was awful, but I noticed he ran a very similar recipe some
months later. Only the best summer tomatoes will do.*

4 large beefsteak tomatoes
4 very large cloves of garlic
6 large basil leaves
1 tsp. salt
6 grindings of black pepper
⅔ cup fruity extra virgin olive oil
1 lb. bucatini or perciatelli

Core and chop tomatoes coarsely, between ¼ and ½ inch.
(I never bother to peel them, but you can.) Put the tomato and all its
juices into a large bowl. Peel garlic and smash with a chef's knife if you
want to remove it before serving, or mince two of the cloves if you
want to leave it in for a more intense garlic taste. Add garlic to
tomatoes.

Cut 3 of the basil leaves into fine ribbons and add to tomatoes.
Add salt and pepper. Stir in olive oil. Cover and let sit at room
temperature for 8 to 10 hours, stirring occasionally.

Cook pasta in a large pot of boiling salted water for 10 to 12
minutes. Drain in a colander, reserving a third of a cup of pasta
cooking water in the pot. Return pasta to pot and toss with reserved
liquid. Ladle into soup bowls. Remove smashed garlic from tomatoes
and ladle over pasta. Sliver remaining basil and scatter on top. Some
will want a flurry of fresh grated Parmesan; purists will not.

Serves 4 as a main course, 6 as a first course.

7

COMFORT ME WITH CHOCOLATE MOUSSE

WHAT MIGHT HISTORY HAVE BEEN IF EVE HAD TAKEN THAT APPLE AND baked it into a *tarte tatin* and shared it with the snake? For Don and me, having tasted the fruit of the foie gras, there was no turning back.

Back home, the pursuit of cuisinary perfection became all-consuming. We worked, yes. You need money to dine well. And Don was ambitious, a committed newspaperman. For me, journalism was just a hobby, providing running-around money till I sold that novel. But novels take forever. By then, I was in weekend-warrior attack mode on the three hundred pages of a novel not even I quite understood. Meanwhile, to cook a great meal was instant gratification.

I cooked following the catechism of Craig Claiborne. I whisked yolks into zabaglione in my copper bowl and whipped the cream over icy water, per the counsel of Julia Child. I conquered my fear of dough with six lessons from the English cooking teacher Dione Lucas in a studio above her shop, Once Upon an Egg, later O'Neal's. I mastered boning a duck without breaking its skin, stuffing it with assorted ground meats, and baking it in a pastry blanket. Helping Dione stretch my twelve inches of strudel dough till it overhung a six-foot table and you could see through it was thrilling. That she sent her nylon stockings to the laundry and they came back ironed was impressive, too. I never did either at home.

Our friends were possessed early foodies, too. When I recognized the dark-haired woman buying a boodle of serious cheeses at Fauchon in Paris as a woman I'd met at a Burgundy Society Tastevin dinner in New York, and then ran into her twice again in the next four days—at the legendary shop selling copper pots and pans in Les Halles and at dinner on the Côte d'Azur—we both took it as a message from the fates. Naomi* and I are still soul mates, now forty years later. It was she who persuaded an uncle in the cheese business to create American crème fraîche with instructions she brought home from France. For neophytes with only a vague notion of what crème fraîche might be and what it was doing in the supermarket dairy case, there was a little folder of Naomi's recipes glued to the container top. The only drawback for me was my insider knowledge, aware from the beginning that the divine ooze was 87 percent butterfat. Even before cholesterol entered the axis of evil, that struck me as dangerous.

As the avant-garde of the gluttony to come, we did dinner parties, my foodie friends and I, wowing one another with whole ducks boned and stuffed, and pistachio-studded pork terrines, devoting long hours to reproducing all the moussemerizing, béarnaising, and vinaigretting we picked up in many rounds of cooking classes and gourmand travel.

We cheerfully commited to shopping that took days and military discipline to organize. Since Don worked mostly nights at the *Post,* he was free to chauffeur me around town in our little red Volkswagen to gather the best ingredients. There was no Fairway then, and Eli was probably still teething on a bagel from the family grocery, Zabar's, which had not yet gone global. We had to cross town to Cheese of All Nations, hit the Village for bread at Zito's on Bleecker Street, double-park outside the Nevada Meat Market for quality veal or lamb, and stop at Esposito's on Ninth Avenue to buy the best ground pork for the pistachio-studded terrine. Don got a shop foreman at the *Post* to cut a lead weight that fit precisely inside my terrine mold to compress my classic pâtés. He immediately had a vision of my dropping the weight on my foot and

---

*I call her Naomi because she is so private not even her doorman knows her name.

made me promise never to weight my terrine unless he was home. Great editors are like that—always anticipating the worst.

I bought my battery of knives from the notoriously terrible-tempered Fred Bridge, famous for snarling at innocents who dared ask uninformed questions in his mythic kitchen-supply bazaar. I tamed his savage bark by buying *oeuf en gelée* molds, and expensive truffle cutters (as yet unused), as well as spring-form pans, charlotte molds, and tart pans with removable bottoms (which I did use). I baked an exquisite, terrifyingly complex *poire bourdaloue* from Time-Life's *Classic French Cookbook*. It knocked everyone out, and then I quite sensibly decided I never had to do that again.

The oenophilic competition of our men grew heated even as our cellars and wine closets were required to grow cool. Don's boyhood friend, Jules the ophthalmologist (who had directed us to La Pyramide), put down seven hundred bottles of the '61 vintage in a humidity-controlled storeroom. Once Jules explained what that meant, Don and I, cellarless but determined to hold our own, found cases of France's most celebrated Bordeaux at Macy's wine shop and brought home Château Margaux, Lafite, and Mouton Rothschild at $225 a case. That was a wanton extravagance then, but they were the only names we knew.

The two of us tried to recapture the rapture of France in Manhattan at restaurants like the Veau d'Or and Café Chauveron. We psyched ourselves to feel comfortable in the Pool Room at the Four Seasons and braved the Coach House, where the proprietor, Leon Lianides, could look right through you if he was in one of his moods, which he clearly never was when favorites like Craig Claiborne and James Beard were lapping up the tripe in avgolemono soup, followed by the fabulous lamb steak with its kidney still attached. Even the great French chef Jean Troisgros was dazzled, we were told, by Maryland lump crabmeat rolled inside Hormel prosciutto, thick Madeira-haunted black bean soup, native sirloin paved in pepper, Comice pears with American cheese, and pecan pie. Troisgros left carrying two iron baking molds and the recipe for the Coach House's grainy little logs of corn bread.

We went to El Parador because Craig wrote that he loved the margaritas and guacamole. And in between these exercises in excess, we ate simply and cheaply at Oscar's King of the Sea, at King Wu in Chinatown, where Don's friends had thrown his bachelor party, and at our favorite

Shanghai local on Broadway at 103rd Street, where we inevitably had the pressed duck—a lushly crusted dish I haven't seen anywhere for decades. We haunted movie revival houses, hating the dip in the middle of the Thalia but driven there by our hunger for movies. But mostly, I cooked. I crisped soft-shell crabs and deglazed the pan with a splash of white wine or shook bay scallops in a bag of bread crumbs and then sautéed them in butter. Sour cream made anything taste better. I invented fabulous frittatas, those layered Italian omelettes, using a week's worth of leftovers from the fridge. And I indulged Don with bananas flambé and crème caramel. We were trim and young. No one had ever heard of cholesterol. Detroit was rocked by riots, in which forty-three died. Away on our honeymoon, we missed the October demonstrations against the Vietnam War at the Pentagon. Home again, we were the Bonnie and Clyde of West End Avenue, with our gourmand swagger. We were so in love.

8

HOW I BECAME
HENRI SOULÉ'S DARLING

AFTER A TIME, IT BECAME CLEAR THAT I WAS AVOIDING CARNAL KNOWL-edge of Craig's favorite, Le Pavillon, creation of the quintessential Henri Soulé. I just didn't have the courage to walk up unknown and unrecommended to the legendary martinet at his podium as he rationed out the royal banquettes at Le Pavillon. I knew from reading *Women's Wear Daily* and Wechsberg's *Dining at the Pavillon* how his glance could turn a poseur to *fleur de sel*. And the two of us—thanks to Don's boyish look and my bargain-basement Ohrbach's couture—were clearly not to the Pavillon born, unlike Jack Kennedy (who got his milk served in an ice bucket). I did not want to be hustled off to the dark nethers of Soulé's Siberia and be fed last week's lamb chops. It would have helped if we could have been introduced by a regular, someone to vouch for us in our untitled, un-best-dressed, un–Dun & Bradstreet shabbiness. But there was no one.

Finally, I realized the way to reach Monsieur Soulé was through my typewriter. I had started freelancing so that our fancy eating would be tax-deductible. I proposed a story to *Ladies' Home Journal*: "A Week in the Kitchen of the Pavillon." Henri Soulé, a flirtatious five-foot-five cube of amiability, was willing. Pouting and posing, an owl who saw himself as an osprey, he instructed his chef, Clément Grangier, to suffer me in the kitchen below for as long as required. I arrived each morning in my tennis shoes, was taught how to flute a mushroom, watched chef Grangier whisk butter to order for a fussy habitué, marveled at the saucier's iron right forearm, and took lessons in *quenelles de brochet*—the delicate whipped pike and cream dumplings that were my favorite dish.

One Friday, Soulé invited me to lunch with him at 3:00 PM. "Say you want *les tripes à la mode de Caen*," he commanded. "It's forbidden by my doctor. That damn Grangier won't even serve it to me." He instructed chef Grangier to hand-chop his usual hamburger. When our food had been dished up from the copper casseroles, and the captain and waiter had backed away in respectful obeisance, Soulé switched plates, generously alloting me a plop of tripe alongside my burger.

I stared at the tripe, a scary nest of anatomical parts in a muddy sauce. It would be a while before my aversion to tripe would evolve into a passion for tripe in all its guises. I didn't have a lot of aversions in the dawn of my gourmand life, but enough that I felt I would have to conquer them. Beets made me gag. I didn't eat olives. I hadn't yet fallen in love with oysters. The worship of caviar escaped me. I had acquired an unDetroiterly passion for sweetbreads but had not mastered brains. I speared the tiniest nubbin of tripe on my fork, doused it heavily with sauce, and swallowed it whole. "Hmmm," I said.

Soulé looked up, fork balanced en route to his mouth. "So you are writing about the secrets of Le Pavillon. You won't find the secret of Le Pavillon in the kitchen," he said. "The secret of Le Pavillon . . . *c'est moi*." He puffed up his pouter-pigeon chest. "Le Pavillon, *c'est moi*."

In May of 1965, Soulé announced he would reopen La Côte Basque, which he had sold in a fit of pique to a confrere who, alas, simply wasn't making a go of it. There was talk of bankruptcy. To recover the unpaid debt, Soulé would have to repossess and run it himself. He had always thought of La Côte Basque as "Le Pavillon for the poor. A place for a man to bring his mistress while he comes with his wife to Le Pavillon."

Don had left the *Post* by then and was happier than he had ever been, caught up in the excitement of the *Herald Tribune,* where he edited Jimmy Breslin and a young red-haired southern fellow named Tom Wolfe, whose prose had a way of ricocheting out of control. I'd quit the *Post* at Don's urging to work full-time on a novel that grew so thorny and dense, I was finally forced to abandon it. I needed my freelancing for magazines more than ever to justify my existence and help finance our gourmandlich wanderings. Don encouraged me to offer the Soulé story to Clay Felker, an editor at *New York,* the *Trib*'s Sunday magazine. Clay, and Shelly Zelaznick, orchestrating amazing flights of unleashed journalism, had everyone talking. My docudrama of the countdown to the celebrity-riddled opening lunch was important; Soulé told me later, "The *Ladies' Home Journal* is okay, but the *Trib* . . . that means something to Soulé. Now you must come often. You and your husband. This is your home."

He lighted up a cigar. I lighted up a cigar. We puffed away.

About that cigar: After five sessions with the hypnotist, I had stopped smoking on New Year's Eve. Ten days later, Don bought me an exquisite tortoiseshell and ivory cigarette holder he'd found in a small antiques shop. I didn't want to hurt his feelings, but I wanted desperately not to smoke again. "You didn't notice I'm not smoking?" I asked.

"You can smoke little cigars," Don suggested. "You don't inhale cigars." He had begun smoking long, thin cigars for the gestures, I thought, and the worldly ceremony. He brought home a small box of pencil-thin Schimmelpennicks, that just fit into the delicate holder.

When Soulé lighted a cigar after our next lunch, I pulled out my little box of small Dutch cigars, slipped one into the mother-of-pearl mouth of my holder, and let Soulé light it. He was delighted.

"I love a woman who smokes cigars," he had said. He insisted I let him fill my purse with small Cuban cigars whenever I came to Le Pavillon. A small stockpile of these hoarded Cubanos found their way to Don's humidor. I never really liked that awful cigar taste in my mouth. I gave them up after a few months because I didn't want to smell like my uncle Max.

I loved those gossipy lunches, the unfolding intrigue of the food establishment, Monsieur Soulé's indiscreet confessions. The lies certain people told to get a reservation when Soulé insisted he was booked. The cosmetic titan who would stop short and refuse to budge if Soulé tried to lead him to a table beyond a certain line in the carpet. The great beauty who had so much to say to her walker and nothing to say to her husband. That's how it was in the fall of 1968, when Felker beckoned me to the new *New York.* I had one foot in my kitchen and a finger already in the Manhattan dining stew. So maybe Clay's casting was prophetic. I might not know enough to criticize anyone's rack of lamb or floating island in *New York* magazine, but I definitely had the requisite hunger.

9

WHEN CRAIG CLAIBORNE
WAS GOD AND KING

CRAIG CLAIBORNE WAS A GOD, MY HERO, MY IDOL. EVEN NON-FOOD-obsessed New Yorkers looked to his Friday restaurant review in the *New York Times* as gospel. Don would go out to pick up the early edition of Friday's *Times* at eleven o'clock on Thursday night and drop into his big green club chair to study what news had been deemed fit to print by the competition.

I sat on the floor at Don's feet—we were always in the same few square feet of space in those early days. (Actually, I liked typing on the floor, my old Royal upright sitting on an atlas, my legs folded Indian-style.) Never mind the headlines, for years I had turned immediately to see what Craig loved or hated. I would give anything, I often thought, to live his life, being paid to eat, being sent overseas with unlimited funds to explore exotic cuisines. I lived his life vicariously through his writing. Craig was always going off to France. He was among the first to hit the dumpling parlors of Beijing when Nixon opened China. He even braved Vietnam during the war, oblivious to politics, properly focused on what to eat on the lemongrass trail.

Restaurant criticism was not the raucous gang bang it has become. There were not swarms of critical gullets in media yet to be invented.

47

And Zagat had not marshaled amateur critics and built their bleats and raves into a media empire. Every New Yorker over the age of six did not consider him or herself a restaurant critic as we do today. True, James Beard had a syndicated food column. There was Clementine Paddleford writing about food in the *Herald Tribune*. And the *Post* had a pathetic column lauding restaurants that advertised in its pages.

I felt a deep, spiritual connection to Craig—fussy, uptight southerner that he seemed to be, he was unabashedly passionate about food. Before Julia, and even after, I used his first *New York Times Cookbook*. His recipes were so modest and plain and undemanding, rarely more than half a page in the book or a paragraph on the *Times* food page, unlike Julia's meticulous, detailed, hand-holding gastrotherapy.

Cooking his recipes was as close as I could get to Craig. His *boeuf bourguignon,* redolent with red wine and caramelized shallots, was a guaranteed triumph. *Redolent* was a Craig word. And the shallot to me was a new, sophisticated onion, unheard of in my mom's primitive Detroit pantry.

Once when the sour cream curdled in a baked zucchini recipe clipped from the *Times* and followed religiously, I dialed the newspaper and asked for counsel. I was stunned when he took the call. Himself. Craig Claiborne, with that Mississippi drawl. "Sour cream will break up if the temperature is too high," he said. Of course. How naïve could I be? In my haste, I'd turned the flame too high. My respect for Craig, the *New York Times,* and sour cream swelled like a popover.

I was a stalker. Not literally (although it might have been a kick going through Craig's garbage), but I did follow in his footsteps, trailing his stars. I was nervous stepping into Pearl's, the midtown den where the smartly dressed Pearl Wong ruled haughtily over her loyal clan of Time, Inc., and Seventh Avenue pets (some of them her financial backers). Word had it that she was a master of snobbery, as arrogant as any French restaurateur. But Craig loved chef Lum's mythic lemon chicken and yook soong, the chicken–water chestnut–red pepper mix to eat wrapped in iceberg lettuce leaves. So I went early one day all by myself, before the lunch wave hit, Craig's review in hand. The maître d' looked as if he wanted to refuse me a table. I berated myself for not spending more money on shoes. But since the room was an empty sea of white, I got a tight little two-top table and ordered everything Craig had singled out for praise in his review—all the spicy, peppery, gingery, chili-detonated stir-fries he loved.

"Very spicy," the waiter warned as he took my order.

"I like spicy. Give me Craig Claiborne spicy," I said. I dropped a chopstick load of Szechuan beef with bits of tree ear and lotus root into my mouth and gasped. Oh yes. It was spicy. The shrimp was a killer, too. I choked and sneezed and coughed, tears running down my face.

"Something wrong, lady?" the maître d' asked.

"No," I said, wiping my cheeks and my forehead. "It's wonderful. It's perfect."

I had to find a way to meet Craig. I was more than just a fan, after all. I was a writer. I would write a profile of the great *Times* critic. How could Claiborne resist? I pitched the idea to an editor at *Look* magazine and he gave his blessings. Craig seemed amused, even pleased, by the idea of a profile in *Look*. He agreed I should start by coming along on a reviewing lunch to see how he did it. We met downtown in the Village at a funky little Spanish restaurant. Craig was fussy and proper and very southern, just like he sounded in the *Times,* scolding the waiter in his soft, rolling drawl because the plates weren't warmed.

I tried not to seem gauche. "Oh yes," I said, feeling the plate with the back of my hand as if it were a loved one's fevered brow. We were the only customers in this little joint with its one waiter. I am sure he had never heard of warming plates, but he warmed them.

I was deeply impressed by Craig's seriousness. He told me how he had suffered that week, agonizing over the stars he awarded—very rarely four, but sometimes three, many twos, and often one. "I was up all night, tossing and turning, trying to decide if I'd given the Gaiety Delicatessen three stars instead of two because [his bosses] Abe Rosenthal and Arthur [Gelb] like the Gaiety. Or does the place deserve it?" He crinkled his nose as if to say, Silly, isn't it? All that fuss over a deli. But I could hear the anguish in his voice.

Craig thought it was important for me to see the yin and yang of his territory as a critic. He'd long ago given three stars to Quo Vadis, a clubby, upper-crust spot in the Continental style, and he thought I should taste its superior food. There was much racing about with platters of the daily specials to tempt him. At his side on the banquette, I basked in the aura of such unctuous ooze. Would Mr. Claiborne like that sautéed in butter? No butter. Olive oil? A new oil has just arrived from Tuscany, smuggled in by a cousin. (No one spoke of virgins or extra-virgins in those simpler, less promiscuous times.) A little puddle was poured so Craig could taste. He ignored it.

The tame old-world edible feel-good stirred up by the two Parma-born partners, Gino Robusti and Bruno Caravaggi, bred intense fidelity from Quo Vadis loyalists, I learned. There were the musical Italians — Tebaldi, Corelli, Tucci. On the day of an opera performance, Cesare Siepi would put away a dozen and a half oysters. Quo Vadis habitués were likely to witness such affectionate reunions as Gen. George C. Kenney embracing Mrs. Douglas MacArthur at a table with Eddie Rickenbacker, John Paul Getty and a scion not talking much, and Baron Rothschild rinsing his hands with water from a goblet. The house was known for a few Belgian and Italian signature dishes—the eel in green sauce, a heroic *bollito misto* (boiled meats with a spunky salsa verde and candied mustard fruits)—and for subdued classics like bay scallops meunière or a wholesome calf's liver with bacon, nutritional sanity for the Geritol set, sexagenarian capitalists, and aging warriors.

Gino and Bruno danced their pas de deux for Craig now in the antimacassar parlor elegance of chintz and crystal and clichéd bronzes on marble pedestals below the fabulous painted palazzo ceiling. I was wowed by the fondue Bruxelloise—deep-fried batter-wrapped pockets of creamy cheese, sprinkled with a shock of fried parsley. But I noticed that Craig seemed seriously disturbed by his *anguille au vert*—eel poached in white wine and mulched in fresh herbs. "It needs salt," he said. I tasted. Indeed. When Craig grabbed a salt shaker and corrected the lapse, I could see both owners go white.

A shallow copper cocotte of kidneys Bercy was presented for Craig's nod, sauceboat alongside.

"Enough," Craig said as Gino dished them out. "Enough. No, that's too much." He frowned. And to me: "So gross."

Too much? Gross? I never knew there could be anything like too much. Too much was always just barely enough for me. But Craig ate very sparingly—savoring each morsel if it were properly seasoned and skillfully cooked. And the kidneys were splendid that day. He closed his eyes and smiled beatifically. He nibbled and sipped his wine, leaving a third of the kidneys on his plate, as if he was actually full. Full, that was another new concept for me. Life was never about full. It was about "Oh my god, how delicious this is." I would soon realize it was drinking that gave Craig his neat little potbelly. He loved his martinis, fine wine in beautiful crystal, and, oh, those margaritas (only fresh-squeezed lime would do for his perfect margarita). I wrote down the recipe, looking forward to thrilling my friends at my next brunch with the perfect margarita.

Look's photographer and I drove out to Craig's weekend house on Long Island to shoot him and onetime Pavillon chef Pierre Franey preparing a recipe for their Sunday *Times* magazine column. I was beside myself with anticipation—Craig Claiborne and the great Pavillon chef cooking for me. Craig lived in a modest two-story prefab that he'd bought from a catalog and parked alongside a modest pool with great views of Gardiner's Bay in the Springs, that low-frills exurb of East Hampton where so many painters worked, not far from where Jackson Pollock was buried.

As a devotee of what soup opera got covered in the very staid *New York Times,* I knew Pierre Franey had stunned Manhattan's close-knit colony of Gallic expatriates by quitting the mythic Le Pavillon (the ultimate great restaurant of its time). He'd felt slighted by Soulé and left for Howard Johnson's and more money, where, Craig reported to me, he was contentedly upgrading the canned gravy and stews, and was the genius behind HoJo's ginger ice cream. Was Howard Johnson's coffee ice cream uniquely brilliant? It was, I learned, because Pierre had insisted they use espresso coffee. Indeed, Claiborne-Franey recipes occasionally might call for a can of Howard Johnson's gravy, a veritable sauce espagnole by any other name.

Pierre had been the invisible eminence in Craig's recipes for a long while and ultimately came to share the byline on their Sunday column. On this afternoon, he bustled about Craig's open kitchen—a sturdy, suntanned Frenchman, fiftyish and sexy, with emphatic black brows and that flirtatious manner that seems to run in French genes. His intimates and maybe the world knew that Craig was gay, and everyone not in their immediate circle of intimates wondered if Pierre was gay, too. It was clear to me that Craig adored him. Pierre stabbed some lobsters, flamed them in cognac, and began to create a soufflé Plaza Athénée—the classic layering of lobster and grated Gruyère with cream and whipped egg whites that would balloon in the oven and brown into a glorious cloud.

Craig stationed himself on a stool at the counter in front of his portable typewriter, counting the eggs as they cracked and occasionally grabbing Pierre's hand so he could measure how much flour or how much salt the chef was about to toss into the bowl.

As dinnertime neared, Craig began pouring Dom Pérignon into Baccarat crystal flutes for all of us. Still freshly hatched and an ingenue in the world of the grape, I was not used to drinking from a flute. The fragile crystal in my bridal trousseau included saucer goblets for champagne. (I'd grown up with the myth that a perfect breast would fit into a champagne goblet, and mine were embarrassingly Burgundy balloons. Certainly the flute banished that conundrum.)

Betty Franey arrived with the three little Franeys. I figured they were all haute chowhounds. "Oh, if only," she said. Jacques, at five, would eat only canned SpaghettiOs and hot dogs, she confided. She flashed me a quick glance of the Entenmann's chocolate cake hidden in her bag for the kids' dessert. "Don't let Craig know," she whispered. "He'd have a fit." I didn't see what the children did with their soufflé. Maybe they didn't get any. Maybe they hid it under a leaf of lettuce. There were two billowing, glazed, picture-perfect poufs—one for the five of them, one for me and the photographer—each bite a savory surprise, every mouthful different: a fragrant fluff cloaking a chunk of lobster, an ooze of cheese-scented cream, or a pungent patch sporting a crunch of crusted Parmesan. It was as complex as T. S. Eliot on the plate.

After dinner, Craig was still pouring, cognac and brandy now. He played recordings of Broadway musicals from a huge collection of everything I'd ever heard of, played them loud, and when *West Side Story* began, he had to dance. "Maria. Maria, Maria." He knelt at my feet, acting it out. He danced with me and then he danced off alone. And when he tumbled down the spiral staircase, blood running from a cut on his head, he laughed as if delighted. He'd drunk enough to blur the pain.

We left for the long drive home. I felt flushed and manic. My heart was racing. I was high on soufflé and champagne in Baccarat crystal and my glimpse into this rarefied world. Only later did I learn that Craig had spent the next few hours in the emergency room. My profile ran in *Look* that August, just weeks before Clay Felker summoned me.

10

THE INSATIABLE CRITIC

THE GROUND FLOOR IS ABOVE ALL APPROPRIATELY GRAND," I WROTE IN A piece called "Paley's Preserve," my first review in the infant *New York,* November 11, 1968. "It is slick, rich, calculated, spare, intimidating. It is Contemporary Wasp. You would hate to break open a roll for fear it would scatter unprogrammed crumbs. It is understatedly snob. There is no Bronx phone directory. Manhattan, of course. Brooklyn, yes. Even Queens. But no Bronx. You sense this slight to the Bronx is no accident. Nothing here is accident. Armies of interior designers have measured, computed, engineered. Even the sugar bowl is part of the statement. Granite plays against rosewood. . . . Shiny black matchbooks wear stark portraits by Irving Penn of nuts and clams. The quarter-round molding that borders the powder room carpet is gold . . . but not just plain gold . . . Florentine gold.

"The Ground Floor is a perfect room to end an affair in. The tables are far enough apart to announce the break in a firm voice, and the ambiance is stern enough to discourage sloppy emotionalism. Not many Beautiful People get this far west before curtain time. There is no one o'clock flutter of Dr. Laszlo's 'girls.'* Even Babe Paley (the boss's goddess

---

*Erno Laszlo was the Hungarian skin wizard whose costly potions silkened the epidermi of those who could afford them.

wife) is less than prudently faithful. But Leonard Lyons* moves through the grill, antennae clicking off the celebrities du jour—actor Donald Pleasance, a famous author drinking breakfast, Barbara Walters, Johnny Carson, Jock Whitney. And good grief! Bob Dylan's manager Albert Grossman, tieless, unjacketed, grizzled grey locks to his shoulder, Ben Franklin specs . . . the oldest hippie in the world."

As a coda, I ended my dissection of the Ground Floor with a nod to CBS boss Paley's more folksy canteen, a regal let-them-eat-franks gesture, the snack bar in Paley Park on Fifty-third just east of Fifth, "an unequivocal triumph since they turned the waterfall on. . . . Here you can start the affair you will end at the Ground Floor," I wrote, "over franks and Coke, root beer or Fresca served in lettuce green paper cups. Ambiance: urban stunted nature with an assist from neighboring incinerators and traffic fumes. But a joy nevertheless."

That was my debut, complete with the addictive ellipses, the verbal "ahem" copy editors decided to tolerate. The various attempts by CBS and William Paley to warm up the calculated cool at the Ground Floor belatedly might not have seemed all that important in the context of war and assassination and social upheaval spotlighted up front in *New York*. But the magazine had already connected with committed media watchers and powermongers, raising political antennae all the way to the White House. Now they would notice that *New York* had a restaurant critic. Some food-world professionals were dubious, even bitchy, asking where Clay had dug me up. But he seemed pleased. It was his idea to dub the column "The Insatiable Critic." I wasn't sure that I liked the rubric at first. Insatiable? I was not insatiable. Was he suggesting I might be a nymphomaniac? I knew I was sufficiently satiable for polite company. Finally, I decided the title was ambiguous and provocative without being specifically damning. And Don just laughed.

*The diminutive but powerful *New York Post* columnist.

Plum Rum Conserve

I put up this conserve as a Christmas gift for friends.

1½ cups white raisins
1¼ cups currants
⅔ cup rum (preferably dark rum)
3 medium seedless oranges
6 cups sugar
3 lbs. cherry or prune plums

Steep raisins and currants in rum for several hours, turning occasionally.

Peel oranges, removing the white membrane, and dice pulp.

Boil orange rind until tender. Remove all the white part from the rind and then julienne the zest into one-inch slivers. Sprinkle with ½ cup of the sugar.

Pit and dice the cherries or plums. Combine with rum-steeped fruit, orange pulp, and the rest of the sugar. Cover this mixture and the orange rind, and let both sit overnight in the refrigerator.

Combine the fruit mixture and the orange rind the next day in a heavy saucepan and bring to a boil. Cook 30 minutes or until thickened, stirring frequently.

Pour into 6-oz. jars that have been sterilized by submerging in boiling water. Stir to release air bubbles. If you have no patience for paraffin, store in the fridge and tell your lucky friends to refrigerate your gift at once.

Makes 10 to 12 jars.

11

PLANTING THE SEEDS
OF SENSUALITY

I WAS A DECADE AHEAD OF AMERICA'S SENSUALITY EXPLOSION IN THE fifties and leaped into the foodie vanguard in the sixties. I didn't know much, but I already knew Vienne was not Vienna, and there were six flavors of mustard from Fauchon aging in my fridge, when everyone else stocked feeble ballpark yellow. I would not have predicted that in a few years great armies of New Yorkers would be trotting off to France carrying *New York,* determined to order the dishes I loved in Lyon and Mougins, or that the young and affluent New Yorker would soon be as obsessed with cooking and great dining as I. Nor did I foresee that by the eighties, half of them would want to own restaurants and everyone would be trying to outdo Jane Fonda at high-impact aerobics. I am not a futurist. I almost never recognize a trend until it starts annoying me— like confectioner's sugar on the cuff of my best silk shirt from the pastry chef's compulsive sprinkling. (I am especially vexed when the totally clueless powder the paper doily *under* the ice-cream-sundae dish.)

In just a few years, with New Yorkers in the vanguard, Americans would move on from tuna melts and well-done prime rib to quiche lorraine, *tarte tatin,* and sole Véronique. It would take only a few years more to advance from croque monsieur to mousse of pigeon, *sole ballotine en brioche,* and *noisette de chevreuil grand veneur* with, of course, quixotic counterculture brown rice deviations and tofu breaks. And then quickly in the sybaritic seventies, the nouvelle cuisine would unleash duck with raspberry vinegar, an ocean of beurre blanc, haricots verts lashed together with scallion ribbon. And out in California, an Austrian import, Wolfgang Puck, would lead us to new frontiers with heart-shaped smoked salmon–crème fraîche pizza. And Alice Waters would discover the rapture of a fresh baby string bean.

Yes, the ease of travel—new cheap transatlantic flights—took us to France, and Julia Child translated French food for dummies here. But the mouth revolution could never have happened quite so quickly or with such passionate gusto except for sex.

The sexual revolution had begun, untethering Americans from prim constraints. Even those not necessarily inspired to indulge in free-range sexual high jinks could not help becoming more aware of their senses and their bodies and the quality, if not the quantity, of their orgasms, thanks to film, fashion, disco dancing, and the feminine mystique.

Russ Meyer's abundantly breasted beauties found an audience at the drive-in. Sexual candor from Ken Russell and Roman Polanski, and in films like *The Damned* and *The Night Porter,* was available at the nearest cinema art house. Adventurers in porno chic would file two by two into Manhattan's Majestic Theater to see *Deep Throat.* As boring as it was with its endless in and out, certainly it offered new angles of masterly fellatio for budding sensualists in 1972. *Behind the Green Door, Inside Marilyn Chambers, The Devil in Miss Jones, The Opening of Misty Beethoven* explored the sexuality of women, with varying degrees of male chauvinism or moral rectitude, but they did seem to confirm that women were sexual, too.

The Feminine Mystique and the women's movement were not just about jobs and equal pay. They encouraged the cry for equal orgasms. Make that better and more orgasms. Maybe I would split the check with my date, or grab the door and open it myself. That meant I could sit on top and find my G-spot even if he couldn't. The best-selling *Sensuous Woman* with her aerated whipped cream and the endlessly quoted *Total Woman* greeting her guy naked at the door and swathed in plastic wrap might not have been universal role models, but we knew they were out there. You might decide, Yes, I will try whipped cream, or think, No, I'll have my foreplay pure.

Fashion peeled away layers in the sixties. Girdles went, along with little white gloves. Bras went, too. Men's hair got longer and skirts got short. Hot pants, rear cleavage–baring minis, Rudi Gernreich's breast-baring monokini, sheer, see-through, clinging jersey, skintight tank tops. Dancing, the flaunting of movement, and the anything-goes nightlife of the seventies. All just another kick in the ass to gentility.

Sniffing, tasting, touching, skin, fingertips—the Me Generation was absorbed in itself. First the twist and later disco with its throbbing heart-beat and transporting rush added to the body worship and self-awareness. Marijuana for those who inhaled intensified the senses. LSD took the senses to another dimension. When Grace Slick sang the refrain to "White Rabbit," "Feed your head," didn't it follow that rum raisin ice cream or chocolate truffles could be my drugs of choice?

Francesco Scavullo's photograph of the bare-breasted Contessa Cristina Paolozzi in *Harper's Bazaar* became infamous. And *Vogue* dared Helmut Newton's sadomasochistic, Sapphic, Peeping Tom intimations, "without which the story of fashion couldn't be told," the *New York Times* observed recently. Tina and Michael Chow in a bondage pose. Lisa Taylor with her legs spread wide, eyeing a topless model in American *Vogue*, "epoch-defining," as the *Times* put it. Offended readers canceled their subscriptions, but, too late, they'd seen it, and for the rest of us, a frisson of sexual danger lingered in the expanding awareness of what sex could be. The naked but airbrushed girl next door in *Playboy* and the vixen exposing her prettily manicured bush and pink-petal pussy in *Penthouse* provided shock therapy, even a challenge.

With a constant media barrage and swinging sex clubs just down the street, even prudes and late bloomers couldn't help but get in touch with their senses (or, at the least, be appalled by the idea of it). As I often observed when interviewers questioned the metaphors of ecstasy I used in my reviews: "The same sense that registers pleasure at the table measures the delights in bed: the eye, the nose, the mouth, the skin, the ear that records a whimper of joy or a crunch of a superior pomme frite." Budding sybarites were getting my drift. A little high-risk adventure in food did not demand a major rebellion. Moving from smoked salmon to gravlax to tuna sushi did not demand leaping off an erotic cliff.

But in 1968, the sexual and gender upheaval was far ahead of what was about to evolve at the table. There were no American star chefs in

1968. The chef of New York's standout American restaurant, the Four Seasons, was Swiss. Nobody knew the names of the black chefs who turned out the refined striped bass in its saintly broth and the celebrated chicken potpie at the Coach House on Waverly Place. Parsley was the fresh herb of winter. There were no free-range chickens, no such botanical as a baby vegetable (except small peas in cans). Vinegars did not come in thirty-three flavors. Olive oil didn't need to be chaste. No one cared, because most of us gourmands and everyone French cooked in butter. No one had ever heard of tiramisú or zinfandel. Salsa had not yet triumphed. There were no Thai restaurants, no Vietnamese. Mexico was underdeveloped, pretty much the exclusive turf of El Parador and Casa Moneo, an early emporium on Fourteenth Street for south-of-the-border ingredients. In the great restaurants—and they were usually French—fish was striped bass, salmon, or sole (real sole from Dover or flounder blithely billed as sole), and possibly trout. Dessert was not crème brûlée, it was crème caramel, chocolate mousse, and, my favorite, vanilla ice cream with candied chestnuts scooped from the jar.

There was sherbet everywhere, but the only sorbet was chef André Soltner's powerful cassis sorbet at Lutèce, where a sculpture of a schooner in fried bread sailed in on the tray that delivered your *tourte régence* ($4.95). And Lutèce's irascible creator, André Surmain, in a bluff sartorial mix of tattersall, houndstooth, and Hush Puppies, could rip up a check and eject some hapless peasant in a blink.

At the Four Seasons, the staff still changed the upholstery and the foliage and the waiter's cummerbunds to herald the season—green in spring, pink in summer. But Joseph Baum, the greatest creative restaurant genius of the century, would soon be rudely dismissed by Restaurant Associates (even tossed out of his Park Avenue apartment, a company perk) because his genius wasn't registering on the bottom line. Baum's most dazzlingly original works—the Forum of the Twelve Caesars (centurion-helmet ice buckets, Romulus and Remus espresso spoons), La Fonda del Sol (splendid folk-art collection and design by Alexander Girard), the Tower Suite (where each table was tended by a butler, maid, and footman), and Zum Zum (upscale counter with dauntingly authentic sausages)—wowed the critics and set new standards in design and graphics, but most did not compute in a Chock full o'Nuts world and soon disappeared.

Soulé was gone, having dropped dead of a heart attack in the ladies' room of La Côte Basque during a fatal conniption on the phone over union demands. I imagined him carefree and cardiologist-free in heaven, savoring tripe stew. His heirs, two generations of expatriate Frenchmen and Soulé's own mistress, Madame Henriette at La Côte Basque, carried on the tradition of arrogance, ambience, and aspic learned at the Academie de Pavillon in restaurants and haughty bistros with red velour banquettes across town. Everyone had assumed Madame Henriette, the silent cashier of Le Pavillon, was Madame Soulé. But, in fact, she was the mistress. Far away in France, an actual Madame Soulé existed to inherit all and Madame Henriette bought La Côte Basque from the estate, quickly becoming grander than grand.

Of course I was intimidated.

Craig Claiborne had a degree from the Hotel School of Lausanne, his tuition financed by the GI bill. All I had was my hunger and a few cooking lessons from Dione Lucas. "So you are the little housewife who is writing about restaurants now for *New York* magazine," I was greeted by Roy Andres de Groot, then *Esquire*'s gifted chronicler of fine dining. We'd met in the greenroom before a radio interview we were sharing in those early months of my reviewing. It was my first radio show and I was so stung by the "little housewife" barb that I let him roll right over me. De Groot was blind, a master of vivid, visual description, and the object of speculation because of the young girls he hired to escort him around and whisper pertinent information in his ear. "I see you're wearing hot pants today," he greeted me at another encounter. (I won't apologize for the hot pants. It was one of those rare moments since miniskirts when fashion smiled at me and my aerobicized thighs. I wasn't going to waste a fleeting second of it.)

A modicum of menu French and the satisfaction of knowing that, no matter the abuse or insult, I would have the last word were the only weapons I carried into the daunting exploration of La Caravelle, La Grenouille, and the Soulé-less Côte Basque. There, the prix fixe lunch was $7.95 and the lacquered blond ladies iconized by *Women's Wear Daily* were miffed to be charged fifty cents extra for coffee.

In the beginning, I focused on the sociology and psychology of Manhattan table games. With *WWD* as my crib sheet, I could actually recognize a lot of the players in situ and I knew who begat whom, what manucurist had married well, and where Daddy Onassis and Jackie had supped. I hoped my reviews would amuse readers who didn't give a fig about great food or couldn't afford to dine upscale. As I plumbed the mores of the native upper crust, eating crow and humble pie myself, I offered fellow naïfs advice to help them brave the frostier latitudes. I was initially respectful of my betters—most of these European chefs had been cooking since they were twelve or fourteen, an age when I was content to pig out on macaroni and cheese. I hesitated to criticize anyone's food for a while, but then one day, my taste buds curled in a cringe. Thank you, Dione, Craig, Julia, Alain Chapel, and the babes in the kitchen at La Pyramide. My head was full of taste memories. I knew what was amiss when it was amiss. Would I dare tell André Soltner his frozen praline soufflé was grainy and a bit weary? It was and I did. From then on, I aimed my fork and let them have it.

12

BITE: A NEW YORK
RESTAURANT STRATEGY

OR HALF A CENTURY THE COLONY WAS AN APOGEE OF GLAMOUR," I
could write and the fact checkers could confirm. That was history. "It was
an international sanctuary for disadvantaged royals and fabulous pretenders,
for the newly rich, and the lately rich, and for nibbling little ladies in flowered hats who parked their corgis and Pekes in the ladies' room. There,
Clara knew which boxer had to have chocolate ice cream and which pup
must have nothing but chicken gismonda." By the time I got to the Colony,
it was "like eating lunch at Forest Lawn except that here most of the flowers are plastic," I reported in a 1971 review called "Colony Waxworks."

True, the young and dashing Sirio Maccioni could be seen bowing
and kissing the air an inch above the knuckles of Mrs. Astor and Babe
Paley, and keeping Sinatra and Onassis from slugging it out over the
prime table each claimed to own at the Colony. But I was shocked to see
the apogee of glamour scarred by a captain picking his nose, a waiter nibbling toast, the owner cleaning between his teeth with a matchbook. So
Last Year at Marienbad. As for the one-dollar charge on the check for "B&B
et Céleris," I fumed that there was no celery in sight, which averaged out
to fifteen cents per bread stick or melba round. Sirio would never quite
forgive me for what he feels hastened the Colony's last gasp.

Clay Felker saw service as *New York*'s strongest mission. So, soon I was writing "How to Melt the Glacial Sommelier." Order a half bottle of Château d'Yquem with dessert. Be justifiably indignant if the cellar only has it in the full bottle. In "How Not to Be Humiliated in Snob Restaurants," I urged the genetically insecure to: 1. Write a best-seller. 2. Get named corespondent in a fancy divorce case. 3. Change your first name to Prince. 4. Let the reservationist think you are taking Happy Rockefeller to lunch. 5. Greet the maître d' by name (so that he is thrown off balance struggling to remember yours). 6. Demand a table in "that little back room where you put the tourists." (Since you're going to get it anyway.)

The response to *New York* in those early years was staggering. We had only a few hundred thousand readers, but they were the most outspoken and influential readers in town. My piece in *Ladies' Home Journal* on "How the World's Great Beauties Stay Beautiful" (good genes and plastic surgery) brought me a huge fee, but no one I knew actually read it. Everyone in media was reading *New York*.

Inspired by Tom Wolfe's prose bravura in "The Kandy-Kolored Tangerine-Flake Streamline Baby," which shook up *Esquire* readers, I began writing in my own voice, too, with all the pauses, the verbal acrobatics, and the tics and parentheses. It wasn't Wolfe, nor an attempt to imitate Tom, but it would never have happened without him. "I love your writing in *New York*," said Helen Gurley Brown, for whom I'd written dozens of articles. "Why don't you write that way for *Cosmo*?" The answer was that no magazine would have let me, till I found my voice in *New York*.

Dinner was a masochist's dream and my nightmare at La Grenouille. Frankly, the service at the table nearest the kitchen in what *Women's Wear* called "the Catsup Room" was sorely lacking. Cramped and crowded, virtually without aisles, thus "no room to sauce or flame or carve." The rolling cart could not roll that far. For more than a decade, I would get dumped at that same table, as if the unapologetic owner, Charles Masson, would rather keep me in my place than butter me up in hopes of a better review. "You don't have to be a full-blown masochist to love New York, but it helps," I wrote. The delphic *Women's Wear* had written: "With a sense of the superb, one can deliberately seek out the darkest corner in the room and make others seek you out . . . . one can turn the Catsup Room from a liability into an asset." I settled on my asset, but all pretense of thriving in back-room exile faded when my companion decided to wrestle the arm of the waiter rushing little doilyed dishes of adorable cookies to pets in the front room. "You better bring this table cookies, too," she cried. The waiter pretended not to hear. It was clearly forbidden: a cookie status test to let you know your pitiful rank among the chosen.

Being tall and blond like the iconic wild-woman model of the day, Verushka—with a blond fall, I could almost mimic the hair—I decided to try my best Verushka imitation. I strode boldly through La Caravelle's narrow status alley, heading toward a table in Outer Mongolia as if it didn't matter. Of course it mattered. Waiters rarely wandered that far into the icy climes. Wave a finger for help and the stone-faced proprietor, Robert Meyzen, smartly trained at Le Pavillon, would look right through you. "I don't care if you call three weeks ahead," Meyzen snapped. "When I can have [society stalwarts] Mrs. Lytle Hull and Mrs. Burden, why should I take Mrs. Nobody from Kalamazoo?"

I rated bottled waters blind and found New York water the tastiest. With leads from crime reporters, I put together a "Mafia Guide to Dining Out." "Little Augie Pisano was shot to death with Gian Marino's recipe for clam sauce in his pocket. Grazie a Dio. Little Augie departed still garlicky and glowing from his last supper." In "Brooklyn, Come Hungry," I rated haunts that belonged to my husband's childhood: Peter Luger, Gage & Tollner's, Lundy's, Bonaparte, Monte's: "Eating in Brooklyn restoreth the soul. You *can* go home again, no matter how homogenized your diction, no matter how alienated your spirit. Lundy's chowder . . . fried clams at Nathan's. . . . Shatzkin's many splendored knishes. Nostalgia anesthetizes all critical judgment. What counts most is LOTS. Twenty years ago Portnoy's mother held a knife at his throat to get him to eat. Tonight, back in Brooklyn for dinner, she can't get him to stop."

I documented "The Graying of '21.' " "If there is a greening of America, it has yet to send one tiny verdant tendril through the asphalt of West 52nd Street at the '21' Club, the establishment speakeasy that Jack and Charlie built, stolid in middle age, a shade past its prime, but still a magnet of power. The rites of belonging survive," I reported. "A friend of '21' is greeted by name . . . kissed (if the gender is appropriate), serenaded on birthdays by the remnants of what was once the glorious Chuck Wagon Glee Club. If he is an ailing General Sarnoff,* a menu will be im-

---

*CBS's founding father.

provised from his diet chart and dispatched to the hospital twice daily. If he is Governor Rockefeller, he will be alerted when the first oyster crabs of the season arrive.

"For the stranger, however '21' can be a dreary disappointment, a bore . . . and expensive. The demanding palate is sadly neglected. . . . Still, thanks to the arid recession of summer 1970, the tables are spottily populated and it is not impossible to claim one unless you are smashed, or suspiciously hirsute or too blatantly not-our-kind-of-people. Guardian-of-the-Gate Chuck Anderson may be stern if you arrive with your brother-in-law the Ox in his white socks and buffalo sandals.

"Upstairs is the dining room favored by Onassis, (Air Force ace) Eddie Rickenbacker and the unshakeably secure. But we are marked for Siberia, a tiny alcove in the rear, just a bit south of the Arctic. I begin to get a sense of belonging," but, alas, "to some untouchable caste.

"Here the salmon ringletted ex-flappers don't even shed their ennsy mink shrugs to eat. Four stolid businessmen are sipping milk with their boiled beef. And at the next table a fresh-faced drum majorette is asking her elderly companion, 'What is anarchy anyway?'

" 'Gael, we're in the wrong room,' cries my status-savvy escort, used to dining with Ava Gardner or Michael Caine in tow.

" 'Well, what is Kahlúa?' Miss Apple Cobbler of 1967 is asking.

" 'Oh God, Gael, did you hear that . . . what are we doing here?' "

Many bruised New Yorkers relished taking their vengeance through me for neglect and indifference and the ghostly cookies that failed to find their tables in the town's haughtier canteens. I got letters cheering me on; letters begging to join me at lunch; letters from regulars at the houses of snub, offering to take me back to the places that had iced me, where, with proper credentials, I would see how wonderful they could be. Of course I accepted. I needed to witness a ray of charm and grace, to give my tales of woe even greater weight.

La Caravelle's steely Robert Meyzen couldn't find a fair-enough hors d'oeuvre on the rolling cart for me the day I lunched with lock and safe mogul John Diebold, a regular at the corner banquette. So the dark-browed Meyzen brought them all, treading on tippytoes, his mouth stretched in a simpering smile. Who would have thought he could actually crack that granite face?

I knew the couturier Jacques Tiffeau only as seen through *Women's Wear*'s "Eye," but I phoned him anyway, and he was game to let me share his prime banquette at La Grenouille. "Enter Jacques," I wrote. "Seconds before he reaches the table, the waiter stations his aperitif, martini on the rocks in a Baccarat balloon goblet. The mini baguettes are swept away and toasted ovals appear. He orders Petrus, and a mollet (soft-boiled egg) in the middle of his cheese souffle. The patron, Charles Masson, is summoned to hear the specifications.

" 'You look so well, Jacques,' says a frozen-in-silicone blonde two banquettes away.

" 'Who is that?' I ask.

" 'Hmmm . . . what's her name, a rich lady . . . I don't give a shit who they are. Hello. Hello. Hello.' He speeds an ax-murderer's smile across the room to the industry's dowager Queen of Flack, Eleanor Lambert. 'Oh you are in luck. Here comes what's her name . . . that rich old lady . . . Woodward, Woolworth. That shaky one. Oh, today you have the cream of the cream. You see that old movie star . . . now she does the Compoz commercials. And well, look who is sitting with John Fairchild. Monsieur Cardin and Madame Alphand.* Don't you think she looks like a manicurist? And that one over there . . . she must be some whore in the garment business. I never remember the names. I don't give a shit who is here. When I finish, I put on my shadows'—he pats his dark aviator goggles—'and I run. I come here like it is my little pension.' He drops his fork. 'The souffle is too cooked. Where is my mollet?'

"I gulp. I have just eaten it."

Publicist Mimi Strong gets me invited to join Millie Considine (mate to Hearst columnist Bob) at the George Jean Nathan table to the left of the bar at "21." Millie arrives and is greeted with a white carnation. Credentials discovered, Mimi and I are also immediately carnationed, too. "That's why the babes all come here," says Millie, nodding toward the men three deep at the bar drinking lunch. "This is the room that counts," says Millie. "Back there they put the semidreck . . . not the dreck-on-dreck, but people from nowhere who've earned their tables."

*Madame Alphand was the wife of the former French ambassador to the United States.

She insists I ask for chipped beef in a baked potato. "It's the dish to have." Apparently, the aging moguls at "21" like to revisit the deprivation of their boarding schools.

"Once I asked a captain, 'How can you charge five dollars for that?' says Millie. 'It's thirty cents' worth of chipped beef, ten cents for a baked potato, and ten cents worth of cream sauce. Half a buck at the most.'

" 'That's true,' he said, 'but you get to eat it at "Twenty-one." ' "

As those early *New York* covers show, Clay Felker was fascinated with the city's power grid. His star writers charted and analyzed the giants of finance, government, media, crime, real estate, the arts. He sicced his stable of masterly reporters on sociological trends that grew into books, movies, catchwords that would forever define the period. THE ME DECADE. THE POWER BROKERS. BLACK POWER CHIC. PASSAGES. Writer Julie Baumgold was immortalized in four poses, sitting on the throne in one of Milton Glaser's dazzling covers for her article that made chopped liver of the Jewish Princess. Clay reveled in the tumult a splashy cover and a pungent piece created where his power pals lunched. Back in the office later, he was quick with compliments. "Everyone is talking about your piece," he would say. "They love it."

It was Clay's idea that I do a feature called "How to Beat the Menu Rap." Could the reader on a budget be happy eating soup for lunch and little else at the town's snootiest and most expensive restaurants? I did my best, ordering just the $3.75 cheese soufflé with a salad at Quo Vadis and the $3.25 omelette at "21," but I found that the bread and butter charges and the humiliation tended to dilute any small triumph.

What was important to me and obviously to Clay was that the magazine's business staff was not permitted to communicate with me. I never suspected that Longchamps, an important restaurant advertiser, had twice canceled their contract after damning reviews I'd written. The ad staff had apparently spent two years wooing them back after the first hostile retreat, only to have my carping notice of Longchamp's Gauguin Lounge atop the Huntington Hartford Museum appear that very week. I found out years later when a copy of a speech Clay had delivered to the Advertising Council landed on my desk.

"And what did you do to get your job?" people would ask, as if demanding at what great fork I had studied . . . with whom did I sleep.

Well, I did not sleep with Clay Felker. Rumors said he had slept around and about among those on *New York*'s masthead, and I did spot him tête-à-tête with a senator's wife at Le Madrigal. ("It's a perfect restaurant for illicit lovers," he told me. She tells me it was strictly platonic.) Gossip is right at least half the time, or half right most of the time. Certainly I've been given credit for conquests I never coveted or contemplated. I guess we'll just have to wait for more memoirs. Or the ultimate roman à Clay.

The truth is, Clay loved writers and writing. He surrounded himself with writers (marrying Gail Sheehy, one of the best-selling of *New York*'s many best-selling authors). One day at a brunch sometime in the late seventies on the back veranda of their East Hampton house, Clay looked around the table and his eyes lighted up.

"How many books do we have sitting at this table?" He went around the table and we counted: Peter Maas, Ed Epstein, Gail, and me (I can't remember who else was there—just eight of us, counting Clay). Three books, four, two—he added it up and announced it triumphantly like a kid with a Matchbox car collection: "We have eighteen books sitting at this table."

I learned Clay liked telling his friends and the powerful whose brains he picked every day at lunch that he'd fished me out of nowhere . . . that I'd never eaten a hot meal before becoming the magazine's restaurant critic. The conceit was too cute to contradict.

Meanwhile, my unfinished novel moldered away on the floor of a closet. I didn't even feel guilty ignoring it. A whirlwind of celebrisociety was emerging in Manhattan, churned up by Clay, with the magazine as its weekly locomotive, and by the emerging, increasingly aggressive ink-stained media gossips. I seemed to have become a boldface name myself, a minor league star, invited everywhere, indulged by the restaurants I'd come to love once they recognized me, suffered grimly by those I'd panned, and indulged anyway. I had dreamed of being a movie star. I had imagined critics invoking Scott Fitzgerald or Ford Madox Ford in extolling my novel. My neck would never be as long as Babe Paley's nor my pedigree as fine, but I had dared to hope restaurateurs would find my ass as kissable. I'd not set out to be a power of the food world, but that seemed to be what I had become. So quickly. And it was fun. I fell for it totally.

13

Ma Vie avec le Grape Nut

WHEN HIS BEST FRIEND, JULES THE OPHTHALMOLOGIST, CAME HOME from military service in France with a huge cache of '61 Bordeaux to "lay down" and explained to us what that meant, Don was determined to create a wine cellar, too—if only in our front closet. Soon he was caught up in the deeply occult scientology of the grape, trying to memorize Schoonmaker's *Encyclopedia of Wine*. He quickly learned three of the most important things to know about wine: Château Lafite Rothschild, Château Mouton, and Château Margaux.

He developed a passion for great Burgundy, specifically Richebourg of the Domaine de la Romanée-Conti, when we stumbled into a small, unknown bistro in Lyon one night in our early days of seeking nirvana abroad. To show the ancient sommelier he was not the callow youth he appeared or just another uncivilized American, Don had ordered a dusty treasure at a princely twenty dollars the half bottle, far beyond our budget. "A noble Burgundy," the old man said, congratulating Don. "A *bon complement* for monsieur's rack of lamb." The man trembled as he decanted the Richebourg and poured a taste. Don sniffed, swirled, sniffed, tasted, sighed, and seemed drunk already just on the fumes. Although he later turned out to be discreetly unfaithful to me, my darling husband was true forever to Richebourg, long after it became so expensive that neither of us could afford it.

Actually, Don's palate showed early promise. One night our dinner host, the learned and self-confident über-Hungarian, George Lang, invited us to taste a trio of champagnes poured in the kitchen into numbered glasses. "I like number three," said Don. "Is it Taittinger blanc de blanc?" Impressed? George was visibly shaken by such sensitivity from the taste buds of someone he regarded as a philistine. In fact, the two of us had developed a taste for Taittinger early on and had sipped it at dinner only the night before. (Of course, no need to tell George. It was fun to see the mighty Lang visibly rocked.)

But now as a restaurant critic, I needed to be a wine expert, too. I needed to learn about wine and I had to learn fast. It wasn't enough to recognize Lafite, Mouton, or Château Margaux at Macy's—wines I wouldn't dream of ordering even in the seventies on my seemingly unlimited expense account. I needed to navigate a restaurant's wine list smoothly, to recognize a wine that was ready to drink, to find a beautiful wine at a reasonable price—and in those days, the wine was most likely French. In the innocent dawn of the seventies, no one east of the San Fernando Valley took California wines seriously. Was the wine corky? Materized? Over-the-hill? How would I know?

New Yorkers, even masters of the universe and the widely traveled, often knew as little as I did at the dawn of the revolution in dining, and, like me, they quaked when an arrogant sommelier handed them the unintelligible wine list with a sneer that said, This is going to hurt you more than it hurts me. True, a handful of experts were writing about wine then: Schoonmaker, of course, Alexis Lichine, Hugh Johnson. I surrounded myself with their weighty tomes.

A self-satisfied snoot of early grape nuts, like early foodies, found one another. All it took was money, the male chromosome, the right connections, and a cellar lined with status Burgundies or proper Bordeaux to win a spot in the local chapter of France's exclusive wine societies—the Commanderie de Bordeaux, the Chevalier du Tastevin. There, the chosen ones knighted one another with a dull sword and celebrated their superiority. Wooed by ambitious importers and indulged by restaurateurs who feared to deny them discounts, they spit and drooled and tasted, one-upping one another at bring-your-own bottle bashes. Women were distinctly not welcome, except at the once-a-year galas open to wives, mistresses, and female restaurant writers.

But life was heady for *New York* magazine's Insatiable Critic. Wine collectors collected me. There I was, basking in the spotlight of my reviews just as our town was unzipping its puritanism and discovering there was more to dinner than well-done lamb chops and orange sherbet. My unabashed passion for eating made great cooks I'd never met want to feed me, and great collectors dangled guest lists of luminaries to tempt me to dinners designed around their greatest bottles. I got out my black velvet ball gown (Oscar de la Renta on sale) for their fancy dinners. And I tasted. Tasting great wines won't necessarily guarantee a sharp palate. But it makes for a divine kindergarten.

Meanwhile, wine makers and importers—the whole spirits industry—were conspiring to wean Americans from scotch, Coke, and highballs to the grape. Marketing experts were sure that if they could lead Americans to Chardonnay, they could make them drink. I was invited to countless wine seminars and I went because clearly the best way to learn was by tasting wines side by side, comparing flavors, labels, and vintages. The experts were so deft and full of esoteric information, I felt mastering wine was only slightly more difficult than brain surgery.

I would mention loving a wine in a review—La Doucette, a sauvignon blanc, for instance, and watch the prices soar. (Well, a name Americans could pronounce without mangling was always a plus.)

Soon I knew a little, enough to spike my reviews with helpful wine chat. I put together a list of Bacchic bon mots that an apprentice oenophile could toss out nonchalantly to impress and thaw a glacial sommelier, and was bold enough (or obnoxious enough) to use them myself.

Innocent pals would watch, mesmerized (or even embarrassed), as I squeezed the cork, swirled the wine and sniffed, swirled again, sipped, and chewed. "I find it acid . . . astringent . . . balanced, bitter, brilliant. Clean, isn't it? Cloudy, coarse, common, dull, earthy, nicely flinty . . . a bit flat . . . hmm." I could parrot my betters' alphabet of joy or dismissal: "Powerful, ripe, rounded, soft, steely, stemmy. And young. So young."

When the mythic and magisterial Gregory Thomas (president of Chanel in America and a revered *Feinschmecker*) stood up at a small and ridiculously exclusive wine dinner at the Four Seasons to dismiss a fruity little Beaujolais as "a simpering teenage cheerleader," I felt learned enough to leap in and defend my sex.

"Oh, really, Gregory," I began. "I find it more like a young lifeguard with his nose peeling from sunburn."

Soon I was summoned to perform onstage with my mentors. Actually, I think Danny Kaye and I were cast for comic relief among the Establishment pros in a tasting panel *Time* magazine put together in the late seventies to compare the new, aggressively marketed California wines with the long-respected bottlings of France—blind, of course. Even blind, I recognized Gallo Hearty Burgundy at once. It was a cross between Beaujolais nouveau and strawberry Jell-O in a jug, and Americans, including me, adored it. "I know this is just a little California jug wine," I whispered to the vaunted expert Frank Schoonmaker on my right, "but I like it."

"I do, too," he said, and to my shock, the loftiest wino of them all cast his vote for Gallo Hearty Burgundy.

Now when we were out at reviewing dinners, Don would hand the wine list to me. "You know what you want," he might say. The day my wine knowledge surged ahead of his, someone less myopic than I might have seen the small gray cloud floating over our marriage. Not me. I was too much in love.

For so long, we agreed we had the best marriage. I remember friends envying us. Our high ceiling with the cherub frieze, the living room's big bay with double windows like French doors, the bed on the balcony with its wrought-iron railing, terra-cotta floors, and the row of tall stained-glass windows. How close we were . . . what fun we had . . . trips to Vermont each fall to see the colors, collecting antiques and Early American folk art, the precious little dinners we cooked, and our annual Christmas Eve open house. Don was unabashedly romantic. He found vintage diamond earrings for my birthday. He left love notes everywhere with wonderfully sappy love names. We never put each other down in public as our friends sometimes did. We never fought. Should that have been the giveaway that something might be wrong?

Very early, I realized that neither of us wanted children. We agreed we would never have children, so we could always be children ourselves and not be forced to move to the suburbs for better schools or change our carefree ways for lack of a nanny. I wrote about the "Joys of Not Having Children" for *The Saturday Evening Post*. The editor called it "A Vote

Against Motherhood," a more inflammatory title. He made me promise not to have a child for at least a year from the date of publication.

"Do you think this is a joke?" I asked. "Or that I would write this just for the money? We are not having children. I can promise you."

My mother was deeply disappointed. "But you love dolls and baby clothes."

"For other people's children," I said.

I received more than five hundred letters from *Saturday Evening Post* readers, most of them urging us not to miss out on parenthood, although many said, "You don't deserve children; you're too selfish." The saddest letters were from women who'd had children and deeply regretted it.

The intimacy Don and I shared seemed organic, touching, a miracle. Don reading the morning papers in the club chair, with me sitting a foot away on the floor.

"Promise me you'll never leave me," Don would say.

"Promise me we'll grow old and gum our gruel together," I said. We promised.

I had never imagined I could love someone so much or that I would be so loved. So why was it we rarely made love? I don't remember when the sexual heat began to cool, just that often I was sleeping when he came home and he didn't wake me, or I was waiting up with a late supper and he was too tired for sex. We hugged and kissed, swore eternal love, wept, and cuddled, sleeping like two spoons, tucked into each other side by side, chaste and miserable. I couldn't understand what had happened. I knew he was frustrated and unhappy at work. When the *Trib* folded in 1966, and was about to be embraced in a bizarre threesome with the former *World-Telegram* and *Journal-American* after a bruising strike, he'd gone to the *Times*.

After years of synchronized opinions and agreeing about everything, our playful weekends had been strained by my ideas on how to restore the little church we'd bought on top of a hill outside Woodstock. I believed in do-it-yourself and he, true child of Brooklyn apartment living, believed in calling the super. But he acquiesced. He always seemed to come around to my way of thinking. Don bought *The New York Times Handyman's Guide* and read it till late at night, well after I'd fallen asleep.

No sex? Not even on the weekend. I snuggled against him in the little bedroom that had once been the Dutch Reformed Sunday school, attached to our precious church. He didn't snuggle back. "This is how you fix a running toilet," he said, reading aloud to me.

I had always wanted a doll's house. Now our church on the hill became my dollhouse. The family who owned it had put up walls everywhere, creating a warren of rooms. As we smashed down the Sheetrock, the church got smaller and smaller and more beautiful. We took out the picture window behind the altar and installed a baronial fireplace salvaged from the men's room of the Paramount Theater on Broadway, condemned and about to be demolished. It cost us seventy-five dollars. Don built shutter frames and I stretched red-and-white workman's bandannas across them to let in light through the bathroom window. I dipped rattan in tea to make it look aged and covered the sink cupboard with it, framing the seams with bamboo that I antiqued with a blowtorch to match the Victorian bamboo hat rack that held towels. Don mitered the corners, marveling at the crude miracle of an old miter box and the saw that came with it. Every drawer in the house was lined with something—vinyl, gingham, book-binding paper, felt. Was there some Freudian implication? I glued lining into every box and drawer in sight.

"Look at this, darling," I said, showing him a small article in the *Woodstock Times*. "You can buy twenty-five trees for ten dollars from the New York Department of Environmental Conservation. We can fill in the spaces between trees on our hill and one day the church will be invisible from the road. . . . Won't it be wonderful to be hidden by pines?"

Did we need to borrow a truck to bring our saplings home from the post office? No. They came in a tiny package, not much bigger than a rolled-up rubber bathtub mat. The tiniest seedlings.

"We'll be dead by the time these twigs are trees," Don said, wanting to toss them in the garbage.

But we planted them. Half of them died. And the rest of them grew. By the time the marriage was dead, the church was indeed invisible from the road.

Don always deferred to me, sweating in the heat, getting splashed and burned as he stood on a tall, rickety ladder, stripping the woodwork with some toxic liquid . . . storing up the suppressed rage I would only later discover. He worked all week, out of place, he felt, at the *Times* and spent his weekends trying to be a handyman in a ripped shirt while I mixed wallpaper glue to dress the entrance with marbled book paper from Italy. Wasn't it fun? Why spend money to hire workmen when you can do it yourself? I was blindly caught up in my fantasy of the exquisite little church on top of the hill.

And with its eight-dollar potting-shed table stripped and stained, the needlepoint dining chairs, the massive stone fireplace, the turn-of-the-century stained-glass windows, and the custom-made kitchen with its handmade copper range hood, it was a showpiece. *House & Garden* came to photograph the two of us in the open kitchen and get my recipe for mushroom–cream cheese strudel and cold tomato–sour cream soup.

One Saturday, the gifted photographer John Dominis and reporter Anne Hollander came up to photograph our place for a *Life* magazine feature on churches transformed into other uses. They were on their way that afternoon to the Woodstock Festival, which had been forced to move to Max Yasgur's farm in Bethel because Woodstock's town council had refused a permit. They invited us to come along.

"It's supposed to rain," I said. "And I hear traffic is backed up for miles."

"But *Life* has a trailer with air conditioning, a bathroom, and ice cubes," Anne said.

What was the matter with us? We said thanks but we'd pass. I cannot remember why. I think we were both pleased with our prescience when we saw the photos of mud-wallowing bodies. What was happening to us? We'd promised to be children together forever, loving, spontaneous. How had we gotten so stodgy?

Then, on a freelance assignment in Los Angeles, I let the unthinkable happen. Half a bottle of red wine, two desserts in that dimly-lighted Hollywood restaurant. I was nervous. He was too good-looking, my friend's ex-husband, wonderful Irish face, blue eyes, and a romantic shock of thick black hair. It could only have happened in a far away zip code. He kissed me and I let him. He touched me and I burst into flames. I let myself. After nine and a half years with just one man, just Don's touch, just that familiar smell, just that one cock, I was invaded by a stranger. I was trembling, unable to stop, scared, keening and giggling and feeling alive again.

When Don called the next day from New York to say good morning, I could barely talk, my throat paralyzed by guilt. "Laryngitis," I croaked. "Let me call you back later." How would I ever face him? I had thrown away the best thing in my life . . . for what? For a hot night with a man I'd never see again. No. I'd done it for sex. To feel sexual again, to emerge from a cocoon of nothingness, where I felt isolated and ugly. I looked in the mirror to see if what I'd done was somehow written on my face. I saw a little abrasion from his unshaven stubble.

Don would know at once, I was sure. He would see it in my eyes, just as I would see it in his at once if he were unfaithful. I got home from the airport before he came in from the office—late, as he often was those days. I offered to do a frittata for dinner. He'd eaten, he said. I chattered away inanely about the shoes I hadn't bought and the irresistible date and nut chocolate ice cream at Wil Wright's. I'd bought a pint and eaten it all, one spoonful at a time, I confessed.

He looked at me.

"You're cute," he said. "I really missed you."

We made love that night.

Once I'd taken the unthinkable step, it was thinkable. There was no retreat. I dedicated all my philandering to my marriage. If a man was attractive and interested, we found a bed or the backseat of a taxi, or a hotel suite. I didn't have to nag or make Don feel my need. . . . I would find sex where I found it and love my husband forever. I talked about this in my head and it made so much sense to me. I became an expert on foreplay and fork play and, once again, a scholar of married men. I reasoned that a married man had as much motivation to be discreet as I did. That didn't mean single men were necessarily out of bounds. At times when I came home, I was sure Don could smell the pheromones and the sex even after a shower. And then he would want me and we would make love. And even when we didn't, there was always so much hugging. So many times we said "I could never live without you."

Danish Meat Loaf

This meat loaf started life as a meatball recipe in the Times.

6 slices of dense square packaged pumpernickel (Wild's Westphalian is perfect)
    or 3 ½-inch slices of bakery pumpernickel
2 large eggs
2 tbsp. Worcestershire sauce
2 tsp. coarse salt
1 tsp. freshly ground black pepper
3 medium yellow onions (1 cup) finely chopped (not minced)
2 cloves garlic, minced
¾ lb. ground beef
½ lb. ground veal
¾ lb. Italian sausage, squeezed from casing. (Sausage can be sweet or hot.
    Guess what? I prefer hot.)
Plain store-bought or fine homemade bread crumbs to sprinkle on top

Preheat oven to 350° F.

Soak bread in warm water for 3 or 4 minutes. Squeeze out water and tear into pieces.

Combine lightly beaten eggs, Worcestershire, salt, and pepper in small bowl. Using a big mixing bowl, mix bread and egg mixture together, then add onions, garlic, and the meats, and blend together with a wooden spoon or your hands.

Pat into an oval or square baking dish or a loaf pan, then sprinkle with bread crumbs. Bake 1 to 1¼ hours or until instant-read thermometer registers 155° F.

Remove from oven, pour off excess fat, and let it rest for 10 minutes.

Serves 6 to 8.

14

MEN I JUST
COULDN'T RESIST

I WAS LIKE A TEENAGER AGAIN, EXCEPT IT WASN'T THE REPRESSIVE FIFTIES, where I'd felt like a wanton aberration. It was the "anything goes" seventies, and I wasn't wasting a moment.

Years later, I would glance at *Time* magazine and my breath would catch in my throat. There were two men on *Time*'s January 9, 1978, cover and I had been to bed with both of them. No, no, not Anwar Sadat and Menachem Begin. I wasn't sure how I felt. Even in the freest sexual moment of this century, I thought I would die if anyone knew, and at the same time I wanted to shout it out. I was a woman of appetite. I wasn't afraid to feed my hunger. Still, I was surprised to see the two of them, linked . . . not by bedroom antics, but by movie box-office magnetism.

It means a lot to me that I never went to bed with anyone to get the story. I do confess that once in awhile in the middle of pursuing a story, I just couldn't help myself. But in the several years of my double life, when I convinced myself I had found a way to save my marriage, out-of-town assignments came with built-in possibilities.

Clint Eastwood had been working all day in the Mexican desert when I arrived on the set of *Two Mules for Sister Sara*, delegated by Helen Gurley Brown in 1969 to dig beneath the studio pap for a profile of the charismatic cowboy. I felt awkward, too dressed for the desert dust, shy, experiencing a surge of the little girl from Detroit who still lived inside my Manhattan persona, intimidated by being that close to a movie star. His manginess, the unkempt hair under his flat-topped leather sombrero, the sweaty rubble of beard, and a mangled stub of a cheroot clenched in his teeth dimmed his unbearable good looks, but not much. He seemed to be cashing in on the silent antihero image of the spaghetti Westerns that had rescued him from Hollywood's indifference.

"At least it's me doing my own bag and not someone trying to imitate me," he said, defending himself when I asked.

Between scenes, he stripped off his shirt. His jeans rode low on bony hips. I'd read the clips. The man was clearly not into food. My flutter of early fame as *New York's Insatiable Critic* would mean nothing to him. I had a feeling that if he knew my slavish devotion to sweetbreads and smelly cheeses, he would keep his distance. Six foot four of skinniness, he lay collapsed on a canvas chaise—his langorous off-camera self— silently stroking a baby rabbit, unwound, obviously content. Everyone I had interviewed in preparation for meeting him had alerted me: "He loves animals; he has a gentle reverence toward animals." I interpreted this to mean animals are easier than people, especially nosy women with notebooks and tape recorders.

Suddenly, there was a commotion behind his trailer. A crowd of Mexicans had roped an iguana and were dragging it to the prop tent in hopes of cashing in. Clint recoiled. "I sometimes wonder who is the zoo. The animals or the people," he said. He disappeared, returning with the writhing iguana, getting slashed by its whiplash tail.

"I bought it for five pesos," he said, hitching the beast to an awning stake. "What do you think they eat?" After lunch, struggling to set the beast free, he backed into a cactus. The makeup crew was still plucking quills from his back when I hitched a ride back to the hotel to cool off.

I could see the man was exhausted by the time we met for dinner on the terrace in near darkness at Hacienda Cocoyoc, the resort where the films stars were lodged, an hour's hairpin ride south of Mexico City. The terrace was not lighted, to discourage mosquitoes, I supposed. I wrestled in the darkness with knife and the pork chop I'd foolishly ordered. One bite told me the pork was almost raw. Will I die immediately of trichinosis or later in horrible pain? I brooded, feeling my forehead. Yes, I was warm. But it could have just been proximity to Clint and not imminent death. Clint tossed most of his food to the dogs ringing the terrace, before I had a chance to see what he was eating. I quickly got rid of my chop, too. I kept trying to draw him out. Nothing I asked provoked an insight, or even more than a bored response. I'd already read most of the history he portioned out in brief phrases. But that voice . . . that iconic lazy, breathy voice. I found myself transfixed by it, not registering the words. I had no plan, not even a fantasy. He was handsome, yes, and, for most women, a heartthrob, I supposed, but I felt his indifference, his distance. I'd not ever known a vegetarian, and I doubted any vegetarian would be attracted or attractive to me.

I wasn't any more comfortable in this charade than he was. But he wasn't giving up yet. I got the message that he had committed to this interview as the price he must pay for a profile that would inspire millions of *Cosmo* girls to see his movie. I followed him back to his cottage suite, where he stretched out on the sofa beside me and glowered at my tape recorder. He was still Clint Eastwood, and I found him more appealing in the low lamplight than I had in near darkness. I asked a question. He didn't answer. I looked up from the notebook. He was asleep.

I'd never had anyone fall asleep in the middle of an interview before. Engelbert Humperdinck had been late and rude, so I said, "Forget it," and walked out. But Eastwood had been unfailingly polite. I touched his arm to wake him.

"Let's go to bed," he said.

I guessed he would do anything to escape talking. I realized that I absolutely did not care about his motivation. We made love, gentle and easy. I remember the sweet smell of soap and the sun smells of his skin, the feel of his beard, how lean he was, how tall, the long muscles wrapping his bones. How dark he was against the white sheet. We lay there afterward and he started to talk. I didn't say a word, for fear of stopping him. He answered questions I would not have dared to ask.

Would I have done it just for the story? Ridiculous question. I wouldn't have not done it for anything. At that moment, I wanted him. I liked that it was his idea. A few months later, I was in Los Angeles again on another assignment. He came to my room at the Beverly Wilshire. I opened the door and my knees buckled from the impact of his Clint-eastwoodness. He seemed even taller than I'd remembered, clean-shaven now, his sun-streaked hair trimmed. The blue shirt made his eyes even bluer, or did his blue eyes make the shirt seem more blue? One wall of the room was all mirrors. I was a puddle of Jell-O. I forgot any questions I thought I needed to ask. I'm not sure we even spoke. It never occurred to me that what we had might have gone on beyond the Beverly Wilshire. It was wonderful sex in an era of wonderful sexual possibilities. I still believed I was having sex on the run to be a better wife to my husband. And anyway, I don't think I could have lived with a Republican. Or a health-food addict. And in Clint's case, shared him with those ex-wives and mothers of his children. So, no regets.

The other box-office centurian? I'll get to Burt Reynolds later.

Infidelity Soup with Turkey and Winter Vegetables

This will be even better the next day or the day after, so you can leave it in the fridge to comfort your mate if you're feeling a little guilty about playing around out of town. If you don't have a turkey on hand, use chicken bones or a ham bone, or even chicken stock.

Stock:
Carcass of a 10- to 12-lb. roasted turkey, broken into pieces
1 large yellow onion, sliced
3–4 celery ribs
½ tsp. dried thyme or 3–4 sprigs fresh thyme
1 bay leaf
1 tsp. whole black peppercorns

Soup:
1 package of 16-bean mix, soaked overnight in cold water to cover
2 cups reduced turkey stock
4 cups cubed winter vegetables: carrots, turnip, parsnip, sweet potatoes, and red onion
2 to 3 tbsp. chili powder, to taste
Salt, to taste
Freshly ground black pepper, to taste
2 cups leftover turkey in largish bite-size cubes, preferably dark meat
Optional: 1 cup ribbons of kale, cabbage, or romaine lettuce
Optional: 1 cup cooked fusilli or penne
1 or 2 tbsp. freshly grated Parmesan and a drizzle of good olive oil per bowl of soup

To make the stock:
Put turkey carcass, sliced onion, celery, thyme, bay leaf, and peppercorns in a stockpot and add cold water to cover. Bring to a boil,

skimming away and discarding any scum that floats to the top. Lower the heat and simmer uncovered for 60 minutes. Pour the stock through a fine strainer, discarding all the solids. Set aside 2 cups of this stock.

Return the remaining stock (you will have about 10 cups) to a 4-quart saucepan and boil uncovered until the stock is reduced to 2 cups (about 45 minutes).

To make the soup:

Cook the beans in a one-and-a-half-gallon stockpot or as instructed on package (after prescribed soaking), using 2 cups of stock to replace 2 cups of the water.

After 35 minutes, add the cubed winter vegetables and bring to a boil, then lower the heat and cover so the mix simmers. Add unreduced stock as necessary to maintain a rather thick texture of soup. Simmer for about 45 minutes.

When the beans and vegetables are just barely tender, season the soup with chili powder, salt, and pepper, to taste, add the cooked cubed turkey, and the optional kale, cabbage, or romaine lettuce. Stir occasionally so bottom doesn't burn. Continue to cook until the greens are tender and the flavors have melded (about 15 minutes longer). Refrigerate if not serving immediately.

Fifteen minutes before serving, bring soup to a gentle boil. You may need to add additional stock or water to keep a semblance of soup texture. Stir to prevent burning. Add a handful of cooked fusilli or penne (if you wish) and simmer till soup is hot. Taste again for seasoning, adding more salt and freshly ground pepper according to your taste. Serve each portion topped with freshly grated Parmesan and a drizzle of good olive oil.

Serves 6 as a starter, 3 to 4 as a main course.

15

THE WOMAN WHO GAVE ME
FRANCE ON A PLATE

I HAD BEEN A PLEBE IN THE AVANT-GARDE OF FOOD-OBSESSED AMERICANS that would eventually become an invasion, trekking across France in the late sixties and early seventies, gobbling, trading addresses and cuisinary gossip, stopping at Fauchon in Paris to stock up on exotic teas, fancy preserves, tins of candied chestnuts, and the inevitable gift for those left behind—wooden crates of exotically flavored mustards exactly like those that already cluttered the traveler's fridge. We couldn't help ourselves. Zabar's had not yet gone global and SoHo was still forbiddingly industrial, with an invisible scattering of artists camping out in vast lofts, Dean & DeLuca not even a vision in fantasy. So it was worth whatever Fauchon charged to collect preserved prunes of Agen, Mirabelle jam, tins of duck and wild boar pâté, lavender, and herbs de Provence in clay crocks, shipped home in wooden crates, mostly to disappear in the shadows of kitchen cupboards, where just looking at the labels was fulfillment enough.

I was an outsider, an ingenue, a cartoon of an American hopelessly enamored with eating—the French seemed to find our obsession with their great restaurants endlessly amusing in its unabashed enthusiasm. And at home, people who didn't commute regularly to France could not hope to comprehend our fervor. We were fiercely serious about our pleasure, and soon considered ourselves more knowledgeable than the seasoned toques who indulged us. Apprenticed to the range in adolescence, many chefs rarely got to eat or drink as we did. Any number of dedicated couples who explored the truffle circuit two or three times a year in the late sixties and early seventies took notes and graded dishes, sending copies to like-minded friends and, of course, to me. These enraptured souls did not call it spring and fall. They called it mushrooms and game. And they scolded chefs overstuffed with stardom for having lost their concentration. I still have the newsletter one couple mimeographed; it carried a copyright and a stern admonition that they and it not be quoted. This vigilante avant-garde noted the fumbles and divined the stars months ahead of poky old Michelin. And the ecstatic noise carried like jungle drums, a rattle of pots and pans igniting what would soon become a feeding frenzy.

Even after the fall of 1968, when I went professional at *New York,* I was just an American parvenu abroad. That was about to change.

In the spring of 1971, the name on every gourmand's fois gras–stained lips was Michel Guérard. Little known and unbankable, Guérard had launched himself in a cramped low-rent spot in Asnières, a working-class suburb on a faraway edge of Paris. Quickly discovered by the French press, he soon found his twenty seats claimed months ahead by an international cognoscenti. I tried every tack I could think of to book a table at his tiny Pot au Feu, but in vain. I called weeks ahead from New York. No hope. The concierge at my modest hotel lacked clout, too. A foodie friend urged me to get in touch with a woman he'd met on his last Paris jaunt. "A great beauty, exquisitely dressed," he said. "She drives a silver Rolls-Royce and she knows all the chefs. You two were born to be friends."

I phoned Yanou Collart. She was a well-connected publicist for many causes, most of them, it seemed, edible, drinkable, or matinee-idolizable. "Can we meet?" I asked. "Can we have a lunch or a dinner at . . ." I hesitated, not wanting to be too obvious. "Le Pot au Feu?"

"When would you like to go?" she asked. "Tonight? Tomorrow?"

"But they say it's fully booked six weeks ahead."

"Tomorrow lunch, then," she said. "I'll pick you up at your hotel."

Yanou Collart pulled up in her gleaming Rolls. She was Belgian, it seems, but looked very French to me, unabashedly braless and flashing sapphires and diamonds on various fingers. I could see the perfect cleavage in the deep V of what had to be a couture suit, fitted to skintight perfection. I got a distinct impression her gems were real. She was at ease in adorably fractured English, with an accent that made even her longest bawdy jokes wildly funny.

Yanou seemed to know everyone—movie stars, couturiers, famous writers, the lions of business—and in my honor, she was full of gossip about Paul (Bocuse, *naturellement*) and Roger (Vergé) in Mougins, about the amazing Jacques Manière at Au Pactole and why Michelin still gave three stars to La Pyramide long after Fernand Point's death. She promised I would have no problem getting into the Tour d'Argent, one of four Michelin three-star restaurants in Paris that year (dinner cost from fourteen to twenty dollars, exclusive of drinks and service). She had only to phone the dapper owner, Claude Terrail, and I would have a window view of Notre Dame.

At Le Pot au Feu, Guérard's woman, the *belle* blond Jacqueline, greeted Yanou like a long-lost sister, a movie star, the ambassador of global *publicite* she was, and Michel came out of the kitchen to kiss the air that kissed Yanou's cheeks. Was she their official publicist or just a friend willing always to help a friend? Even when I got to know her well, it was not always easy to make the distinction. She was the most charming facilitator I'd ever met, as well as a clever publicity counselor to the gastronomic superstars. ("The best-connected person in France and all of Europe," Pierre Salinger described her. "She is a magic wand who can launch a chef through promotion like a boxer, or a couturier or a film," *Food Arts* would quote Paul Bocuse in awarding her its December 1993 Silver Spoon Award.)

The chef sought to gauge Yanou's pleasure. Small, with a shock of dark hair, a quizzical smile, and a long pointed nose, Guérard looked like Pinocchio in a human phase. "Shall I just make you a dinner?"

The chef's impromptu tasting? Of course. Yes. Yes. Yes. We both agreed.

We shared a bottle of red—Yanou drank only red, usually a significant Bordeaux, often with a name even I recognized. After the lofty Château Pétrus she favored, her everyday choice was a Ducru-Beaucaillou from a respectable year. Did she ever ask for a check? I don't remember, and anyway, no chef in his right mind would present one. Since the French critics were by reputation mostly incurable freeloaders, it was a while before she would understand that certain American journalists had the endearing but rather imbecilic notion that free meals for critics were immoral.

The food emerging from Michel Guérard's kitchen that day was unlike any other I'd ever tasted. His *merlan braisée après Fernand Point* was typically bold. Whiting, while definitely low-caste, was nothing I'd ever spotted on a menu in an ambitious *maison*. In homage to the great Fernand Point in Vienne, where many of the three-star chefs had prepped, Guérard's firm wraith of whiting rode to the table on a bed of tomato, shallot, and mushroom bits—in a pool of its cooking liquid, reduced to an intense bouquet and then thickened by the whisking in of a ton of butter. Our uncontrollable whimpers of pleasure escalated with the first shock of a gossamer *mousseline de brochet*—nothing but pike beaten to a pulp with cream, so light that it seemed to float right off the plate, its free-form dive arrested only by nubbin of lobster in the Nantua sauce.

Fricassée de volaille au vinaigre seemed daring, too. It was the first time I'd confronted what would eventually become a nouvelle cuisine cliché—the bird thrillingly moist, its sauce gaspingly tangy. I imagine even now I am tasting for the first time Michel's riff on sweetbreads— batons of the delicate organ, tossed with sticks of truffle, foie gras, and ham, the nutty warmth of cream that filled my mouth. I'm not really sure why I loved it so much. This dish was cute, while the rest was astonishing.

Guérard had begun his kitchen career at the pastry station and won a rare Meilleur Ouvrier award in pâtisserie, so his desserts were remarkable. I remember square balloons of puff pastry more delicate than any I'd ever tasted—shards of buttery leaves filled with the unbearable lightness of crème chantilly cushioning a layering of pear, each slice beatified with a tinge of caramel. And the piercing sorbets, cassis that day, that not only revived the overwhelmed palate but cleared every corner of the brain, so that somehow it was possible to enjoy the coda of mini-tarts and chocolate truffles. As for me and this appealing woman, the harmony of our irrepressible cries was striking. I felt we could be the Supremes of the table.

I was never a hapless tourist in France again. From that moment on,

I found myself adopted by Yanou Collart, mythic mover and shaker in her world. She was irrepressibly self-involved yet astonishingly generous. I was now a favored nation, a VIP—or as we say in France, *un grand fromage,* a big cheese—wherever I went on Yanou's advice and her staff's reservation. It was a delicate balancing act for me because, of course, it was no secret that Yanou was the chefs' noisemaker—that's what she did for a living and her client list grew over the years: restaurants, hotels, spas, films and theater, movie stars. Her inventive campaigns and a highly personal touch with demanding movie stars paid for the vast office/apartment on the rue François Premier, a floor or two below Alain Delon's. She had everything I wanted—glamour, sapphires, closet space, couturier samples, a waistline that belied her appetite, tits that stayed up all by themselves, and a refrigerator with nothing inside but champagne, water, orchids, and boxes of chocolates. I never saw her with a special man, and I had my loving husband—I still thought—even though he seemed reluctant to tear himself away from work to sit by my side on these obligatory overseas tours of duty. But she was always with friends, fermenting delicious fun, and never seemed lonely.

It wasn't possible to know if Lionel Poilâne, the master bread baker, and the proprietor of L'Ami Louis (the ultimate joint even today for food that is only about quality and season) and the sculptor Cesar (she wore his rectangle of smashed gold on a chain around her neck) were clients of Yanou or simply good pals or admired artists crucial to her matchmaking prowess. Did she represent Regine? Somehow, Yanou could always get a last-minute table. If a movie star wanted a table and a restaurant wanted a movie star, voilà. Call Yanou. She took care of a constellation of movie stars. (Jack Nicholson told *Food Arts* that in twenty years he'd "seen her move more people around better than the Chicago Bears." Later, she would work for the pope and the Dalai Lama, but in those early days she was just creeping into our hearts, establishing her image as an adorable fixer.

I knew she needed me as much as I needed her. My reports from abroad in *New York* brought cuisinary ingenues clamoring for tables. So we both pretended we could keep it pure. Or at least I did, probably being a shade more naïve. And she became my guru, a confidante, the woman whose coaching and coddling were prepping me to be the knowing guide to *New York*'s affluent foodie readers. She claimed she always respected my need for anonymity, making my reservations in the *nom de fourchette* on my credit card. But who was kidding whom? I struggled to keep my critical faculties clicking while chefs pretending not to know my provenance and mission fussed and dispatched little extras from the kitchen.

Lists of what was new and hot, clients or not, were ready each time I arrived in Paris, printed in the pale brown ink of her typewriter ribbon, and her assistant stood by to demand a table in overbooked rooms at the prime dinner hour. Perhaps if the restaurant wasn't a client, I might actually be anonymous, but even so, maître d's tended to flutter and the chef's welcoming giveaways, *amuse-gueles* (before the phrase was gentrified to *amuse-bouches*), tended to multiply. Faithful readers could organize their own truffle tours, carrying *New York* magazine clippings, ordering what I'd loved . . . poised to feel the earth move. Oh, it was heady stuff.

When visiting Paris solo, I often stayed at Yanou's, with its soft, sink-into velvet sofas and piles of cushions, the Art Deco vases and floor lamps, her collection of pocket watches under glass, the mirrored consoles and the mirrored bath with hundreds of dollars' worth of fancy soap piled in a giant seashell. I slept in a camp bed in the guest room, surrounded by dozens of photographs of Yanou, stylish Yanou, Yanou in hats, in Patrick Clark's buttons the year of his couturier *succès fou*, in all the evolving hairdos of the decades. Yanou with her friends: Yanou and Clint, Yanou and Charles Aznavour, Yanou and Yves Montand. Yanou with Bocuse. With a dozen stars I recognized from French film, male and female. With Sean Connery, Jack Nicholson, Kirk Douglas and his wife. With James Coburn, Peter O'Toole, Michael Caine. Sometimes she is gazing at them in rapture. Sometimes the gaze is returned. I don't mean to suggest for a moment that this might be a rogue's gallery of romantic conquests. Not at all. I have no idea if Yanou slept with any of them. On this aspect of her past, she was uncharacteristically discreet. There was a mysterious someone, I knew, but we'd never met.

Over the years, the Yanou documentary collection grew, obscuring the walls. There she was with Danny Kaye. I introduced her to Danny (I'd met him through his daughter Dena, a writer friend who lived across the street from me in New York). Danny seemed quite smitten with Yanou. Of course, he was a certified food nut, too, and a food lover's life with Yanou pulling the strings was addictively delicious.

I also introduced her to Craig Claiborne. Now that I think of it, that was worth a few of the hundred phone calls she made for me. Entrée to the *New York Times*. What a coup. Yanou took Craig on the fast train to Lyon to meet and interview Paul Bocuse. Escorted by Yanou, Craig was first to write about Alain Ducasse, newly installed at the Louis XV in Monte Carlo's Hôtel de Paris, where he would gather three Michelin stars faster than any chef ever had.

Craig was putty in Yanou's hands. He was in love with Yanou, too. A friend who played host to Yanou many Augusts in East Hampton recalls Craig almost falling into the pool the first time Yanou leaped up from her chaise to greet him topless. Topless sunning was rare in the Hamptons then, but on Yanou, petite and slim, already bronzed, topless looked fresh, rather like the demure nudes cavorting on the walls at George Lang's Café des Artistes. Even though Craig's sexual yen was for men, he seemed to have a special fondness for women's breasts. I suppose it could have had something to do with southern fried chicken, *poulet de Bresse,* his mammy, or even his mother, but I won't even try to guess.

"I think that if I could have been happy with any woman," he once told me, "it would have been Yanou."

One evening, Yanou and I were descending a restaurant staircase after having dinner together, when I recognized Omar Sharif surrendering his coat to the cloakroom attendant below.

"Oh, Yanou," he cried. I stood there, my heart pounding at the sight of his beauty—he was even handsomer in three dimensions—as he caught her up in his arms and kissed her on the mouth. I walked ahead, the soul of discretion, as they gabbled away in French. Then she came up beside me, smiling and aglow.

"I can check into a hotel for the night," I offered. "No problem, honest."

"Don't be silly," she said. "I would never be unfaithful to . . . you know."

My prime position in Yanou's bulging Rolodex brought one sybaritic revel after another. She included me, and Craig, too, among a handful of journalists invited in the winter of 1977 to join a gaggle of two- and three-star Michelin chefs from France, Belgium, and Germany to tour India and discover the genius of Indian cooking, courtesy of the Taj Hotels. What a glorious boondoggle. The Taj people created whole villages with dozens of artisans and hunting camps with waiters dressed as gun bearers to amuse us. In Bombay, we mingled with movie stars, politicians, and bejeweled gentry at a faux Parsi wedding feast minus the bride and groom. In Jaipur, elephants waited to carry us to the Taj Rambagh Palace as young boys in exotic dress and on horseback heralded our arrival with drums and horns, and sari-wrapped beauties danced on the front steps, waiting to drape us in jasmine and carnation leis.

That night, we found sequined chiffon saris in our rooms and a call to join Jaipur society at the maharajah's palace for dinner. The maharajah ("Bubbles" to his intimates) signaled everyone to join him cross-legged on the floor along the edge of a vast brightly colored rug, a thousand and one nights of weaving and big enough so the entire cast of a hundred or so could sit, knees grazing, while servants distributed dinner—mysterious stews, fiery pickles, and puffy breads—on individual round silver trays.

As always, Yanou was a star, trailing scarlet chiffon, rising gracefully at the end of that dinner when the maharajah said something in Hindi as well as in English and a dozen young women, all in yellow saris, got up to dance. Gamely, Yanou imitated each step and gesture of the lithe beauties as the locals rolled their eyes and giggled. "It is the dance of the virgins, you know," my neighbor confided, "the virgins' salute to spring." I like to think no one spoiled that moment by telling her. Yanou was bigger than spring. She was bigger than life.

16

CAN THIS BE LOVE, OR
IS IT AN INTOXICATION
OF BUTTER?

COMBUSTIBLE LUST WAS NOT ALL THAT MOTIVATED MY SEXUAL BRAVADO in the early seventies. I was finally driven to begin scouting another mate. I still loved Don. I could not imagine not loving him. I had told myself we would be together as long as it was good, and I'd come to count on this perfect "we" as the foundation of everything I did, my strength, my security. But clearly something was wrong. We handed over our psyches, each to our own therapist, and together we saw a marriage counselor. But I felt his deep unhappiness eating into my energy, bringing me down.

For me it was like winning a key to the city when *Times* managing editor Arthur Gelb nominated Don to be culture editor. As kultur maven, Don rated second-night tickets to every Broadway show that opened, gallery invitations, house seats at the ballet, and dozens of new records every week (the Doors, the Tramps, the Beatles, Ray Charles—cellophane-wrapped, free). But Don, who had thrived at the *Trib* in its most creative period under Jim Bellows, was really a tabloid kind of guy. "It's like working at an insurance company," he had complained. But he was proud to have opened a window and swept out a little fustiness. He fought for theater critic Clive Barnes's use of the word *cunnilingus* in a review of *The Beard,* a play that featured exactly that—onstage.

"Isn't there a scientific word we can use?" Arthur Gelb had asked.

"Yes, that's it," Don told him. "*Cunnilingus.*"

The decision went all the way up to Sulzberger, and *cunnilingus* it was. But from what Don told me, there were not many triumphs that came close to that one.

In Detroit, my sister, diagnosed with breast cancer, had refused a mastectomy, standard treatment at that time, and found a hospital to excise just the tumor. But her disease was unusually virulent and she'd had a recurrence. After a childhood of intense competition, Margie and I had become close, by telephone mostly, only in the previous few years, when, after years of sexual prudery, she discovered extramarital adventure and turned to me as the expert.

Terrified and threatened—devastated to lose the breast and the lovely cleavage she had displayed in deep décolletage for some years—she had decided to leave her husband and live as passionately as she could in the time she had. Her three young children were in a panic. First cancer, then divorce. I flew to Detroit to see her and be there for my anguished mother.

Suddenly, it seemed that life had no reward for procrastination. What was I waiting for?

I never suspected Don had actually been unfaithful. Even while I was flitting around like a happily deranged hummingbird in a field of lilies, I never dreamed he was playing around, too. If I'd known, I might have made a strong move sooner. I was sure I had convinced him he was incapable of lying. "Your pupils dilate when you try to lie," I told him. "I can always tell."

And he would agree: "I can never lie to you."

One Monday, he called from the *Times* to say he'd be home late, not to bother with dinner, because he wanted to see *Joe Egg*—a Broadway show I'd already seen and raved about.

"Oh great," I said. "You'll love it."

I felt vaguely uncomfortable. Something was not right. I looked at the newspaper. Of course, the theaters were closed on Monday.

"How did you like *Joe Egg?*" I asked as he came in the door and tossed a *Joe Egg Playbill* on the table. Good grief. Even a *Playbill.* No trick at all for the culture editor of the *Times.*

"Great. Wonderful. So sad."

"The theater is closed on Monday," I said.

He fell into his chair and covered his face with his hands.

"So where were you?"

There was this young woman in his department. With a crush on him. So vulnerable. So troubled. So needy. He'd agreed to have dinner at her place.

"Did you have sex?"

"Of course not."

I looked at his eyes. His pupils were very small.

"Did you kiss?"

"Nothing. A kiss."

"What did you eat?"

"Lamb chops."

"That's it? Just lamb chops? Not even a vegetable? Nothing green?"

He stared at me. "Pumpkin. Darling." And he pulled me into his arms.

Even though I was blind to what should have been obvious, with all the wise therapists and know-it-all-marriage counselors tending our psyches, I was forced to see a certain corrosion. I'd been playing around all this time without his guessing, but still I thought I knew him too well not to know. Since I had so much emotional stock invested in this "we," I needed to believe there was another man for me somewhere just around the corner, perfect for me as Don had been so perfect, and he wouldn't be haunted by eighteen-year-old bodies as Don confessed he was. For a long time, I thought that man was Murray Fisher. What is it about editors? He was a brilliant one. Maybe writers just need editors.

We met in Chicago, where I was promoting my book *Bite: A New York Restaurant Strategy* in 1972. *Bite* was ahead of its time, too—unbridled foodiness was not yet the epidemic that it would become, and pitifully few copies were sold. But serious restaurant criticism, which barely existed when I took my first bite for Clay Felker, was growing more common.

Producers of a local television news show had asked me to review three Chicago restaurants and report my findings on the air—a nice little chance to boost my book. I wanted company for my reviewing meals—to taste more dishes—and I didn't know many people in

Chicago. I decided to invite the editor of *Playboy* to lunch. *New York*'s impact was so powerful even this far into the hinterlands that I felt I could invite anyone I didn't know to lunch and they might be curious enough to accept. *Playboy* top gun Arthur Kretchmer demurred, didn't have a jacket in the office that day, or so he said, and he suggested I take Murray Fisher instead. Murray Fisher. Not an auspicious name. He would look like an accountant or a copy editor, as if he never saw daylight. I didn't expect anyone that handsome, very tall and slim, with the mane of a lion. Fisher—a brilliant editor, as he told me himself in our first fifteen minutes of breathing the same air—loved food and always had a jacket. That day it was sky blue.

All I remember about that lunch at the top of some Chicago skyscraper is that it was the sexiest and most intimate conversation I'd ever had . . . sexier and more intimate than a lot of the sex I'd had.

Fisher was full of himself, cocky and funny, and challenging and smart, and, yes, married, to a young and beautiful wife. Oh well, I was married, too. That needn't stand between two lusty adults and a bed, I believed. Murray had strong opinions about everything and he wasn't one to dillydally long with small talk. One spoonful of gazpacho and we were talking about . . . sex and love and infidelity. In response to his cutting probe, I was spilling my deepest anxieties. I admitted I was feeling more and more abandoned by Don and thought that I should be looking for a real connection in case my marriage was finished. Murray was in love with his wife and didn't believe in playing around, he said. He was a missionary's son and was perfumed with an air of righteousness. He held my hand as he said it and electric shocks went up my arm.

We were talking about skin and breasts, and whether I had ever eaten Chinese chicken salad, and if it was good to trade sexual fantasies in bed. I felt myself blushing all over. I was hot. Was he that cool? I wondered. Fortunately for my TV commitment, I found a few scribblings on the lunch in my notebook, because otherwise I would not have remembered even eating. I didn't want him to go. It was almost four o'clock. Did he really have to go? What about dinner? Yes, he really had to go.

Don seemed much happier now that he had left the *Times* for an executive niche at *Newsday*—"the tabloid in a tutu," they called it. Not even the draining daily commute to Garden City, Long Island, diluted his enthu-

siasm. We settled into our warped little domesticity, weekends in Woodstock, weeknights dining with friends on my reviewing rounds. Our circle of tasters loved the free meals but were grumpy when I insisted they
order what I needed to taste, and if the meal was a bomb, someone might
say, "Now you owe us a really good one." Don was a contender for a top
job at *Newsday* and he often worked late. I played games with my once-a-
week wine merchant lover. He wrote crazed and highly original poems
and mailed them to me, and between bouts of quite enjoyable sex, he did
a nonstop monologue on the wine business. So I could say I was sharpen-
ing my grasp of wine marketing. Thus our affair was not simply deliciously
high-risk, aerobic, and fun in the late afternoons but also good for my
taste memory in my palate's formative years. An unshakable Francophile,
I was sure I'd never taste an Italian wine beautiful enough to make me
weep. That all changed the evening he brought a Gaja Barbaresco of dig-
nified age to go with the carryout pizza we planned to share in front of a
fire in his country chalet. A swirl of the glass (of course, he brought those,
too, a pair of balloon goblets) threw the scent of berries and truffles into
the air. The first sip was bombastic, three baritones in simultaneous as-
sault, but after a bite of pepperoni and cheese, and a few minutes in the
glass, the deeply regal red warmed and softened, complex as a poem in a
foreign language, like satin on the tongue. And I wept.

Nixon went to China. Clifford Irving admitted his Howard Hughes
book was a hoax. Mrs. Aristotle Onassis sued photographer Ron Galella
to keep his distance. "Honor Thy Pasta," my survey of northern Italian
restaurants—Romeo Salta, Nanni's, Aperitivo, Giambelli 50th, Trattoria
da Alfredo, San Marino, the Italian Pavilion, Giovanni's, Nick & Guido's,
Ballato, and more—inspired a cover with naked New Yorkers swimming
in a giant bowl of fettuccine. Don came along on the pasta binge—after
all, it was for him I'd begged Marcella Hazan to share her technique of
making fresh pasta by giving me a private lesson. But my onetime partner in delicious excess seemed less enthralled with the endless quest for
the new and the sense-reeling. He needed to watch his weight, he insisted. He begged off my next eating swing through France. He couldn't
afford three weeks away from *Newsday,* he said, so I should find someone
to go with me. A pal of ours from the *Post* said he would pay his own way
just to share my dinners.

*   *   *

One early spring afternoon, Murray Fisher called out of the blue. I felt the blood rushing to my face. I stammered. Everyone from Chicago was in town for some Playboy Club event, he said. I suggested we meet at the Flower Drum, one of the more ambitious Chinese restaurants in town. Maybe they would do Chinese chicken salad. He had said he loved Chinese chicken salad. It seemed to be a West Coast fusion. He insisted on sitting next to me on the banquette. I ordered, but I can't remember what or if we ate. Knowing me, I probably did. Murray was depressed and angry. Indeed, he was indignant. His wife had left him for her ski instructor in Aspen, he said.

"What does that mean?" I asked. Surely the snow would melt and she'd come back again. He went over all the things he'd done for her and how she'd misinterpreted every caring word and move as obsessively controlling. Ungrateful bitch, I thought. Lucky me.

"Well, you need to get away," I said. "You should comfort yourself with truffles. Come to France and do this incredible trip with me. All you need is a plane ticket. The magazine pays for meals and hotels and our car. We'll start in Paris, do Bocuse, Père Bise on Lake Annecy. Oh, you can't imagine how beautiful it is. Then Troisgros. And we can stop in Les Baux—once, it was the medieval court of love. Oh, it will be magical."

"We just ran a story on the Troisgros brothers in *Playboy*," he said. "I edited it. Did you read it? The title was 'Is This the Greatest Restaurant in the World?' "

"Well then, you'll make the reservation at Troisgros," I said. "Then I can be anonymous and we can be lionized anyway."

He was making love to my hand again.

"Let's get out of here," he said. "My plane leaves in a few hours. Can you come to my hotel?"

I was supposed to meet Don at some *Newsday* gathering. "Let me call Don and tell him I won't be there."

I stepped into the phone booth. Don had already left for the party. For some insane reason, I was convinced I *had* to meet him. I can't imagine why now. Murray and I kissed and rubbed against each other like teenagers. Amazingly, the phone booth didn't melt. I pulled my clothes together, grabbed a cab, and left him panting on the curb.

In the seventies, sex was so carefree, so up-front, so ever-present, at least for me both before and after Don, it was easy to just leap off cliffs. At least it seemed so to me in the years since I'd started being unfaithful. Foreplay did not get much respect. Not that men hadn't become more sensitive lovers. During the almost ten years that I had been faithful to just one man, the women's movement had not only freed women to realize their sexuality; it had freed men, too. A lot of men suddenly got the drift of female anatomy. They seemed to know what it was and how to find it and what to do when they got there. Indeed, for me the two greatest discoveries of the twentieth century were the Cuisinart and the clitoris.

What seemed to be lost was classic old-fashioned foreplay, a courtship over time. A ritual game of seduction . . . with obstacles that keep two people from jumping into bed at the first little tickle. And that's what we had, Murray and I, a long-drawn-out, wondrously torturous, and sizzling anticipation.

I didn't cool down for days after he returned to Chicago, except briefly when a writing deadline or a fact checker interrupted my pornographic reveries of sharing foie gras and beds all over France with this complex and intriguing man.

I'd been banking my lust for weeks. Murray's plane was due to arrive in Paris early in the morning. He would come directly to L'Hôtel. I'd never stayed there before, but it was the Left Bank inn of the moment, located in the heart of Saint-Germain-des-Prés, with rounded walls and turn-of-the-century airs, legacy of denizens like Oscar Wilde and Mistinguett.

I set my alarm clock to wake me an hour ahead so I could bathe, put on makeup, fluff my hair, and slip into an unwrinkled sheer chiffon nightshirt and pretend his tap at the door had awakened me.

His knock kicked up my pulse.

Murray dropped his suitcase and swept me into his arms. He was wearing a double-breasted gray flannel suit, and I could feel the buttons and the scratchy wool through the chiffon. It came to me suddenly that this was a total stranger sliding his hand under my nightie—a man I'd never made love to—and we were committed to ten days of intimacy. What if it didn't work?

Well, there were a few shocking revelations. Murray didn't really like fish. And he wouldn't eat anything with a face on it—like shrimp, crab, or lobster. Needless to say, sweetbreads, tripe, kidneys, and brains were unthinkable. And two of his favorite colors were purple and orange. What can I say? The hippie sixties didn't really go away till far into the seventies, and psychedelic prints on polyester brightened his wardrobe.

But what might have been insurmountable conflicts were nothing really, small inconveniences in the glow of glorious astonishments. I'd always defined a great meal as one you couldn't possibly make love after and had advised readers on the truffle trails to make love before dinner. I was wrong. We made love before and after every great meal. Sometimes I would wake before dawn, not sure where I was, and then becoming sure . . . we would make love again.

We so exhausted ourselves making up for lost time that first day in Paris, we almost missed dinner. I'd reserved at Lasserre, not because I had that much faith in its Michelin three stars for great food but because I remembered it as unrelentingly romantic—luxurious and old-fashioned, with a ceiling that opened on balmy nights.

When I tried to stand up to dress, my legs were trembling.

"We don't have to go," said Murray. "I'm not that hungry."

"Of course you're hungry."

I staggered to the bathroom, bruising my hip on the jutting Empire dressers and vintage armoires crammed into that tiny room. I remember the dress was black, with a deep V that showed an edge of lace bra, and I was wearing black suede Roger Vivier cutout slingbacks—what Don called my "Joan Crawford fuck-me shoes." I remember sipping a champagne aperitif in the bar at Lasserre while Murray's hand caressed the arch of my foot, my insides fluttering. And I think possibly, probably, there was a meringue swan for dessert. We talked about what we had done in bed and how good a lover he was and what we would do in bed later, how perfect we were together, how amazingly suited for each other we were, nothing that would have amused anyone eavesdropping, but, for us, it was as if we were still in bed . . . and soon we were.

Chocolate Wickedness

This is a recipe adapted from Paula Peck's Art of Fine Baking, *with my own sauce. Kept in a jar in the freezer, it is always available for emergencies. (These instructions are for hand-beating, which I still do sometimes for nostalgia's sake.)*

1 cup heavy cream
1½ lbs. semisweet chocolate
3 egg yolks
½ cup brewed espresso coffee or 1½ tsp. instant espresso dissolved in ½ cup
     boiling water
½ cup crème de cacao
6 egg whites
Pinch of salt
¼ cup sugar

Using a wire whisk or electric beater, whip cream until thick. Refrigerate until ready to use.

Put chocolate in a large heatproof bowl over a pot of simmering water. Do not let the bottom of the bowl touch the water. Heat until chocolate is melted. Stir in egg yolks, coffee, and crème de cacao. Mix until smooth. Remove from heat, and cool.

Beat egg whites with salt until they stand in soft peaks. Add sugar, a tablespoon at a time, beating after each addition. Beat several more minutes until very stiff. (If beating by hand, it will take at least five minutes.)

Fold whipped cream into egg whites and then fold chocolate mixture into that mix.

Pour into a large glass bowl or 10-cup soufflé dish. Freeze for a minimum of 4 hours. Let sit at room temperature for 15 to 20 minutes before serving.

Serve with mock crème fraîche, made by blending ½ cup heavy cream, whipped into gentle peaks, with the ⅔ cup of sour cream and 1 teaspoon of vanilla. Refrigerate until ready to use.

17

A GASTROMANIACAL
INTERLUDE

Y OU NEVER KNOW WHAT IS ENOUGH UNLESS YOU KNOW WHAT IS MORE
than enough." William Blake had it right.

Murray had thrown himself into the delicious, artery- and liver-
challenging excess that defined my assignment. Meals alternated with
sex like a preposterously rich mille-feuille pastry—layers of sensuous
pleasure. He seemed dedicated to extending the parameters of my orgasmic potential and I celebrated his dedication, exhausted, sometimes
aching, and worn to a frazzle, but thrilled and amazed to discover this remarkable new me. I was staggered to be on this sensory roller coaster—
great food, evocative wines, high-wire sex, and once in awhile an
intellectual thought. It felt like paradise to me. Could one actually live
like this in the everyday world? And write and shop and remind the dry
cleaner to pay special attention to the food spots?

We had moments of supposed sanity. Skipping an occasional lunch
meant dashing through small towns, collecting crusty baguettes, sliced
sausages, a hunk or two of duck-liver terrine, and some cheese for a picnic alongside the road. This may not have been a wholesome savings in
calories, but picnics did come with exercise, a short walk and lovemaking under a tree, with only a few drowsy cows to see.

Occasionally, the outside world intruded, a few words in a newscast, Governor Wallace paralyzed by gunshot, American planes bombing Hanoi. But that cacophony was noise in a distant room. Essentially, we remained isolated in an erotic cocoon, endlessly focused on sex, trading histories and markers, his first this or that, my first whatever . . . as if we'd both just escaped from a sexual drought.

Farms passed in a blur of green and narrow stone walls. A few shops with crates of fruit outside marked tiny villages as we drove the roads that stretched between meals.

"Oh look . . . poppies," I cried, catching a blur of red flowers on my right. "The whole field is full of poppies. Like *The Wizard of Oz*." Murray swerved and slammed on the brakes, pulling me out of the car. He pushed me down on the fender. "Hey, hey, wait." I was laughing as he ripped off my panties and fucked me, surrounded by poppies on the side of the road.

We were not in Kansas anymore.

In those weeks of fiercely serious eating—research verging upon obsession—from the numbing joys of La Pyramide in Vienne and the creative vitality of Paul Bocuse, with his exquisitely etched pastry-wrapped *loup de mer,* to the blush-fleshed *omble chevalier* in a divinely humble butter bath at Père Bise. Les Frères Troisgros, in a little nowhere town called Roanne, one Alka-Seltzer east of Lyon, proved to be the most ingenuous sorcerers of all.

I insisted we arrive at Troisgros with an edge of hunger, stomachs empty, even though assorted senses might tingle with use and abuse. Let loose in the very heart of gastronomic freak-out country, Murray thought any attempt at moderation unseemly, but he acquiesced.

"Nothing in the solemn dignity and clarion discipline of France's gastronomic temples quite prepares you for the sweet silliness of the maison Troisgros," I wrote at the time. Brother Pierre in his tall white toque sat playing gin rummy in the middle of the dining room, where the awed pilgrims left over from lunch still nibbled petits fours, as we checked in. There were Troisgros dogs sniffing and champagne corks popping and old auntie asleep, propped on her elbow.

Well, of course, the important *Playboy* editor was expected. Though dinner was just a few hours away, the Troisgros family would not take no for an answer. "What do you mean, no late lunch? Are you thirsty? No? Well, here is a glass of icy Sancerre. Hungry? No? What a pity. Then you will have only one giant triangle of *clafouti* [sublimely simple pear and custard tart], not two." And as this was a town where manufacturing shoes was the hot ticket, visitors with time to linger might find themselves shooting baskets with the sociable Troisgros brothers or tagging along on food foraging expeditions between lunch and dinner. And so we did.

The two of us, with our very long legs, were stuffed into the backseat of a smallish car because the front was reserved for brother Pierre and a giant wheel of almond custard tart. First stop, the house of Bonnin, Roanne's most elegant delicatessen, just to schmooze with good friends. The Troisgros brothers, Pierre and the squarer, more reserved Jean, with his country gentleman beard, and hangers-on from the minicar in tow behind, headed directly for the cellar, where brother Jean tried to get his red-eyed hunting dog to climb into an empty vat by climbing in himself. There was champagne, a bottle of Burgundy—"Yes, just a small glass, just a taste, yes, you must"—and Pierre divided the almond tart with scissors. So much for our grim Spartan denial. Perhaps an hour of sleep would produce the hallucination of a reasonable number of hours passed without food.

Nine o'clock. A fine sharp air of expectation—not the electric voltage of formal dining, but something related to it—awaited. Pierre and Jean roamed the dining salon, serious now, but relaxed, champion athletes running a cinch race. The room was ringed by transient pilgrims of the palate, atingle with awe, like an alchemist's aphrodisiac, stirring them and us, too, into a frenzy of expectation and desire.

Instead of the signature $13.50 dinner, the pilgrims came to worship—the Troisgros brothers had choreographed a numbing parade of seasonal dishes for us. "Just a little of each, just to taste."

I felt uneasy out of my usual brown sparrow anonymity. I did not think they recognized me as a critic, but as the appendage of this *Playboy* editor, I was definitely sharing a regal fuss.

First came the snails, supersize mutants and amazingly tender, nourished by crunching on the leaves of the Burgundy grape, Jean pointed out. They had been snatched in adolescence, sautéed, braised, and somewhat blandly sauced in a swirl of herb-scented butter—a last-minute liaison requiring consummate timing, Jean observed: *"Très difficil."* Murray ignored the animals and blissed out on the sauce.

Pierre was about to disclose the sex life of a snail, when the next plate interrupted: a billowing pastry *feuilletée* filled with fresh foie gras and tiny batons of poached turnip. A mellow Meurseult was poured with the copper *cassolettes* of crayfish: tender little beasts curled in a tarragon-spiked broth. Burgundy labels flashed before our eyes; glasses filled—"just a soupçon"—emptied, and disappeared. New glasses appeared.

The barely cooked salmon on its gleaming sorrel-flecked pool was supernal, surpassing even rose-prismed memory from my earlier visit. Just in time to revive hyperindulged senses came a goblet of bracingly tart lemon ice flecked with citrus zest. What sorcery. Just enough. Not sweet at all. I found myself contemplating raging-rare slices of Charolais beef as if it were a new day, with fresh reserves of appetite.

I did not hesitate to consider cheese, "for research sake," I whispered into Murray's ear. I found myself able to nibble a few crumbles of Fourme d'Ambert, salty, soft, uncharacteristically gentle, a prepubescent *bleu*. And from the dessert cart, strawberries in a raspberry puree, an Everest pouf of floating island, satanic chocolate truffles, macaroons, the flat butter cookie called "cat's tongue" for it shape. By that time, champagne corks were popping again—a blanc de blanc with the Troisgros label. Seriously smashed, Murray and I smiled helplessly. "Rude to resist," he whispered to me, slipping a few inches lower in his chair.

The two of us descended, still rocky, the next day at noon, Murray very pale and unusually silent, our bags packed and ready to move on. *Absolument non. Impossible.* The family would not hear of it. Papa Troisgros had just returned from his very first cruise ever and wanted to meet us. Papa, at eighty, dapper and ruddy, flirtatious behind his lightly tinted shades, waxed ecstatic about the cruise-line food as if at home he existed on saltines and gruel. Pierre insisted we must join Papa at the family lunch before the regular service. You might have thought Papa had returned from a year in the Crusades, the way the clan fussed over him. He was a natural, the patriarch holding court.

"We shall taste the first of the 1970 Burgundies just arrived yesterday. Are they cool?" he asked the captain as the Chambolle-Musigny was decorked, and then a Bonnes-Mares. Coming from a rigid tradition of white wines chilled, red wines cellar temperature, I was surprised to learn that the Troisgros drank their young Burgundies slightly chilled.

Papa nodded and sipped. "This wine rains kisses in your mouth," he cried, throwing his arms in the air with the delirious pleasure of first love.

"You wouldn't want to wait to let it age a few years?" I ventured, ambassador from a country that had just moved from lemonade and Ovaltine to Cold Duck, Hearty Burgundy, and the hushed worship of great French reds.

"Wait?" Papa cried. "Wait for what? Do you wait to eat an old radish? Wine, like radishes and women, is best young."

Last week's radish wilted.

Murray leaped to the rescue. "But isn't it true that a great woman, like a great wine, improves with age?" he ventured. Papa wasn't listening. He was ooohing and smacking his lips over an oblong of tissue-thin pastry billowing high, spikes of asparagus emerging. The sauce was ever so faintly tart, liquid silk, elusive—just butter, cream, a dash of lemon, and bits of foie gras, Jean was explaining. He looked like a schoolboy bringing home a lamp from shop class to please his father.

"It is a *nouveau plat*," Papa Troisgros announced. "With a *nouveau plat*, you must cross yourself and make a wish."

Jean's wife, Maria, was summoned to taste. Pierre tasted, too. Papa wanted more. But the celebration was interrupted by a giant aluminum cauldron with two young bass in a steaming clove and coriander–scented bath, perfumed with olive oil and flecked with parsley.

"Serve all those vegetables. All of them," Papa commanded the captain. "All, the carrots, the onions . . . all." Everyone gathered to taste as Papa looked on, sipping his chilled red Burgundy. He seemed to sense our unspoken question. "I never drink white wine with fish," he said, "I save white wine for cheese. Little white wines for goat cheese. Montrachet [that rarest of rare Burgundies] goes with the cheese of the cow," he explained. "People will say old Troisgros is crazy. But it is not the reds that are too strong for fish. It is the whites. Try it blindfolded. You will see."

Now the two chefs and both wives settled down for a small joint of the chicken in a tomato-scented vinegar sauce, served with the Troisgros hashed browns dosed with a clove of garlic still in its *"chemise,"* as Papa observed, adding, "Just a touch of garlic, a hint."

He scowled at the cheeses. "When it is the time of the red fruit, it's not the good time for cheese," he lectured, signaling the waiter to bring on the Pont Neuf, a giant puff pastry pizza filled with almond-fortified frangipane cream. And his favorite, giant prunes—"de Californie." He bowed his head in our direction, as if bestowing on us the Légion d'Honneur for the prunes. There were chocolate truffles again and more champagne.

And then somehow we had been shoveled into the car and were backing out of the courtyard, Jean and Pierre waving good-bye, Pierre's wife, Olympe, standing out on the street, halting traffic. Then just as we shifted gears to pull away, the two brothers came running, waving something in a white paper wrap.

"It's fresh Marcigny cheese. It just arrived. It will not last. You must eat it tonight." Jean handed me a moist, dripping bundle of creamy soft goat cheese. Olympe signaled. All traffic snarled, roses twirled, red-eyed pups nibbled almond tarts, snails were munching through the vineyards, and Papa was savoring the last of the new Bonnes-Mares.

All was balmy in Troisgros country.

I'd plotted a zigzag circuit for us dictated by the mouth . . . touching down at heart-stopping tables, longtime favorites, and an inn or two that might be a discovery I could write about in *New York*. So much of what we did was a rerun of earlier debauchery with Don. I felt odd about that. I had enough of a hangover of love for Don and an almost superstitious need to believe in the perfect marriage, even if I had to squint to shut out the fissures that seemed to be dividing us. Perhaps that's why I felt a twinge of guilt now and then, sharing the very same delights we'd discovered together with another man now. Sex was a lark, but the Troisgros thrush terrine was sacred.

It would have desecrated the memory of my nights here with Don to sleep with Murray in the same Auberge de Père Bise suite in Talloires. So Murray and I looked out at the crystal clear Lake Annecy from a room in the nearby Hôtel de l'Abbeys while he made love to me from behind. Faithless wife dances with the angels, balancing on the head of a pin.

I was wooing this man now, hoping to seduce him to my way of life,

even while I was hoping Don and I could somehow heal the breach between us. Murray might be a less neurotic choice, I thought. He did not
strike me as likely to be intimidated by a strong woman. He was grown-
up, confident, opinionated, bossy (annoyingly bossy even), hmmm . . .
maybe even too much like me. Could I live with a man like that? Did I
really have an innate need to always be in charge? Wouldn't it be wonderful just to relax and let someone else make the decisions? Did I have
to decide now? Was there anything to decide?

Skeptics, those less sexually driven than I, might like to read that at
some point in the week, perhaps between blond chicken livers at Alain
Chapel in Mionnay and the baby lamb with herbs de Provence at Bau-
manière, the crazed sex cooled and Murray and I could talk of other
things. But for all those who want to believe sex that hot can't possibly
last, I have to note that, in fact, the sexual intensity only grew. Murray in
bed was full of surprises: songs and commands and silences. I felt free to
be as wanton, as demanding, as raw and perverse and out-of-control as I
had never guessed I could be.

But, of course, there were the in-betweens and the autoroute and the
hours at table. Murray was a big talker, a raconteur, a debater, full of confessions and questions and demands for opinions I didn't always want to
think about. Sometimes as we drove, I would pretend to be asleep just to
escape.

"Isn't it time for a chocolate?" he would ask, his voice waking me.
Like people who convince themselves they aren't truly alcoholic because
they don't drink before 5:00 PM, we agreed we would not have the first
chocolate of the day before 4:00 PM, when a little caffeine really helped.

So we talked. I learned about Murray growing up the son of a missionary in China, what he read, how he was perceived at school, what
food was like at home, and how he'd come to discover great wines—in
his crowd, he was the tastemaker. "This chocolate is good, but it's not as
good as a Frango." A Frango was a Chicago icon, a deathless chocolate
mint. He would send me some, he promised.

Murray had edited the *Playboy* interview each month, since it was
conceived as a way to add intellectual heft between the girlie stuff. He
had discovered Alex Haley's writing, assigned him to interview Malcolm X,
and was helping Haley with *Roots*. He was wild about Shel Silverstein's
writing and had brought a couple of his essays from *Playboy* in his brief-

case. He read them aloud to me . . . before and after making love, before and after chocolate.

"Do you have a plot for the novel you're writing?" he asked me one day as I sat pressed close to him in the car. I took my hand off his thigh. I had talked so many years and so vaguely about the novel I would write that I never thought much about what the novel would be, or when—that is to say, if. I remembered being really annoyed and a little deflated when Françoise Sagan's *Bonjour Tristesse* made such a splash. It was already too late, even then, for me to be a prodigy.

"Well, my heroine is a successful writer." I began inventing. "A film writer. She has a wonderful marriage and a husband she adores, who lets her be whatever she wants to be . . . and he loves her success."

"And then?" He sounded like my crotchety high school Latin teacher: impatient, relentless. "Yes, and then? She meets another man," he prompted. "She is instantly attracted. His wife has left him for her tennis instructor."

I laughed. "We're disguising the characters here to protect the innocent, are we?" I thought for a moment. "And then they escape together to France, where she is rewriting a film for a director who treats her rudely because she's a woman. They drive through France, eating in all the best places, making love. And her husband doesn't know. Or maybe somehow her husband finds out."

"What are you waiting for?" Murray asked. "You're almost forty years old. Time doesn't go backward, kiddo, so if you're going to write a novel . . . write it."

He was such an editor. Editors think it's so easy to write. "Just write," Don would say. "If you don't know how to begin, begin in the middle." But Don was always so gentle. Murray was a drill sergeant.

"You're right, of course, Murray. I will write it."

"When are you going to write it? This fall? This winter? You'll need to take a leave from *New York*." He had a way of holding his head at an odd angle, with his nose in the air, as he drove. Suddenly, he was not attractive at all. He looked like a turtle. "If you're not writing it, maybe you should stop talking about it." I looked at him. Smug smile. Smart-ass. I wanted to slap that silly superior grin off his face. But I've never been a slapper.

I was silent.

"I didn't hear what you said."

His voice was mean. I was itching and my stomach ached. Why was he ruining everything?

"Darling, let's not discuss exactly what will happen when I get home. I owe *New York* a certain number of reviews a year. I want to write the Troisgros story, and *New York* is paying my way home on the *France,* so I owe that column, too. I like your plot. . . . Your ideas are fabulous. I'm really excited about the plot. I feel . . . inspired. I will write the book. I can't wait to sit down and do it. I will do it. Please. For now, let's just be here."

18

HAUTE AFLOAT

MY LIFE IN SEARCH OF THE BEST TO EAT, NEVER MIND THE PRICE, WAS a total contradiction of all the heroic counterculture movements of our time. A Woodstock friend had sworn to eat only organic. She picked Jerusalem artichokes from alongside the river, made her own yogurt, and had forsaken éclairs for unsulfered prunes. Other women were discarding bras and forsaking alimony in the name of liberation. All about me, husbands and wives seemed to be destroying one another in the name of honesty. Incensed by gas-guzzling imports, patriots were riding bicycles. Well, I figured I had been a feminist before *The Feminine Mystique,* so I didn't feel a need to woman the barricades. I'd signed the abortion statement that ran in the first issue of *Ms.* magazine and I hoped that Gloria Steinem would remember and count me among her founding Valkyries.

Long before PETA came along to divide furistas from antifuristas, there was John Hess's graphic report with photographs in the *Times* on the force-feeding of geese to fatten their livers. Foie gras was becoming available year-round in Paris restaurants in 1972 and impoverished goose herders were getting rich. GEESE ARE TOO SMART TO OVEREAT, BUT SCIENCE IS FIXING THAT read the headline. That was an end to foie gras innocence and denial. I did feel lingering pangs of guilt for those poor birds, but not enough to give up foie gras as long as the farmwives of France were willing to do the dirty work.

In my consuming passions, I was hopelessly out of sync. I'd always longed to experience the luxury of a transatlantic crossing on the S.S. *France*. Craig Claiborne's transatlantic diary in the *Times* had called it "the greatest restaurant in the world." Was it really all that exclusive? Where else could a middle-class salaried American live like a Rockefeller or a Vanderbilt for a mere $180 a day, tips and port tax included? I'd read the *France* would be doomed to dry dock one day soon. That seemed reason enough to persuade Clay Felker to finance my float of unashamed decadence.

I thought it would be a serene coda to our escape from reality before Murray and I had to part—he returning to Chicago to provide socially redeeming value between the Playmate pinups, and I to yet another marriage-counseling attempt to glue Don and me contentedly together. Don had called to say he would be waiting for me at the pier in New York. He did have a way of falling in love with me all over again when I was out of town long enough, I realized. I wasn't sure how I felt.

Stifled by the steamship's predictably geriatric crowd, Murray and I struggled against the ennui of an ocean voyage. Well, yes, there was squash, swimming, shuffleboard, stock market classes, sunning, pinball machines, a small seizure of teenagers in the discotheque, predictable nightclub acts, and French movies without subtitles. But eating seemed to be the primary sport.

We made the rounds of heaving decks, endlessly trying to burn the calories of nonstop feedings with only sex and Ping-Pong to keep us alive. The fresh orange juice wasn't fresh, but cheese was served in six-ounce wedges. If you asked for apricot jam at breakfast, it came to your room in a quart jar. Croissants traveled only by the dozen.

Alas, in the years since Craig's exuberant endorsement, the kitchen had clearly faded. Up close, the boat itself was tacky, 1940 motel moderne, the dining room too bright, the stemless wineglasses too small, the cheese cold as marble. Craig had written that the kitchen would honor special orders—anything whim or gluttony might command. "That's true," our waiter, Michel, confirmed. He suggested we order a quiche for lunch. A quiche? Hardly an exercise to dazzle the gastronomic saints, but all right.

"Is it possible there is no extra charge for these special-order demands?" I asked. "If I ask for duck tongues and quail eggs, won't there be a bill?"

"*Absolument non.* No extras," Michel promised, seemingly quite pleased to be involved in stirring up the kitchen.

I gave the chefs every challenge I could muster. And someone out there picked up the gauntlet and threw it back. Astounding architecture and sculpture in ice and sugar emerged from the steamy caverns below. Sugar matadors, fruit baskets, windmills. The branch of a tree in spun sugar, with four candy birds perched above sweet frivolities. A simple request for grapefruit sorbet provoked a perfect globe of fruit in a spun sugar hairnet with green pulled-sugar leaves—off came the top and inside was a heart of silky grapefruit sorbet.

Ancienne cuisine ruled. A simple *canard au vinaigre?* The chef had never heard of it. So his bejeweled bird was Elizabeth Taylor dressed for a Venetian ball—fluted lemons and truffle rounds strung on a silver skewer, and a necklace alternating delicate chicken dumplings and little ovals of foie gras mousse, plus a few pastry puffs filled with apple.

We were winning, but we were losing.

At times, Murray and I had to drag ourselves up the stairs for our brisk deck walks, and we hogged the Ping-Pong table for killer games (mostly me running to pick up the ball slammed by Murray in an effort to be athletic). It was almost like being married the night neither of us was up to the effort of arousing the other after dinner.

"Making love is aerobic," I said.

"Why are you doing this to me?" he moaned.

"Nobody said we had to finish everything on the plate."

"I have to clean my plate," said Murray. "It's like a religion. Don't forget, I grew up in China."

Before we'd been overstuffed ourselves, I'd had fantasies of a tour de force for the final evening and had challenged the kitchen to do a pot-au-feu in the style of Dodin-Bouffant, the sensualist Brillat-Savarin-like hero of a novel by Marcel Rouff, *The Passionate Epicure.*

Halfway across the ocean, Michel reported sadly that the pot-au-feu of Dodin-Bouffant could not be found in any cookbook in the ship's vast collection. Every day I asked and every day he grew gloomier. But at lunch before our last day at sea, he announced the recipe had been found.

Daddy as
Clark Gable

Princess Moi and Sarah Lee

Intrepid *New York Post* reporter
(in front of my last self-portrait)

In my dollhouse, 1968, with the
mantel rescued from the men's
room of the condemned
Paramount movie theater

My author photo for *Don't Come Back Without It,* 1959

It wasn't easy leaving Don . . .
here we are at my sister's
wedding a few months after
our final breakup.

The church on the hill in
Woodstock, 1966

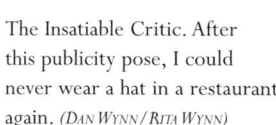

The Insatiable Critic. After
this publicity pose, I could
never wear a hat in a restaurant
again. *(DAN WYNN / RITA WYNN)*

At the Mondavi Cooking
School in 1976 with (*from left*)
Jean Troisgros, Joel Grey,
and Michael James

Gilbert and Maguy LeCoze
at Le Bernardin

Lunch at a garden table with André Soltner at Lutèce (*Sue Marx*)

A wintry day at Versailles with Jamey Gillis

A memory of that wonderful summer on the bay in East Hampton, with
the mischievous Craig Claiborne and Pierre Franey *(DAN WYNN / RITA WYNN)*

Citymeals-on-Wheels celebrates America's food legends. Front row, *left to right:* Famous Amos, Joe Baum, Mrs. Brennan from New Orleans, Julia Child, Craig Claiborne, Ben of Ben & Jerry's, Pierre Franey, George Land, Murray Klein from Zabar's, and me in the hat. *(WAGNER INTERNATIONAL)*

At the Citymeals-on-Wheels annual
party at Rockefeller Center with
David Rockwell (*left*) and
Drew Nieporent (*right*)
(© 2003 VIRGINIE BLANCHÈRE)

The happy ending. Steven Richter
keeps us moving in our houseboat
on Lake Powell.

They had cabled Paris, I figured. I was thrilled. The only challenge was making a dent in the stunning platter that arrived.

An excess of pot-au-feu was not the only reason I slept so badly that night, waking once from a threatening dream. I clung to Murray, and in the morning after a quick, hot wake-up fuck and a long, slow, languid, sensuous tango of love, I wept. And he held me a long time. The ship was already docked at the Forty-fourth Street pier. We had put our big bags outside the night before and now baggage handlers waited in the corridors to help the last first-class passengers disembark.

We agreed Murray would leave first and I would wait a few minutes, collecting myself to meet Don. And if we saw each other on the dock, we would not speak.

The customs inspector sniffed my herbs de Provence. Well, it did look like marijuana. "What exactly is in here?" he asked.

"Parsley, lots of parsley," I said, hoping to hit a familiar note. "And herbs like tarragon, sage." He was distracted by a tin of wild boar pâté.

"Boar. That's pork. Pork's not allowed."

"Unless it's in a can," I said.

In the distance, I saw Murray striding by Don, heading out into the street to find a taxi. Don was watching me parry with the customs officer. He waved and walked toward me. He grabbed my carry-on and caught me in a hug. I felt him shaking with tears. I was crying, too.

I was remembering a favorite line from a friend who'd fallen for a Don Juan: "Killers always cry." What had she meant? Poor Don. Poor baby. I could feel his terrible sadness. I could scarcely breathe feeling his pain.

It seems he was in love with one of his reporters. He finally found the courage to tell me a few days later. He hadn't meant it to happen. I recalled his favorite cynical romantic's motto: Fucking Leads to Kissing. It was true. She was twenty-two years old. A brunette, of course. I didn't ask about the fullness of her lips. Enough torture already. He needed to be with her. And yet he couldn't bear to leave me. Poor baby.

"Well, go then," I said. "You're impossible to live with like this."

"Just for the summer," he promised.

Good grief, I thought. He's taking a summer vacation. I had a whole summer to taste what life would be like without Don. As I might have guessed. It was fun. And it was unbearable.

19

UNDER COVERS

IT WOULDN'T HAVE BEEN HELEN GURLEY BROWN'S *COSMOPOLITAN* WITHOUT the usual wondrous cleavage on the cover. April's exotic vixen in 1973, captured by Francesco Scavullo, was framed in the twin pillars of brilliant teasing headlines that Helen Gurley Brown invented (and the more sedate sister magazines ultimately copied). I swear these are not made up. They are that April's actual come-ons.

The (Tricky, Sticky)
<u>Male</u>-Menopause—How <u>His</u>
Can Affect <u>You</u>.

How You Can
(and Will)
Live Through
an Anxiety Attack

Stephen Birmingham
Probes the Lives of
Very Rich Girls
and Their
Bizarre Hangups

Are
Younger Men
the Answer?

What It Takes
to Be a
TV News Girl

Could a girl (or even a woman) possibly resist putting down a dollar at the newsstand for all that hand-holding and psycho-burping? Inside, Nancy Friday told how to buy a man's suit. Thomas Meehan exposed "The Brain Manipulators." Walter Reade revealed "Love Affairs Are Good for You." But the pièce de résistance (in every sense) that month was my profile of a Hollywood hunk. The cover line promised:

The Burt Reynolds
We Didn't Uncover.

The aftermath of the Watergate break-in consumed Americans. Gordon Liddy had been given a twenty-year sentence for refusing to answer the Watergate grand jury's questions. The Vietnam War was officially ended even as White House warriors were insisting that it was right to bomb Cambodia. But, as always, frivolities distracted and consumed us. In New York, Halston's pantsuits aroused longing in those who couldn't afford them. Voyeurs devoured peeks into the glamorous life of Diane and Egon von Furstenberg.

Long before *New York,* I'd written for Helen Gurley Brown at *Cosmopolitan*. It was income, I told myself, money to finance our eating out, overseas travel, furs. I had a weakness for fur. I found a talented furrier who made me an American broadtail coat that fit like a dress, a V-necked brown broadtail blouse that zipped down the back, and a cheetah suit that Don loathed. It was hard to break the freelance habit, even though Don had urged me to devote all my free time to the novel. With his salary, he could easily handle the bills for all his addresses—ours, hers, and Woodstock, where the two of them would spend summer weekends while I bunked with friends in East Hampton. I knew he was right. But I liked having that extra money. Before I could exit cold turkey, I agreed to one last request from Helen: a profile of Burt Reynolds. Well, I was curious.

Burt Reynolds was filming *White Lightning* in the stifling heat of Little Rock in August 1972, when Helen sent me off to pin him wiggling to the canvas. I went through the press clippings. One year earlier, the buzz about Reynolds's powerful performance in *Deliverance* was so feverish, it had made him nervous. If the picture lived up to the hype, it would be a breakthrough for the actor, who'd been fired from Universal and had slogged through television action series—*Riverboat, Gunsmoke, Hawk*—only to find an audience being himself, sardonic and self-mockingly funny, on the late-night talk shows. Just before I met him, he'd been offered one million dollars to play James Bond for three films and had turned it down as a dead-end career move. "I know what I want because I've waited fifteen years to get it," he said. He was several years away from sharing the cover of *Time* magazine with Eastwood.

Then came the *Cosmopolitan* centerfold. Burt had astonished himself, Helen Gurley Brown, and the world by posing nude on a fur rug for *Cosmo*'s first centerfold. Now sexual propositions came at three o'clock in the morning. Incredible mail poured in—Polaroid photos of naked supplicants taken in the mirror, a lock of pubic hair in wax paper.

His affair with Dinah Shore, nineteen years his senior, was certainly intriguing. Younger man, older woman. I liked that. And I thought the centerfold was a wonderful spoof. From the clips and quotes, he struck me as a man who didn't give a damn what anyone might think. I could see the years in his eyes, a little puffy . . . and the lines in his forehead. I found them appealingly decadent.

"You could even see the blurred scar where doctors removed his spleen and put him back together after the accident that killed his dreams of a professional football career," I would later write. I found the scar on that beautiful body "moving . . . a symbol of vulnerability, unbelievably sexy." Was I born to write for *Cosmo*? Helen thought so. Clearly, women were lined up to jump into his bed. I was not attracted by that. It was too obvious. I promised myself that I would not be one of them. All's fair, I thought, but I didn't want to be the kind of woman who would fool around with Dinah Shore's guy. I needed to find him attractive to write the profile Helen wanted, but I didn't need to uncross my legs.

*   *   *

I found Reynolds in the Sam Peck Hotel bar with a string of locals warming the bar stools and the imported movie talent cooling down after a day on the set. He was dark, heavy-browed, his sulky lips involved with a vodka and tonic. He smiled and tossed off a few one-liners, flip, nervous maybe, sizing me up while playing Burt Reynolds the self-mocking wag. He was big as life, which is never as big as celluloid or fantasy, thinner than he seemed in photographs, looking fresh-scrubbed and Saturday Night Feverish in a skintight striped body shirt open at the neck and lean black stretch pants.

This was work for both of us. He'd been slammed around on the set since 7:00 AM. But the rules of this movie-star interview game say you both pretend it's fun. He needed to win me if he hoped to like his image months from now in *Cosmopolitan*. In those first few minutes, his leg was already pressed against mine. I imagined the leg was saying, I am a man and you are a woman and we're stuck with this artificial intimacy, so let's go with it.

Okay, leg, I thought, not moving away. I don't mind being treated like a sex object by a sex object. Let's talk. We started with *Deliverance*. Supposedly, Burt Lancaster and Marlon Brando had wanted the part, but the director, John Boorman, had asked for Reynolds after seeing him on the talk-show circuit. Burt suggested we move to a table. He ordered a club sandwich, annointing it with catsup, and tolerated a dozen interruptions from passing fans rather sweetly.

"Don't you just want them to go away?" I asked.

He shrugged. "I sat there for fifteen years while people reached across me to get someone else's autograph, asking me, 'Are you somebody too?'"

I had developed a style for writing magazine profiles. I liked to hang around for a while, watching my subject, or my victim, as it might turn out, at work and play, eavesdropping, lobbing a question or two from time to time, saving the actual interrogation for later, when I knew the person better. So that's what I did. The heat was oppressive the next morning, the mosquitoes bigger than chickens, twenty minutes outside of Little Rock. Burt, as moonshine-runner Gator McKlusky, would tangle with a gang of toughs, the cops, and the sheriff in the dusty rubble. The crew was boldly bared in the heat, women in shorts and halters, the grips bare-chested. Burt would be shoved, pummeled, fly through the air, and wind up hanging in the crook of a tree. No stuntman here.

"Everybody thinks I'm an ass for doing my own stunts," he told me. "Number one is that I like doing it. And in the long run, I'll be a better McKlusky." The movements had to be precisely choreographed, rehearsed, rehearsed again. Between each take, someone handed Burt a glass of vodka spiked with Gatorade.

Just as the camera was lugged into place again, the sun disappeared. Burt lounged during the break, admiring his costar's legs. "Cyd Charisse's are even better," he volunteered. "And for the best keester in Hollywood, it's Vera-Ellen and Mitzi Gaynor. As for boobs . . ." He pondered, watching me take notes. "There's a problem. Big boobs are wonderful, but after six hours you get tired of them. Small little boobs, they just sit there and stare at you. They're wonderful, too." I couldn't decide if he thought he was amusing me or just playing Burt Reynolds, and who cared what I thought? It was his Johnny Carson persona.

We moved into the star's dressing room—not the giant luxury trailer I would have expected, but, rather, a cramped tin can on wheels, left over from a low-budget shoot. Nothing long enough to stretch out on, just a few feet of seating, skimpily padded in plastic. Rotting squares of cheap carpet. Wheezing air conditioner. Burt propped his feet on a rusty metal locker after blending an alchemy from its contents—frosty vodka, limes, near-frozen tonic nestled in a bank of ice. I excused myself to check out the medicine chest in the john: Blistex, Snow Tan bronzer, piles of knee and elbow pads, acid-balanced hair spray, styling set, Solar-caine (which could also be used to prolong erotic ecstasy, Burt annotated later).

I picked up a paper fan and unfurled it. There was a letter written on it: "Dear Burt, you really should work for the space center. Your letter sent me into orbit without a rocket. Hope this fan keeps you cool. I'm available to operate it."

"Isn't that cute?" said Burt. "I love things like that."

Now he was confiding why he would resist an affair with his leading lady. "You get too protective." He reminisced about the loves of his life, about the importance of ending a relationship with honesty. Of not pulling "every bullshit trick every man tries to pull." I was not sure what to make of this uninhibited outpouring. Eventually, I noticed that a lot of it sounded familiar. I'd read it already—his canned confessions—in the movie-magazine clips supplied by the studio publicist.

The sun broke out again. The crew scattered peat moss over brush and scraggle to soften the falls. Burt unzipped his dungarees and started stuffing padding around his flanks. I couldn't help but notice—I guessed I was expected to notice—that the *Cosmo* centerfold did not do him full justice, hiding that perfect derriere. Oh dear. I had to pull myself back to reality, remembering that I was not going to be just another pushover.

So why did I suggest that we have dinner in his apartment atop the Sam Peck Hotel that evening? To escape the dining room's constant intrusions, of course. I was wearing a white satin jumpsuit covered in a wild floral print—evening pajamas almost, but not quite—with a zipper down the front, *Cosmo* cleavage, but, most important to me, impossible to get out of gracefully. A fashion statement as chastity belt. Know thyself.

Burt looked fresh and relaxed, taut in his body shirt and stretch pants. We stood on the terrace, watching lightning cut fissures into an elephant gray sky, when the buzzer sounded. Oh. Yes . . . a female wanting photo and autograph. Then another.

"Do you think we could pretend there's no one out there?" I asked.

He agreed we could ignore the buzzer.

"Want to see the horse I bought today?" He handed me a photo of a spindly freckled colt. "I bought him by telephone." Burt picked up the phone and asked for room service. Two vodkas and tonic for Burt. Two glasses of white wine for me. "That's what money is for," he confided. "Room service. Horses. Flying your friends in to visit the set." Money had bought the 180 acres of Florida ranch, the house built by Al Capone, where his parents lived, the land in Gatlinburg, Tennessee, the California house and its gate with the giant fretwork *R*.

This time, the knock announced room service. We sat there in the darkening room of the dimly lighted apartment, impersonal except for the handsome abstract paintings he had rented for the duration of filming. The waiter wheeled in a table covered with a long white cloth. Burt lighted candles.

"I called Clint Eastwood to check you out," he told me, leaning back on the sofa, sipping his vodka.

"I guess he said I was okay." I wondered what Eastwood had told him.

All the time I was listening, taping, sipping my wine, and analyzing the man, I was trying to remember why it had seemed so important to stay vertical. Suddenly, instead of a smart-ass cocksman, I was imagining some element of insecurity in this hypersexuality. Oh no. Vulnerability. My weakness. His leg was touching mine. His conversation was sexier than the actual seduction moves of most men. And I let him talk, let him alternate between superstud and sensitive Mr. Wonderful. I was quiet, sipping my wine but not drunk at all, thinking about the line between the compulsive Don Juan and a man who clearly loves women.

"I'm getting talked out," he warned. "I told my agent I can't do any more of these interviews. I don't want to talk about anything for three months. I've just been so f—— honest."

I was talked out, too. To hell with denial, I thought. If my life depended on it, I couldn't remember why it was I was not going to make love to this adorable man. I moved toward him and offered my mouth. His lips were soft. He let me kiss him. Oh, what a wonderful surprise. He really knew how to kiss. And everything else.

At the risk of seeming shallow, I have admitted to a certain compulsive bedability. But in defense of my highly selective promiscuity, I want to note that I turned Helen down when she asked me to interview Robert Redford, because I didn't think he was sexy. It was my theory, and hers, too, that if I found the subject hot, the reader would, too. Someone else was dispatched to profile Redford. At Helen's request, I met Marcello Mastroianni in the bar at the Pierre to talk about the possibility of a profile for *Cosmopolitan*. He scowled, looking weary, wrinkled, and defensive. Suspicious of being misunderstood by the *Cosmo* Girl reader. "I am not a sex symbol," Mastroianni kept saying. "I am not sexy at all. I am a tired, boring actor." I thought he was probably right and told Helen I'd pass.

20

TRAIN GAMES

BURT DID NOT CALL. FUNNY, ISN'T IT. YOU THINK YOU CAN HOP IN AND out of bed casually like a man, and then twenty-four hours later, you're a woman wondering why the bastard hasn't called. I told myself Burt was too busy to call. Getting battered on the set every day. A pileup of appointments back in Hollywood or a horse stampede in Florida or . . . I couldn't imagine. Rather, I *could* imagine. He was Burt Reynolds and he'd have to beat his way through a pack of babes vying to get into his pants just to reach a telephone.

Murray called from Chicago now and then, but that felt like a dead end, too. He was very uppity and businesslike on the phone. Pushy, or, I suppose one could say, encouraging, about my novel but not about any future for us. His wife had come home from Aspen and he was determined to revive their marriage.

Not that I had time to pine anyway. There were restaurants to explore, reviews to write. Don was home again after the summer's trial separation. He'd missed me so much, he said. We'd found yet another marriage counselor. I could see that Don was filled with anger, deep, barely contained anger, but it didn't seem to be about me. How could it be me? He had left me to live with his twenty-two-year-old for a summer and had come back. Didn't that prove neither of us could live without the other?

There was some experimental cancer treatment in trials at Sloan-Kettering. I got my sister into the program. She had taken a wine-tasting course and fallen in love with the instructor. They were going to open a wine shop together. I was amazed and moved by her courage.

Don and I had survived Christmas in Woodstock together and were doing well, I thought, laughing again without immediately breaking into tears. For Christmas, he bought me antique diamond earrings with baroque pearl drops. The new marriage counselor had a train game he wanted us to play. We each controlled a train. One of us had to back up to avoid a collision. I backed up.

He made us do it again and again. Each time, I backed up just as the trains were about to collide.

"Why do you always back up?" the therapist asked.

"Because I have to save Don from crashing. There is no alternative."

"But there is," he said. And he showed us a simple deviation to the side track.

We stared at each other in silence.

"I can't believe I didn't see that," I said.

"Well, I didn't see it, either," said Don.

We laughed.

None of this turmoil invaded the writing of *New York*'s Insatiable Critic. For the first couple of years, I had not let the reader know my gender. It was still a time where being male or female made a difference, with less respect for the opinions of women. And I did get mail addressed to Mr. Gael Greene. Even after I came out of the closet, I still had secrets. I wanted the reader to think of great eating as unadulterated joy, to aspire to my truffled highs as I had once aspired to Craig Claiborne's. I might hint at erotic playfulness but would never confide too discomfiting a reality—like a few unexpected pounds the morning after an excessive weekend or a straying husband. From the mail I got and the people I met—"Are you *that* Gael Greene?"—I imagined a following of novitiates, eager to convert to my faith.

"The Decadent Delights of Breakfast in Bed," an ode to unabashed indolence, appeared in 1973, during that troubled spring. It really was about us, the gamekeeper who came home from summer with his twenty-two-year-old inamorata and brought me sacred offerings on a tray. "Breakfast in bed is one of those unnatural acts that can be supremely delicious when performed by two consenting adults," I wrote. "I should have been a pampered courtesan . . . muse to some mad creative genius, a woman of modest intellect, great wit and fine consuming passions. But given the mean and ascetic boundaries of democracy, I struggle and contrive. I play geisha to his prince, slipping softly away to bring fresh-squeezed orange juice and homemade bread and smart, smelly Reblochon or runaway Brie . . . left on the counter overnight to mellow. And sometimes he is the weekend gamekeeper; splitting logs while I sleep the last precious hour, then coming into the bedroom dark with Hostess Twinkies, fresh bitter espresso, purple and green grapes in an old Shaker basket and the *Times Book Review* in the pocket of a squat-legged wicker tray scavenged from the Woodstock Library Fair for $3.

"Perhaps I have a faintly unrealistic attachment to bed. Some of us are bed nesters. Eros tangles our love lives with Oh-God-the-birds-are-awake-what-am-I-doing-in-bed mates. I cannot bear to leave the cocoon. He leaps awake to 76 trombones. Who are these anal-compulsives who will not suffer breakfast in bed? Imagine! A man who can start the day without coffee. A New Yorker traumatized by a dab of sour cream. An army of eager achievers, wary of spills, ill at ease in a mountain of pillows, frazzled by a stranger with a bed tray, spooked by a crumb.

"I am not intolerant. I accept the fact that there are some who prefer to read in a downy club chair and those who work best at a desk. There are romantics who scribble love letters at an escritoire and naturalists who favor breakfast beside the lake and sensationalists who prefer to make love in a bathtub.

"I'd rather . . . in bed."

New York magazine was all about service. I listed nine sources that promised to deliver breakfast. And yes, Don did understand that I needed to wake slowly and would bring me goodies and deep dark espresso with the *Times Book Review* on the wicker bed tray even till the end. No wonder I was confused. In all the years since, I've been waiting for the man who understands my need for breakfast in bed.

The Morning-After
Orange Fruit Soup

I don't remember where I got the recipe for this refreshing and delicious fruit soup. If I stole it from you, please forgive me.

1½ cups water
2 tbsp. quick-cooking tapioca
1 tbsp. sugar
Pinch of salt
½ cup frozen concentrated orange juice
2 cups fruit (see below)

Mix the instant tapioca into water in a small saucepan. Cook over medium heat, stirring constantly, until it comes to a full boil. Remove from heat. Add sugar, salt, and orange juice concentrate. Stir to blend. Let cool for 15 minutes, then stir again. Cover and chill for at least 3 hours.

Just before serving, fold in fruit. In winter, you can use orange sections with the membrane cut away, sliced bananas, half grapes (seeded), frozen and thawed peach slices, and the best berries you can find. In summer, you can choose a mix of sweet and tart summer fruit—plums, peaches, nectarines, and, most especially, berries. Don't forget the banana.

Serve in chilled bowls or balloon goblets.

Serves 4.

21

THE SCENT OF A MAN

DON HAD AGREED TO JOIN ME IN EARLY SPRING OF 1973 FOR A GOUR-mand swing through Italy. I thought of it as the last reconciliation at-tempt. I believed we both did. He loved Italian food, and most of Italy was unexplored territory for both of us. If handmade pasta did not work a healing magic, what could bring us together? I was counting on getting an ocean between tearful regrets over leaving his twenty-two-year-old HER and the shared joy of spaghetti carbonara.

I'd written the Reynolds profile. It was in galleys, but there were a few holes here and there. Questions I needed to ask, I told myself as I dialed his Hollywood office. I'd be strictly professional, not even hint at how his silence had hurt.

"What are you wearing right now?" he began.

I ignored that and started going through my queries. They all seemed suddenly lame.

"That husband of yours come back yet?" he asked.

I told him about the overseas trip Don and I were planning. "One last reconciliation attempt," I said. We would meet in Nice. Don was di-recting a *Newsday* team of investigative reporters documenting the heroin path from North African poppy fields to laboratories in Mar-seilles to the streets of New York. He would spend a week editing the first half of the series and then we would drive north to Milan, Lake Como, and Turin.

Burt was on his way to Europe, too, he told me. Paris first and then a publicity tour of Scandinavia. Why not meet him in Paris, he suggested. He gave me the dates when he'd be at the Plaza Athénée.

"Promise you'll come," he said. "Let me persuade you to come to Sweden with me."

I don't know what I was thinking. A night in Paris with Burt Reynolds was not exactly a fruitful way to begin a trip meant to jump-start a stalled marriage. Maybe I was as burned by Don's yo-yoing as his young friend seemed to be. Perhaps his silences and his sighs and the sadness of his love notes—I kept them all, the farewells, the "love you forever," the "please forgive me," and the "I don't know what I'm doing." Maybe I knew already these last months were a gathering of strength by both of us to let go.

I had stopped playing around when Don came back. (I told myself Burt didn't count because that was out of town.) But sex between us was unbearably self-conscious and infrequent. I persisted in self-delusion. Surely I should have known we were doomed when, during a rare moment of making love, he answered the phone and got into a conversation with Jimmy Breslin. I told myself we'd be two different people in Italy. Yet I would lie in our bed at night remembering the screaming intensity of other beds. I felt that Paris with Burt could only be a lusty parentheses, but I did long to be in bed with that man again. It felt like the difference between being a beautiful, desirable woman and being last year's rejected hag. I left a week before Don to visit an ailing friend in Venice, allowing a night or two in Paris before we were scheduled to meet in Nice.

Someone, a studio assistant, I guessed, let me into the star's vast suite at the Plaza Athénée, where dishes from a late lunch sat congealing on a roll-away table. A couple of men in shiny suits looked at me quickly with a dismissive "just another bimbo" glance, or so I thought. I was not introduced. Burt was dressed and stretched out in bed as if exhausted. I wanted to believe it was jet lag and not the quickie before me.

He sat up and pulled me over for a hug and a kiss. "Do you think you could go out and buy me some of that French aftershave?" he said into my ear. "I just need half an hour with these guys and then we're free." He pulled a bunch of franc notes out of his pocket and tried to stuff them in my hand.

I shook his hand away. "I have francs."

I decided not to make a federal case out of being dismissed like a gofer. And I left. It was a longish walk, but I knew Le Drugstore would be open on the Champs Elysées. And I sure as hell didn't need to come back too soon and be dismissed again. I sprayed first one and then another men's cologne on my wrist and sniffed. I smelled Eau Sauvage. Perfect name, I thought, but it wasn't Burt. I tried Zizanie. My father had liked Zizanie. Not right. And it was too late to get into bed with Daddy. I spritzed a whiff of Paco Rabanne on my elbow. No question. That was how Burt should smell.

He was alone when I returned. The room was dim, the curtains tightly drawn, with just a crack of light from the street.

"Come here," he commanded.

I unbuttoned and unzipped and ungartered.

"Give me your arm," I said.

"Give me your boobs."

"No, arm first." I spritzed his wrist. "Is that you or isn't it?" I was proud of my nose. And why not? My professional nose. Without the nose that knows, the palate is nothing much.

Burt sniffed the air. He sniffed my skin. He pulled me down beside him and he began to make love to me. In the *Cosmopolitan* profile, I would quote his ex-wife Judy Carne for discretion's sake, but I could have said it myself: "Burt is a wonderful lover. He's a very sexy close-to-the-skin man. He's not a man who makes love to get his rocks off. He's a giver. And how he gets his rocks off is how much you're getting off. Do you know what I mean by the difference?"

Yes. Oh yes, I knew. There are men like that. Men who love women, really love women . . . men who get into a woman's head and play you like a violin prodigy, sensitive to every nuance of the female response, of one female's specific response. A man who takes you out of your mind, sends you somewhere you've never been, shows you the sexual woman you can be. Usually superlovers are the most ordinary men, short or bald, attractive perhaps but not likely the classic Adonis, certainly not the movie-star sexpot with box-office allure. Or so I would have thought.

I lay back on the pillow, stunned for a while, then shivering, basking in all the sensations. I caught a glimpse of the clock on the nightstand. "We should be going," I said. "It's late, and I reserved for dinner in a place you'll love."

He groaned. "You don't really want to go out, do you? Let's just stay here and be lazy and have room service." He had his hand between my legs. I could see where we were going, and it was not to my favorite bistro, L'Ami Louis.

We sipped champagne from the minibar and I ate chocolates for dinner. I wasn't sure if it was morning or night when I got dressed to go back to my hotel. "I want to give you my schedule," he said. "I am sure you and your husband will be fine, but, just in case, if you need to get away, this is where you'll find me." He gave me a list of dates and hotels.

"Sweden is full of gorgeous blondes with big boobs," I said.

"I mean it," he said. "You'll be with me."

I tucked the piece of paper into my bag. "Will we have lunch in the Tivoli Gardens?" I asked.

"You'll come?"

I spritzed a little Paco Rabanne on my wrist, and sniffed it. "I can't possibly forget you now."

22

THE YO-YO UNWINDS

WE DID NOT HAVE LUNCH IN THE TIVOLI GARDENS. I DID NOT GO TO Copenhagen. I did not get to Sweden. Those ten days in Italy with Don was our life in a microcosm—half the time, we were lovingly in delighted cahoots, half the time we were snapping and ripping each other apart. He was exhilarated by the week spent editing the drug series in Nice. He knew it was good. (Though he didn't know it would win a Pulitzer for *Newsday,* for himself, and for the investigative team.) Don loved being an editor. He loved newspapers. That positive energy brightened our time together at first.

In Milan, Signor Buccellati himself and a saleswoman pulled out brooches, rings, a string of pale gray pearls in the jewel-box shop of the great Italian jewelry family. I slipped a wide gold cuff on my wrist. It was a leaf with a raised stem in the middle, etched all over with the finest lines, in the classic Buccellati style, just $330. I had to have it. Don grinned with pleasure and hugged me. I'd made a decision. I had found a bracelet I loved and I didn't make a big deal about the price. I put it on immediately.

A disappointing meal at a classic favorite of Milan in the Galleria brought us down. A couple of wonderfully al dente pastas at lunch brought us up. I insisted we walk a mile on tiny backstreets to find an antiques dealer who no one had heard of, and he dented the car trying to park. What did we fight about? I can't remember. Perhaps it was my pitiful Italian. I could ask directions but I didn't always understand the answer. We were lost in a net of one-way streets. He expected me to know everything. He slammed out of the car and walked away, leaving it in the middle of a narrow street. I pounded my fist on the windshield.

He came running back, grabbed my hand, and kissed it. "I'm sorry. I'm sorry. Look, your sweet little hand is hurt."

We drove into Turin, both of us sulking for some reason I cannot remember, except that nothing was working, not even pasta. It was gray. We were gray. By that time, all the hope I'd never stopped clinging to had vanished. Holding the map upside down in a vain effort to figure out what direction we were going, I said left when I meant right. He screamed at me. He said every terrible thing he could think of. That he hated me. That he loved Her. That it was no fun to be with someone who knew everything. That the joy for him was showing the world to someone who didn't know anything. I did not answer. I did not look at him as we finally checked into the hotel.

I would leave, I was telling myself. My mind was racing. I would find Burt in Scandinavia. Let Don stew in Turin. Let him find his way back to Milan, to the airport, to New York. I sat on the bed, leafing through a folder, looking for Burt's itinerary. I sat there staring at the phone number, staring at the phone.

Don doesn't speak Italian, I told myself. How will Don manage to get back to Milan without me? He lay beside me in the bed, facing the wall, weeping. "It's over, isn't it?" he said.

"We'll go home," I replied.

We went back to our three therapists—his, mine, and ours—but we both knew now we were just seeking the strength to say good-bye.

Burt Reynolds didn't like the piece I wrote for *Cosmopolitan*. Why would he? In it, I had scolded him for trying to be both a serious actor and a cheap pinup. He didn't take my calls. I never saw him again.

"Why were you so tough on him?" my therapist asked years later. "You didn't treat him as a serious person."

"But what I wrote was true," I protested. "I am a journalist, you know. He had just made *Deliverance*. He'd shown he could act. And he was sending fans photos of himself half-naked."

"So that was your fine journalistic integrity?" she asked. "You could be living with Burt Reynolds."

"Oh Mildred," I said.

"You didn't need to tell the truth," she said. "Not if you cared for him. It was not the *Times,* after all. It was only *Cosmopolitan.*"

23

IT'S NOT NICE TO FOOL MOTHER KAUFMAN

O F COURSE I LONGED ONE DAY TO BELONG TO NEW YORK'S LITER-acracy. But being an eater, later a dancer, and not much of a drinker or lounge lizard, I came to Elaine's literary nursery late. An unabashedly seedy neighborhood bar at 1703 Second Avenue, near Eighty-eighth Street, it was simply not on my radar in the sixties, when I marched along, blinded by the fog of my Francophilia. At some point in 1963, the door of this simple saloon had yawned open and Nelson Aldrich, then a teacher, later an editor at *Harper's,* wandered in and lingered. Next night, he brought a poet friend. A drift of lean Off-Broadway playwrights set-tled in. A nonstop poker game evolved. And Elaine, the young earth mother, nursed them along, loving nanny, trading gossip, taking confes-sions. By the seventies, life was sheer gold for Elaine.

She had already evolved into her complex character (Mother Goose, tempestuous Madame Defarge) by the time I first documented the literary lemming crawl—"It Must Be Calf's Foot Jelly, Because Cannelloni Don't Shake Like That"—for *New York* in 1971. When *Women's Wear* found the Elaine's mix compellingly chic, historians, sociologists, anthropologists, poseurs, and wanna-bes were forced to notice. It was that defining moment when journalists and writers came to be seen as sexy, Manhattan's rock stars.

The playpen of the quality media quickly became an obligatory scene. "The Beautiful people clotted there, light bouncing off perfect capped smiles, making midnight Second Avenue bright as noon," I wrote. Limos double-parked in the grimy no-man's-land, spilling superstars— Mastroianni, Clint Eastwood, John Lennon, even Jackie. Lynda Bird with George Hamilton and her Secret Service shadow demanded a prime table, I reported. Elaine stood them at the jukebox.

"Inevitably came the third-string royalty, and the second-string rich, the politicans and flacks, the sycophants, the voyeurs, the grubs and slugs and drones, the curious, you and me," I reported. "Blueblood dandies and Dun-and-Bradstreet-adored dudes screamed for see-and-be-seen tables but Elaine kept them iced at the bar—a gorgon, guarding those sexy front stations for her 'boys,' the ink-stained regulars."

You didn't need to call your broker, your bookie, or your divorce lawyer to find out how much you were worth. "One had only to stand at Elaine's bar with a watch, timing the wait for a table, smiling big as if the telltale drag on the minute hand weren't all that painful. As if a wave to the back room wasn't really fatal," I wrote. The front-row flaneurs were thrilled the night Elaine kept Henry Ford and his dazzling Christina cooling at the bar, then exiled them to the Ragu Room, her Siberia. "She's just a middle-class Italian," I quoted Elaine.

Divorces were doubly cruel. Who would get custody of Elaine's? In a moment of mock tragedy after splitting with Dan Greenburg ("How to Be a Jewish Mother"), Nora Ephron dared to voice the unthinkable. "Do you think Dan gets Elaine's in the separation agreement?"

People came expecting a floor show. Jason Robards weaving on his chair, denouncing a reporter for writing that he was known to take a drink now and then. Richard Harris lunging at a total stranger in the bar. "People go hoping to see Robert Frost in his cups or Solzhenitsyn decking Kurt Vonnegut or Norman Mailer in a violent Maileresque moment," I quoted David Halberstam as saying. But the truth was that Elaine's special pets were not all that recognizable. A. E. Hotchner, Hemingway's biographer, was an insider's icon. I certainly could not have picked Bruce Jay Friedman (*A Mother's Kisses*) out of the scrimmage or Mario Puzo before *The Godfather*. Even Elaine didn't recognize Antonioni. Exiled him out back. Mike Royko was a big deal in Chicago, but how would Elaine know? Royko needed to come back with Jimmy Breslin, Jules Feiffer, and Mayor Lindsay to rate a perch where he could handicap the crowd.

There weren't all that many front-row tables along the wall to jockey. Protecting the big "training table" for her boys, bouncing drunks, and shouting down sassers was a full-time job. In fact, it was another variation on the sadistic tables games French restaurateurs played in those days. When Gay and Nan Talese walked in late one night with the actress Teresa Wright, Elaine went up to the two Englishmen she had seated after an interminable wait. "It's been such an awful night for you, you won't be surprised if I move you to another table," she said, shuffling them off toward the rear.

"I would never run a joint that way," said Danny Lavezzo, who ran P. J. Clarke's, often in absentia. "People aren't even hungry. They just come in to find out how they rate. It runs you jagged."

Jagged, Elaine would rip up checks. "Out. Out. Get the creep out," she would say, exiling some real or imagined offender. When a waiter took pity on the actress Cloris Leachman standing famished at the bar during an extended wait and brought her a piece of bread, Elaine screamed insults too primitive to print in *New York* magazine. Leachman didn't move. When Suni Agnelli's kids wanted Cat Stevens's autograph, Elaine closed in, snapping, "I won't have my customers annoyed." When Ben Gazzara left a ten-dollar tip on a one-hundred-dollar check, Elaine screamed, "How dare you stiff my waiters?" One by one, Gazzara's drinking companions—Pete Hamill, Nick Pileggi, John Scanlan—got up, slipped behind Elaine, and disassociated themselves from Gazzara's gaffe. "Her strength is everyone's fear of the irrational mother," theorized my *New York* colleague Anthony Haden-Guest.

But when Elaine aimed her ire at *Women's Wear* editor in chief Michael Cody, he took his vengeance. Elaine's ceased to exist in the gossipy "Eye" column of *Women's Wear*. That was the summer of 1975. I tagged along with friends who loved Elaine's—there to document the fallout. "Unless Patty Hearst is captured playing croquet on the White House Lawn or Golda Meir is trapped having breakfast in bed (bacon and eggs in a pita) with Anwar Sadat in a hot sheet motel on the Gaza Strip, it looks as if the summer of '75 may come to be known for the Great Saloon War," I wrote.

It was an argument over money that provoked Elaine's majordomo and silent partner, Nick Spagnolo, to break away, moving into Nicola's at what had been the Foresters Rendezvous at 146 East 84th, taking along her third chef, a waiter or two, a dishwasher, the name of her baker, and the formula for her squid salad. *Women's Wear*—with a constituency the size of Ruritania, it somehow wielded the power of an H-bomb in those days—proclaimed Nicola's the best "joint" in town, hailing it for "fast becoming the IN place to go." Thus began the tug-of-war between literary Manhattan's wet nurse and her right-hand man for the hearts and minds, floating bar tabs, and heartburn of Elaine faithfuls: the loitering literati, the filmflam, the commuting celebs and their heaps of Uriahs, the masochists, the gofers and hangers-on.

Irwin Shaw, Chanel mannequin-turned-designer Jackie Rogers, Lily and Douglas Auchincloss, Arthur Miller, Robert Altman, Larry King—*WWD* gave the roll call. Soon the scrubbed little rich kids and Bloomingdale's overreachers were standing summer pink and beautiful at the bar as Nick fussed over defectors from Elaine's: Rita Gam, Jules Feiffer, Nora Ephron and her husband-to-be, Carl Bernstein.

As if those betrayals weren't cruel enough, it was Gay Talese, Elaine's very special darling, who couldn't help observing to David Halberstam, as I reported, "The food is really better here."

Halberstam, choking slightly, pointed to a potted palm: "Shhhh. She may have the place wired."

Elaine's pets were pinned wiggling in the spotlight, as Suzy, the Ernie Pyle of frontline hometown war correspondents, filled her *Daily News* column with names. Dare one brave a veal chop at Nick's for fear of exile from Elaine's? Soon there were faint tracks in the sidewalk from Elaine's flock skulking, swaggering between the two fueling stands. Spaghetti carbonara at Nick's. Nightcaps at Elaine's. Beef paillard at Elaine's. Then Nick's till a boozy 2:00 AM. Everyone wanted a decent beef paillard and Elaine's devotion, too. Did Elaine know? Would she explode? Should one . . . confess? The journalistic titans of our time cowered and burped.

Certain passionate Elaineastes refused to cross Nick's threshold. But a lot of the old true blues quite frankly liked Nick, too. "Elaine gave us a sense of community and Nick was part of that feeling," I quoted Halberstam. He hesitated, pondering the boundaries of loyalty, remembering that Elaine herself had narrowed the turf during the bitterest moments of the *Harper's Magazine* rebellion "when she seated that miserable son-of-a-bitch Lewis Lapham at the very next table."

"Elaine's is our club, but Nick's is a restaurant," saloon commuters cried. "Nick's veal is spectacular," one assured me. "His salad is fifty times better," reported another. "I have been watching Elaine's veal chop," reported one of America's most lauded investigative journalists. "It's getting smaller." Men of courage, women of conviction, brave journalists who had boldly taken on the president, the Pentagon, the Mafia, *New York Post* publisher Dorothy Schiff, and assorted other great American institutions, begged not to be quoted by name.

Now Nick's was all booked, unless he happened to know you. Friends of the house got seated fast. Strangers held up the bar, eyes darting in paranoia as they watched socialite (later publisher) Carter Burden rushed to a vacant table. They screamed. Nick screamed back: "Go. Don't wait. I told you it might be two hours." He stalked away.

Had he not learned about the restaurant business at Elaine's elbow? Nick had the Walter Cronkites, Muriel Resnik (*Any Wednesday*), Lee Radziwill, even Elaine's very special darling, playwright Jack Richardson. And film director Frank Perry with writer/editor Barbara Goldsmith. Elaine had Kurt Vonnegut and his wife, photographer Jill Krementz, the Schuyler Chapins, Frankie Fitzgerald, and David Halberstam two nights in a row (with Burt Glinn Tuesday, with Tammy Grimes on Wednesday). Elaine had society's design duo, Mica Ertegun and Chessy Raynor. And Suzy, breathlessly reporting the heroes and casualties of the nightly skirmish.

One night, Elaine bounced two guys and was moving back to her check-toting station at the bar, when one of them sneaked back in and kicked her in the derriere. Was it an act of isolated boldness? Was it the beginning of the end?

"Does the cosmic angst of this saloon ado escape you?" I asked my readers. "If your adrenaline is unspiked by minor masochism, if you're not susceptible to narcissistic mortification, if you have never quite understood the need to escape from your wife, the seven drinks before supper, the fear of closing your eyes, the terror of intimacy, the horror of being alone, then it is difficult to explain the spiritual imperative of a refuge like Elaine's." "How amusing," writer Michael Mooney mused (fortified by seeing the cover of his new book on the wall at both Nicola's and

Elaine's. "That Elaine Kaufman should be the Madame de Maintenon of the age."

Despite assorted seismic fissures now and then over the years, Elaine is still there in her saloon every night, bigger than life. She never really looked young, so she doesn't look old. Three decades later, she indulges the survivors, mothering a new generation of press punksters and bold-face parentheses, hosting their book parties and exclusive opening-night after parties, their new DVDs and Grammys, and now and then she'll open in the afternoon for a wake, where we look around to see who's alive, who's a blonde now, who's had a face-lift, who's still eating out on somebody else's check. It's power beyond chic, beyond fashion, beyond generational divide. Mama knows.

As for Nick, well, Nicola's is still there, but I can't recall the last time anyone spoke of it.

24

NOBODY KNOWS THE
TRUFFLES I'VE SEEN

PRESS JUNKETS AND FREE MEALS WERE STRICTLY FORBIDDEN TO *NEW YORK* magazine critics and contributing editors. But there was no way I could refuse the totally elegant hustle Yanou called to propose. Ten of America's greatest writers would be invited to the grand *bouffe* of all *bouffes,* choreographed to show off one of her clients, La Grande Cuisine Française, a new collective of France's star toques. The Young Turks, as they had been dubbed by Raymond Sokolow, Claiborne's replacement at the *Times,* would soon become the shock troops of something called the nouvelle cuisine. We would crisscross France's gourmand plains at harvest time in the two company jets of our hosts, Moët & Chandon.

It was 1973, the year of Watergate revelations, and heavy U.S. air strikes in Cambodia. Nixon's secret tapings were no longer a secret and all my friends wanted to be on his enemies list. Editorial writers were in a snit because France had ignored worldwide protests and exploded a nuclear device in the South Pacific. But serious eaters are notorious for not nursing grudges. And I could not imagine a richer way to do the gourmand truffle hop than among Yanou's chosen flock. I also saw the excursion as a chance to escape from the gloom at home, where Don was either melancholy and clingy or melancholy and distant, and where my mother tried not to sound teary on the phone when she spoke of my sister, whose cancer had started to eat away at her bones.

Yanou told me she'd already invited Tom Wolfe and wanted to know whom else to ask. I gave her a wish list of the literary giants I'd most love to break bread with: Truman Capote, Norman Mailer, John Updike, Philip Roth, William Styron, Kurt Vonnegut, Gore Vidal. I got goose bumps just thinking of the wit that would flow with our Dom Pérignon.

To protect my journalistic integrity, Clay Felker agreed that I should pay for the transatlantic flight and my hotel rooms. Yanou promised to ask each chef to give me a bill. Most of them understood the magazine's rules, but a few just laughed. Pierre Laporte in Biarritz returned my check for thirty dollars with the amount crossed off and "thirty kisses" written in its place. The bills were a pitiful sham, to be quite honest. I would have had to mortgage our little church on the hill in Woodstock to pay for the private-jet hops and the avalanche of champagne, but expensing the magazine for what added up to a pittance made me feel less of a freeloader.

Why was I not shocked to learn that my nominees for a winged salon of great writers were otherwise occupied? Still I assumed similar greats had been gracefully substituted by Yanou. I was taken aback, on boarding the plane, to spy Al Goldstein, editor of the tawdry sex journal *Screw,* sipping champagne as if severely parched. "I'm not supposed to mention *Screw* on this trip," he confided, noting that he was a recent graduate of the Four Seasons wine course, serious bona fides for this excursion. As his last act on earth, he had sent a copy of our itinerary to his Weight Watchers group leader. "I'm probably fourteenth choice," Al said, brooding. "I'm probably a stand-in for Mailer. I'm Jewish. I'm from Brooklyn. Actually, though, I've never stabbed any of my wives." Not that he couldn't have, since he was carrying saccharin in an ejector pen.

Nora Ephron had come directly from covering "The battle of the sexes" in Houston, where tennis power Billy Jean King had routed Bobby Riggs in straight sets. *New York* magazine regular Jane O'Reilly was ostensibly aboard, eating for *Ms.,* Gloria Steinem's brand-new publication, which had yet to recognize the importance of anything as frivolous as food or wine. There was a very junior editor from *House Beautiful;* a bourbon-loving science expert, who was writing a book on why infinity isn't; photographer Dan Wynn (the favorite food photographer of *New*

York then), and Bob Guccione's sister, who had a pretty serious Coke habit. At least *New York*'s wine writer, Alex Bespaloff, had serious credentials. Yanou informed us that a British wine journalist and Danny Kaye ("because he is so crazy about cooking") would join our coven in Paris. To a generation that might only know the great comic artist from movies on late-night television, where he appeared as Hans Christian Andersen, I should note that Danny was a certified foodie, celebrated for his fine Chinese cooking. He kept three helpers slicing and chopping for his star-studded dinner parties in his professionally equipped eat-in kitchen in Beverly Hills. There, he presided over a giant wok with flamboyant gestures, as if he were conducting a symphony.

"This is like a ship of fools," Goldstein observed, bright-eyed and eager. "No one is with his mate. Do you realize what potential there is for lust?"

I suggested he sublimate his lust and concentrate on this glorious exercise in gluttony—advice I was actually giving myself. All over France, the great chefs had been hoarding the fattest duck livers for us. Awash in a torrent of bubbly, we would jet from foie to foie, collapse on silken sheets in luxury hotel rooms, fighting the cholesterol rush, absently nibbling exquisite chocolates. Never quite sober on our seven-day mission, we groaned as the small corporate jet's fridge was opened to reveal fresh bottles of Moët every morning before lunch . . . and drank it anyway. Each night, another Michelin-laureled chef would have us at his mercy. From the sound of the plans, I felt I would need a wheelbarrow to transport my own liver back home.

Bleary from jet lag that first morning, we were cheered on by Yanou with an oyster and champagne breakfast at Le Duc, a seafood spot run by the Minchelli brothers, whom Yanou was grooming for stardom. The panache of sea creatures was stunning, like nothing I'd seen before: giant Belons and sharply briny oysters from the Ile de Re. Crackling baby shrimp to eat shell, feelers, eyes, and all, brilliantly peppery. Outsize crab, sweet and tender, with full meaty stomachs and exquisite coral roe. Tiny snails, actually barnacles, with wormlike bodies, which had to be pulled from their shells with a straight pin. Tenderest langoustines steamed in a pepper- and fennel-scented broth. And for dessert, raspberry tart. "I was only going to eat two oysters," I said, moaning over the Everest of shells on my plate.

*   *   *

Next morning, Yanou divided us up to board two small jets, each assigned over the next seven days to visit a different Michelin two-star spot for lunch and a three-star for dinner. I knew I had landed with the A team when I saw Yanou settling in next to Danny Kaye. Al Goldstein was not happy: "I can just see the headline if this plane goes down," he complained. "DANNY KAYE KILLED IN PLANE CRASH. Five Others Perish with Full Stomachs."

First stop, Tours, in the Loire Valley. Gastroholics making the cuisinary hajj in those days often overlooked Charles Barrier's three stars in Tours. Not us. Barrier didn't quite look like a chef, but like an ear, nose, and throat man, Danny suggested. And the place was done, done, done, but styleless. The chef's mousse of fresh duck liver, a recipe he'd worked on for two years, Barrier confided, glowed rosy-pink in its large white china basin—bold, provocative . . . a triumph of voluptuousness in my mouth. I looked around, wanting to share my "Oh my God" sentiments with someone similarly struck. A few of America's great writers were unwilling even to taste it. The problem was that it looked disturbingly raw.

"I promise you it's delicious," I whispered to Goldstein. "Incredibly sensuous." He shrugged. "You should be ashamed. . . . Aren't you considered a master of eating pussy?"

He brightened. "I hadn't thought of it that way. It would help if you'd press down on the back of my head."

After half a dozen courses—from electrifying to stultifying—lotus-tea sorbet in a big balloon goblet bobbed into view like a life raft afloat in a sea of butter. Looking across the table, I caught a glimpse of newsprint and a photo of a naked thigh. Yanou and our Moët escorts were leafing through an issue of *Screw*.

Al had been unable to bear anonymity another minute. "I expect to go to jail within a few months under the new obscenity laws," he was confessing. "I want to go on a full stomach." He started collecting addresses, promising to send subscriptions to everyone. "Do you realize *smut* spelled backward is Tums?" he marveled.

Not even Truman Capote could have defined the moment as tellingly.

In off-season Biarritz, we slid into a relaxed and warm welcome at Café de Paris, and fresh duck liver, of course, this time sautéed with apples. Guccione's sister, Jackie, had developed a taste for Dom Pérignon by then. Well, it's fizzy, after all, just like Coke. "They should send us a case of this when we get home," she suggested, "so we can taper off gradually." Rich rillettes of goose with fat cracklings were a challenge at breakfast the next morning. A challenge met.

The next night, after a long and impressive feast at Roger Vergé's handsome stone-walled Moulin de Mougins, there was sweet wine to sip with the tiny petits fours, something movingly chocolate, and shockingly tart red currants. And an intoxicating pear liqueur.

"You could get pregnant just from drinking this *poire,*" Danny announced. Danny alternated between Mr. Congeniality and Rumpelstiltskin. His bawdy high jinks quickly disillusioned the young flower from *House Beautiful*. She was shocked to realize that her childhood idol, Hans Christian Andersen, was actually a real man, a Hollywood actor, actively trying to bed her.

I found myself sleeping most of the time between meals. Perhaps foie gras was a soporific. And maybe foie-drugged sleep was a good way to escape memories. I felt Don like a ghost in so many of these rooms. We had made this same voyage of discovery together when everything was new and we were new. Increasingly, I felt woozy from sensory exhaustion. We were all eating like pigs, some of us piggier than others. Clearly, the great chefs of France were vying to stun our taste buds.

I must admit we were less than grateful to our benefactors at Moët & Chandon. There was champagne at every course. We were drowning in it. In rebellion, a few of us demanded red wine. Of course, champagne was James Beard's prescribed cure for overindulgence. Jim never specified what to do if the overindulgence happened to be committed primarily in cascades of champagne.

"Everybody cover your head with a napkin," Yanou cried as she demonstrated *ortolan*-eating etiquette at Troisgros in Roanne. These were the first *ortolans* of the season, plump little birds crisp-roasted but rare, to crunch and eat whole, everything but the beak. The napkin was to catch the flying juices. But in the isolation of his linen do-rag, Goldstein slipped the fat little creature into his trouser pocket, where the tattletale grease dribbled down his leg. (Later, when France outlawed eating the threatened bird, the napkin at forbidden *ortolan* feasts would also serve to hide the evidence.)

The uninhibited Troisgros brothers found a perfect playmate in Danny, who tilted a white toque atop his blond hair and pulled a chef's jacket taut over a pillow potbelly. At one point, a French photographer marched through the dining room, holding a pig's head aloft and insisting it was a calf's *tête*. Most of us were too sloshed to argue. We were all deliciously drunk on food and silliness.

Lemon ice spiked with Bacardi came along to tease our palates into craving still more foie gras, this time rolled into a cabbage leaf, along with partridge and a great red Burgundy, puckery with youth and slightly chilled, the way the Troisgros family liked their local grape. Carts bearing *le grand dessert* converged from every corner, but by that time, all I could manage was a portion of Papa Troisgros's beloved prunes poached in port and topped with a plop of crème fraîche. Did I say that's all? And a few cookies, candied grapefruit peel, little tartlets—no one was counting.

Now Moët's *bec-fin* house publicist, Jean-Marie Dubois, was challenging all comers to a boozy champagne game called Pomponette, pouring golden bubbly into pyramids of glasses piled high like a fountain. Even the champagne antagonists were chugalugging Dom Pérignon. Glasses were flying across the table. Five were smashed. "This is the most decadent night of my life," Al Goldstein cried. Quite a tribute, coming from a man who had just invited us all to his next orgy.

A stop at Paul Bocuse was not on our itinerary (our confreres in the other jet had Bocuse on their dance card), but how could Yanou say no when Bocuse insisted? Besides, Collonges au Mont d'Or, outside Lyon, was only two hours away and we—well, certainly I—were already working up a hunger. Great food is like great sex: The more you have, the more you want.

Bocuse insisted we drive right up to his catering hall to hear his collection of circus calliopes and fortify ourselves with a small *mâchon lyonnaise* for a snack. The maître himself was waiting for us, hawk nose flaring, head held high in the tall toque, arms folded across his broad chest. He stood like a god beside a table laden with the air-dried leg of a pig, countless foie gras canapés, and two kilos of caviar on ice. He shouted a command, and there we were popping sturgeon eggs to the pounding choruses of "The Star-Spangled Banner" played on the calliope. "God Save the Queen" and "La Marseillaise" followed.

"Don't eat too much," the chef cried long after we had all eaten too much. "Now comes lunch." Lunch? Wasn't that lunch?

The restaurant itself glowed in soft, filtered daylight. Half a dozen chickens were roasting before a blazing fire—poor little bruised birds. On closer viewing, I realized the bruises were giant disks of black truffles slipped under their skin. To be sure we all fully appreciated the first course, the chef tossed live crawfish on the table . . . but, happily, no live chickens.

Bocuse merely smiled when Yanou warned that we had to run or our plane would be late for the farewell dinner at Michel Guérard's in Paris. He opened yet another bottle of costly Richebourg to go with the cheese. We submitted to a blitz of desserts.

Al sighed. "Do you know anyone at *Gourmet*? I've decided to quit *Screw*."

Bocuse wouldn't let us board our jet without a giant wicker basket of country bread, sausage of Lyon, wine, cheese, and every leftover chocolate in sight. "In case you get hungry on the plane. Eat. Eat. Who knows if you will get much tonight chez Guérard," he warned.

That night, at Le Pot au Feu, my hunger was raging again. With our two flying squads united, plus a few luminaries from Moët and a sprinkling of Yanou's celebrity chums, we filled the tiny restaurant. Guérard spoke haltingly, head down, as innocent as a schoolboy: "I ask myself what can I feed you after all the great chefs of France." He made a gesture of helplessness. "Something supremely simple is what I decide. A simple fish. Some pigeons raised by a country woman in a most admirable manner."

The Spartan fish arrived naked on a bed of seaweed in the black iron cocotte it had steamed in. Seaweed—that was a breakthrough for France, I noted. And then—what a revelation—the acid of a shredded raw tomato sauce was the perfect foil for the sweetness of this ascetic *loup de mer*. I sat there as the plates disappeared, savoring the taste of the sea that lingered in my mouth.

There was a *feuilletée* of course, Guérard's supernaturally gossamer puff pastry filled with lobster and sweetbreads in a bordelaise sauce. A waiter passed with a basket of rolls. I waved him by, but then I sensed I would need bread as a kind of anchor to survive yet another bout of excess.

"I smell liver," I cried.

"It's probably your own," said travel writer Horace Sutton, who had joined our group for the finale.

Well, I would not have been surprised if a few of us needed to be carried home on stretchers. But there was indeed liver in the sauce of the pigeon, which was arranged on the plate with the geometry of an Aztec emblem: precise angles of fork-tender breast, a triangle of toast coated with liver puree, the head of the bird split precisely in two in case one wished to eat the brain. At the tail, a mound of onion marmalade (a first for me of what would become a nouvelle cuisine standard) with its hint of aged vinegar made a cunning counterpoint to the dense richness of the bird.

The roll was hot. I broke it open. Inside, a black truffle big as a golf ball had been baked into the roll, its juices permeating the bread. Guérard grinned, pleased with his witty triumph. I sat there, the intoxicating bread pressed against my nose, inhaling deeply, totally wowed. "My bread is spoiled," I heard someone say. Poor innocent, I thought. Guérard, in the unspoken competition's most daunting position, had met the challenge. And, amazingly, so had our motley crew.

25

GETTING TO KNOW CRAIG

I HAD ACTUALLY WRITTEN ONE HUNDRED PAGES OF A NOVEL, THE ONE Murray Fisher challenged me to write during our stolen time in France. I had hidden away at the MacDowell Colony for five weeks the winter of 1974, and what I'd written was good enough for me to be offered a contract from William Morrow. I was calling it *Skin Flick*. Now there was a real deadline, with money I would have to return if I didn't get serious. I would take the summer off to write the next one hundred pages. It was crucial to escape from the distractions of Manhattan.

As a child growing up in Detroit, summer, to me, had always meant a cottage at the beach. For most of my childhood, our entire extended family—aunts and uncles and cousins—moved en masse to a funky cottage colony on Lake Huron. My cousins and I simmered in the sun. Our mothers played mah-jongg. And the fathers drove out on weekends to play gin rummy and drink Moscow Mules in copper mugs.

My first summer in New York, I'd discovered Fire Island, where I rented a no-frills cottage with friends from college. Don never shared my feelings for the beach. He preferred rolling hills and woods. When we decided to buy a house, he convinced me the country was more practical than Fire Island, where a hurricane could wash our property away overnight. As much as I came to love our little church outside Wood-stock, I had always missed summers beside the sea.

My city existence had become complicated and emotionally drain-ing—the lure of new restaurants opening, the boy toys I used to prove how hot I was, my lingering attachment to Don. I had said the word *di-vorce* one morning not long after we returned from Turin, and Don had quickly pointed this out. "You said it, not me. You said it." And so it was agreed that he would move out sooner rather than later.

I'd balanced for three years on an emotional seesaw, waiting for Don to realize I was the one. I'd absorbed dozens of bracing and ego-shellacking sessions with Mildred, my charismatic therapist, and endured thorough behavior battering and restoration attempts from not one but two rela-tionship counselors (one yin, one yang). "He's not leaving you. You are leaving him," Mildred had kept telling me. "*You* are leaving him because you don't want to live with a man who wants eighteen-year-old bodies."

"Right. *I* am leaving *him.*"

Still, there were many mornings when I curled up in the curtained darkness of my/our balcony bedroom, wanting to be invisible, unable to drag myself out of bed. How ironic that just when life had become so de-licious and writing so rewarding, I was being abandoned. What cruel irony. I had once written an article for *Cosmopolitan,* "How Not To Get Dumped on His Way Up. " Now I was being dumped on my way up.

Every time I opened the top drawer of the Italian commode in our living room and saw the fragments of the ceramic angel from our wed-ding cake that he had shattered against the wall, I hated him. But I couldn't bring myself to throw the pieces away. And I knew I would love him always once I stopped remembering the explosions. It would help, I thought, if I got the cherub fixed.

Since Don had walked away from West End Avenue, leaving everything in the apartment behind, it seemed only right that we use some of our savings to furnish his new walk-up in the Village. Still, I couldn't help feeling annoyed that we were buying Early American antiques and folk art. His living room was becoming a small museum. The home wrecker, as I liked to think of Her, had refused to see him till he had the divorce papers in hand. He would make a quick trip to a divorce mill in the Caribbean in September. We made love on his new bed, and the sex was easier and hotter than it had been in years. As if life weren't confusing enough.

Don and I flew to Detroit together in June for the marriage of my sister, Margie, to Walter, the wine merchant, the new love of her life. She clearly adored him. They were both dressed in yellow. She had never been so thin. She looked fragile and glamorous in a sunshine voile garden hat and sheer yellow shirtdress. The dress bloused to hide the back brace that she wore because the cancer that would kill her ten months later had already eaten into her spine. A guitarist played the Kris Kristofferson song, "You Make Me Feel Brand New." A woman sang. Margie and Walter looked into each other's eyes as if they had forever. I wept. I couldn't help myself. I couldn't stop. I wept so loudly, people stared. Don held me tightly. Yes, I wept.

So it was summer and chance put me practically next door to Craig Claiborne. Our paths had crossed now and then as competing critics. But even though I'd grown more confident after six years of professional eating, the envy of the town's growing ranks of foodies wishing they could be me—or at least eat with me—I still felt like an imposter next to Craig. I was a lapdog to Craig's Saint Bernard. Once, Craig had complained that the most unlikely people suddenly became food writers or cookbook authors after he'd written about them for the *Times*. "Like that Boy Scout I interviewed," he had muttered dourly. "Now he has a cookbook contract."

I was sure he thought I used my *Look* profile of him to get my job. When anyone asked, I was properly modest. By profession a journalist, I'm just an amateur, I'd say, in the true sense of that word. I figured it would be best for me to say it before they did. Dan and Rita Wynn's weathered gray cedar house in the Springs, a few doors down the beach from Craig's, was mine for the summer. Dan was the food world's favorite photographer by preference, particularly his own. Many of the photos we see now that evoke the last years of James Beard are Dan's. I treasure the shot he took that summer—with me standing between Pierre Franey and Craig, Craig's hand under my blouse, reaching inside my bra, a huge grin on his face. That was the summer I got to know Craig, his joy and his aloneness.

*   *   *

"I tried having sex with a woman," Craig confided one night over his peppery fried chicken, just the two of us at dinner in his house. "It was awful." He screwed up his face. "Yech." That didn't mean Craig wasn't sexy. After a drink or two, he could be naughty. Breasts and crotches, it didn't seem to matter. He would grin and grab. People either loved him or pretended not to mind. He was warm and funny, generous and vulnerable, the ringmaster of glorious, celebrity-riddled parties and gourmandisiacal larks—and, admittedly, much too important to offend. So most of us ignored his roving fingers or brushed his hand away.

After a couple of vodka martinis and a stinger or two, Craig reminisced. "If you only knew how many heterosexual men I've had sex with, you'd be astonished," he told me. "Right there. In that steam bath." He refused to name names, though I swore never to tell. So I don't know and can't say. But a parade of luminaries danced through my brain, sloshed and amiable, possible objects of Craig's advances.

I imagined the lineup: food-world cronies, Hamptons' pals, chefs and restaurateurs grateful for his write-ups, loose enough after several drinks to let Craig give them a blow job in the steam bath. He was so sweet, after all, and the instigator of much delicious excess. As for hypermacho Paul Bocuse: Paul's eyes were crinkling with fun as he French-kissed Craig's ear in the photo Craig had hanging in his guest bathroom.

Weekdays, when most of my friends were in the city, I sat at my portable typewriter. I felt isolated in the gray house, a slave to the antiquated keyboard of my Royal. I needed people to talk to at the end of a writing day. Craig was often alone, too. One evening, he invited me to meet him at Casa Albona, his favorite Italian spot on the highway, where they knew how he liked his martinis. He was fond of the linguine with clams.

"You and I have a lot in common," he announced a martini and a half into the wind. "We both love men. But you don't need to worry about competition from me. I like older men. You should see some of the hunky high school boys who try to pick me up. But I'm not interested." He wrinkled his nose and flashed that sweet smile of his. "And unlike you, I'm not interested in love. I think love is icky. When I have sex, I can't wait for the guy to get up and go home."

"Love is the best thing," I said. "I wish it for you." I often felt like cracked crockery—a ghost of myself. I imagined Don in his new life, our apartment empty. I'd begged him to use the Woodstock house weekends. He had started to cook. Don, who never cooked. I imagined him cooking for someone, maybe even Her, my recipes being prepared in my black iron skillets. It was impossible to erase the images. I saw him entertaining our friends, making my risotto in my yellow Creuset casserole. I saw him burning the pot. At least he will know not to use Brillo to clean it, I thought, consoling myself. Was I crazy?

"If you ever fall in love, Craig, you'll understand what I'm talking about," I said.

"I'm a Virgo," Craig said, telling the waiter to bring us two stingers. "Virgos like sex, not love."

"I don't drink after dinner, Craig," I said, begging off, looking for the waiter to cancel one stinger. "I can't drink and drive." He couldn't either, but that didn't stop him (until the town finally took his license away).

"I hate puritans," he said, closing his eyes and wrinkling his nose in distaste. "It's mostly white crème de menthe anyway. It's not going to hurt you."

God forbid anyone might mistake me for a puritan. I sipped my stinger. It warmed the brain, blurred anxiety, and tasted a lot like melted mint chocolate chip ice cream. "Oh Craig," I moaned. "I love this drink. I'm high already. Did I tell you I'm a Capricorn? Capricorns like to be in control," I said.

In spite of his avowed aversion for lovers who linger, Craig was, in fact, endearingly romantic. On my first week in the Wynns' cedar house, I had met a man. "He's not your type," my friend Naomi said, telling me her accountant would call, "but he's smart, he's divorced, he's out in East Hampton for the month, with his sons part of the time, and maybe he would be fun for dinner." He was fun and funny at dinner, but I had decided to become more cautious now that I was single. I promised myself I would get to know a man before leaping into bed. I would wait till the second date. So I fought the powerful attraction I felt to Andrew,* the accountant, that first evening and shoved him out the door after an hour of play that left me aching and him in need of a quick dunk under the cold-water faucet so he could drive home.

I felt like a teenager again, burning hot, blood pounding, rediscover-

---

*Not his real name or true description, except for the amorous prowess.

ing the aphrodisiacal power of foreplay. The next day, we lay side by side on the beach, touching, kissing, confessing past amorous diversons. By the time we got back to the house and jumped into the shower together, we were wired to explode. Would we flood the bathroom? Would he drown on his knees in the shower? He was a volcano in bed. In the next few days, before his sons arrived for Daddy's two-week July custody, I had to force myself to get out of bed and move to the typewriter for half an hour between torrid interludes in the blue bedroom. Gray beach light filtered through sheer white cotton curtains on bodies damp and sticky, wondrously exhausted by what seemed to be a match dreamed up by some Aphrodite overdosed on Prozac. No wonder the sex scenes in my novel (ultimately to be called *Blue Skies, No Candy*) seemed unbearably charged and vivid. I fucked. I typed. I fucked. I typed.

One evening, I called Craig to ask if Andrew and I could have a swim in the pool before dinner. "I'm going out," he said, "but no problem. Come. Just swim. I'll be getting dressed." The two of us were naked at the far end of the pool, testing whether you could do it underwater, when Craig came out of the house.

"I'm not looking," he said, setting a bottle of Dom Pérignon in a bucket of ice at the edge of the pool, along with two crystal flutes. "Stay as long as you like."

Some years later, Craig announced he was in love. No apologies. No song and dance. No revisionist jive. He seemed to have forgotten Virgos never fall in love. He had spotted the man one evening walking near the Plaza Hotel—a wonderfully handsome man, straight, he said proudly, with five children, but of course his wife didn't know yet. They'd met half a dozen times since. The loved one lived somewhere outside Boston and had many family obligations, but he promised to visit as often as he could. The two of them exchanged Hallmark greeting cards all the time. Craig showed me a card with a flowery poem. "Corny, isn't it?" he said, clearly quite pleased with the sentiment. Later, as we were sitting down for dinner, the phone rang. "It's him," he cried. "Wait, " he told his caller, and he raced to put on the stereo. "I'm playing our song."

About Pierre . . . as so many wondered. Given the speculation about him and Craig Claiborne, Pierre Franey may have felt pressed to prove how heterosexual he could be, but I prefer to believe he was simply very

French and very hot. I like to think he was romantic, sexy, and full of hormones, like so many of the food people I knew, and that he was enjoying one or any number of the dark-eyed ladies who clung to him possessively when his wife, Betty, wasn't around.

Lunch with Pierre was a postgraduate seminar in New York dining history and the state of the art, larded with the most outrageous gossip. He was so innocent (or so it seemed to me), he didn't realize he should not be spilling the dirt. I felt I had to protect him by not passing his gossip along (unless it was about someone I disliked, and then how could I help myself?).

One August afternoon just before sunset, when I was summering and writing in a rented A-frame on the beach in Wainscott, I watched a lone fisherman pulling in bluefish. He offered to gut a big one for me if I wanted it, and I called Pierre for grilling advice. He offered to come by and cook it. Setting the two long fillets on a bed of glorious August tomatoes, crushed and cooked down with bits of softened garlic and onion, he brushed the fish with mayonnaise he had just whisked up.

The mayonnaise puffed up and browned under the broiler like crème brûlée—a mini-soufflé—and the fruity acid of the tomatoes cut the natural oiliness of the blue. It was like eating summer. As sensual and remarkable a revelation as the bluefish was, it was not followed by sex. But I always got the feeling that Betty Franey thought we were lovers, the way she hoisted her nose in the air and looked past me whenever we met.

When the world of food exploded and the *Times* single food page became first the "Living" section and then the demanding Wednesday "Dining," there were many columns to fill. Pierre wrote his weekly thirty-minute dinner, but Craig tangled with his editors. He never seemed happy with their assignments. He would have been content to hold court in his huge new house on Clam Shell Lane in the Springs. It was designed for the big dinner he loved—the vast commercial kitchen, complete with a tandoori oven, and a dining area that took up two-thirds of the entire space. He slept on a Murphy bed that pulled down from the library wall. The great chefs and rising stars of New York and the world drove out to cook with him and Pierre and to see their recipes featured in the *Times* Sunday magazine column.

But the editors had other ideas. They were editing a weekly food "magazine," after all. Craig was stubborn—baffled and annoyed by their proposals. So he quit. He would live on his royalties. But the newsletter he and Pierre put together failed to make money. He had heart problems and gout. He was knocked down by a taxi. He grew increasingly frail. His great love had promised to buy a house down the street and move to East Hampton, but he never did. Craig was discreet about the details but clearly disappointed. He seemed to be estranged from some of his closest friends—even Pierre. Pierre had his own expanding career in books and television and was happily caught up being the Franey patriarch and grandfather, as well as coach to the new food critic at the *Times,* Brian Miller.

In the late eighties, I left the Hamptons behind and began spending summers in Aspen, so I was shocked to see how frail Craig looked when I picked him up for dinner one night at his small Manhattan flat in the Osborne, on West Fifty-seventh Street. He smiled, suffered a kiss, and berated himself for the long, painful minutes it took to shuffle from the elevator to the front door. The cabbie, nastily chewing me out for making him wait, took one look, shut up, and helped Craig into the taxi.

Eventually, Craig was confined in his cramped pied-à-terre—mostly in bed—with a full-time caretaker, seemingly abandoned by many of the fine-feathered pals who had feasted for years at his table. A few restaurateurs who had witnessed his decline sent food. The premier restaurant critic of New York (perhaps the land, if not the world)—the man whose craving for chili peppers had led a generation of timid eaters to savor the Szechuan pepper, to revel in Tex-Mex and Thai, and to tour the world in his wake—seemed forgotten.

I'm not sure if it was before or after *The New Yorker* referred to him in error as the *late* Craig Claiborne that I proposed to Warner LeRoy and a few food-world cronies that we invite a hundred friends and admirers to "A Hug for Craig" at Warner's Tavern on the Green. Craig was wheeled in. He grinned like a spoiled child on Christmas morning as he gazed around the room at the familiar faces: his secretary Velma Cannon on his right, Joel Grey, Mayor Ed Koch and Pauline Trigère at one table with his ex-*Times* editor, Joan Whitman. Valerie and Joe Heller. The owners of the *Times,* the Sulzbergers. Ruth and Joe Baum, Sirio Maccioni, Betty Comden, the Batterberrys.*

*Michael and Ariane Batterberry, creators of *Food & Wine* magazine, are now publishers of *Food Arts.*

Many of us stood in turn and told a Craig Claiborne story. Craig couldn't stop smiling. It was like being at his own wake . . . only better, because he got to eat the caviar, the white truffles, and the crème brûlée.

Some interviewer had once asked Craig that inevitable question, what he would like to have for his last meal. I remembered he wanted grapefruit sorbet. So the sorbet came before the crème brûlée and "a dessert storm" from Le Cirque, and a brandy Alexander tart after.

The last time I saw Craig, cookbook writer Ruth Spear and I invited him for lunch at Trattoria Dell'Arte, across from Carnegie Hall. He was in his wheelchair. Craig ordered a vodka martini. I didn't know what to do.

"Are you sure you're supposed to be drinking, Craig?" I asked. In a flash, I imagined that lunching with me might be the death of Craig Claiborne.

"Of course," he said. "And who are you?" he asked Ruth.

"You know me, Craig," said Ruth. "I wrote the last *Ladies Village Improvement Society Cookbook*. You wrote the introduction."

"I don't remember," he said. "But I like your hair. . . . where is the flat bread?" he asked the waiter. "That crisp bread you always have."

The waiter apologized. The crisps were only served at dinner.

"You always give me those crisps," said Craig.

"Could you look around and see if they aren't a few crisps left from last night?" I begged the waiter. He disappeared.

"What are you drinking?" Craig asked.

"It's a glass of red wine. A California cabernet."

"I'll have one, too," he told the waiter.

"Oh Craig," I said, remembering now that his doctor had once told him to drink only vodka. "Are you sure it's good to mix vodka and wine?"

He ignored me. "You have beautiful hair," he said to Ruth.

I noticed that Craig, normally right-handed, had been using his left hand to drink the martini, so I moved his red wine to the left.

"That's not right," he snapped at me, frowning in distaste. "Etiquette says the glass goes on the right." He moved it. "Where is my martini? Who took my martini?"

"I think the waiter thought you were finished with it when you asked for the wine."

"I was not." He pursed his lips.

I called for the waiter. "Is it possible Mr. Claiborne's martini is sitting on a side table somewhere . . . ? Could you bring it back?" I pleaded.

The waiter apologized profusely.

"It's proper to ask first before you clear," Craig scolded him.

Craig ate a chicken liver from his small appetizer portion. A fresh, full-blown martini appeared. A man righteous and vindicated, he sipped it. Now Ruth was looking anxious, too.

At that moment, a man came bustling in the front door with a grease-stained brown paper bag. "Flat-bread crisps just out of the oven," he announced, asking a waiter to put them in a basket for Mr. Claiborne. "I went up to Fiorello* myself to get them."

Craig was beyond flat bread. Ruth and I broke off several shards, then ate some, crumbled some, and hid a few to make them look sufficiently appreciated.

I realize I'll never know whether the Trattoria crew was being sweetly indulgent to a fragile ghost in a wheelchair or trying to please me. I like to think it was an homage to the power Craig had been. Because, after all, fame is fleeting, the liver is frail, and one never knows if *The New Yorker* will seal your coffin before the grapefruit sorbet.

Years later, Pierre and I had a last lunch together just weeks before the cruise he didn't come home from in 1996. He was full of good news— new grandchildren, a new million-dollar two-book contract, an upcoming swing through all the famous kitchens of France that would be the framework of his new television series. "And I have three pensions, too," he said, "one from the *New York Times,* one from Social Security, and my pension from France."

Betty was with him on the ship when he was stricken with a heart attack and carried ashore. He died the next day. Friends were shocked, deeply sad to lose him, so young and vital at just seventy-five. It was indeed tragic. He was so full of life. He might have gone on, beloved grandpapa of a growing progeny, racking up sales, hitting his numbers, charming viewers across the land with his easy cooking, gathering his lobsters in Gardiner's Bay, spilling the juiciest gossip. His memorial din-

*Another restaurant in the Shelly Fireman portfolio that includes Trattoria Dell'Arte, Redeye Grill, and many more.

ner at Tavern on the Green was a bacchanal, a lovefest, an outpouring of affection.

Yet I kept remembering Craig. Becoming testier and angrier as he grew more frail, lingering in that wheelchair, not always recognizing the few old friends who still came, Craig barely lived at the end till he died in January 2000. His closest intimates (I among them) discouraged admirers from turning a memorial service into a $350-a-plate charity benefit, and no one seemed to have time to organize a more modest memorial, until Dorothy Hamilton opened the French Culinary Institute to a gathering of Craig's friends.

Pierre died the happiest man I ever met.

Mushroom Strudel

This is a recipe from my young bride days, before cholesterol was a health concern. But I believe holidays are the perfect excuse for excess. If you serve sixteen with this recipe, you'll feel half as guilty. I did four of these for Craig Claiborne's riotous sixty-seventh birthday party, where so many great chefs cooked that few guests even noticed my effort.

2 lbs. mushrooms
¼ cup minced shallots or green onions
6 tbsp. butter
2 tbsp. oil
Salt and pepper
2 8-oz. packages cream cheese
8 sheets frozen strudel or filo dough, 16 inches x 22 inches
¾ cup melted butter
Bread crumbs

Preheat oven to 400° F.

Mince mushrooms and squeeze them dry in the corner of a towel.

Sauté with minced shallots or green onions in butter and oil over moderately high heat, stirring frequently. Cook until pieces separate and the liquid has evaporated. Season to taste with salt and pepper. Blend in cream cheese.

Spread a sheet of strudel or filo dough on a damp towel, narrow end toward you. Brush with melted butter and sprinkle on bread crumbs. Repeat with second and third sheets, stacking them on top of the first sheet, then butter, but do not crumb fourth sheet. Put half the mushroom mixture on narrower edge of the dough, leaving a 2- to 3-inch border at the sides. Fold in the sides, then, using the edge of the towel, roll. Prepare the second strudel.

Put strudels on buttered baking sheet and brush with melted butter. Bake in oven until brown (about 20 minutes). The strudel cuts easily with shears. Strudel can be made and baked ahead, stored in the refrigerator or in the freezer overnight, and then reheated.

Serves 8.

26

I Lost It at the Baths

Don's haste to get the finale in writing was rude. But there was no speedy divorce in New York State then. I signed the separation agreement and told him he could take it from there. "Just be sure the judge gives me back my maiden name," I said.

Don had picked a day in September, just weeks away, to fly to the Dominican Republic—mecca of no-fault divorce at the time, no questions asked, no waiting. I was back from summer in the Wynns' gray house, triumphantly toting the hundred pages I owed my publisher. Andrew, the accountant, confessed that he was torn between me and the woman he thought he was hopelessly in love with before we met. Where had I heard that before? It was painful at home, wandering the scene of the crime.

A sybaritic and restorative retreat dangled by Yanou seemed divinely timed. I would escape the comforting of well-meaning friends while Don was securing our quickie divorce. The previous winter, just before I locked myself into the MacDowell Colony, my Parisian publicity genie had persuaded me to write about a client's torturous slimming cure and had joined me in near starvation in the mountain village of Crans-sur-Sierre in Switzerland. Now she called to trumpet that days of spa torture were over. Michel Guérard, definitely her client now, was defatting soufflés and lightening sauce with an amazing new alchemy all his own, having dedicated himself to the creation of a *grande cuisine diététique*.

Michel, the brilliant sorcerer I knew from Le Pot au Feu, had fallen in love with tall, slim, otherworldly Christine Barthélémy, daughter of a thermal-spa dynasty. He'd already lost five kilos from sheer joy, Yanou reported, and the family's medicinal waters had trimmed even more flab. He had shuttered Le Pot au Feu in the suburbs of Paris forever. The two had been married in vintage dress, then retreated to the countryside to create a stylish inn they were calling Les Prés et Les Sources d'Eugénie, near the Barthélémy family's spa. I should bring my fragile person to their little nowhere town in the southwest of France at once, she urged.

Given the headlined famine and drought around the globe in 1974, I couldn't help feeling uncomfortable about the excesses that led me periodically to detox for a week or two in some expensive spa. Alas, no matter how genuine one's social conscience, or how many charities you supported, among grand bouffeists, the search for slimming miracles never ceased, and I felt the obligation to report them. Yanou dangled the exclusive rights to be the first to test the chef's dramatic breakthrough.

Christine Guérard, with her pale, unpainted oval face and straight black schoolgirl hair, was a wraith from another era in turn-of-the-century lace and ruffles. It was she who had created the stage set, the glorious Victorian inn with its Napoléon III touches, ridiculously charming bric-a-brac, fresh flowers everywhere, and thick towels in the wantonly luxurious bathrooms. The dining room was all painted wicker and fringed Victorian silk shades, candelabra—no two alike—velvet walls, and, in an airy alcove looking out to the meadows, tiger-striped velour and a banquette of kelly green hugging a table draped in Indian paisley.

Everything in the room—except for the few subdued cure takers gloomily anticipating painful deprivation—was witty or beautiful, or both. Christine insisted on keeping me company at that first lunch. We sipped the dieters' aperitif, a tea brewed from the beards of corn husks, pine needles, cherry stems, and heather, served in a tall glass garnished with long curls of orange and lemon peel, a slice of fig, half a strawberry, a half-moon of peach. "It will make you want to sleep," she said. "And pee pee."

Lunch was breathtaking to look at and delicious, too: a perfect poached egg crowned with tomato coulis and snippets of chive, and beside it, slivered chicken riding in an artichoke heart on a cool pale green sea of cucumber puree. A concerto of texture, color, and taste. Okay, I thought. Nice lunch. But there was still more. A second plate, a statement in beige: thinnest slices of duck in a rich pepper-studded sauce, with sautéed apples.

"Can it be cream?" I asked. No, Michel insisted, looking wounded that I would suggest such perfidy. What looked suspiciously like a cream sauce was the result of whisking zero-calorie white cheese with duck stock and water in a blender.

"But surely the apples are sautéed in butter?"

"Absolument non," Michel cried. "It is my pan of Teflon that does that." Dessert was yet another still life: a trembling little mold of delicate coffee custard capped with a crunch of espresso ice, beribboned with candied orange peel and a punctuation of ripe currants. I'd eaten a total of precisely 445 calories. Or so the posted menu claimed.

I thought of the desolation of dinner at last year's Swiss spa, one gassy braised green pepper. Of course there was a downside at Eugénie-les-Bains. I had agreed to submit to the prescribed waterlogging spa rituals every morning, the soakings, the measured sippings of vile sulfuric liquid, the strafings of needle-sharp water spray designed to shock and melt the cellulite.

Spa culture had not yet became the rage nor the routine it is today in America, though we had our Maine Chance and the Golden Door. Sitting in radioactive pools or sipping sulfurous waters was totally bizarre to most Americans. But on the far side of the Atlantic, if Lourdes failed you, the thermal bath was an alternate faith.

Now with Michel Guérard in residence, Les Prés et Les Sources would also become a detour on the serious dining circuit, as well as a mecca for plumpies. Chef pals, Parisian chums, a scattering of gastronomic groupies, and the local bourgeoisie were already showing up for Sunday lunch, primed for that old full-blown gourmand Pot au Feu magic, and the kitchen delivered. Thickening matrons in conspiracies of two and four, a scattering of young beauties with nondieting husbands in tow, one delicious nymphet with a brittle-thin mother overseeing the child's "cure"—we were the pampered *curistes* exploring the eight-dollar decalorized menu.

In the parlor, friends of the Guérards were toasting one another with champagne. I could hear the crunch of their foie gras—laden toasts across the room. I sipped my virginal tisane. No need to be consumed with envy, I told myself, not when one is eating what tastes like a rich cream of fresh garden vegetables served in tall covered porcelain cups, herb-marinated rabbit with a zesty tomato puree, and mint-splashed melon—only 392 calories.

A few years later, I realized we had been the guinea pigs of early experiments that Michel would refine into the *cuisine minceur* that brought him international fame and spawned an expensive cookbook in countless languages. Did anyone ever cook from this book? Not me. But looking at the photographs was less fattening than eating.

He hadn't dreamed up the name yet, but every day at Eugénie brought new tastes on the Villeroy & Boch plates: chicken poached in parchment, a leg of milk-fed lamb baked in meadow grass, remarkable soups and vegetable purees peppered with deliberation, like his foam of spinach blended with pear (it would be copied everywhere), an eggplant starter resembling a Cubist still life by Picasso, a *tourte* of cabbage leaves. I remember the first time I saw Michel's flat apple pizzette, the thinnest-possible pastry, which became the maquette for skinny tarts still seen today in far richer versions everywhere. I thought I detected butter, but very little, and apples so thin and so sparsely sugared that he easily had wrung hundreds of calories from the classic.

Days at Eugénie evolved into a lazy ritual. The French did not believe in exercise for slimming. Indolence was the rule. One hundred grams of springwater upon rising, breakfast in bed, then coffee and a soft-boiled egg with tiny asparagus tips to dip into it, or creamy white cheese or yogurt and fruit were the dieter's options, but the innocent chambermaids couldn't stand to see suffering, and they insisted on serving doubles of everything to everyone. Then to the foul-smelling baths.

The scale indicated the drill was working. I was losing a pound a day. After lunch, reading, walking through Eugénie (a small village, barely a seven-minute exercise), and sunning at the pool were de rigueur but rigorless. In the kitchen, Michel demonstrated how to whisk a *diététique* sabayon that would make a meager ration of fish taste wantonly rich later that evening.

"I hate the word *régime*," he said. *Régime*. French for diet. "It sounds so military." He cocked his head quizzically, searching for a poetic alternate. Alas for me, the journalist determined to stick to the low-cal plan—the better to embark on my new single life—his fatal flaw was his subversively tender heart. "Give her one sip of this beautiful wine," he would tell the sommelier. "Give her just a tiny portion of that goat cheese."

One evening, I was invited with a handful of Guérard pals to dine with the son of the Darroze restaurant family in his living quarters behind the pharmacy nearby. A caravan of cars was commandeered to transport a gang of us. Michel carried a diet dinner in a giant basket for the *curistes*. The Darroze kin and friends oohed and aahed over the exquisite detail of our near-calorie-free watercress timbale filled with snails and ringed with Teflon-sautéed frogs' legs, and the braised calf's liver sauced in a clear juice pebbled with minced carrot, onion, celery, and tarragon.

Michel pretended to hide his eyes as our hosts insisted the *curistes* must also taste the foie gras, a few wild cèpes, a morsel of dove, and, of course, that fatty little bird, the *ortolan*. Take two; they're small, we were told. And yes, we must sip the '47 Talbot and the '29 Cos d'Estournel, because who knew how many times again in this life such wines would come our way. And who could deny us a dab of Roquefort and at least one swallow of ancient Armagnac, a smooth, throat-warming relic of 1900. I'd almost forgotten what a thrill it was to eat much too much and sip more than one sip of a magnificent wine.

The scale halted its gentle descent. "This is not going to make a very good article, Michel," I complained, depressed to see days of prudence destroyed by one night of madness.

Michel got the point at once. He sentenced me to sip bouillon for the next two days and eat salad tossed with mineral oil—that old laxative trick. There was so little time left to hit my goal of five kilos. I had to settle for nine pounds as I departed with a kiss on each cheek from Michel and Christine, bound for a weekend gathering of chefs and food-loving friends to celebrate chef Roger Vergé's third Michelin star at the Moulin de Mougins. A voyage from cozened deprivation to wholesale abundance. Well, after all, it was my job.

What could Vergé possibly feed the cuisinary all-stars gathered at Mougins? Cleverly, he gave us a *grand aioli* that first afternoon. It required no cooking at all, just garlicky mayonnaise and everything meant to dip in it. But that was just the aperitif. The weekend binge went on and on.

By the time I got to a scale at the Restaurant Bocuse, my next stop the following Monday, I had regained five pounds, although it did seem to me that my cheekbones were nicely chiseled. That would definitely help in my new life as a single woman. Paul Bocuse, who'd driven us both from Mougins, had been dieting, too, and didn't like the scale's telltale news. He punished us both by plying me with tempting morsels till I thought I would burst, and then it was time to catch the train to Roanne. I'd promised the Troisgros family I would stop by on my way back to Paris.

27

DROWNING MY SORROWS
in CHILLED BURGUNDY

I MOURNED MY MARRIAGE IN THE SUNLIT GARDEN AT EUGÉNIE. EVEN THE bees ignored me. I brooded about my fate between ham baked in meadow grass and other delights. Was I too old to fall in love that way again? Reading Updike novels at the pool didn't help. Adultery didn't seem any more elegant in New England than on West End Avenue. Even now, in my advanced wisdom, it doesn't strike me as so naïve that I thought considerate adultery could help us stay together. So many of our friends seemed to get away with it.

Now on the train to Roanne, I imagined Don in the Dominican Republic, not speaking Spanish. I wondered how he would get along. Meaning, of course, without me. I'd always led the way overseas with my brave bits of French and Italian. And where was I going on my own? I hadn't been single for more than ten years. I hadn't been great at it then, though I suppose a conservative bystander might think I hadn't been all that great at being married, either. But I'd been wonderful at being married. I still believe that. I thought Don was brilliant at it, too. Indeed, life with Don had often felt like playing house, carefree and precious, exactly what I treasured. I berated myself for not doing more to save us. But what could I have done? Plastic surgery? Fat lips and thin hips. It would never have been enough. Even after he packed his bags and left forever, he was writing me sobbing notes of undying love and regret. (Am I nuts? I kept them. I have the craziest beside me as I write this, but I'll spare you.) Yet a moment later, he was talking about twenty-two-year-old skin. The shallow bastard. Mildred was right; I had to leave him. Now I felt less crazy and very alone. Don had promised to call from the island to let me know when it was official. I wondered if he would take Her along for a romantic Caribbean weekend. Could he be that cool? That uncaring?

There was an attractive man sitting across from me. He was wearing a wedding band. I think it's nice when they advertise. And anyway, it would make no sense for me to fall in love in France, I thought. I offered him one of the chocolates Bocuse had insisted I take with me.

In Roanne, Pierre and his vivacious Olympe greeted me like family. It was a much-needed distraction. There was no way they could guess how much I wanted to curl up and be comforted. They had heard about Michel's *cuisine diététique* and were curious but dubious. "A great chef cooking *cuisine diététique* is good for the *presse*," Olympe said. "Good *publicité,* good for the business of the spa." And *certainment,* I did look thin, observed Pierre.

Jean Troisgros was quiet. His wife, Marie, had committed suicide some months earlier, but I didn't know any details. Unlike Olympe, always bubbling and seemingly happy at the reception desk, Marie, as I remembered, stood in shadow, usually silent and indifferent, or maybe just shy. I wandered out to the kitchen to watch Jean salting a piece of beef, testing the heat of a skillet, snapping commands to a cook. I'd never really looked at him as a man before. I'd seen him as one half of the fun-loving *frères* Troisgros, teasing and grinning, and not all that serious in the dining room, waiting for a moan, a sigh, a cry of approval for a new dish. I'd been here with Don and then with Murray and later on the Moët & Chandon junket with Yanou. But now with an empty chair opposite me and a husband signing off on our marriage in the Caribbean, I saw Jean. I saw that in spite of his graying beard, he was younger than I'd first thought, and handsome. Did I imagine he was flirting with me? He seemed to hover by the table, filling my wineglass from the pewter *pichet,* turning a plate the waiter had set down off center. His eyes sparkled. The beard was sexy.

There was a phone call for me at the desk.

"The lawyer fucked up," said Don. "By the time I found him, we got to the court late. The judge decided he couldn't sign the papers till tomorrow."

"Oh, poor baby," I said. "What will you do?" Here I was, comforting my husband because he couldn't divorce me fast enough.

He was alone. He would get a room. He missed me. He was sorry we had stopped working. It was all his fault. He started to cry.

"It's my fault, too," I said my eyes filling up. "So tomorrow, then," I said. "I'm not sure where I'll be. Maybe en route to Paris. You don't need to call again. I'll just know it's done tomorrow."

"I'm so sorry, pumpkin."

I hung up. It was too late to "pumpkin" me now.

The waiter explained he had taken away the braided-fish dish in my absence so it wouldn't get cold. Jean came out of the kitchen with a *cassolette* of scallops. *"Très simple,"* he said, "raw, the way you like it." He was teasing. I always asked for my scallops and fish *"pas trop cuit"*—not too cooked.

"Can you sit a minute?" I asked in French. "Talk to me." I was not sure we had anything but food to talk about.

"Sorry," he said. "I excuse myself. I must go back to the kitchen."

"After the service, then," I said in French. "Come to my room."

I thought he seemed shocked. He did not answer. I felt stupid. Then the waiter came to fill my glass again. Jean took the moment to disappear. I tasted the scallops, but the sauce seemed sickeningly rich.

It was Pierre who came to see if I was pleased with the lamb. And Pierre who supervised my choice of cheese, adding a wonderfully smelly epoisse steeped in marc and a chèvre wrapped in cinders—new, "from the neighborhood goat lady," he said. I watched Jean chatting with a couple across the room, stroking his beard, standing on one foot, with the other tucked behind it, as if exhausted.

I needed something citric and pungent. I waved the pastry cart away and asked for sorbets—plum, pear, tangerine, *pamplemousse* (that marvelous word for grapefruit)—and then managed to put away two thousand calories in cookies, mini-tartlets, and chocolates.

I felt a little queasy as I went up to my room.

I bathed, perfumed, rouged, and powdered . . . slipped into a pale blue nightgown that held everything that counted in the right place and skimmed the rest discreetly. Just in case. The knock at the door woke me. I let him into the room. His hunting dog bounded ahead of him. We kissed . . . and his hands tried to brush the gown off my shoulders. I undid his belt, unzipped his trousers. I slid into bed as he sat to remove his shoes and then turned to me.

At this very moment, the judge is signing the papers, I thought. Don is feeling lost and sad. People are talking to him in Spanish. I'm divorced. He will marry Her and she won't let him see me. I don't want to think about it now.

I reached for Jean, touched his beard, put my fingers into his thick hair. He rolled on top of me and made love to me. The dog rested his muzzle on the edge of the bed and watched.

28

OF JAMES BEARD AND
ENCOUNTERS WITH
GODDESSES

I WAS NEVER IN THE INNERMOST CIRCLE OF JAMES BEARD CONFIDANTS, protégés, and sycophants. What with deadlines, the strains of wounded domesticity and later divorce, rebirth, and a devotion to disco dancing, I didn't have the free time to hang out in his charming Village pad. I adored him mostly from afar. Now I can see that I was also intimidated. He was the founder of our church, the all-knowing wizard. I was grateful that he was very generous in his comments about me for publication. I knew he had a rapier wit and could be bitchy in private. I felt he could see right through me, and I worried that he saw an imposter.

Picasso had to learn to draw before he did those Cubist tricks. And here I was, scolding a two-star Michelin chef because his vanilla cream was too strongly scented with rose petals and chiding André Soltner at Lutèce for a vapid *crème renversée au caramel.* Yet in my brief years as an amateur cook, I had never tackled sweetbreads or cleaned a squid and had failed utterly in my one attempt at trying to duplicate Le Pavillon's *quenelles de brochet.* The stink of abused fish had lingered in our kitchen for two days.

To feel on firm ground when critiquing Chinese restaurants, I had taken a series of Chinese cooking classes. I'd studied with the dowager queen of the wok, Grace Chu, then with sometime actress Lilah Kan and, later, Virginia Lee, coauthor with Craig of *The Chinese Cookbook.* Mrs. Lee had us endlessly marinating chicken and meat in cornstarch and egg white for her velvety stir-fries, so there were always bowls of abandoned yolks. One day, she tossed three dozen yolks into a puddle of oil in a hot wok and scrambled them for the class. It was the essence of egg . . . eggs on speed. Richer than foie gras. Nobody died that night—as far as I know.

When I tried to sign up for Beard's advanced cooking class in 1974, I was flatly rejected. "No one can take the advanced class till they've done the introductory," his assistant told me. There was no argument, no string to pull. How embarrassing. The restaurant critic was required to join the novices in his teaching kitchen, struggling with the bizarre burnerless glass stovetop that we all hated. (But Corning was a client, after all, so that's what we cooked on.) Jim would perch on a tall stool in one of his red or black cotton tunics, tree trunk–like legs splayed for balance as he took our measure, pairing us off—two by two—with an assignment for the evening to put together the various courses of what would be dinner.

One day, he decided we should test whether freezing meat sabotaged the flavor or texture, research for a magazine article he was writing. We would roast and pan-sauté a series of matching beef cuts, half of them fresh, half of them thawed from the freezer. What a shock: Contrary to the epicurean's innate disdain for the freezer (good only for ice cubes, homemade bread crumbs, and to store bones for making stock), we discovered no difference at all.

The class was all about pleasure and fun, a mad dance dodging one another's knives in the crowded kitchen, vying for an approving grin or wink. Every once in awhile, Jim would put his gigantic hand on top of yours to correct a knife chop or a whisking movement.

Tasting, endless tasting. Beard was a legend for his extraordinary taste memory, the ability to retain and recapture a dish's distinct tangle of scents, flavors, and textures, not unlike a great musician or composer's perfect pitch. And he could convey a sense of the joy of a new discovery with the details of the stories he told. My favorite image from class is that of Jim standing at the kitchen counter in the old house on Patchin Place, carving a slab of seared brisket, slipping a chunk of fat into his mouth, and laughing. "I'm a fat boy myself."

Garlic was our mantra. I remember one class that called for garlic in every dish except dessert. If an innocent dared to ask, "How much garlic, Mr. Beard?" he'd boom out the answer: "Half an acre." One evening, I was in the duo charged with rolling a boned leg of lamb studded with garlic into a sling made out of a clean dish towel. It was to be suspended from the handles of a large oval enameled iron cocotte, then steamed over garlicky broth till the thermometer registered rare. After a suitable rest, the roast was unwrapped and sliced. Beard wanted it served with a fast-cooked garlicky tomato sauce and gremolata, the classic garnish of osso buco—grated lemon peel, minced parsley, and finely chopped garlic . . . raw garlic. The turnips Anna, a variation on the French classic potatoes Anna, slathered with butter—crisped and baked in a flat metal pan—were aggressively dotted with minced garlic, too. I forget what got tossed with garlic for a first course. I tried to scrub away the garlicky stickum on my fingers with lemon juice. A faint earthy scent lingered.

I would not have imagined that boiled anything could have been as lush and flavorful as that lamb. I stole the gremolata mix and used it that next summer as a feisty staccato on cubed swordfish that I crumbed and then seared in a black iron skillet. Even though I could measure how much butter it took to melt the turnips into sweet submission, turnips Anna still seemed less fattening than scalloped potatoes, and even now they pop up at my holiday dinners.

Andrew, the boyfriend left over from the magical summer in the house on the bay in the Springs (I continued to share him with his fiancée, his children, his work, and his guilt months later), came by to pick me up after class. Later that night, we were locked in the addictive embraces that drew us to bed long after we both should have known he would marry the all-forgiving "other woman."

"What have you been eating?" he cried from somewhere near my knee. "It's like garlic is coming out of your skin." I found my inner arm not far from my nose and sniffed.

"Oh my God, I think you're right."

Andrew was not a lover of garlic. But he was a lover of women. That carried him through what must have been quite a challenge.

I regret I was not around for the early rumbles of revolution in California cookery. In the seventies and early eighties, I was always looking east, flying off for a quick fix in France as often as I could get Clay Felker to foot the bill. Fortunately, Clay understood my mouth needed this constant rehabilitating ecstasy. Although I admired their work from afar, I didn't come to know Alice Waters or Marion Cunningham, Jeremiah Tower, Jonathan Waxman, and Wolfgang Puck till much later. And I never shared an oyster or a confessional cup of tea with the mythic M. F. K. Fisher. Perhaps if I'd spent more time on the West Coast, I might have earned a share of that intimacy and jumped on the grow-your-own-vegetables team earlier. It took a while before I noticed that a fresh bean was superior to a French bean. And it took even longer before a fresh bean was a local bean.

It was Jim Beard—congenitally bicoastal and beloved on both—who introduced me to the goddesses. I first tasted Alice's food at dinner with Jim and my friend Harley Baldwin in the café above Chez Panisse. I had arrived in San Francisco fresh from worshiping the exquisite finesse and refined complexity of Frédy Girardet in Crissier, outside Lausanne, and Michel Guérard in his remote fiefdom in southwestern France. Frankly, I wasn't expecting much.

"Shall we just cook for you?" Alice asked, relaxed and confident, bubbling with affection for Jim. (Jim brought out a lot of bubbling in his female acolytes and protégés.)

I remember thinking, Okay, show me. And to my astonishment, she did. There was something radically daring in the simplicity of every perfect vegetable, the pristine leaves of baby greens that had not yet hit kitchens in New York, the clarity of an oddly shaped tomato. Until that moment, *heirloom* meant a hideous vase you dare not send to the thrift shop because it had been your grandmother's. If there were zealots reviving forgotten species of tomato or twenty strains of heirloom potatoes on the East Coast, I was not yet aware of it.

"I have only three scallops left," Alice said. "They're very special."

We each had a scallop still in its shell—unheard of back east at that moment—slicked with a bit of butter, a drop of lemon, a turn of the pepper mill. It was like eating something just born, hatched a moment before in the sea just for us.

Alas, I definitely came too late to my first audience with the aging and ailing M. F. K. Fisher. One afternoon in the mid-1970s, I walked into the dining room at the Stanford Court in San Francisco and spied James

Beard, a huge smiling Buddha in a blue denim mandarin jacket, impossible to miss. I ran over to give him a hug. He was lunching with an elderly woman draped in brown, her face rather dour and unexpressive. I looked at her and nodded.

"You don't know my friend Mary Frances?" He seemed surprised. "Mary Frances Fisher."

It took a few seconds before it sank in and I realized this swollen, clearly unwell creature was the famed, beloved, unsurpassed writer of food and love, the sexy siren (as food historian Betty Fussell describes her) . . . M. F. K. Fisher.

"This is Gael Greene," Jim said. "She is the very enthusiastic restaurant critic of *New York* magazine." (Jim had a way of saying something positive about me that could also be negative when you thought about it later.)

That day at the Stanford Court, I imagined I could see M.F.K.'s young beauty from her portrait on so many book jackets, although it was almost lost in the doughy puff of her medication-distorted face.

"I'm having trouble with my *New York* magazine subscription," she said.

I bit my tongue and smiled. "Well, if you send me the sticker from your last magazine, I'll get that fixed for you the minute I get back to New York."

It was in Jim's beginner class that I met Jane Freiman, a fine-arts major then in publishing, who would leverage these classes, a passion for food, and sheer chutzpah to become a cookery teacher and cookbook writer when she found herself unemployed in Chicago due to marriage.

Together, Jane and I were formidable. How else to explain where I found the chutzpah to invite James Beard for dinner? The two of us fussed and debated the menu, elaborating and revising, testing and refining. Jim seemed comfortable enough sipping champagne on the cushioned window seat in the back room of my apartment. I'd set up the foldaway aluminum table and draped it in dark blue corduroy cloth to the floor—regal backdrop for service plates and candlesticks from my collection of pewter. We brewed pumpkin soup so I could use my antique pewter tureen and ladle. It took two tries, but I mastered lush ricotta and spinach gnocchi from Naomi Barry's Tuscan cookbook. The leg of lamb that followed—generously pierced with slivered garlic cloves—was exquisitely rare, perfect with a '66 Mouton Rothschild from the cellar riches Don had generously left behind in Woodstock.

The climax was my version of Paula Peck's deeply dark chocolate velvet under drifts of sour cream folded into whipped cream for an approximation of crème fraîche, and meltingly buttery Viennese cookies. Jane's lush bittersweet chocolate truffles arrived with coffee and cognac.

Jim sipped and looked thoughtful. I guess we all felt some comment was called for.

"This is the richest dinner I've ever eaten," Jim said. All I heard was the superlative. And I glowed with pride. Next day, I chewed over the ambiguity of his statement. I finally decided not to brood about it.

29

SPLENDOR IN THE FOIE GRAS

EARLY AMERICAN SYBARITES AND EMBRYONIC GOURMANDS WERE RUN-
ning loose abroad now in the seventies as the larder at home grew more
sophisticated and uptight tradition began to evolve. No one had ever
thought of cheesecake as sinfully wicked till I urged them to try Miss
Grimble's über-chocolate Grimbletorte. A band of feminists liberated
McSorley's men-only bar. The Whole Foodier Than Thou folk ate tofu and
sprouts. It was 1971. A man named Carl Sontheimer wanted a small venture to occupy his time in retirement, so he began importing a French
machine called the Robot-Coupe. Marketed as the Cuisinart, it was soon
chopping up New York. The bloated bellies of starving babies in Biafra
nightly on television haunted our growing appetite for excess. There was
a five-year waiting list to get into James Beard's cooking classes. Carrot
strips became crudités. I tapped into the trends, documenting and fan-
ning the flames.

McDonald's finally invaded Manhattan and Nixon chopsticked in
China. Détente encouraged China to open its own Chinese Pavilion on
the East Side. *New York* analyzed the home kitchen as an erogenous zone.
Truly serious epicurians carried small silver pepper mills in pocket or
purse. At least I did. General Mills introduced Tuna Helper in 1972.

Bloomingdale's made parties after hours in department stores imperative with a five-course sit-down pheasant dinner for thirteen hundred on its one hundredth birthday. Some people left town rather than admit they hadn't been invited. Though worried that expansion would clean up its appealing clutter, Zabar's let itself sprawl all the way down Broadway to the corner of Eightieth, but even so, it seemed more cluttered than ever. Balducci's, in the Village, grew and met the challenge with radicchio.

Determined not to die on his feet, a slave to the kitchen in Lyon, Paul Bocuse recruited his chums from their salad days in Vienne, chez Point, to form La Bande de Cuisine in 1972, a marketing arm for themselves and their products. They were up to something, these Young Turks. *"La cuisine du marché"*—cooking inspired by the market—was Bocuse's banner. Gault and Millau, France's sassy duo of restaurant rating, gave it a name: nouvelle cuisine. The life of the fussy mouth would never be the same.

In New York, the growing ranks of sincere and sometimes near-demented foodies took cooking lessons. We were making our own hot-and-sour soup, and *poulet au vinaigre* and our own chocolate truffles, ahead of the crowd. I remember hanging sweet marinated spareribs from S hooks in my oven to roast Chinese-style and spending hours scouring away the baked-on mess. The seventies were a time for spinach salad, César Chávez and the grape boycott, cornichons, raspberry vinegar, a rainbow of peppercorns, and goat cheese—crumbed, grilled, sautéed, au naturel, even in ice cream. Hardly anyone wanted a whiskey sour anymore. We drank kir; a splash of cassis made bar plonk sexy. The Shun Lee folks opened Hunam (as it was mispelled), where we choked and sneezed on the incendiary peppers of Mao's birthplace, and prepped for Thai, Cajun, and Tex-Mex to come. Americans discovered frozen yogurt and haricots verts. No one would ever take an ungainly overgrown string bean seriously again.

Olive oil was French, and conspicuous consumers wanted to have walnut oil, too, rarer and more expensive. Without Soulé, Le Pavillon had lost its soul, and its consortium of owners closed it forever in October 1972, making way for the Women's Bank, with not even a small plaque to commemorate the mythic *quenelles de brochet*. The canny Riese brothers—Irving and Murray—gobbled up fast food–chain franchises but made their fortune in real estate by signing leases for hot midtown corners, preferably for ninety-nine years. Tony May (later to lift the town's Italian restaurants out of a sea of red with Palio and San

Domenico) staged an "Italian Fortnight" at the old Rainbow Room, importing chefs from his homeland, and for two weeks there was great regional *cucina* in our town—the first carpaccio, homemade ravioli, chocolate tartufo.

Paul Bocuse flew in like a movie star, trucking pigs' bladders for a dinner at the Four Seasons to promote his Beaujolais. I knew he didn't speak English, so I spent mornings for two weeks before he arrived trading kitchen talk with a French teacher in order to write the story. Paul draped me in his signature apron and instructed me to peel the truffles. Cutting away even the thinnest stubble of a costly black truffle was a luxury only he could afford. But what did I know? Forever after when I tasted an unpeeled truffle in a dish, I rapped the chef.

France's foie gras–mongers knew who buttered their bread, and they popped into town at the drop of a truffle to woo the affluent and the influential. (Lucky me.) France's celebrated master pâtissier Gaston Lenôtre opened a bakery/café around the corner from Bloomingdale's in 1974, proposing to cater all of New York's celebrations. That flirtation didn't last very long. But New Yorkers would never again confuse sherbet with sorbet.

Eli Zabar left his kinfolk on the Upper West Side and crossed town to open E.A.T., catering to hungers we never dreamed could be quite that expensive.

Sirio Maccioni triumphantly sneaked fresh porcini home from Tuscany, carrying them through customs in his briefcase, for the opening of Le Cirque on East Sixty-fifth Street in March of 1974. The landlord, William Zeckendorf, we heard, had offered the space rent-free to the defunct Colony's suave ringmaster and chef, Jean Vergnes, counting on Sirio's society and show business flock to lend cachet to Zeckendorf's new Mayfair Regent Hotel. Winos with a nose for a bargain as well as for pinot noir were swift to discover that Zeckendorf's own cellar of treasured old Burgundies had landed on Le Cirque's wine list at affordable prices. But for me, critiquing the instantly fashionable new spot, chicken gismonda and creamy stuffed crepes in the retro Colony style were hopelessly dowdy. It would take a year before Le Cirque's kitchen found its own identity and society's bouffant-coiffed blondes blooming on the front-row banquette would make Sirio a legend.

*   *   *

It seemed to me that Paul Kovi and Tom Margittai, dedicated Hungarians from the early heyday of Restaurant Associates, might have been born to save the Four Seasons. With the city in a financial doldrum, they opened the Bar Room at the top of the stairs in 1975. It had its own discounted grill menu and itsy doodads, *amuse-bouches* by any other name (crafted by the small hands of Japanese women, they told us), for expense-account lunchers to nibble with white wine. The three-martini lunch seemed to be on the wagon. Everyone drank white wine. Are you old enough to remember gravlax, the dernier cri in marinated salmon? The Bar Room, now the Grill, had its core of regulars claiming every table. *Esquire* would call it "the Power Lunch." Regulars would call—not to reserve, but only if they couldn't come.

Fairway opened. It was all about fruit and vegetables then and not yet a provocation to Zabar's. The Quilted Giraffe was in out-of-town tryouts in New Paltz.

Michel Guérard flew in and even the city's tabloids started to sputter in French: Guérard's diet cooking, "Cuisine Minceur" (1975), was the headline of the day. On his own after the rejiggering of Restaurant Associates, über-Hungarian George Lang invented a new profession—restaurant consultant—and put his stamp on four hundred hotels and restaurants around the world from Manilla to Thessalonica, or so he boasted. But dusting away the cobwebs and restoring the playful nudes on the walls at the Café des Artistes was his gift to the city. Warner LeRoy, of the Hollywood clan and creator of Maxwell's Plum, now gave us Christmas all year round by resuscitating the crumbled Tavern on the Green with his own phantasmagorical vision.

Defections from the house of Elaine that had begun with the opening of Nicola's in 1975 soon led to Parma and Elio's, then Petaluma and on into the next generation—Vico, Sette Mezzo, Vico Uptown, Lusardi's, Due, Triangolo, Luke's, Primola, Girasole, Campagnola, Azzurro, Brio—uptown's Little Italy.

The pasta persuasion was child's play. Slightly more sophisticated than the spaghetti and meatballs of a middle-class childhood, it was good for weekdays in the neighborhood. But matriculating gourmands were ready for new tasting diversions, sophisticated tangles of flavor, ever so slightly scary new textures, serious wines, and, every once in awhile, a sensuous dining ceremony worth an outrageous price.

30

SWIMMING IN BORDEAUX

IT'S A MIRACLE ANYONE'S LIVER SURVIVED THE MANY SEDUCTIVE POURINGS that blotted out our afternoons in the seventies when France's wine makers found affluent New Yorkers so ripe for temptation. The grandiloquent grape-juice peddlers flew into town to woo retailers and indoctrinate the growing bubble of wine journalists. And we were ripe to swallow imported wisdom.

Eric Rothschild, the new generation running Château Lafite Rothschild, was young and beautiful and single when we first met in Paris. One thing led to another, as it often did in the sybaritic seventies. Now he'd come to New York to show off a dozen vintages of his family's great Bordeaux to a froth of wine press and trade at Seagram's, his distributor. Eric had a business dinner but agreed to meet my friends and me at a club in midtown where men and women—naked except for a few bundles of grapes attached strategically—lolled on nets suspended from the ceiling. My friends had expected a Rothschild to be stiff and uptight, but Eric just laughed at the silliness of it all. We had a drink at the bar and then I spirited him off to dance at Xenon.

The next evening, Eric was expected at a dinner of the Commanderie de Bordeaux, hoity-toitiest of a hoity-toity lot of men-only wine societies. "They won't let me come because I'm a woman," I complained to Eric. "It's a disgrace. Make them come into the twentieth century, Eric," I begged. "There are so many women winemakers and wine writers now. If *you* insist that I come, no one will be able to object." Eric, as always a diplomat, was not a candidate to commit cultural terrorism.

"Those dinners are so stuffy and boring," he insisted. "You'd hate it."

"I hate more that they don't invite women."

"I'll just go to their dinner for a course or two and then I'll come to you," he said.

"You'll only see me if I'm not out doing something better," I replied petulantly.

It was after 11:00 PM when my bell rang. I walked to the door in a sheer black nightgown.

Eric bounded up the one flight of steps to where I stood, a bottle of Lafite in each hand, his Commanderie de Bordeaux medal bouncing on a ribbon around his neck, and kissed me. Kissed my mouth, my ear, and my neck. He followed me to my balcony bedroom. He was a charming, graceful lover, exactly as I remembered from Paris. He lingered for an aristocratic few minutes, murmuring pillow talk, then scrambled back into his tuxedo, tucking the tie into a pocket and reaching for his medal. I walked him to the door, naked in the light of the streetlamp.

"I think I deserve that ribbon," I said.

He laughed, then solemnly placed the ribbon around my neck, where the medal fell between my breasts. He kissed me lightly on each cheek.

That's how I finally got my ribbon from the stubbornly chauvinist Commanderie de Bordeaux.

31

HOW THEY ATE IN POMPEII

F OR THOSE OF US BY STOMACH POSSESSED, THE GREAT GLORY OF THE SEV-
enties arrived in April 1975, with a fifty-dollar prix fixe, wines priced
for an emperor, cognacs so rare that a sip could cost forty dollars. The
Palace, an apogee of arrogance and excess, was dreamed up by Frank
Valenza, a onetime actor we knew from his ads begging to seduce us with
Bloody Mary soup and Lemon Melting Moments at his pop restaurant
success, Proof of the Pudding. "Morally the Palace is an outrage," I wrote
in a review called "How They Ate in Pompeii Before the Lava Flowed." "If
only my mouth were not so numbed with joy." The Palace arrived with
a case of terminal decadence. It was hardly the moment to launch the
most expensive restaurant in town. The Dow Jones was so low, its chin
pinched its toes. Breakfast was bitter, eaten with the specter of swollen
Mauritanian bellies haunting the news. New York City had teetered on
the edge . . . a fat rotten apple. It was a time to buy gold, talk poor, post-
pone the new sable. A gossipy cabal of French restaurateurs sneered.
Bronx-born, a failed actor, Valenza would never pull it off, they predicted.

From the Melting Moments promoter, I had expected superficial
pomp. But doubts evaporated as I took in the gentle understatement: no
doorman, inside a beige temperance, pastel flowered carpet, graceful

love seats. The splendid details: ivory rosebuds with petals edged in coral, silver candlesticks . . . incandescent lighting capable of sweeping away decades of too-vivid living. The shock of the kitchen's brilliance took me by surprise.

Early on, chef Claude Baills already seemed a fitful wunderkind, even though the dining room was still a prep school for a cadre of rotating rookies. I watched a waiter confiscate a glass of Lafite Rothschild left behind by departing moguls and walk off sipping it. After a few nights when no one came, Valenza was finally forced to give up the conceit of an unlisted phone number. He never could stop talking about how much he spent . . . what each luxury cost. The faceted crystal stemware (not ideal for wine but voluptuous in the hand). Gold-rimmed china. Splendid porcelain dessert and coffee service with scattered forgot-me-nots. A silver trolley that cost slightly more than a Cadillac. The royal table set for eight, canopied and tasseled like a four-poster bed as yet unclaimed by any king.

One night, we were only sixteen mouths to feed. "Yi yi yi yi, nights like this," Frank moaned.

A sympathetic gourmand tried to comfort him. "It took Lutèce years to start making money."

"Yes, but André Surmain* had a rich wife," Valenza responded.

Everything on *l'écriteau* (fancy French for menu) was written in the original Old French. A tightly wound maître d', speaking without actually opening his lips, made sure we had noticed. Would we have caviar— a gift of détente from Russia—firm and sweet? Lobster and artichoke heart in a nutty vinaigrette? *Zephyr de sole catalane?* Capon truffled from here to there? Of course it was silly, *opéra bouffe,* over the top, undeniably ridiculous. But I loved it. Each dish arrived with its own spectacular pièce montée—an architectural folly or sculpture that would have wowed the great master Carême. Escorting the lobster was a fisherman's wife sculpted in lard and wearing a skirt ruffled all around with lobster-tail petals. A Leaning Tower of Pisa built out of uncooked spaghetti loomed over a dish of pasta. And glorious petits fours were piled in a basket—not wicker, but woven in pastry wrapped round with sugar roses.

---

*Lutèce's creator and original owner.

Valenza himself was wowed by his creation. He stood tall in black velvet, back arched elegantly, one too-long shirt cuff hanging out. His ingenuousness was actually appealing; the passion for perfection remarkable. "But he must learn not to pronounce foie gras faux gras," I wrote.

I loved the Palace. There were stumbles, and misunderstandings. But I loved it. Loved the Scottish salmon rolled around crème fraîche. Loved the magnificent cream of mussel soup with threads of saffron and tiny bay scallops bobbing. Swooned over the angel-hair pasta doubly truffled in a chiaroscuro of black and white, the aristocratic *côte de boeuf* with classic truffled chicken dumplings afloat in its Madeira sauce. Too much. Too much. Too much. Just enough.

William Blake must have dreamed it himself when he wrote, "The road of excess leads to the Palace of Wisdom." The pillars of the food and wine world loved the Palace. Craig and Pierre went there often. James Beard was delighted to be a fixture. I saw *Forbes* magazine's favorite critic, Malcolm himself (who trusted his own capitalist palate), as well as wine-society stalwarts. Of course, oiled Arabs were grateful to have their wallets lightened. Six customers earned the house's eighteen-karat-gold credit card by spending ten thousand dollars. In late 1977, France's influential food magazine *Gault-Millau* rated the Palace "the best New York has to offer and without any doubt the finest in the U.S.A."

By that time, Chef Baills was gone. He had stalked out one night when Valenza dared to upbraid him for starting to make gazpacho from scratch for a restaurant critic in the middle of the dinner service. Michel Fitoussi, a small nervous wraith with supreme confidence, had calmly taken over the kitchen, lashing thin logs of carrot and zucchini with ribbons of scallion, and astounding us all by blowing molten sugar as if it were Murano glass into green apples and stuffing them with white chocolate. (To my regret, a few words from me on white chocolate led from that one cloudy pouf to an avalanche of soapy white chocolate that still persists.)

I spent many paragraphs apologizing for loving the Palace. "Some people buy emeralds. Some people have children. I am good to my mouth," I wrote. But I understood why it was so easy to hate. And I worried each time the *Times* judged it harshly, once by a critic who admitted preferring fish well done, and then by a critic who confessed she could not eat pink chicken livers, described cassis as blackberry liqueur, and referred to a vanilla butter cream and crème pâtissière–filled truffle as "a cocoa-dusted ice cream ball." (It was my good fortune that *New York* had fussy fact checkers and the *Times*, apparently, did not.)

Each time the *Times* reviled it, alloting one star (based, I thought blindly, on value for money), I wrote yet another updated celebration in *New York*, a call to rally affluent gourmands. "The Palace tells us more than we may care to know about who we are," I wrote. "I am not Albert Schweitzer or Mother Cabrini. I have yet to meet a single saint in this town sworn to vows of poverty, chastity and cottage cheese. There are men and women, noble and true, dedicated to research or music or evangelism or chasing the bogeyman from traumatized psyches, and many spend their disposable income on horses and houses and Halstons and hatcheck girls."

Though it never made a profit, and filed for a Chapter 11 bankruptcy, the Palace was finally undone by Valenza's angry wife. Enraged that Frank had fallen in love with another woman, she turned him in. How the tabloids loved it: Valenza's indictment on sixteen counts of assorted fiscal sin made big black headlines. His acquittal on all but one count (later overturned on appeal) was reported in a paragraph on some dull back page. All the actors in this drama went on to whisk and sauce again, but the leaning tower of spaghetti never got another airing.*

But even the Palace seemed like small-time decadence when Craig Claiborne and Pierre Franey sat down to dinner at Chez Denis in Paris— dinner for two anywhere in the world was the prize offered by American Express in an auction to raise funds for Channel 13. Headlined on the front page of the *Times,* the four-thousand-dollar dinner was trounced on as a scandalous act by the Vatican. Oh, how I wished I had thought of it.

Impressionable grape nuts of the seventies, on easy sipping terms with French wines, were eager to know more. What did New Yorkers see in zinfandel? Well, for one thing, they could pronounce it. Now with wine authority Gerald Asher beating the drum, the great California wine

---

*His savings decimated by legal fees, Valenza worked as a consultant and staged periodic comebacks, dreaming always of a revolution that would end his exile. In the nineties, he tried everything from a twenty-dollar prix fixe to costly redundancies of truffles at 222 on West 79th Street, reluctantly admitting defeat in 2004.

makers flew in for the Four Seasons' first Barrel Tasting in 1976. Soon Chardonnays and cabernets from what wine writer Anthony Dias Blue called "the auteur school of wine-making," would be whipsawing the French by winning much-publicized competitive blind tastings in Paris.

The French were not discouraged. In May of 1976, Regine opened a flashy mirrored boîte on Park Avenue, with Michel Guérard coaching the kitchen. Purists were aghast at the tackiness of linking great food and disco. But it made sense to me. We could eat Guérard's astonishing egg (caviar) and egg (scrambled) in an eggshell and dance it off till 4:00 AM. And wasn't it ecumenical of Regine to put two American kitchen acolytes to work: Larry Forgione, a graduate of the Culinary Institute of America, and Patrick Clark, just out of NYC Technical College.

An aristocratic expatriate, Marina de Brantes, designed the Coup de Fusil on East Sixty-fourth Street* with the chef Yannick Kam. It was dedicated to the nouvelle gospel. Nouvelle cuisine was wildly contagious. Soon impressionable eaters were caught in a quicksand of purees. Plates got bigger; portions got smaller. What was raw got cooked; what had been cooked was now raw. Vegetables were laid out as if they were precious jewels, a carrot, a brussels sprout, a turnip carved into a baton. Dinner was a still life on a plate.

Fresh-turned pasta was a fetish of the seventies. We early foodies made our own fettuccine at home, but then the first Pasta & Cheese shop opened in 1976 and cloned itself in the neighborhoods. French chefs had looked down their noses at the cooks of Italy for generations, but soon they had all borrowed ravioli. Anything could be stuffed into ravioli—goat cheese, ratatouille, even garlic puree. Sirio Maccioni, passionately Italian at Le Cirque—what he disarmingly called his "French bistro"—got his congregation to eat pasta primavera, except for the calorie counters and X rays who lived on chopped salad.

Restaurant Associates' exiled wizard Joe Baum's magnum opus atop the much-reviled World Trade Center, Windows on the World, had the city looking up in the recessionary spring of 1976. I spent two weeks watching Baum worrying the details and was wowed by what he and his architect had wrought on the 107th floor of the north tower. "If money and power and ego and a passion for perfection could create this extraor-

*It was located where JoJo is now.

dinary pleasure, this instant landmark . . . money and power and ego could rescue the city from its ashes," I wrote. It was the most optimistic moment in architecture since the Rockefellers gave us Rockefeller Center at the height of the Depression. To make the point, the magazine's cover showed just the restaurant, as if suspended in the air, minus the tower beneath. This was another clever idea from *New York* art director Milton Glaser, who just happened to be the graphics designer of Baum's dream, as well. Reading my piece now, I do sound a bit gaga. I admit I was gaga. I was thrilled by the astonishing views and felt a wave of mild acrophobia because the glass wall went down to my feet. Every vista of the city seemed brand-new, a miracle. I wrote, "In the Statue of Liberty lounge, the harbor's heroic blue sweep makes you feel like the ruler of some extraordinary universe. All the bridges of Brooklyn and Queens and Staten Island stretch across the restaurant's promenade." Even New Jersey looked benign from up high. Helicopters and clouds floated below.

It was not merely a time of economic pain. The streets were rife with uncontainable crime and there was not enough money to sweep away the grime. But from above, I observed, "Everything to hate and fear is invisible. A fire raging below Washington Square is a dream, silent, almost unreal, though you can see the arc of water licking flame. Default is a silly nightmare. There is no doggy dew. Garbage is an illusion." A few months later, a *Daily News* headline would record the president's indifference: FORD TO CITY: DROP DEAD.

Joe Baum was everywhere at that first meal. "This is one of my favorite tables," he said to me. I reacted as if it were a posthypnotic suggestion. We were as far from the prime window seats as could be. Yet, I had to admit the view was remarkable. The interior had been layered so that every table would have a view.

"They didn't put enough sugared pecans on your strawberry-rhubarb compote," Baum complained, pounding the table to summon a waiter.

"No, Joe. They did. I ate them."

He bent down to pick up a cigarette wrapper.

The magazine's cover line on my story was pretty gaga, too: "The Most Spectacular Restaurant in the World." Amazingly the world (long before SoHo and TriBeCa would beckon) was willing to go all the way downtown even for lunch.

*   *   *

The gentrification of notoriously grungy and dangerous Columbus Avenue began in the mid-1970s, too. Its booze-soaked sidewalks were seized by Yuppies seeking low-rent apartments and by merchants eager to quiche and white wine them. Michael Weinstein wasn't planning to be a restaurateur till he opened the Museum Café on Columbus and a few critics appreciated his pop menus. (But with success at Saloon and Ernie's and later America, his company, Ark, would go public and eventually buy Lutèce.) The Silver Palate was scrunched into a closet-size storefront, with catering by Sheila Lukins and Julee Russo. (It would grow into a factory selling relishes, jams, and flavored vinegars, and then an all-time-best-selling cookbook.)

Macy's Cellar got grander and more global. And the first Greenmarket opened. Not long after, Dean & DeLuca lured us downtown with the market as art gallery on Prince Street. The corner superettes, long mom-and-pop acts, often Jewish, were bought by Koreans, and suddenly we could find fresh flowers for sale twenty-four hours a day.

Flying Foods downtown, wholesaler and broker of exotica, brought in out-of-season greens from other hemispheres, exotic mushrooms all year round, and a rash of radicchio. Back in Detroit, my mom, Saralee, refused to venture beyond iceberg, but the mesclun revolution was making waves across the country and certainly in her supermarket.

The year 1977 brought an MSG scare, and no wonder. With three master chefs in residence in New York City, Chinese food had never been more beautiful or more exciting. At Shun Lee Palace, master T. T. Wang orchestrated supernal hot-and-sour soup and cold appetizers so searingly peppered, some of us broke out in a sweat. As addicted as I was to peanut butter as a child, I now became fixated on Shun Lee's peanut buttery sesame hacked chicken. Uncle Lu dynamited heads off with torrid stir-fries at Hunam on Second Avenue, a side venture of Wang, with a young Michael Tong as his clever sidekick in the dining room. Uncle Tai perfected slithery caramelized venison and cold peppered rabbit, mysterious and fiery, sweet and silken at David Keh's blue-painted Uncle Tai's Hunan Yuan on Third Avenue. Tai's voluptuous orange beef became the signature of his second, Chef Ho, who went off to open Fortune Garden.

David Keh's feng shui must have been working in those years. Keh had a sweet, shy charm and a knack for pleasing fussy celebrities, though he often left majordomos to run his dining room while he went out to play. He had arrived in America in 1965, headed for Seton College from China's remote Anhui province. One hundred dollars borrowed from a San Francisco friend of his father let him cross the country on a ninety-nine-dollar Greyhound deal with a sack of hard-boiled eggs. He found his way that first night to the Chinese Pavilion of the World's Fair in Queens. There, he cleaned toilets and slept on a bench till he could afford a room.

Waiting tables at Four Seas in Wall Street, he met Lu Hoy Yuen and teamed with that brilliant, natural cook to open Szechuan Taste on Chatham Square. New Yorkers rallied by our magazine's Underground Gourmet—then Milton Glaser and Jerome Snyder—went bananas for that fierce chili heat. Szechuan uptown on Second Avenue made Keh rich and Lu famous, but Lu was lonely and soon disappeared. David Keh's ambition was to open the Lutèce of Chinese restaurants, he told me. That was what he had in mind for Chung Kuo—Rosenthal china, fresh red roses on every table—in the space that had been Longchamps on Third and Sixty-fifth. Someone pointed out that the name had twenty-eight strokes, an ill-fated number. He changed the logo to David K and his temple of luxury took off in spite of prices unhead of for Chinese food. Later, David would launch the unknown Zarela Martinez in architect Sam Lopata's brilliantly shadowed Café Marimba below his David K in a move to get the union off his back.

Once midway through appetizers at his Uncle Tai, I noticed three men in long black coats over kitchen whites walk in the front door and march straight to the kitchen, summoned from who knew where to bolster the troops for my dinner. Though Keh could be distracted by mahjongg, a pretty face, and good times with cronies in Hong Kong and Taiwan, he didn't miss a trick, certainly not a restaurant critic.

Late in the seventies, New Yorkers who thought tuna came only in cans began to discover sushi. Scattered Westerners joined the Japanese businessmen at the sushi counter in Nippon and Hatsuhana and learned to say *"omakase"*—"Let the chef decide." With my friend Joel Grey as my sensai, my first *omakase* at Takezushi—a "Hallelujah Chorus" of seafood crunch and mystic rice—was a revelation.

Between rounds of excessive feasting, millions went on the Scarsdale diet. Soon it became a book, and it found new life on the best-seller list

when its author lost his life, shot by a disheartened lover after she discovered his infidelity. (His bedsheets gave him away, she said. He should
have changed the sheets, outraged feminists agreed.)

After fourteen years bumping heads with the city's bureaucracy,
Buzzy O'Keeffe opened the River Café in 1977—a major waterfront
victory, lashed to a barge, with a lyrically romantic eye on the Manhattan skyline. Soon it would nurture a line of thoroughbred cooks, Charles
Palmer (later at Aureole), David Burke (who would perfect his playful
ways at Park Avenue Cafe), and the dessert master Richard Leach. There
were critical boos for the food in the first few months, but then chef
Larry Forgione arrived with free range from O'Keeffe to buy only the
best. Not long after, a poultry farmer, with subsidies from Forgione's
budget, was raising chicken in a revolutionary old-fashioned way. "Free-
range" it said on the menu.

Sometime in the summer of 1977, I couldn't help but notice that Le
Cirque's kitchen was finding its own new identity. No way could I miss
the sunny evolution, because I happened to be keeping occasional company with the proud new *chef de cuisine,* Jean-Louis Todeschini. He loved
to eat. He loved to dance after his crew scoured the kitchen at 1:00 AM.
But after spending two weeks with him that fall touring France, I worried gossips might question anything I wrote about Le Cirque. Rather
than wait for the bitches to chatter, I titled my mostly enthusiastic review
"I Love Le Cirque, But Can I Be Trusted?"

The city broke out in a rash of sun-dried tomatoes. Anyone who didn't
jog signed up for aerobic dancing. Some took fitness seriously. The rest
of us worked out religiously so we could eat. Die-hard traditionalists in
the fancy French restaurants still sauced and carved tableside, but our
own nouvellistes arranged plates in the kitchen and sent them out under
shiny silver bells—inspiring cloche-lifting choreography that provoked
oohs and aahs and nervous giggles.

My dear friend Naomi called, always looking out for the welfare of
my lovelorn heart, since she knew Andrew, her erotically charged accountant, was still keeping me dangling. Her husband's cousin had met a
recently divorced "perfect man for you." I invited real estate developer
Harley Baldwin to join me for a reviewing lunch that lasted till five
o'clock, when we walked home through the park, still talking nonstop. I

left him at the Dakota to change for dinner. He was tall, with an athlete's long muscles and the face of a Gerber baby—pale blond, blue-eyed, pink cheeks. It was clear at once we were soul mates, but after three consecutive evenings of dinner, dancing, a black-tie benefit, and chaste kisses, Harley finally set me straight. He was not the perfect man for me. "I have a lover named Peter" was how he put it. We became pals, constant companions, sometimes the two, often the three of us. I tried everything I knew to straighten him out.

"It's so much more psychologically mature to be bisexual," I lectured him. "To be able to respond sexually to either gender." Though he conceded that in certain crucial sexual acts I was almost as good as a man, he had divorced his adored wife, made a strong commitment to his gay side. I should have met him in high school, he said.

Harley had been named the designated developer of Bridgemarket in the crumbling but gorgeous space under the Fifty-ninth Street Bridge used as a garage by the Metropolitan Transportation Authority. His plan called for a Greenmarket, rows and rows of ethnic shops and bakeries from all known countries and any yet to be discovered, and a restaurant or two. The architect's sketches looked like they'd been drawn by Palladio. His days were spent fencing with the community and the bureaucracy. Evenings, he wooed the great cooks he wanted to move into Bridgemarket. He'd been born in Chicago but had done a few deals in Aspen. He became the Rocky Mountain Sybarite, a character in my reviews.

"Come with us to Harlem for barbecued spareribs," he said one afternoon.

"You're kidding. You are not Cole Porter. I am not Helen Morgan. These are not those bad old good old days when people like us had fun in Harlem."

It was 1979, and to be frank, I wasn't sure how welcome I'd be fried chicken–hopping in Harlem with a duo of aging blond preppies. Two whiter WASPS, I'd never seen. Harlem had not been all that welcoming to white forays since Rosa Parks refused to sit in the back of that bus and the civil rights struggle began. Black Power had pretty much drawn a Maginot Line. You could feel the tension in the subway without going all the way to 125th Street.

But off we went for glorious ribs, transcendent candied sweets . . .

and the warmest welcome at Sylvia's, on Lenox Avenue, just north of 126th Street, a neighborhood both shabby and forlorn, if not forbidding. "Sylvia Queen of Soul Food," as it said on the menu, was there to greet Harley when we returned one Saturday for breakfast. He had his mind set on luring Sylvia to Bridgemarket. Breakfast was an adventure, a bargain, a lark. The grits were impeccably smooth and full of that nutty hominy flavor. Two eggs with grits and homemade hot biscuits cost only a dollar. We tried the sausage and slab bacon, too, a salmon croquette, and the pork chop, smothered, of course, in gravy goo.

"Harlem on My Mind" in *New York* enticed eager downtowners up to Lenox Avenue. And soon Sylvia had expanded into the two stores north of the narrow little counterette. Long ago (before she opened a jazz supper club on the corner and tourists started busing in for gospel breakfasts), Sylvia Woods gave me a plaque commemorating my ode to her sassy ribs, sometimes hot, sometimes hotter. It should have gone to Harley, of course.

What a sense-reeling joyride life in the seventies was for a restaurant critic. I watched the fever spread as pilgrims from French kitchens arrived and scored or stumbled and retreated while self-taught Americans in love with French cooking dared dramatic diversions. In 1979, I heralded Le Plasir as the debut of the year. A Wall Street analyst named Peter Josten, and Steven Spector, a well-meaning dilettante and dabbler in real estate and art, had created a peach-glow cloister on 969 Lexington Avenue. Each table had its butter in the shape of a small bird, homage to Griggstown Farm, where the partners raised aristocratic quail for the town's fussy chefs. And there was Claude Baills, late of the Palace, in the kitchen. Good word of mouth filled the house almost at once, but too soon, during a major snowstorm, the temperamental Baills walked out, abandoning his innocent moneymen. The house was fully booked. Veteran restaurant consultant Barbara Kafka realized that the Japanese sous-chef, Masataka Kobayashi, had the skill to carry on but lacked the confidence. She found him a partner overseas.

What a shock, then, when Le Plasir reemerged and quickly hit its stride. It seemed that the overly modest Masa had the right stuff after all. Everything he did was rare, lightly cooked, barely poached, sparingly seared—tender, bursting with a natural sweetness. "This is the Japanese sensibility of the nouvelle cuisine, splendidly executed," I wrote in a bit of seventies gibberish. "Happily, the idiom is almost second nature for Masa. It's in his bones. If the sauces do not always sing, they hum on key."

Too soon, the keeper of an inn in the Napa Valley came along, tempting the chef to go west. Masa announced that he would move to California so his children could have a better life. The twice-wounded partners did not have the heart to start over yet again. Le Plasir died. Masa went off to became a San Francisco star. Ironically, given the security he sought, he found violence. His murder in November 1984 has never been solved.

Thanks to Paul Bocuse and his merry pranksters, professional cooking had new cachet. But unlike the Bocuse born-to-the-whisk band, the new American chefs were former marine biologists, lawyers, engineers. Barry and Susan Wine brought the Quilted Giraffe from New Paltz to a Greek coffee shop on Second Avenue. Karen and Bobby Pritsker came from Boston to open Dodin-Bouffant. Karen and David Waltuck made Chanterelle into a beacon of light on a desolate stretch of SoHo.*

A year after founding *Food & Wine* magazine in 1978, Michael and Ariane Batterberry organized a first-year-anniversary gathering of rising stars and celebrated chefs at Tavern on the Green. "It was the first time American chefs cooked on the same footing with European chefs, at a time when the term *American chef* was still an oxymoron in most people's minds," Batterberry recalls. "And all the products were American. The French came expecting to knock people dead with their nouvelle cuisine and there was Alice Waters, doing very similar things. Paul Prudhomme received a standing ovation and he in turn saluted Alice, who, he said, 'sure beat the pants off those Frenchmen.' " The press that followed seized on the American triumph. *Food & Wine,* Batterberry believes, was the "visionary magazine in what was becoming a visionary age of food."

For a while, it might have seemed I was a hopelessly elitist voice speaking for a manic minority, but now we were hearing from newly-hatched sybarites in Minneapolis, New Orleans, Santa Monica, Berkeley, Chicago, all across the country.

*See Chapter 40, "Cuisines from Three Marriages."

32

BLUE SKIES AND CANDY, TOO

SUMMER—WHEN THE BOOK WORLD USED TO SPACE OUT AND NAP IN lawn chairs—was not prime publishing time. And in that summer of 1976, not much else was coming off the press, so William Morrow thought my first novel, *Blue Skies, No Candy*, could make a splash. They had bought the long-gestating opus on the basis of the one hundred pages written at the MacDowell Colony after Murray's goading. It had taken me three more summers to finish my story of the screenwriter Kate, who seemed to have everything a liberated women could want— adoring husband, well-adjusted child, enthusiastic afternoon lovers— and yet it wasn't enough. Kate's narrative would begin in bed, I had decided, because that's where Kate felt most womanly. I wanted even male readers to know what sex could feel like to a woman. So I used all the senses, all the sensory words I used to describe food—the taste and smell of it, the sound and heat. I would put the reader into bed with Kate. It had not occurred to me that not everyone would be comfortable there.

Certainly there was already a buzz. People who thought they knew the real me from my rants and ravings in *New York* seemed to be curious to see what a restaurant critic could do in a novel.

Even so, I never anticipated that devils would be primed to pounce.

One week after the official publication date of *Blue Skies* exposed my brave Kate and her joyful hobby of adultery in the afternoon, the novel was cruelly shredded in *Newsweek* and by both Anatole Broyard in the daily *Times* (ironically, he prided himself on being the paper's self-appointed champion of sensuality) and by an outraged Donald E. Westlake on Sunday. "Kate's fantasies, or her lovers . . . sound like Krafft-Ebing in a Classic Comics translation," Broyard wrote. *Newsweek*'s critic seemed equally offended: "It's just like all the Nurse Barton books and those crazy career-girl romances you're crazy about—except it's really dirty." "According to this book," Westlake carped, "not only are women's sexual fantasies as banal and repetitive as men's, they are men's."

Three strikes, I was out. I was devastated. Cooler heads than mine might have asked why I was so surprised at the barbed response: all that graphic coupling, the zipless fucks, the wet pussies, and the heroine's pride in her art of fellatio. No, no, no. I truly thought there was an audience out there ready to discover a woman's sheer carnal joy. I never took into account that the odds of an unabashed sensualist being assigned to review my book were slim to zero.

I had been struggling to finish the novel two years earlier, when Erica Jong's *Fear of Flying* landed with an explosion of publicity. (I couldn't call it *Skin Flick* anymore because someone had published a book called *Kinflicks* and it wasn't *Blue Skies* yet because I couldn't settle on a name.) Jong's book made me nervous. Now my book would not be unique. It would be a symptom, a trend, yet another sticky-paged sexy romp by a woman. I wanted to read Jong's novel, but I was afraid I would be influenced in some way or maybe find myself paralyzed, unable to finish.

I asked a publishing friend to read it and tell me whatever I needed to know. "Don't read it till you finish your book," he said.

"Is it too late?" I asked. "Has she written the same book?"

"Not at all," he said soothingly. "It's totally different. I just think you shouldn't let it distract you."

I didn't believe him for a minute. Oh damn, Erica has written my book, I thought. Later, when I finally read it, I laughed at the similarity—two sets of lovers driving though France, madly coupling. But her lovers had menstrual periods at inopportune moments and got bitten by mosquitoes. Mine melted into molten joy and had multiple orgasms. Of course, Erica had better bloodlines. She was an intellectual and a poet. I was merely an ex–newspaper reporter who had found God in the details of *uni* sushi and truffled fettuccine.

Now in the summer of unleashing *Blue Skies,* smarting from three public spankings, I was devastated. I crept into bed and languished in the dark for three days. Then Murray called from California. It was Murray's fault. He'd misled me in every way. Since that wild euphoric fling through France, our romance had played out like "Send in the Clowns." He was free, but I wasn't. I was free, but he wasn't. He was free. Oh, forget it. One of us was always up in the air when the other hit the ground. Murray had dared me to stop talking about writing a novel and write it. He had bossily dictated the plot that afternoon on the road between Lyon and Les Baux. And he had line-edited the final edited version three years later. What could he have been thinking?

"How could you let me publish it?" I cried. "If it's such stupid Nurse Barton crap, why did you let me publish it?"

"But it's not porn," he said. "Listen to me, sweetie. It's wonderful. It's powerful and funny. . . . It's a woman writing about a woman's erotic feelings. Don't you get it? These three critics attacking you are all men. It's so obvious. They are terrified by a sexual woman. Women will love this book. Talk to your publisher," he urged. "Get women you know to write their comments. Let them run it as an ad."

The ad ran—a tombstone, two long columns the length of the *Times* daily book page. NOT SINCE HENRY MILLER HAS A BOOK ABOUT SEX CAUSED SUCH A FUROR, the headline read. "The Men Can't Take It" was printed atop the first column, above the cruelest excerpts from the three male critics. Below that stretched a yard of white space. The other column was captioned "But Women Love It," followed by positive quotes from a roster of well-known women that ran all the way to the bottom of the page.

"A super talented writer has taken a completely original voyage into the lushness of women's sexual longings. I think of Greene as a contemporary Colette," wrote the novelist Ruth Harris. (Should I have been embarrassed running these quotes? Yes, she was a pal.)

". . . Greene has written about sexuality the way she has always written about food—as a necessity of life which can also be sublime," cookbook writer Paula Wolfert commented. (A longtime friend, too. Well, so what?)

"If it's Philip Roth, sex is fine and fun," Gloria Steinem wrote. "If it's Gael Greene, its 'psychopathology.' Read this book . . . you'll see these male reviewers are reviewing themselves." (Gloria would never lie.)

The ad ran once. That was all the budget allowed. But, in fact, the devastating reviews—echoed by attacks from newspapers all over the country—had boosted *Blue Skies* onto the *New York Times* best-seller list. I had fantasized being banned in Boston. That would have been almost fun. I could have rallied the ACLU. These attacks on my writing really hurt, but it was having a positive impact on my bank account. Every few weeks, Morrow would order another printing.

Though I had never anticipated the furor *Blue Skies* provoked, I think I realized I could never have published the book if my father had still been alive. As for Mom, well, Saralee was a survivor. The two of us had often conspired to protect Dad from painful realities. But now as I flew home to Detroit on my book tour, I was anxious. All my aunts and cousins and Mother's canasta pals were lined up at the Bloomfield Hills bookshop to buy my book and get it autographed. Aunt Rynee was already pursing her lips and tut-tutting: "I hear it's even dirtier than *Forever Amber.*"

"What are you going to tell them, Mom," I asked, "when they say how could you raise a daughter that would write such filth?"

She smiled and handed me a homemade chocolate chip cookie, from the stash she'd baked to send to my doctor brother in Chicago.

"Don't worry, dear," she said. "I'll just tell them that's what you have to do to sell a novel these days."

Much later, when she'd read it and I got the courage to ask what she thought, her only comment was, "I'm glad I read it. Now I know other people do those things. The blow . . . you know." She couldn't bring herself to say it. "I always thought it was something your father invented just for us."

In certain rarefied circles, I had been a food goddess. Now I was a sex queen, I discovered, as I flew from one city to the next to promote the book. My legs were everywhere. Kindly photographers showed me how to cross them for the ultimate legginess. The big black wide-brimmed hat I hide under for publicity photos became famous. There was a pink one with flowers, too. I was as likely to be photographed lying down as not. Bill Boggs interviewed me on his noon TV show, with the two of us lying on a double bed . . . fully dressed and not touching, of course. Interviewers were shocked or amused or outraged. One reporter dismissed me as drab and mousy, dressed like a librarian. Another thought the same slit skirt and ankle straps were a bit sluttish. What questions they asked. Suddenly, I was a sex expert. This was about the time the media was discovering and celebrating (or poking fun at) a source of female pleasure called the G-spot. Many women had always suspected there had to be something going on down there. Certainly my heroine, Kate, knew. Now my opinion on such matters was in demand. Anyway, it was called the G-spot, but not after me.

Warner Books launched a spectacular publicity campaign for the paperback of *Blue Skies, No Candy* in the fall of 1978. One of the top women runners in the New York City Marathon crossed the finish line wearing a *Blue Skies* T-shirt. (No, she wasn't first. Maybe she stopped to make out along the way.) A giant billboard went up in Hollywood. The cover, the title, and my name winked on and off in colored lights on the screen above the moving headlines on the tower in Times Square.

I was on the road again, barnstorming for the paperback, when I got a call saying the Metropolitan Transportation Authority had banned my ads and pulled down eight thousand subway cards and three thousand bus posters with a version of the book's undeniably racy cover: a photograph of a woman's manicured hand tugging down the zipper on a pair of jeans "obviously worn by a man," as the *Post* reported. WCBS was quick to telecast complaints about this moral transgression, and the MTA quickly caved in.

I was never really comfortable with that cover. When I first saw it, I was so upset that I begged publisher Howard Kaminsky to do something not quite so raunchy.

"This is a brilliant cover," he insisted. "I promise you this cover will sell an extra million copies of your book."

I dabbed at my tears. "What can I say, Howard?" I replied, surrendering. "You are the expert at publishing."

When the first small carton of books arrived, I ripped it open and screamed. No one had shown me the back cover. There was the cloudy blue sky and the jeans again, this time with my portrait emerging from the unzipped fly.

It was Saturday. I called Kaminsky at home. He was watching a football game. But for a hysterical woman, he pulled himself away and came to the phone.

"How could you put my face in that crotch?" I cried. "I agree the front cover is brilliant, but I can't go out on the road to sell a book with my face in the crotch."

So Warner Books went back to press with a new back cover immediately, in advance of my road trip. Kaminsky never forgave me, even when the book did go on to sell millions. (I'll never know if this was my temper tantrum, the arrogance of my daring to give him an ultimatum, or my insensitivity in interrupting the football game.) Years later, when I noticed a few of the original paperbacks floating around used-book stores with my face emerging from that crotch, I was told that rather than shred the offending edition, it had been sent overseas to be sold in PXs. (War did not break out that year, so I cannot be blamed.)

Kaminsky said he was shocked the MTA could be bullied into ripping down the "tastefully provocative" posters that had cost him eight thousand dollars.

"I'm shocked and disappointed, too," I said, having been reached in Chicago by the *Post*. "If the MTA is worried about filth, let them clean up the dirty subway cars."

Back in New York, I persuaded WCBS to send a cameraman with me into the subway. "I'll show you filth," I said to the camera as I led the way into the scabrous underground. "What about these hemmorhoid ads? And look at that poster with a man pulling down a woman's slip strap. It's obscene if it's a woman unzipping a zipper, but it's okay if it's a man undressing a woman."

My indignant five minutes ran on WCBS twice that day, at six o'clock and again on the eleven o'clock news. Half a million copies moved out of bookstores in a week. Months later, Ross Wetzsteon took a thoughtful look at *Blue Skies* in the *Village Voice*. It was my first, maybe my only, serious review.

When the book's respectable ride on the *Times* best-seller list got me a huge advance on my next novel, *Doctor Love,* I could easily have afforded that three-bedroom apartment at the Dakota, the one I didn't buy, as it turned out. I decided I should have a mink, and instead of my initials embroidered into the lining, I asked the furrier to put "Blue Skies, No Candy" in royal blue, with a bright red comma. I might have taken a leave from *New York* or quit, taken advantage of the momentum, written the new novel quickly instead of taking five summers. But I was afraid. Afraid

I might never have another publishing bonanza and I would lose the apartment. Afraid I would dissolve and disappear and editors would stop calling to ask my recipe for grilled eggplant or how to cure marital boredom or what I was reading at the beach that summer. I was a shallow and vulnerable woman.

Writing is lonely. And I was living alone. I needed the tumult and mayhem of the restaurant world and the magazine's constant deadlines. I liked inviting friends and strangers to dinner. The book would take years, and then maybe no one would like it. I was addicted to instant gratification. In fact, that was one reason I cooked—the triumph and applause invariably came before coffee.

Scallops with Salsa Cruda and Gremolata

Don't make this dish unless you have great summer tomatoes. It also works with really fresh swordfish cut into 1-inch cubes.

Sauce:
4 great large beefsteak tomatoes
¼ cup minced shallots
1 tbsp. olive oil (to cook shallots)
2 tsp. minced cilantro or parsley
1 tbsp. olive oil (to flavor tomato mix)
1 tsp. lemon juice
¼ tsp. coarse salt (or to taste)
Freshly ground pepper, to taste

Scallops:
12 large sea scallops
½ cup very fine fresh bread crumbs
¼ tsp. salt
Freshly ground pepper, to taste
3 tbsp. butter

Gremolata garnish:
2 cloves garlic, minced
Optional: 1 tsp. olive oil
4 tbsp. minced parsley
Zest of 1 lemon, grated

To make the sauce:

Peel and seed tomatoes; squeeze out juice (reserve for another use). Chop; drain on sideboard.

Sauté shallots in olive oil until soft but do not let color. Stir into chopped tomatoes. Stir in cilantro or parsley. Season to taste with good olive oil, lemon juice, salt, and pepper.

To prepare the scallops:

Shake scallops in brown paper bag with bread crumbs, salt, and pepper. Sauté in hot butter very quickly on both sides and edges till they are golden, warm, and still rare inside.

To prepare the garnish:

Mix together garlic, parsley, and lemon peel. Garlic may be sautéed lightly in a little olive oil if raw garlic frightens you.

33

LIFE IS A CABERNET

ONCE UPON A TIME IN THE DIM DAWN OF ORAL HISTORY, THERE WAS NO Williams-Sonoma international bazaar of kitchen and tableware in every mall, no De Gustibus famous chefs cooking classes at Macy's, no Food Network, no chefs hotter than rock stars. James Beard taught a few classes on television in the fifties. You could buy springform pans and madeleine molds at a few high-end kitchen shops or from snarly Fred Bridge's professional cookware hideaway. There were cooking classes, of course, Dione Lucas, Grace Chu, and Helen Worth, whose method was to teach one student at a time, standing over you like a benevolent mother-in-law and saying, "Rinse the spoon—cold water, please. Now hang it back in its place next to the whisk." Then in the late sixties and early seventies, the newly food-obsessed fought to get into overbooked cooking classes.

The city was straining to get out of the financial doldrums. Yet no one stopped eating or stopped aspiring to a mastery of the kitchen. Food was a comfort most of us could afford. The rest of New York seemed to be latching onto obsessions once confined to us early foodies.

For those with leisure and money, "we blessed souls who live to love and love to eat and eat to love and love to delicious excess," as I described us, the dream escape was a great chef's cooking class far away. "True, gastronomic cravings are as varied as the libido's yearnings," I wrote. "Some long for Mother's cooking, for soul food, for the prepubescent banana split. Others yearn for the simplicity of a perfect raspberry. To be immersed in pasta. To be assaulted by chocolate. To dive into a tin of caviar. To be attacked by a running Brie. But surely a universal food-world longing is to apprentice in the kitchen with a French chef of the vaunted three-star tradition." All it took was a transfusion of money.

That fall, the fantasy came to life in all its wine-stained, butter-oozing reality in the Napa Valley. Roger Vergé, the brilliant chef-proprietor of the Moulin de Mougins, north of Cannes, had been enticed to make his debut into gastronomic showbiz. He would teach a weeklong cooking course at High Tree, a luxurious Victorian house nestled among the vineyards of Napa. I had been hired to costar as critic and raconteur by the school's impresario, Michael James, because, to be brutally frank, he thought only I could persuade Vergé to come.

As a young Romance languages major, Michael's fixation on languages had led right to the table, and to classes in France with Simone Beck (the legendary Simca of the Julia Child *Mastering the Art* consortium). At twenty-six, Michael was beautiful in a silkily turn-of-the-century way (dark eyes, trim mustache). He looked as if he might take off and jeté across the floor at any moment. But inside, ambition simmered, and buttressed by the business sense of his earthbound partner, Billy Cross, he had concocted the Wine Country Cooking Course, first with Simca at the stove and later Jacques Pépin and Marcella Hazan—all sellout successes.

Vergé and his lively red-haired wife, Denise, liked the idea, as I explained it to him, of being paid to discover the Napa Valley, with only a few hours in the teaching kitchen as the price.

Billy had negotiated to have twenty pounds of the best butter flown in from Wisconsin. I was to bring sixteen pounds of crème fraîche packed in dry ice on my flight from New York. Vergé would shop in San Francisco the morning before the students arrived, poking the fish himself to verify its freshness, and admiring a prime rib in the city's grandest supermarket as if it were a Brancusi. Vergé had never seen a supermarket quite so sprawling or grand before. He picked out two plastic-bound chunks of bright orange cheese *"pour les sandwiches."*

"I'll do bacon, avocado, and cheddar on toast," he said. No one dared tell him he had just invented what was already a California luncheon classic.

Students flew in private jets for the privilege of sharing Vergé's secrets. We strolled toward the house that first afternoon on a path covered with overripe figs fallen from dozens of trees, making an organic squish that thrilled those of us used to nothing but pavement. It was an amazing haunting smell, as if the whole world were nothing but Fig Newtons.

Actually, my French was severely limited. I was not the ideal translator for Vergé, who did not speak much English then. Indeed, I often mistranslated. That seemed to amuse and disarm the class. And several took pleasure in correcting me. "Monsieur Vergé said 'never,' " they would cry good-naturedly, "not 'always.' "

Most of us, even those, like me, who often cooked by instinct without recipes, felt threatened as Vergé simply began to cook, grabbing pots, chopping, slathering, sloshing wine, pulling pans off raging flames, never saying how much, how long, how hot, why or when, and with no written recipes to follow. Bemused by the class panic, Vergé, surprisingly shy, eventually paused to explain. The duck stock, how to do it, the browned bones, the chicken wings, the clarified butter, how and why. Reduction . . . the beginnings of his demi-glace. Bring to the simmer. Reduce. Reduce. Reduce. The last-minute blob of cold butter he would swirl in to make the sauce shine. Michael James bobbed and danced a running interpretation.

Vergé peppered.

"How much?"

"That much."

He nutmegged.

"How much?"

"A bump and four grinds."

Vergé lopped a half-pound lump off a five-pound block of fancy butter into the saucepan.

"Oh no," a student cried. "All that butter."

"What about cholesterol?" asked the slender blond actress with a shudder.

"It's not the butter that's bad for you," Roger replied. "It's butter blended with flour that can hurt you." It was a tenet of the nouvelle cuisine faith. The actress stared, eyes wide, wanting to believe. Oh, if only . . . we all strained to believe.

Champagne was poured. From humble kitchen peons, we became

royalty at the dinner table. There were candles everywhere and an extravagance of bright flowers, fragile crystal, someone's inherited china. Billy Cross wore black tie, and the waiters were spiffy in their gold-braided officers' mess uniforms. A parade of Napa wines was presented to taste, and the fruit of Vergé's mystifying legerdemain: sublime crayfish in a delicate buttery bath, duck tender and rare in a sherry-tinged sauce.

And so it went. An academic exercise quickly blossomed into a house party, escalating finally into a sensory blitz. Buttery croissants at breakfast. Sublime local and imported cheeses at lunch. Vergé's *tarte tatin* made with High Tree's own walnuts. We—well, some of us, myself for one—were actually learning the technique of the chef's fragile vegetable timbales and the simple sorcery of bass fillets in a vermouth-spiked cream.

"If they poke us with a fork, we'll spurt butter like chicken Kiev," lamented an architect's wife.

When we weren't actually cooking or eating, our students were thronging the local cheese shop or invading the Court of Two Sisters, a Yountville bakery that posted a stern warning: "No smoking please. Butter, cream and fine pastry at stake."

The exaggerated stylishness of High Tree was reflected at the table. One evening we arrived to find one hundred votive candles flickering. At lunch, a flock of ceramic ducks celebrated the duck barbecue. That night, dozens of candles in paper bags lined the walks, the mantels, and the sideboards. The staff all wore Moroccan caftans, or French sailors' blue-and-white-striped jerseys, or naval uniforms. One night, I found a daisy lying on my pillow. One afternoon, an exuberant pink begonia was floating in my bath.

I loved living in this fairy tale. I imagined this was how I would live if I were Grace Kelly; clean sheets every day, damp towels spirited away by invisible servants and returned smelling of Ivory Snow. Great chefs somehow fathoming exactly my mood for dinner. I had to admit I'd come a long way from the Velveeta cocoon.

At dinner each night, there were heated philosophical debates, a litany of the en masse folly of gourmands that we were. . . . We discussed which was the best dumpling house in San Francisco and whether truffles, the dark tubers that could not be cultivated, might be found on Catalina. One evening, an incredibly handsome guest took my hand, gazed meaningfully into my eyes, and said, "Have I got a chocolate cake for you."

Even the *New York Times* crossword puzzle seemed in sync. The clue one day read "Home on the Range." And the answer, "Julia Child."

Life at High Tree was pure fantasy, dangerously rich. Still, my life at home as a restaurant critic and cheerleader for indulgence was rich enough, beyond anything I could have imagined for myself. So reentry was only a slight shock, but soft—like landing on down pillows.

34

AM I BLUE?

I STOOD IN FRONT OF THE OLD BRENTANO'S ON FIFTH AVENUE AT A TABLE piled high with copies of *Blue Skies, No Candy*. Wouldn't anyone stop and buy? Where were the Insatiable Critic's fans? Eating brunch, I supposed. It was an autumn Sunday at the 1976 New York Is Book Country street fair. I noticed him at once—first that jaunty stroll, his "I'm not rushing anywhere" walk, then the tousle of shiny black ringlets, the faded jeans and dark plaid shirt, opened just one button too low. He smiled. I smiled. He looked familiar. Of course, an actor.

I recognized him from my porn-film excursions with Andrew, the accountant. It was before VCRs, home video, and porn-on-demand television. Andrew's affection for porn took us to shabby movie houses, where he always worried someone would recognize him.

"Walk out backward," I once suggested. Andrew would pull up the collar of his raincoat and slip on dark glasses as we emerged from some Eighth Avenue sleaze center into the rain like ill-fated lovers from a Hemingway novel. He wasn't even liberated by a bleep of porno chic when adventurous couples braved the semen-sticky seats and lurking masturbators on the aisle to check out *Deep Throat* at Forty-ninth Street's New Mature World Theater. Just before the summer we met in East Hampton, the FBI had arrested Harry Reems on an obscenity charge.

Could we be caught up in an FBI sweep? Never mind. Porn turned Andrew on. And seeing porn with me alongside made him even hotter. I had nothing to lose and everything to gain from Andrew's stoked-up BTUs.

So yes, I had recognized that face, the shiny curls, the off-duty bad boy from porn movies.

"You're that actor," I said, "from those movies."

He smiled. He was young and shy and even better looking in person.

"You know my movies." He seemed surprised and pleased.

I struggled to remember which film. Oh yes. I flushed. "You were wonderful in *Misty Beethoven,*" I said, suddenly recalling the boots, the black leather, and the riding crop.

"That was fun to make," he said. "I liked the woman in that one."

"And what do you do when you don't like the woman?" I asked, feeling warm and strangely nervous.

"I just get myself in the mood," he said, looking me straight in the eye.

What a concept. My mind flashed to memories of men who were too tired, too tense, too busy watching the Knicks. I liked that: a man who was willing, and able, to get himself in the mood. He gazed out into the passing crowd as if he was looking for someone. Then he picked up a book from my pile of unsold *Blue Skies* and started to read. He laughed. I was pleased. I meant the book to be funny. "What made you laugh?"

"The hero has my name," he said. "Jamie. I know you. You write about food in *New York* magazine."

"Give me your phone number and I'll take you along on a reviewing dinner," I said.

He found a piece of paper in his pocket and tore it in half. He wrote the name Jamey in a childish scrawl and a telephone number. So he was Jamie in the movies, but for some reason, he considered himself to be Jamey.

"I met the actor from *Misty Beethoven,*" I told Andrew later that night after dinner and after his complaint that he was too stuffed to make love, followed fifteen minutes later by our usual amazing, brain-numbing, sense-stirring sex. He was catching his breath, blowing gently on my skin to dry our mingled sweat.

"You should call him one of these days," said Andrew. "He probably knows the kind of woman who would have sex with us." Andrew longed to share a bed with two women, and sometimes he crankily blamed me for not making it happen. I realized not only that I'd led him to believe I was game—yes, I was game—but that I had only to approach a lusty friend and he would be wrapped in multiples of silken thighs.

What really occupied my mind when I wasn't distracted by writing and eating—the mystery, as I described it to my beloved shrink—was why Andrew couldn't see that two people as in love with sex as we were made for each other. Here I was, single during the full blossoming of the sexual revolution, making the best of it. But I panicked if the phone didn't ring, if I didn't have a plan for the evening.

"Sex is great," I would tell my shrink, as if she didn't know, "but I want love. I'd trade it for less sex." She made a gesture of disbelief.

"No, really."

I was only scared when I stopped to think about it. I wouldn't feel secure and fulfilled until I found love again. But mostly, I tried not to think about it, not to get enmeshed in recriminations about having done something wrong to let Don fall out of love with me.

Sexual adventure was the way to Andrew's heart, I decided. I'd already amazed and amused him weeks earlier, arriving at his apartment just before midnight in only stockings and a garter belt under my fur cape. The cape had slits to the elbow and required two hands holding it together not to stupefy the cabbie or the doorman.

"Oh, I'm sure this guy from *Misty Beethoven* knows a few porn stars we could share," I said, shamelessly dangling a lure he couldn't resist.

I put the scrawled "Jamey" paper on top of a pile of business cards on my desk and replayed his film in my head. The same old endless in and out of most X-rated movies left me cold, but there was almost always at least one scene that made me hot. By 1976, X-rated movies were becoming increasingly ambitious, having set designers, romantic kissing, teasing foreplay, humor, and plots that might not compute but at least tried. What I had liked about *The Opening of Misty Beethoven*, a porno *Pygmalion* with Jamie Gillis as a whip-snapping Professor Higgins, was that Misty was beautiful even in close-ups, her skin flawless. There were luscious dominant women, teasing threesomes, female twosomes who didn't seem to be feigning enthusiasm, and Jamie's character alternating between S&M, first the dominator, then the slave. One could certainly admire such flexibility.

I dialed the number he'd given me. It was his service. I left a message, but he didn't call back.

My writer friend Audrey had just broken off with her steady guy. The two of us survived the holidays, dancing, flirting, and going to movies, as well as planning a big party that would launch us to a fresh start in 1977. We would ask all our single women friends to invite wonderful men they were willing to recycle, and we'd also include a significant balance of couples so that our scheme wouldn't seem too obvious. We called it "Whip the Januaries" and asked everyone to bring their worst Christmas gift to trade for something better. My occasional boyfriend, Le Cirque's *chef de cuisine,* Jean-Louis, said nothing was happening that week in the party room. He would prepare us a feast for ten dollars a person.

That made me nervous. What's the point of turning down a few glasses of champagne offered by restaurateurs before dinner if you accept a party at Le Cirque for practically nothing? "Jean-Louis," I protested. "It's bad enough everyone in the food world thinks they know something about us. I certainly can't accept a free party."

"It is not free." He was indignant. "I give you everything cheap, cheap, cheap," he promised, pronouncing it *chip, chip, chip.* He would do mussels vinaigrette to start. "Mussels cost me ten cents a pound." I wanted the house's famous pasta primavera. "Vegetables, spaghetti—that costs nothing, and I give you kiwi tarts for dessert." (The kiwi had just been discovered and was not yet a joke fruit.) We could save money, too, by bringing our own wine, he agreed. I was in so deep already with Jean-Louis (insisting, and believing, that not even a little hanky-panky could blur my critical faculties) that it was a cinch to convince myself that ten dollars per person was totally reasonable for mussels and noodles, and not perhaps the most unethical thing I'd done to date.

New York's wine writer, Alex Bespaloff, agreed to take me to a Sommelier Society wine tasting to find drinkable wines within our budget, and, to my amazement, there he was, Jamie Gillis, with a goblet of red in his hand.

He'd come with a friend. He had been out of town doing a movie. He'd decided it was probably too late to return my call. Pretending not to notice his friend, I invited him to the party at Le Cirque. He wrote the address and time on yet another mangy scrap of paper. I didn't really expect him to come.

It doesn't matter who you are, major culture hero, boldface name, social scion, in New York, as anywhere else, people tend to stay glued to people they know at parties. But given the challenge to wander the party room at Le Cirque, trying to trade a hunk of trash for a treasure, strangers were instantly caught up in provocative dialogue. Someone who hated a Tiffany pottery platter for strawberries and cream was thrilled to trade it for paisley pajamas with someone who loved pottery and strawberries. One of my personal candidates for recycling brought his gift in a plain brown paper wrap. Convinced from the shape of the box and the swapper's innuendos that it was a vibrator, an actress friend eagerly traded a burgundy cashmere scarf, then laughed on discovering she'd gained a curling iron.

I was surprised when Jamie walked in, wearing a gray velvet suit and that same plaid shirt unbuttoned at the collar. I admired the air of confidence he wrapped himself in. It was as if he had a wonderful secret.

"You didn't bring your worst gift," I said, sitting down beside him and making sure he had grated Parmesan for his pasta.

"I have two tickets to the burlesque to trade." He patted his pocket.

"I didn't realized burlesque still existed," I said.

"Oh yes. For an extra five dollars, one of the girls will sit on your lap."

"Maybe you'll take me one day," I said.

He smiled.

Liz Smith's beribboned toilet-bowl cleaner was voted the worst gift, and she won the prize, a ride home in a horse-drawn carriage we had hired that was parked outside. Everyone danced. It was like the prom I should have had. Instead of the bored boyfriend I had borrowed from an older friend so I could go to my high school prom, I now had a succession of partners.

As the room began to clear, I took stock of my options, my dancing partners, the seductive whispers. It seemed that I had a choice of three men to go home with: The dauphin of a wealthy upper-crust family, who was between wives. The unabashedly promiscuous Jean-Louis. Or the

porn actor I'd met at the book fair. I thought about my mother. Yes, I did.
I thought how Saralee would love the rich man's son, smart, talented,
dashing, a suitable age.

But Mom knew me better than that.

Jean-Louis was waiting. "It was a dream party. Thank you, and please
thank Sirio, too," I told him. "I'll see you soon." His mouth dropped open
in surprise. The charming scion, waiting for me near the door with his
coat over his shoulders, seemed dazed, as if too drunk to rise in protest
as I kissed him good-bye.

Jamie Gillis took in the small drama and seemed bemused. I took
him home and had my way with him on the living room floor. He let me
have his lips. He let me force his lips open with my tongue. He let me
loosen his belt and unbutton his shirt. He was there. He'd gotten himself
in the mood, as advertised. He was the most passive man I'd ever met.
The total opposite of his cinema persona. How odd. What a challenge.
Quickly, I was hooked.

35

THE PRINCE OF PORN AND
THE JUNK-FOOD QUEEN

I WAS FASCINATED BY HIS STORY. I WANTED TO KNOW WHAT HAD LED JAMIE Gillis, née Jamey Gurman, from a cum laude degree in English at Columbia University and then acting school to reciting Shakespeare while performing live sex at the Show World Center on Eighth Avenue. His father got the name Jamie from Tyrone Power's pirate in *The Black Swan* and that's how he spelled it, but his mother—the two were separated— insisted on Jamey.

"When I check into a hotel, I never know which name to use," he confided. "I feel responsible more and more for Jamie Gillis, since I created him. I had no control over Jamey Gurman. I used to think I was a prince left by mistake. This couldn't possibly be my family." I watched him play Jamie Gillis out in public with me, turning on the self-conscious strut, the velvet confidence of his voice. Inside, I believed he still felt like Jamey Gurman, myopic, unathletic, failing at high school, no one to take to the prom. We were both Cinderella. Immediately, he became that deprived child, Jamey, to me.

Jamey was hungry. His hunger made my hunger seem quite tame. He was fascinated with tasting. He seemed to get an almost sexual thrill— his nose would twitch like a cat's—from a new taste he had never experienced before. His dream, he told me in all seriousness, was one day to invent a fruit.

Does that sound goofy? I thought it was sweet and saw my role in this drama. I would be the cherished facilitator, setting untold delights on his plate, finding my joy in his joy. And he would open an underground world of sexual secrets to me. Granted, he was a porn actor. But here I was, at the peak of my own sexual power. It was just another ascent. So he fucked for money. Not nearly as much money as the women got, but top money for a guy, he boasted. But he had an innocence, a fresh way of looking at things, that I found appealing. And he seemed remarkably happy.

I don't remember ever meeting anyone quite that pleased with himself. He filled his afternoons with pleasure—treating himself to a jar of lingonberries, slipping into a theater with the intermission crowds to see the second act of a Broadway play, signing an autograph for a fan on the street. What a turn-on, especially if the fan happened to be a woman. Evenings, he weighed his options, so many delightful options that he could never be bored. He loved his life. He was in love with his work. He never ceased being amazed that he was paid for making love to dewy young beauties and aging Lolitas. Even his tears were joyful. Telling me about an early love he'd lost when she fell in love with another woman, he began to weep. Then he wiped his eyes and smiled.

"That felt good," he said.

After Don's melancholy and the deep discontent I perceived in Andrew, Jamey's talent for happiness was irresistible. To some people, the adult-film world might have seemed dangerous, a sordid scene with drugs and Mob money. But I saw a rather naïve guy, young for his age but smarter than I would have expected—Columbia, after all, and the *New York Times* with coffee every morning. He'd been moved by a certain passiveness into what seemed easy money, but he appeared no more sexually obsessed than I.

I took him into my world. He looked dashing at the Four Seasons or at Frank Valenza's wonderfully outrageous Palace in that pinstriped brown flannel suit he'd worn in *Misty Beethoven*. I had to be subtle and diplomatic to convince him that the lapels of his shirt looked better inside the jacket, not open and out, à la John Travolta in *Saturday Night Fever*. He liked to wear a shiny floral tie that still had its strip of masking tape inside, labeled "orgy scene," his little joke. At gatherings of the lit clique, Gay Talese, immersed then in skinny-dipping research for *Thy Neighbor's Wife,* his monumental opus on swinging in the seventies, was clearly fascinated. Jamey already knew Jerzy Kosinski from grungy cellars of sadomasochism downtown in the Meatpacking District. At The Literary Guild anniversary party at the Four Seasons, they shook hands, grinning, like comrades from a secret sect.

Jamey let me know he had a special girlfriend. She was smart enough to give him freedom to roam, he said. I was seeing him once or twice a week, shamelessly playing to his weakness. I am nothing if not competitive. I dangled Lutèce; he couldn't say no. The Cellar in the Sky at Windows on the World . . . a different wine with every course. How could he resist? He'd grown up in poverty on West 103rd Street, one of six children. "The only white boy in my PAL group," he said, referring to the Police Athletic League. He dreamed of one day buying the brownstone he'd grown up in and turning it into a castle. "I'd invite everyone I love to live in it," he confided.

"What happened to your acting career?" I asked.

"I am an actor." He was clearly insulted. "I make a living as an actor. Not many actors do, you know. Five percent, according to *Variety.* I really tried to find something I could do, something to care about besides acting. I took an aptitude test. I thought maybe law, or teaching. I almost did get a job once teaching in a school for bad boys." He laughed. "If it had been bad girls, I would definitely have taken it."

"And porn?"

"I was doing Shakespeare Off Broadway for nothing and driving a cab for a living. Then one day, I saw an ad for actors to do nude photos. The job paid forty dollars an hour. That was what I took home for driving a cab all day. And it was easy. It was fun. Everyone was sweet, and I loved the sex."

For a while, it looked as if sex films were getting better and there would be a breakthrough, he said. Everyone in the business talked about serious actors doing explicit sex in big-budget Hollywood films. "I felt good about being in the avant-garde. I felt like a sexual missionary," he told me.

His story was touching. I was impressed by that English honors degree. Originally, he'd gone to Hunter to enroll for classes, but he found the system too confusing, he said. A friend knew an administrator at Columbia. There, registration could be arranged. Second from the bottom in his New Jersey high school graduating class, Jamey found himself uncharacteristically motivated in college.

"At Columbia, I just decided to do it. I was at the top of my class. Got all *A*'s and *B*'s. Everyone said, 'This kid has potential.' " He hesitated, aware that I might think he had squandered that potential. He looked away. "There's a need being unfulfilled in me," he said, turning back with a grin. "That's part of my charm."

That charm was working on me. I felt he'd never really had a chance. I wanted to do something to help him. I didn't see red lights blinking. Or if I did, I didn't care. I felt I could handle it. I found his dark world intriguing—the movies shot in two days, women rebelling against deeply religious homes and fundamentalist religions, the men mostly Jewish, all of them paid so little in an industry that raked in millions. He didn't seem to think of himself as exploited. He accepted the limitations; indeed, he was proud that he was among the top-paid men in porn, didn't seem to mind that work was occasional, unpredictable. He was happy. He made just enough money to support an unambitious lifestyle. And oh, the girls. "They were so sweet. So juicy."

"You're like a pig in shit," I said one day. Jamey laughed. "I love what I do." But he was a trained actor, after all, I reasoned. Perhaps all he needed was a little push, a few phone calls to open other doors.

"No one has crossed over from porn to straight film," he told me. Did he seem dangerously passive? I dismissed the thought. With my confidence and connections, he would get the energy to pursue it, I felt sure.

"I was thinking about writing an article on pornography," I said one evening. "But your story is much more interesting. It should be a book."

"Funny," he said. "Jerzy Kosinski told me the same thing. I met him once at a party. What do you think? Should I let Kosinski do my story?"

He wasn't ready to trust me. Too many promises broken, I thought.

Whenever we went to dinner, we'd go dancing after at Regine's or Xenon or the Ice Palace, a dark place with pin lights, butch lesbians, and great disco music. We danced apart, we danced close. Moving slowly to Sinatra, I'd put my hand around his neck, fingers tangled in his dark curls. I find it hard to explain what it was about dancing. The high school wallflower became the queen of the prom. I had great moves. I had the best-looking guy on the dance floor. I was transformed. I had never been good at anything athletic, although I'd always loved to dance, long before disco. Now I was a dancer every night of the week. I could imagine the physical abandon, the elation, the kinetic ecstasy of Cyd Charisse, Leslie Caron, of Ginger Rogers matching Fred Astaire step by step, only backward (as Gloria Steinem pointed out).

There would be a long line vying to get by the doorman at Regine's. Someone would spot me. "Let Miss Greene in," the hostess would call out. Someone would take my long fur cape and hand it to the cloakroom attendant over the heads of mere mortals patiently queued. I was given no coat check—two hundred coats, but no check for mine.

"It's rude the way the woman who takes your coat doesn't even see me," said Jamey. "She doesn't acknowledge I'm standing there. It's rude to you."

"You're right. I'll say something."

"Don't do it for me. I know who I am," he said. "In my world, no one would know you, either."

Camille, the very blond captain I knew from Le Cirque,* would put us at a table up front. Jamey would order Perrier. I would ask for ice water. Camille would bring fancy cookies. And we would wait for the movie star–handsome tuxedo-clad waiters, carnations in their lapels— Regine must have hired a casting director—to push back the screens that hid the dance floor during dinner. Then the DJ would switch vibes from supper-club mellow to jump-around disco. And there was the see-through Plexiglas dance platform, with its pulsating neon.

Jamey never seemed to be in a hurry to get home, unlike other men, normal men with jobs. He so rarely worked, he didn't have to be anywhere at nine o'clock in the morning. As it got later, the after-dinner revelers crowded onto the Lucite floor, anonymous bodies pressing against one another. Jamey closed his eyes, losing himself in the orgiastic intensity of it. I saw his hand brushing a passing chiffoned ass. I let my hand wander, too. He smiled and closed his eyes again. One evening, Elizabeth Taylor danced alongside us, orchid eyes glued to her rangy escort as if he were the next Richard Burton. She seemed to move in a halo of light.

*He later opened Chantilly on Fifty-seventh Street east of Park, now BLT Steak.

Often, it was two or three o'clock in the morning when we claimed my cape and then walked home. The sex was never hotter than the night Jamey spent dancing inches from the exquisite goddess of his dirtiest reveries, the adolescent Brooke Shields. "Oh, my precious baby," he crooned, eyes closed—but so what?

His world, a crazy world. I'm writing a book, I thought. This is research. But in fact, I was being naughty and it was fun. I liked doing whatever it took to turn him on. It was hot. I was a new, more aggressive me. I was learning how many women had passed through his life. He spun the tales slowly for my little notebook and the book we'd agreed to write, but, of course, he was rationing his confessions, not sure what I could handle. One day, he spoke of us in the past tense and I got huffy. I realized I wanted to be the one he could never let go. I was sure we had a blockbuster book. "We're going to be very rich," I promised him. The book would bind him to me. I might never be the one woman, but I could be the one woman he really needed.

We were feeding quarters to the porno-flick machines in a cubicle at Show World on Eighth Avenue, a rare afternoon together ("for the book," I'd suggested).

"I remember this film. Oh, these were my babies, my beautiful babies," he moaned, masturbating as he watched himself flanked by what looked like a pair of Lolitas, rubbing against him on-screen. You didn't buy much footage for a quarter. The machine flicked off. He added another quarter. "I can't believe you're taking notes," he said, zipping up to run outside to the cashier for more quarters. Sticky world. I had a new dimension. I did my work. I met my deadlines. I tasted meals not worth writing about and set up photo shoots for the magazine's issue on entertaining. I dated other men. I danced after dinner with other men. But I obsessed about Jamey. My friend Naomi couldn't understand it. "He sounds to me like a giant mouth," she said. Jean-Louis, at Le Cirque, warned me that he could only be trash and might have something contagious. My wise and permissive therapist, Mildred, thought Jamey was just another symptom of my unresolved neurosis. Don was concerned, "though I don't really have a right to be," he said. Why did nobody understand what I saw in Jamey?

Even as intrepid girl reporter for the *Post,* I had avoided the sleaze of Times Square. And now in the late seventies, the neighborhood was scabrous, full of desperadoes, dealers conducting brazen drug sales on Forty-second Street, scantily dressed runaways from Minnesota in white plastic boots offering themselves on Eighth Avenue. One evening, I found myself trailing Jamey through the tawdry scene, among the child whores and winos, as he stopped at Smiler's for the *Times* and his morning grapefruit, my hair soaking wet from nonstop dancing till 3:00 AM after some fancy benefit, wearing my mink, my black velvet gown sweeping the pavement.

"Why don't we go to your place?" I said.

"I didn't have a chance to clean," he warned as he led me upstairs to his second-story apartment.

I gasped and stumbled as he pushed the door open, stung by the chaos.

He saw my reaction. "I like it this way. It feels cozy to me."

I took care to avoid sliding on the scattered girlie magazines and underwear. There was a home-movie projector next to the unmade bed, clothes draped and dropped everywhere, a half-eaten baguette, turned to wood now, handcuffs and dildos and lacy panties, a riding crop, a black stocking draped over the bathroom mirror, open jars of strawberry jam and dregs of wine in bottles sitting amid the fan mail on the kitchen table, unwashed plates piled into the sink. A cockroach I pretended not to see skittered away. I wondered how he could dress at night and emerge so pressed and clean from this chaos. It must have some special meaning to him, I thought.

He ignored me, settling into an armchair with the *Times,* an unlit pipe in his mouth. Above him hung a blowup of himself with a riding crop from the film *Through the Looking Glass.*

I stood there in my coat, disgusted, thinking I might leave. I could catch something in the bathroom, I thought. My fur might pick up a cockroach. I was a woman who had amorous adventures in marble bathtubs in five-star hotels. I used lavender soap from Provence and olive oil bars from Les Baux. What was I doing here? I walked to the door. He said nothing. I decided I would stay and not let myself think about it, not let the mess creep me out, not brood about germs or crawly things. I found a hanger for my gown and a couple of wire hangers that would support my coat. In the bathroom, I touched up my makeup and took off the bra and panties I was wearing under a lacy black satin teddy. I liked myself in his mirror, breasts billowing immodestly in the deep décolletage, thighs and legs looking very long in high heels and the lace-edged slit of the panties. I walked into the bedroom, kicking aside a high-heeled pump lying on a magazine, and stood there.

Jamey got up from his chair, turned out the lights, lighted the stub of a candle next to the bed with a cigarette lighter. The window shade was up and I could see the marquee of the Martin Beck Theater across the street, visible in the streetlight. Jamey settled the pillows under his head. I caught myself wondering how many times a year he changed his sheets, then shook my head to banish the thought.

I dropped to the bed on all fours and purred. He closed his eyes.

I was in my own porn movie.

36

SKIN FLICK

I NEVER FOR A MINUTE THOUGHT I COULD POSSIBLY FALL IN LOVE WITH THE Prince of Porn. Surely he would be the ultimate unattainable man. I was too smart for that trap. For me, it was only about sex. I wanted to feel every nerve ending. I wanted to know everything, to experience all the variations, to taste it all. And so did he. He was eager to bite into birds he'd never known existed, to fathom the mystery of truffles, to guzzle Armagnac for the first time. He seemed not to know he was embarrassing me by picking up a rib eye in a fancy restaurant and eating from the bone. I tried to pretend I found that charming. Finally, I got the courage to suggest it was not good manners to pick up a dinner roll and gnaw it in the middle. And good manners, silly as they might be, counted in the places we went. "I hope you don't mind my sharing a little etiquette from Emily Post," I said. "My mom was big on Emily Post."

"Is that the one who committed suicide?" he asked.

I didn't say he wasn't smart. "Oh, you mean Amy Vanderbilt." I was taking him into my world and I let him know I expected him to show me his. "For the book," I reminded him. Our tastes were often quite similar. Sorbets could never be too tart for him. We could agree on that. Meat must be rare. Wine was red, except for dessert wine. He quickly developed a passion for Château d'Yquem. Our alliance was not merely sybaritic; it was symbiotic in its pursuit of sensuous feasts.

So it was becoming more complex than just hot sex. Of course, most everyone close to me—and I suppose anyone who cared to think about us, across the table or a dance floor, alerted by an item in Liz Smith's column or a sighting in the *Post*'s Page Six—assumed it was all about bodice-ripping, uninhibited, beyond-fantasy sex. Porn fans and Jamie Gillis fans probably imagined black-leather moments and playful threesomes. But I was in bed with Jamey, not Jamie, and prize movie stud though he was—he could always get himself into the mood and bring me along to a grand finale and many curtain calls—he had exasperating taboos.

"Why do all women just want to be dominated?" It was so exhausting, he complained. He adored the woman who led him around town with a string on his cock and tugged it at dinner. Yet he would focus on some woman nearby giving him the eye, or, even more tantalizing, pretending to ignore him. "She's asking for it," he would say. "I would tie her up and make her beg."

"Yes. Yes," I said. "You can tie me up and dominate me—nothing really serious, of course. I'm not into pain."

He refused. "I just don't think of you that way."

Jamey was not a country person, he told me, but I lured him to the little church in Woodstock by promising to cook a feast for us—quail, an aged entrecôte that I would pan-sauté, chicken livers, rare, the way we both loved them, and whatever bottle he might choose from the generous stash Don had left in the cellar. Jean-Louis, though wary of Jamey, didn't seem to mind loaning me his huge van, fitted out for hunting deer, carpeted with fake fur, guns and knives tucked in the rear.

I'm not sure how it happened. We were almost to Kingston on the thruway, when suddenly I lost control of the van. It veered off the highway and started turning over. How many times? Over and over, down an incline. So slowly, I had time to think about what was happening. This is it. We're never getting out of this alive . . . can't possibly not be smashed, maimed, scarred. I waited for the roof of the car to crush us. Jamey was flying through the van. It stopped on its side. He was lying in the debris of Jean-Louis's cooking gear in the rear. I was hanging upside down from my seat belt, shouting again and again, "Jamey. Are you all right? Are you all right, Jamey?"

He crawled toward me. "I think I'm all right." He looked dazed, as if shocked to be alive. People were crawling all over the van. Someone opened the driver's seat door and pulled me up. Someone else unlocked the belt. Jamey handed me my purse. Someone pulled him out. I watched him stretch, testing his bones to see if anything was broken, hopping on one foot and then the other. There was a tiny cut on his rib cage, shaped like a tear. He dabbed at it, standing there looking slight in his navy blue T-shirt.

"I'm a nurse," a woman said. "Everyone get away from the car," a man commanded. "It might explode." We moved toward the road. The two of us collapsed, seated on the gravel and broken asphalt of the thruway shoulder.

"Shall I call an ambulance?" a cop asked.

I had just returned from two weeks in Chicago, where my brother, Jim, a doctor of emergency medicine, had arranged for me to observe emergency technique, research for my new novel, *Doctor Love.* I knew too much about emergency rooms.

"Unless there's something seriously wrong, we'll be stuck there for hours," I whispered to Jamey. I made him tug on my hands to see if one side was stronger. I looked into his pupils for signs of a concussion. The crowd was thinning. Miraculously, the van had not exploded. But they said it was probably totaled. Someone handed me my wallet. A biker helped Jamey pick up all our stuff from the field. "I've got to find the quail," Jamey said.

A friend from Kingston came to take us to my house. "Is it safe to leave you?" he asked. "You're sure you are both really all right?" Once he was gone, I started to shake. If I were with any other man, I would be hysterical now, I thought. But I have to be calm because it's Jamey and he is fragile. I have committed myself to taking care of him. He was so quiet, watchful, staring at me. I could see he was shaken.

"What happened?" He backed me up against the refrigerator. "Try to remember what happened." He pressed the side of his face against mine.

"It must have been a rut in the highway." The pressure of his body gave me a sense the world was not spinning off its axis. I let it be enough. "Here. Help me unwrap the steak."

I ran water for his bath, spilled in bubbles. While he was soaking and trying to calm down, I fetched a bottle of Lafite from the cellar and set it on the counter. I put bacitracin and a Band-Aid on the sink.

"The sour cream disappeared," he said, coming up behind me. "Will the chicken livers be all right without sour cream?"

"But look, the brownies survived."

"You didn't do it just for the book?" he asked.

I convinced him I did not, would not.

"We are the kind of people who think first about the quail." He was coming around. "Good Jamey." He patted himself on the back. "I like to do that when I've been good," he told me.

We carried dinner trays to the steps of what had been the church's altar, sitting in front of the fire I got roaring (after Don's tutorials), sipping the luscious Lafite, which was slightly warmed from its time in the kitchen.

"It's thrilling to eat something as tiny as a quail," he remarked. "I'm not overwhelmed by being taken care of, because I know I control you sexually."

By the time I washed up and put everything away, he was asleep in the bedroom. I lay awake next to him, remembering a series of auto accidents I'd had in my dad's car the year I got my license. Mom, in diplomatic mode, persuaded my father not to tear up the license. I thought of how pleased my father was when Don and I called to say we'd bought a house upstate, though he couldn't understand why anyone would want to live in a church. He died of a stroke at fifty-six and never got to see our home or my dream kitchen, gutted and stripped and polished. Like Jamey, he never understood weekends in the country. I lay there weeping silently. Jamey turned and snuggled close, making a few snuffly sleeping sounds, then making love to me lazily, gently, as if not quite awake.

"Isn't it time to go?" Jamey asked the next day after a short walk in the cemetery that bounded our—I say our, but it was mine now, since the divorce—tiny acreage on the hill outside Woodstock.

"We need more time to recover," I protested.

He looked at his watch again.

"You bitch. Come here." He slouched in the tall covered bishop's chair, legs wide apart. He took off his belt and bound my wrists . . . pushed me down onto the thick fur of the rug, ripped at my panties. He unzipped his jeans . . . he was naked, as always, underneath—and filled me up. He slapped me lightly with the end of the belt. I couldn't help it. I felt so silly. I started to laugh. After all, I'd begged for this. He slapped me again. I gave in to the pleasure.

Afterward, the girl reporter in me couldn't shut up: "Was I supposed to struggle?" I asked.

"You're not *supposed* to do anything but what you feel," he snapped.

"I'm just trying to understand the game."

"It's not a game." He was annoyed, began zipping up, then turned away.

"But it's a fantasy, and I'm just trying to understand. Maybe it's a question of semantics."

He picked up his overnight bag, a brown paper sack. "I like them to struggle a little."

I bit my tongue, trying not to laugh, and went off to pack up the leftovers. "Want the last brownie?" I asked.

He pulled me into a hug. "It's okay," he said. "I tasted arugula and VSOP and I didn't die. I think that means something."

For the first time, I felt the enormity of how close we had been to death. Miracles—that the van didn't crush us, that the engine didn't burst into flames, that Jamey didn't land on Jean-Louis's free-flying kitchen knife. Oh God. What could I say to poor Jean-Louis?

"We lived a lot," I agreed, "considering it was just half a weekend."

I felt I was beginning to touch Jamey, opening him up to the world's possibilities. I felt challenged by his strangeness. How different he was from anyone I'd ever known. Who would play me in the movie? What would we call our book? *When Narcissists Collide?*

Jamey decided to go to France with me on my spring tasting swing for the magazine. I thought he was the dream candidate for the trip. We seemed to love all the essentials—sex, dinner, and dancing. He had two perfectly acceptable suits and a tie. No wife and no nagging job obligations. Alas, he was afraid to fly. Why couldn't I go by boat? he wondered. Wouldn't a boat trip be the perfect time for our collaboration on the book?

"I don't have that much time, baby."

He brooded. "Maybe we could take the *Concorde*. It's new, and they're still trying to make a good impression. They wouldn't let it crash." Once he'd been forced to fly to Britain, he told me. "I couldn't decide if I should go BOAC, with a pilot who did it a million times and knew everything, or on Japan Air Lines, where they might not be so nonchalant." He had finally chosen JAL because they served sushi.

Jamey called an astrologer to ask for dates that might be good to fly. The response agitated him. "The astrologer said, 'Do *not* fly. There's a bad sequence of Uranus in Saturn.' " He weighed cashing in his small cache of stock, everything he owned, to pay for overseas passage by boat. But that would add two weeks to his time away. "When do you plan to arrive?" he asked me.

"Friday the thirteenth."

"I'd consider another date."

"Well, Jamey, maybe you should just forget it, let it go. Now you've got me spooked. I'm not getting on any plane with you." I offered to find him a more professional astrologer. Often, I amazed myself with my patience. I hadn't the tiniest faith in astrology and yet I was financing the hiring of some charlatan to draw up his chart.

We were at dinner. He took my hand. "Tell me again, sweetie. Tell me again what we're gonna do in Paris? Will we go to the Bois de Boulogne at night and fuck in the car while people watch?"

"Yes. Yes. Yes. We'll do it all. We'll do everything." Why not?

"If I fly, I could save twelve hundred dollars. For twelve hours of torture, that's one hundred dollars an hour I'd be saving. Good money. Not even your therapist gets that much."

We were at the Brussels Restaurant, his choice, in honor of his birthday. He found our captain impressive. "I should hire him one day for my staff." He was playing with the idea of getting rich from the acting jobs my connections would bring him. I'd sent him to an agent, who seemed more taken with my interest in him than in his acting career. "It is Circe's fate to live with swine," she said. I thought that rude. But she promised to send him on casting calls.

The appetizer of brains, sweetbreads, truffle, and bean sprouts in a heavy vinaigrette on red leaf lettuce seemed to knock him out. "It reminds me of the French director Artaud," he said. "He wanted to put the audience in the middle and surround them with the actors. A dizzying immersion in spectacle."

He was full of little gifts like that.

Another evening at dinner, Jamey apologized for dragging me into his romantic problems, but he said he needed to let me know that his girlfriend Andrea was unhappy about his going, especially about the money and time wasted on the boat, which would leave no time or money for their planned vacation in June. "She says I want to have my cake and eat it, too. She says she won't be waiting when I come back." I thought it was his backward way of showing how much he was willing to sacrifice to be with me.

"I would have thought Andrea would know by now that loving you is for masochists," I told him. "I thought she understood she'd always be sharing you." Was I speaking for myself? Surely not. I still figured I was above it all. I saw Jamey clear as cellophane. A playmate who would take me places in bed I'd never been. I knew enough not to count on him. There would always be other women. Eleanora Duse had said it of D'Annunzio: "His life is like a tavern. Everyone passes through it." D'Annunzio was hot and a handful. I knew exactly why Eleanora put up with it.

It was several days before Jamey was to leave on the *QE2,* and he really didn't have time to play, he told me when I called. I interpreted that to mean he was saving every moment to jolly Andrea out of her anger. But I had been invited to sample the ultimate in sleepover luxury. Augustin Paege, the thirty-one-year-old Bulgarian host of the Box Tree, a man-nered little restaurant launched in upstate Purdys (its namesake opened later in Manhattan with a five-thousand-dollar loan from Bankers Trust), wanted me to do a test run of new lodgings he'd been gilding above the inn. "He's sending a Rolls to pick us up," I said. "A Rolls in a very English gray." Jamey miss it? I didn't think so.

The Box Tree family was waiting for us. There was champagne on ice— Louis Roederer Cristal. A Lalique flute was pressed into my hand as we entered the small 1775 farmhouse and Augustin Paege welcomed us. Paege, born in "austerity," as he liked to put it, always hinting of connections with the banished Bulgarian royals, had unimpeachable style. He favored the Duke of Windsor look in country dress. His driver, in full livery, would chauffeur him about Manhattan in an open Jeep. Why not the Rolls? The Jeep was easier to maneuver.

Augustin was justifiably proud as he led the tour. Every stick of wood was period or had an impressive pedigree. He'd culled the Farouk estate. Upstairs, there was a bottle of madly expensive Romanee Conti on the table of the Louis XV suite, the private dining room, alongside fruit as shiny and perfect as any in a Renaissance painting.

"I didn't realize cherries were in season already," I said.

The humble innkeeper (as he often described himself) smiled. "They *are* at Box Tree."

There were twin Napoléon beds with opossum coverlets in the Consulat Room, $190 a night. But we chose the François 1 suite at $220, where a canopied four-poster was dressed in bed linens fine as Swiss hankies (one thousand dollars a set from the purveyors to Buckingham Palace). Hundreds of Canadian lynxes had given their soft bellies to make the fur throw. Forsythia and lilacs were bunched in a giant tub. The alarm clock was Cartier. Caswell-Massey cologne, blended for George Washington, filled a jeroboam. The armoire was Louis XIII, its hangers like voluptuous sculpture. There were eucalyptus leaves to scent the crackling fire. Of course a Box Tree bathroom would have a bidet, Paege pointed out, and fat, fluffy towels big as most bedsheets, vast enough to wrap Bob and Carol and Ted and Alice.

"Shall I unpack for you?" asked Kevin, our valet.

Too bourgeois to have a stranger unpack my sex toys, I sent Kevin away. I stripped to my chemise and undressed Jamey as he lay submissively on the bed. I wrapped him in the lynx. He got up and stood in front of the tall pedestal mirror. "I look good in anything I wear."

"Give me that," I said, spreading the fur on the floor. And he did.

Box Tree's kitchen itself needed editing, I noted in my judiciously expurgated review. But there were dazzling details: a too-big portion of Stilton from a cheesecloth-wrapped round and splendid Mexican coffee. Everything was done with style and wit and exaggerated pretension. Jamey looked very country squire in his blue velvet jacket, helping himself to an orange from the bowl on the mantel.

"I bet they are upstairs now, redoing our room, rearranging the hairs of the lynx," I said.

"I wish we were going to Italy," he said. "You'd be wonderful in Italy. You're so ripe."

"Are we like Lea and Chéri, do you think? There's about the same age difference between us as there was between Lea and Chéri. But they lazed away in bed and had all kinds of feasts, and she taught him about women, not that I can tell you anything you don't know."

Colette had written, "*Je suit gourmette, gourmande, gloutone.*"

"Of course, the awful part is that he leaves her to marry that young girl," I said, depressing myself.

"But you forget," said Jamey. "He comes back and she won't see him. She doesn't want him to see her fat and old. And he is the one that's rejected." He took my hand and held it to his cheek. "I feel a little sickly. I think I'll take an orange for later."

Upstairs after dinner, there was more Roederer Cristal in the ice bucket beside the bed, a box of Godiva chocolates, and the life of the Marquis de Sade on the bedside table, rosebuds on the fur throw, giant peonies on the pillows. Kevin drew the bath, scattering salts from the south of France "to exercise the skin," and backed out of the room. Jamey climbed into the tub. There were sponges big as bowling balls, Italian toothpaste, almond soap in the tub, violet soap at the sink.

When I grabbed a towel to warm it in front of the fire for him, the thick glass shelf fell off the wall. It cracked the top of the toilet tank and fell into the tub, just missing him, because he was standing, ready to step out. The noise echoed.

"Maybe they think we're killing each other," he said.

"They are probably out there trying to decide if they should break in or be discreet," I whispered.

"That's what you get when you leave a volume of the Marquis de Sade on the night table," said Jamey.

We crawled into bed, spilling pink peony petals to the floor. In the light from the fire, I watched Jamey lift the full-blown peony to his face. I could smell the scent from my pillow. He buried his face in the flower, purring and moaning. I felt my eyes fill with tears. I lay back beside him. What was wrong with me? Why was I feeling cheated? We'd shared a wonderful, silly, preposterously luxurious evening. Wasn't that enough? I wiped my eyes, getting mascara on the queen's own linens. Jamey was watching me.

"I can't believe you're jealous of a flower," he said.

And incredibly, I was.

37

WHAT I LEARNED
ON SPRING BREAK

ALONE IN PARIS BEFORE JAMEY'S BOAT DOCKED, I HAD TIME TO EAT OUT with old friends, to rewire a light flirtation with Eric Rothschild, and to share a dinner with Julia and Paul Child. Julia swept into the lobby of my hotel. And as she swept, she knocked against the bouquet of flowers on the tall pedestal at the door. It tipped. I gasped. Behind her, Paul Child caught it mid-topple and set it straight. What a team, I thought. Not only did they adore each other, but Paul was always there, seemingly content to swim in her wake, picking up whatever she might bowl over in her exuberant passage through life.

Their love story, as they told it, was almost Victorian, sweetly eccentric. They had met while serving in the Office of Strategic Services during World War II in the Far East. "I was an old maid of thirty," she told me. "And he was an old maid, too." Before they made the final decision to marry, they went home to introduce each other to their families. "And to see if we felt the same way about each other in civilian clothes or if it was just the uniform," she said, eyes twinkling at the preposterous thought. Of course she always made it clear that he was an equal partner.

I had toted all three volumes of *Mastering the Art of French Cooking* in a shopping bag for Julia to autograph when we met for lunch at Le Cygne two years earlier. She signed each one and then passed it on for Paul to sign. "They're his books, too," she said. The how-to drawings had been made from Paul's photographs.

Le Cygne's owners, Gérard Gallian from Grasse and Michel Crouzillat of Toulouse, did headstands to please us. Julia had met Gérard's mother while filming a spot for her show in the Nice market. The courses of our $8.95 lunch kept multiplying.

"I get upset when the kitchen sends out extras and refuses to put them on the bill," I complained, not wanting to make a fuss over the missing items on the bill in front of Julia and Paul.

"I think we should just enjoy it," Julia cried in her wonderful bass falsetto. "Who knows how long it will last."

That afternoon in Paris, I was taking all of us to the Tour d'Argent, on *New York,* of course. I remember we crowded into the restaurant's small ornate elevator, and a bellman pulled a brocade curtain to hide the metal grille, wrapping us in a satin cocoon. Amazingly, the cocoon was air-conditioned, and illuminated by a bulb inside a glass rose held aloft by a cherub. On our large starchily cloaked table was a crystal duck, a box of matches, toothpicks, silver service plates.

Unfortunately, I was no longer anonymous at the Tour d'Argent, which most critics agreed was not the strong Michelin three-star establishment it had once been. The tall, startlingly lean patron, Claude Terrail, wearing his signature blue cornflower in the moiré lapel of his midnight velvet suit, greeted me, executed a snappy bow, and kissed the air above my knuckles. I introduced Julia and Paul, of course, and was shocked to see that he didn't have a clue as to who she was—this legend among American foodies. Indeed, there was an instant buzz of recognition from the many American couples ringing the room in the prime window seats looking out at Notre Dame, fingers pointing, banquette bouncing as they spied their goddess. Julia smiled and nodded, and crinkled her eyes in a wink of pleasure in every direction. Paul muttered.

Even then, the self-important Monsieur Terrail was oblivious, so focused was he on himself and me. It was not a stellar night for La Tour d'Argent. Our duck, unashamed to wear its identification tag, #432,728, was dry. A good enough bean and lentil soup seemed strangely rustic for such a grand setting. Julia, with regret, pronounced her fish, the *barbue,* not just boring, not just a bit old, but rotten. In that voice: "Rotten." And the sommelier, a little old man with caved-in cheeks and a wisp of white hair, got lost after delivering our fine red Beaune wine, and left us to pour it on our own. Our lunch for five cost $135, a princely sum for the time. No wonder I was indignant. America was shifting into the throes of a revolution, learning to cook French with Julia. And France was so full of itself, it hadn't noticed: It had yet to recognize our own fiery Jeanne d'Arc.

Watching for Jamey on the quai where the boat train had lurched to a stop, I saw a bobbing head of curly dark hair. Jamey? No, sorry, look again. It was a young guy, taller, very handsome, and he was following Jamey. Were they lovers? How quickly my paranoia flared. Was this better or worse than a luscious blonde or a brunette with fat lips?

"This is Jon, from the boat," Jamey cried. "I told him all about you. Can he stay with us?" The quick, distracted, perfunctory kiss at the train station got us off to a cool start.

"It's a tiny room, Jamey," I protested. I'd moved to the Plaza Athénée in his honor and been given a cramped cubbyhole.

"We can drop him at his hotel, then," Jamey offered.

"We can't. It's at the opposite end of town. And we'll be late for dinner at Regine's."

There were not enough taxis. I grabbed a door to stop one and threw his suitcase inside, looking around for him. "Jamey." He had disappeared. "Jamey."

He ran toward me, then back to Jon. They stood talking and laughing. The cabbie was going crazy, threatening to pull away with the bag in his trunk. Jamey and Jon were exchanging phone numbers. Jamey yelled, "Why did you do that to me?" He was furious as he settled beside me. My fantasy of our romantic reunion was threatened. "You didn't let me say what I wanted."

"Well, say it."

"I was afraid to say what I wanted."

"Well, you'd better start saying what you feel, or this trip is not going to work. I can't know unless you tell me." It had never occurred to me that I might not want to know all the specifics of what he needed.

He was calmer now. "That was the worst part," he said. "The worst part is over. Now it can only get better." At Regine's, I suggested he choose dinner for us. He was instantly full of good cheer. So many options. How could he decide? The waiter suggested trying a little of everything. Jamey reared up, wiggling his nose like a racehorse. *"Mais oui."* He kissed my hand.

Afterward in our tiny room, I bathed and got into a lacy new nightgown. He lay in bed, propped up on pillows, reading a girlie magazine, ignoring me. I had put myself to sleep—flushed, if not feverish—for the last few nights by imagining this moment. I was so hot. I snuggled close. He sighed. "It's not all it's cracked up to be, is it? Going with a porn star."

"Damn you." I rolled out of bed and onto the floor, pulling the velvet spread along with me. "I don't need you. I have myself."

He turned a page, smoked his cigarette, turned another. Finally, he switched off the lamp, lighted a candle with his cigarette lighter, and slid to the floor. "Bad girl. Bad girl."

In the morning, I nearly slipped on the magazine, catching myself just in time. I studied a few wrinkled pages. What had turned him on? A woman draped over a Bugatti. The woman? Or the Bugatti? I supposed it didn't really matter. We would be fine once he settled down and discovered what a perfect trip I'd planned.

The next night, we had tickets to Crazy Horse after dinner. I'd seen the revue before, brilliantly cast and performed by about fifteen or twenty remarkably beautiful women of every nationality, stripping, dancing, marching in unison, performing erotic skits in daringly suggestive leather bibs and harnesses. All had the same adorable S curve of the spine, and perfect standup tits. Clearly, the producer was an ass man. With one exception, each ass looked exactly alike. But that one was like a full-blown red rose in a tight bouquet of pink buds—the gorgeous bottom of Trucula Bonbon.

I didn't need Jamey, electrically charged beside me, fired by waves of happiness, to know how erotic the show could be. "There's not a flaw there," he whispered. "Maybe I should be a talent scout for Crazy Horse."

Back in our room, he danced with me and kissed me. "Such beauty," he cried. "It makes a man feel unworthy. I would line them all up. It would make a great porn movie. About a man who leaves a great job to work backstage at Crazy Horse. How would it end?"

"Sadly, of course," I said. "Like *The Blue Angel.*"

"You are going to get me Trucula Bonbon," he said. "Yes, you will."

And so there was a second night of mind-searing sex. Was he closing his eyes and seeing images of that ass? I couldn't have cared less. After all, the body in ecstasy was mine.

Jamey was not a morning person. I knew that by then. But we needed to face breakfast soon so we could meet friends for lunch. A waiter wheeled it in. I set out the exotic fruits I had collected for him from Fauchon at ridiculous cost: mangosteen, fresh lichees, passion fruit, his favorite, our favorite, the fruit itself hidden inside its ugly pocked shell. Till now, he'd only tasted the fruit as sorbet. I opened the curtains just enough to wake him. He put on his glasses, glanced at the *Trib,* tossed it aside, then took the rose from its bud vase and sniffed it. "No smell," he said, dropping it on the table. In the morning, he wore glasses until he'd showered and dressed and decided he felt like putting in his contact lenses. He looked younger and vulnerable in his glasses, like a student. He picked up the small brown mangosteen.

"Peel it like this," I said.

He laughed like a child. "A new fruit." He bit off a small piece of an opalescent white segment, and then another. He rubbed the rest of it all over his face. "Oh my. Oh my." He was crying.

His tears reminded me of Don. But anything could bring Jamey to tears, not just sadness. He wept when he was moved by beauty. He was swept by emotion over a taste he'd never experienced before. I've never been with a man so in touch with his emotions. I found it moving that a man could cry over a peach. He was so unlike most men. Of course, his everyday needs were exhausting, too.

"I still need my regular morning grapefruit," he said.

How could I possibly have overlooked the grapefruit?

"Why are you crying?" he asked. "Are you jealous of the fruit?"

"It's good to cry," I said. "Isn't that what you always say?"

We boarded the night train for Lausanne, toting a massive picnic "just in case," though we'd just put away dinner. It would be my second visit to the restaurant of Frédy Girardet, the hot new hajj for cuisinary pilgrims that spring of 1977. As a youth, Girardet had played soccer. He had never done a serious kitchen apprenticeship. He had helped out in the family bistro. Then, on a wine-buying excursion to Burgundy, friends took him for lunch at Troisgros. That lunch was an epiphany. He'd come home to this tiny town to astonish the locals and even himself. Girardet was handsome, with a sensual flare of features, blond hair brushed back from a high forehead. To hear him talk in his slow, almost uninflected deep purple satin voice was to know that he was driven by some transcendent vision.

"Yes, a salmon is only a fish, after all," I wrote. "An artichoke is a thistle; watercress, a weed. But in Girardet's hands a fish, a thistle and a weed become a poem that haunts." I remember langoustines in a green chive cream, their flesh so fragile and tender, they might have been raw, or perhaps merely "cooked" for a minute or two with lemon . . . "as if all other prawns before these had been coarse imitators."

"Come for a week," Girardet had said. "I'll cook you ten different dishes every day."

Now I'd returned, saying very little to Jamey, for fear of diluting the pleasure of discovery. It was crowded at lunch. The restaurant was now often booked months in advance and the chef was not about to turn his Geneva regulars away. We were seated at a table for two, madame on the banquette, of course, Jamey with his back to the room. "Don't they know who you are?" he asked. "We should be side by side at a bigger table."

I promised we would trade seats halfway through so that he could look at the room instead of the wall. Sipping the very ordinary Swiss white wine Girardet wanted us to drink, I felt a certain anxiety. Memory has a way of exaggerating ecstasy. But not this time. With the first bite of a barely gelled sea creature, I relaxed. Girardet had been touched by the gospel of the nouvelle cuisine that had converted most of France, but he didn't stumble into it willy-nilly. His control of heat was uncanny. He had discovered not how long but how little a shrimp or a fish needed to be cooked. The breast of a chicken emerging from his kitchen was so moist and delicate, you might think he'd invented a new breed of bird. He blanched parsley as if it was spinach, then simmered it in butter. A thin peppery broth was studded with small slices of achingly sweet melon and bits of raw salmon and *loup de mer*. Frédy grinned and called it gazpacho. Fabergé might have designed the ballotine, a mosaic of sea creatures with a core that was pale pink, moist, and soft as a ripe peach.

It had to be salmon, but no salmon I'd ever eaten anywhere had quite that astonishing mouth feel.

Tears were falling down Jamey's cheeks. "If there's a heaven, this is what they'll serve the good kids," he said, licking a tear that had strayed to his mouth. He came to sit beside me on the banquette, refusing my hankie. "The tears feel good. When I was eighteen, I went to see Marcel Marceau the first time and it was like this. It was almost a religious experience. Another dizzying immersion. I decided to be a mime, not an actor, but a mime. I took some classes. But that was bold. This is brilliant. The unexpected. So exciting."

After lunch, we walked endlessly, exploring nearby Lausanne, racing across bridges, desperate to get enough exercise before the reckless gluttony of dinner. After all, to come so far and not stay for dinner was not thinkable. It was as if I'd never seen Lausanne before seeing it with Jamey. "I can't believe it," he said, pinching me, then pinching me again. "I have to pinch myself to keep control," he told me. "I didn't realize I was pinching you. . . . It must be a compliment. I'm sharing with you."

I marveled at the intricacies of his thinking. I marveled at how easily I adjusted to it. Well, they were just light pinches. I started seeing everything through his eyes. The women were beautiful. An adolescent girl parked her bicycle nearby and he was mesmerized. He stopped, struck dumb, pulled me close, pinched my arm, kissed my neck. She looked up at us as if she could feel his stare. I pulled him along. At the top of the hill, there was a fruit stand with perfect fruit, exquisitely displayed. "Oh my, what a town. It has everything. Fruit and asses." There was a melon we had never seen anywhere—a green cantaloupe. Called a "honey melon," it was from Israel, the vendor said. Jamey had to have it, and two kinds of passion fruit.

Back in the hotel, there was only time to shower, suck the juice from a passion fruit, and change for dinner. I liked to make love before dinner, and I'd imagined a seduction scenario where I would forbid Jamey to taste the melon . . . until. To most mortals, that would be a non sequitur. But it might turn him on, I thought. The night before, he had ignored me, turned away and lay there reading one of his sex magazines till I finally fell asleep.

"I have needs, too," I said as we drove back to the suburb of Crissier. "Like the way you needed that passion fruit. It was there. You had to have it. I know you need to have sex at least once a day. You told me so. It's in my notes. It's not as if you don't want it, too."

"But I'm happy just jerking off to a magazine," he said, catching my mouth about to go off. "And we do have sex," he said. "You get more sex from me than Andrea. She's content if we have sex every four or five days. I've never been with anyone this close, this intimate for so long. It's not what I'm used to. You do realize that what turns me on are very young girls."

"I thought young girls were just one of your turn-ons. What about the Lindner woman?" I had given him a postcard of one of the artist's cold and menacing women, which he carried in one of his pockets.

"I can get into that, too. But it's really very young girls. Like the twelve-year-olds in David Hamilton's photographs. I don't even know what I would do with them. I would never scare or shock them. Unless they are little sluts, begging for it."

"You're scaring me. The girl on the bike. Is she a slut?"

"It's difficult to tell from far away." He looked at me. "Just kidding."

There was some residual tension as dinner began, though now we were seated at a larger table, side by side on the banquette. "Can't you get Frédy to let us order some French wine?" Jamey said in a baby voice I was starting to dislike. Girardet would not hear of it. Switzerland should have knighted him for forcing all those unthrilling wines on his worshipful clients. We'd ordered the duck for two. But now, Jamey spied a gorgeous rack of lamb being carved by a captain across the room.

"I want to go over and pick up a chop," he said, squeezing my thigh. "Stop me." Fortunately, the artful nonchalance of the maître d'hôtel, Louis, carving our duck breast distracted the gourmand's gourmand. Jamey sat there fascinated, as if he were watching Fred Astaire, his eyes filling with tears. Turned carrots, turnips, the tiniest onions tossed in butter to achieve a caramel glaze surrounded thin, perfect pink duck slices. The legs would be served separately with more of the same vegetables and a certain awe for our stamina.

"It would be nice if we could set aside a few hectares in New York to raise ducks, and maybe lambs and the haricots verts," Jamey said. "I wonder where I get my good taste?" he mused. "Frédy's food is a miracle. I could kill the guy in the kitchen at Regine's, trying to pass off their schlock work." I had to smile, thinking how quickly he had become a food critic. "What I hate is schlock work. I have to work with a lot of people who don't care what they do."

"Is there anyone in porn who loves it as much as you do?" I asked.

"Probably not."

As always, wherever we went, we found a place to dance after dinner. As always we, or certainly I, raised the mean age of the crowd considerably. We were better dancers, too, Manhattan disco pros, looser than these tight little Swiss and even the French. "Dance with whomever you want. I'm going to the loo," I told Jamey, suddenly taken with the idea that letting him go would keep him closer. When I got back, the music had slowed to a Sinatra croon. I saw Jamey holding some twenty-ish thing close, not an inch between them, their cheeks pressed together.

"My turn," I said, cutting in, trying to hide my despair.

He let her go and walked to the bar, lighting a cigarette.

"You gave it to me," he said. "You had no right to take it away. Stupid. Stupid. It was such a wonderful night, and you took it away."

He was like the little girl with the little curl right in the middle of her forehead. When he was good, he was very, very good, and when he was bad, he was horrid. One evening at dinner, a woman came in selling roses. He bought one with his own money, gave her an extra franc. For a moment, I almost melted. Then I realized, of course, he'd bought the rose for himself. He sniffed it, smiled, set it beside his plate. I decided not to take his need for a rose personally.

I noticed he seemed to be taping his diary every day, as he'd promised. He would walk on the street with the tape recorder or stand on the balcony. One day, he couldn't make the recorder work. "I dropped it," he explained. "Maybe if I drop it again, it will start working." He dropped it on the carpet. He dropped it again. Switched it on. "Well, that did it." He seemed very pleased with his technological breakthrough.

He was sulky and wanted to wear shoes without socks to dinner at Père Bise in Talloires. "I came here once with the most romantic man," I said, remembering a night in this same hotel with Murray. "I must have been crazy to bring you here to denigrate that memory."

"I bet my cock was bigger."

"Well, to be honest, actually, it wasn't."

He sat in shocked silence.

There were amazing highs, a stunningly excessive picnic at the side of the road, the stirring dinner at Alain Chapel's in Mionnay, when our every gesture seemed in sync. "I love how needy we are," he said. "You're searching for something rare and wonderful. I'm searching for something wonderful, too. The wonderful thing is that we know when it's wonderful. Some people don't even recognize when they're in the middle of heaven. We do. It's a gift, you know, to live life in the present."

But by the time we reached Cannes, nerves were frayed. Both of us were suffering. With no control over his daily existence, Jamey was starting to unravel. He didn't want to make love anymore. "I'm like a prisoner," he said. "I've never been with just one person for three weeks."

I had not seen the downside of a prolonged play date with Jamey. I was exasperated. "I didn't kidnap you. I invited you for an extraordinary adventure. The boat made it longer." At home, I knew, he picked up street girls, slept with girlfriends and ex-girlfriends, even had sex with the photographer and reporter from *Porn Times*. It was his idea of a perfect interview—and theirs, too. I had it all written in my notes. Yet it had never occurred to me that we couldn't find enough ways to do it to keep him content. I would be the daddy. He would be the little girl. He would be the daddy and I would be the little girl. I was the madam. He was the john. I pretended to hate men. There was no way he could please me. I had fantasies to spare. I was game. But he was feeling more and more deprived, caged, all those beautiful girls on the beach, in the shops, at Dino de Laurentiis's table inches from ours at Tétou, the bouillabaisse restaurant in Golfe Juan. All those possibilities, such a short leash. By denying me sex, he was at least somewhat in charge.

Julia Child invited us for lunch on the hillside of the home she and Paul had built on the property of Simone Beck at Plascassier, overlooking the Mediterranean. The Becks had given them the land with the understanding that the Childs, who had no children, would will the house to the Becks' offspring.

"We're going to have a nice *salade composée,*" said Julia in that rolling profundo that promised if she could cook it, you could, too. And if she dropped the duck and picked it up and wiped it off . . . well, so could you. I read someone else's essay about lunch with Julia, and she raved about the *salade composée.* I must admit I was disappointed. Disappointed? Shocked. What did I expect? Nothing complicated. A lovely cold pork roast. A deviled chicken. I was not demanding a suckling pig turning on a spit or a laborious *ballotine* requiring birds be boned and gelatin gelled. It was a glorious sunny day, perfect for chilled rosé. The baguette was excellent, and that platter of perfect tomatoes, impeccable hard-boiled eggs (not a tinge of green), smart French tuna, and haricots verts at the precise moment of doneness was, I admit, the sensible, even elegant, lunch on a hill overlooking the town of Mougins. We sat under a tree, gazing down to the sea. Paul took photographs of us together. I look serene and happy. To be with Julia . . . it should have been enough. What an ingrate I am to have expected lukewarm *loup de mer* with a sauce *gribiche.* Forever the Insatiable Critic.

Oh what a surprise: In Cannes the next day, we just happened to run into Jon, Jamey's friend from the boat. Not an accident at all, I suspected, but I said nothing and invited Jon to dinner. Jamey took my arm, energized with excitement. "If I can exchange my return ticket for the next sailing, I might stay on and go to Sweden."

"What a wonderful idea," I said. "You'll miss your audition for acting school that the agent arranged, but . . ."

"I've never been to Sweden. Have you? There will be more auditions in the fall. Jon says there are blondes lining the streets, just waiting for bad boys with curly black hair." He planned to take all the cash he still had, a few hundred dollars, and gamble it to make enough money for his trip. I followed them into the casino in Nice. It was shabby and smelled of cleaning fluid, stale smoke, and desperation. Instead of Cary Grant and Greta Garbo look-alikes dressed by Edith Head, there were swarthy sheiks in shiny tuxedos and overbleached blondes with chipped nail polish.

Jamey was cautious, circling the blackjack tables, sniffing out the play, looking for a lucky spot. He would play a chip or two and then, if he lost, move on. It was very boring.

"I'm going to find the disco," I said. In Europe, you didn't need to stand on the edge of the dance floor looking eager, hoping someone might ask. You just whirled in. Even if you weren't young and beautiful, if you were a good dancer, you could find a partner. You could dance with him or drift away without serious insult. A rangy dark-haired youth in a many-zippered jacket skittered my way. We began a rhythmic pantomime of advance and retreat to an anthem of Gloria Gaynor. She was everywhere we went in France that spring, even in a small whiskey bar in an isolated town fifteen miles from Saulieu, where the chef Bernard Loiseau had taken us in his tin can of a car after dinner. He had two stars, and was struggling for three, but Loiseau's water cuisine was too intellectual for his own good, I'd thought.

Jamey and Jon were circling the floor. I saw them in the distance and, saying au revoir to my partner, caught up with them.

"We didn't want to interrupt," said Jamey, "in case you had big plans for later."

"Would we share him?" I asked. "You caught me weighing my options," I teased, using his favorite line. I could scarcely remember the guy's face. Sharp, thin, with a dimple, snapping his fingers. "I guess I'll keep looking."

After Jon sensed that Jamey was distracted, he said good night. We walked on. "I'm in shock," Jamey said. He'd been up almost a thousand dollars and then lost everything . . . lost the four hundred he'd started with. He had maybe forty dollars left.

"I'm so sorry, darling." I squeezed his arm. "Isn't it true it's always fixed in favor of the house? It's so hard to win." He collapsed into an easy chair in our room, as if stupefied. I went into the bathroom to change. He was sitting in the dark when I emerged.

"You are such a bad boy, you can't sleep with Mommy tonight," I said.

"Bad boy," he said, falling to his knees and holding on to my leg. "Bad boy. Sorry. Please sleep with Mommy."

"No. Bad boys can't sleep with Mommy."

He kissed my knee. "Please. *Please.*"

"Well, all right. If you promise not to do anything dirty." I was improvising. Sexual fantasies take two, after all, and he didn't believe in rehearsal. "Shall I read to you?" I picked up one of his *Penthouse* magazines.

"Gina thinks she is a pussycat," I read, flipping a page. "Don't look; it's too dirty for you." He snuggled against me, kissing my breasts.

"Good boy. Good boy. Mustn't tell Daddy," he crooned.

The next morning, I decided to loan him money for Sweden because it seemed so important to him. "After all, to come this far . . . to be so close to all those blondes. I think you should go." He seemed to have forgotten our big plans to make him a star in the straight world. Or maybe the possibility of success was too much for him to contemplate, requiring too much effort on his part. "I wouldn't want to be too successful," he had said to me. "I wouldn't want to be like Paul Newman, so that I couldn't wander around Bloomingdale's panty department without causing a riot." I warned him the agent might interpret his delayed return to mean he wasn't serious. But we both knew there would always be work in porn whenever he got home.

"Come to Scandinavia with me," he said.

"I would never go to Scandinavia. Not even with my husband. I don't need to be in a place where the streets are paved with gorgeous blondes."

"You didn't have the same perversity in your relationship with your husband," he said. "Scandinavia . . . I suppose this is the last gasp of a dying man." He mused. "I should go home and grab Renée [his first love] and marry her, or marry Andrea, or marry you." He didn't look at me when he said it. The sane, sensible part of my brain thought he just wanted me there to make arrangements and pay the bills. "I should go to Iceland," he said. "The girls there are really desperate. Nobody ever goes to Iceland."

"Maybe I should see Sweden," I said. "And Copenhagen, too."

I called Naomi in New York to see if she could put some money into my account to keep checks from bouncing and get her secretary to cancel a few appointments. I was already late delivering a piece. My editor would be screaming. "Your column hasn't been in the magazine for weeks," Naomi said. "That's a mistake. I don't see what you see in this man. He's totally self-centered, contemptible. He's like a self-indulgent twelve-year-old. What disturbs me is that you want so little for yourself."

I defended him. I tried to explain that it was more than just sex. It was about helping him be all that he could be, I explained, although it

looked like he was running away from that. I knew she was right. I had
to go home. It would be less painful to make the break now than to drag
it out.

He was dancing around the room, exuberant because American Express had called to say they were able to book him on the later ship. I told
him I was going home. He went silent, acted sullen.

"I'm not rejecting you, Jamey. I'm not abandoning you. I love you.
You'll be fine. You'll be better without me around. Everyone will want
you. All the blondes will be begging to take you home. I'll loan you the
money."

He disappeared into the bathroom. I heard the sound of his voice.
Was he taping? He emerged, naked, with his new little France-plumped
belly and the recorder. "I've been trying to decide if I should play this for
you." He played it. He'd been on his way back to the hotel yesterday, he
was saying, and he suddenly missed me and wanted to get home. Thinking of the hotel room as home. And he got a hard-on for me, astonishing
himself, thinking how pleased I would be. He shut it off. "You see. You
must come to Sweden with me. Just come for a week."

At first, I was moved. And then I was furious, remembering how the
previous day he'd come into the room, where I was being as calculatedly
sexy as I could be in my rose satin caftan with the slit up the thigh.
"Pretty hot, babe," he had said. And he'd done nothing. He hadn't even
kissed me, or touched me.

There seemed no point in complaining anymore. I felt light, carefree. I felt a surge of happiness. I was going home the next day and I
wouldn't have to want or beg or buy anything from him again.

Alain Senderens came out of the kitchen at l'Archestrate that night to
marvel at how much we had eaten. We'd had the chef's grand tasting
menu, and as if that weren't beyond gluttony, a few extra entrées, too.
"Sometimes I'm nuts about you," Jamey had said when I went along with
his mad need for too much. "Sometimes I think I love you," he said. "But
it's so hard to know if I love you or if it's what you give me that I love."

Senderens signed the menu, a copy for each of us. On Jamey's, he
wrote, "To the gourmand with the astonishing appetite."

"Look what he wrote," said Jamey. "Everyone who knows me will
know it means me."

"Let's not go crazy," I said as we gathered goodies at Fauchon the next day for one last picnic in the room before I had to leave for the airport. "We can only eat so much."

He pouted. "I have to have it all because I didn't have it when I was a child. I didn't have anything. I want to feel I can have it and throw what's left away. I'll pay half," he said, actually spending ten francs of his own for fruit tarts.

I covered the bed with bath towels and we spread out our feast. He re-arranged it a bit. He stood at the foot of the bed, taking it all in, and roared like a lion contemplating a limping gazelle. "It's all arranged in the order we should eat it," he said. He pulled up a chair on his side of the bed and started with the terrine de campagne, ripping off the heel of the bread. "You said you didn't want herring. Last chance, I'm taking it all." And then he was sobbing.

I knelt at his feet. "Darling, what's wrong?"

"Everyone always talks about pain. Women want to possess you. They are always saying I bring them pain. And then I'm the one who gets left alone."

"But all those women loved you." I was crying, too, for fear I was one of them and not really ready yet to quit cold.

"I need unequivocal love. Why is that so difficult?" He dabbed his eyes with the sheet. There was a knock at the door. He wiped his eyes and my eyes, too, and he kissed me. He kissed me hard on the mouth, then again.

The bellman had come for my bags. I looked back to wave good-bye. He looked like I had abandoned him on a sinking ship.

I was feeling shipwrecked, too. But then I took a deep breath, belt barely permitting, and realized I had done it. I was going home. The low-grade knot of frustration in my tummy was already fading. I had cut the cord. Quit cold turkey. I was free.

38

A WINE ROMANCE THIS IS

FLUSHED BY A SUCCÈS D'ESTIME THAT HAD EMPTIED THEIR BANK AC-
counts, Michael James and Billy Cross asked if I would come back to
Napa Valley for another cuisinary high-wire act. Would I help them lure
Jean Troisgros? How could I say no? Jamey was off the radar, harvesting
blondes in Scandinavia, out of sight, out of mind. I was eating again as fast
as I could, dancing away the calories, and flying off whenever booked to
promote *Blue Skies, No Candy*. Napa would be a time out of time, like
stepping through the looking glass, with Jean all to myself. Well, mostly
to myself, I imagined, with only two dozen or so foodies vying for a
sliver of attention. And I'd pocket a nice little fee for just being there and
contributing some pith and patter. "Speak to Roger Vergé," I told Jean.
"He'll tell you what fun it was. And bring your tennis racket."

I had continued to see Jean whenever we were on the same conti-
nent. I am not sure what Jean Troisgros and I were all about. He was single. I was single. We ate. We made love. We talked about food. We had
dinner with mutual friends who spoke French and amused him while I
sat there, sometimes a bit sappy, admiring his face, the big dark eyes almost bruised in golden skin. Most especially, I loved his hands, huge
hands with perfectly formed fingers . . . as if sculpted by a master.
(Look at the hands of the older chefs, chefs who have actually cooked

for years, hands plunging into boiling water, moving hot pots. They are often giant hands, swollen by heat, with muscular fingers.) Jean was not much taller than I—we were probably the same height in my lowish ankle-strap wedgies—and his arms and legs were like steel.

Jean was only in his early fifties then, but with his mustache and beard almost completely white, he seemed older, and he struck me as almost fatherly in his thoughtful, caring, protective ways. But he was a desirable widower, after all, and eventually there was a special woman back in Roanne, as friends who did the circuit two or three times a year made sure that I knew. Jean never spoke of her. Indeed, I do not remember Jean ever speaking of himself, or family, or feelings, or of his son Georges, a journeyman at Regine's on Park Avenue, who was lean and had a full black beard, and would later become a stalwart visible through the pass-through to the kitchen at Lutèce.

Jean spoke little English. My French was never good enough to follow a whipsaw conversation among Frenchmen, never good enough to say anything particularly deep or poetic or funny. As a seventeen-year-old in Paris, I'd mastered the uvular r—I loved that uvular r—so I sounded like I spoke French, and people would chatter back at me till my brain glazed. I never thought Jean was the man for my life or I for his. But between the hurricanes of emotion that seemed epidemic in my new singlehood, he was occasionally there, solid, straightforward, and calm.

Jean was the strong, silent type—he'd spent most of his life in a kitchen, as French chefs did until Paul Bocuse started jetting around the world in 1973, taking his kitchen pals along with him, and making a splash by cooking brilliantly publicized dinners. The kitchen was where most chefs were planted—not exactly fertile ground for intellectual insights or social repartee. When the press quoted Bocuse, it was usually when he had said something bluntly outrageous, blindingly chauvinist, or hopelessly misogynist. And he was the spokesman for his tribe. Jean was reserved, even shy.

I remember telling Jean that the notoriously restless Paul was losing credibility with the food press and the growing ranks of gourmand travelers because he was almost never in his restaurant at Collonges, especially by the time he, Roger Vergé, and the celebrated pâtissier Gaston Lenôtre opened the Three French Chefs restaurant at Disney's Epcot Center in Orlando. Bocuse had left two wives behind in Lyon, one official wife, the elegant and patrician-looking Ramonde, who ran the restaurant, later with their grown daughter by her side, and the other, unofficial "wife," mother of his son.*

"The person who cooks when I am here is the same person who cooks when I am not here," Bocuse responded to the critics. I'd eaten an astonishing meal when neither Bocuse nor his trusted chef stand-in, Roger Jaloux, were in the kitchen. But pilgrims from abroad making that long and costly trek were less likely to drop to their knees over the pastry-wrapped *loup de mer* with scales incised in the dough, and the chef's inimitable floating island, when they didn't spy that famous eagle profile under the grand toque stalking the room.

Jean defended Bocuse. "If I were going to have my last meal, I would choose Paul to cook it," he told me.

The bills for the wanton luxury and drama at High Tree Farms had left Billy Cross and Michael James broke, but by the time Jean was booked to cook, they had found sheltering arms and a properly plump budget for their cooking extravaganza at the Robert Mondavi winery. "I like the idea of linking the wines of California with the cuisine of France," Mondavi said as he launched The Mondavi Wine Country Cooking School. Jean and I would live in the winery guesthouse, a sprawling A-frame, its vast glass facade looking out on row after row of the vineyard that surrounded it.

I managed to get a column ahead at the magazine and flew out from New York with Jean. We spent the night at the Stanford Court so he could supervise the shopping the next morning. He almost provoked a riot in the supermarket when he bit into a daikon radish and, rejecting it, tossed it back onto the produce pile. Jean wanted fish. Where would he find fish fresh enough? Michael James took us to Chinatown. Jean stroked a few likely specimens, looked them in the eye, lifted their gills. He'd never seen sand dabs before. He had to try them. It wasn't even whole fish that he bought finally, but some very ordinary, schlumpy-looking fillets of red snapper. I was certain he was courting disaster. Fillets would never last. Jean instructed the fishmonger to put everything

*A graduate of the Culinary Institute of America in Hyde Park, he is now cooking at the Epcot Center.

on crushed ice and into the trunk for the drive north to the Mondavi winery. To keep those fragile fillets fresh-smelling, he stored them in metal bins on ice in the fridge—frigid but not frozen under wet dish towels that he would change twice a day. Jean barely had time to unpack what he'd brought: a bathing suit, his tennis racket, a two-hundred-dollar can of black truffles, and ten quarts of essence of veal bones (reduced to a demi-glace by his son Georges).

The communicants, nested in inns and lodges nearby, arrived for lunch. They came from Vicksburg, Mississippi, and Kankakee, Illinois, wearing dungarees and major jewels. They were sybarites and everyday gourmands, professional cooking teachers, food writers, and unabashed chef groupies, as well as Augustin Paege (the eccentricly quotable Bulgarian who'd been our unctuous host at the upstate Box Tree Inn) and an amateur cook and food lover who introduced himself as Joel. That was Joel Grey, fresh from winning an Oscar for *Cabaret*. An architect from San Francisco carried his own chef's knife in a leather hip holster. The wife of a doctor (who also built racing boats) wore surgeon's whites and a 12.5-karat emerald.

With his smile and four English phrases—"Thank you," "Hello," "I love you," "More butter"—Jean instantly won them over.

Midway through class that first evening, swiftly slivering cucumbers into crisp, perfect matchsticks, Jean was already communicating easily with the vivid gestures of his kitchen technique. But he was worried about the flour, remarkably different from flour in France. How would he adjust to make his pastry? And what about the butter? he wondered.

Michael tapped the bricks of butter on the counter. "You don't know what it took to find this quality of butter," he said.

Some of the students managed to gulp down their first kidney ever that evening. Dazzled by the posh of the table—waiters in black tie, orchids in glass bricks, cabbage in clay pots at lunch, a parade of crystal goblets by candlelight—a real estate and insurance salesman announced he would leave the business world and open an inn.

"You have to watch everything Jean does," he confided to me. "You have to be here to see him spear a garlic clove with a fork and use it to stir the spinach."

The class seemed enthralled even with such basics as peeling Swiss chard. "What do we do with the chard remains?" someone punned.

After breakfast each day, we raced off to vineyard tastings. Lunch looped into afternoon haze and often more vineyard visits. At Domaine Chandon, where Moët & Chandon was bottling its pioneer Franco-American sparkling wine to go on sale that December, Jean slashed a champagne bottle open with a knife as if it were a sword and poured aperitifs for the class. At Heitz Vineyard, Jack Heitz waited till everyone had arrived to open a bottle of his rare and legendary Martha's Vineyard cabernet.

"You wouldn't open it ahead to let it breathe?" I asked. Breathing was a sacred ritual among the serious winos I knew.

"No," Heitz said. "I want you to experience that first taste, and then we can all see how it evolves in the air." That first sip was so complex and powerful, I had to lean against the wall to think about it. (And I went home a convert, astonishing friends and frustrating sommeliers for the rest of my life by not letting them open a young red till we were ready to drink it.)

Jean would disappear for a few rounds of tennis between winery marathons. One afternoon, half the class got lost on the road to Mayacamas Vineyards. Jean disappeared into the brush and plucked wild plums, lest someone starve between breakfast croissant and lunch.

When the class gathered in the Mondavi winery kitchen at five o'clock to cook dinner, a few imprudent drinkers who couldn't bring themselves to spit expensive Chardonnays came staggering in late. By that time, Jean's lightning-swift knife had chopped turnips, carrots, shallots, kiwis, and grapefruit skin. Jean was a surgeon dissecting the baron of lamb, an alchemist elevating humble Swiss chard to buttery sainthood, and a puzzled man trying to skin an American fish of unknown ancestry.

"If God had meant a fish to be skinned, he would have given it a zipper," a West Coast restaurant critic observed.

The class punster couldn't resist. "This is a zipless fluke."

"All it takes to be a restaurant critic in Portland is being able to tell which frozen cheesecake is Sara Lee," the Oregon reviewer had lamented, confessing how he envied me the richness of my bailiwick.

Joel Grey's face was radiant as he mastered the art of disjointing a chicken. "You must do it in one blow of the knife," Jean commanded. "Two will disjoint your fingers. If you cut yourself"—he looked up from slivering turnips—"be sure to leave the blood for the sauce."

I watched Jean wrestle a twenty-five-pound mattress of puff pastry
into submission for the evening's dessert. Surely it had been years since
he'd had to knead and roll and turn his own dough. Back home in
Roanne, that was a job for the pastry team. Watching him in the kitchen
was like watching Nureyev, I thought, or an Olympic slalom champion.
A master of his métier performing was incredibly sexy. And it was not
just me who found his cooking erotic. I noticed a few of the women
gasping for breath, and I thought, Yes, yes, yes.

Indeed, most of us were so gaga, we missed picking up the real secret of
the haunting fish sauce. Jean would shoo us off to the dining room as he
and Michael and our friend from New York, Naomi Linden, plated the
food. Jean always did my plate himself, Naomi told me later. He would
select what he considered the most beautiful fillet, the most perfectly
rare breast of pigeon, ladle the sauce in a precise geometric swirl, wipe
the edge of the plate, and instruct a waiter to carry it directly to me.
That's how Naomi discovered the fish sauce's crucial ingredient, never
revealed to the class.

"It's the veal demi-glace he stirs into it," she confided to me later. "I
caught him doing it and he made me promise to keep it a secret, just for
myself. But of course I am sharing it with you."

Jean was a model of discretion in class, relaxed and proper. At night, he
was comfortable and affectionate in the big bed we shared on the open
balcony overlooking the soaring living-dining space below. Our friends
Naomi and Greg Linden remained invisible in their bedroom. Sometimes the morning light pouring in would wake us. Sometimes it was the
bustle of the staff setting up breakfast on the table below, shushing one
another not to disturb our sleep. Jean would wake as men often do,
primed for making love. And I would climb on top, riding to my own
rhythm, my arm pressed against my mouth so no telltale cries could escape. Once my breathing returned to normal, I would call out over the
balcony rail, "Good morning, everyone."

Those muffled moments felt naughty and delicious, almost as
naughty and delicious as raspberry pie for breakfast. It wasn't rich
enough merely to have fresh raspberries in an era before berries might
arrive in the market more or less ripe from somewhere around the globe

every day of the year. But to have them for breakfast on pastry cream in an exquisite tart shell baked by Margaret Fox, the woman who ran the Café Beaujolais down the road, that was paradise. Some mornings when the sun had time to dry the dew, the table was set outside and we sat surrounded by grapevines, picking raspberries off the last of the tart.

While we sailed along in the kitchen—with Jean sprinkling flour on everything, including a few irreverent students, and improvising a new dish using the basket of figs that had just arrived—Billy's serving crew created new fantasies at the table. Why were they all so good-looking? I marveled. He had selected them, male starlets, surfers, and runway models, as if he were casting a beach flick. One noon, the table held hundreds of shiny red peppers. That night, branches of orchids bisected the crossed tables as local VIPs joined us. Another day, roses and tulips bloomed in a hundred tiny Asian vases, one to a vase. Or sweeping branches of fruit blossoms in tall weighted glass bricks might stand dipping low to the corners of the table. Live crayfish in laboratory beakers provoked manic delight and outrage. (By evening they were dead, having given their ultimate gift to Jean's *cassolette de queues d'écrevisse*.) And always candlelight. Nothing but candlelight. The Mondavi dining room's famous glass ceiling above was cranked open to let in the sun at lunch and to reveal the full moon at dinner.

One of the women brought a copy of *Blue Skies, No Candy* along for me to sign. "Would you read aloud to the group after lunch?" she asked.

"Oh yes," several others chimed in. "Read to us."

I leafed through the book, looking for a section that would stand on its own . . . something funny perhaps, something food-related. I looked out at their smiling faces, at what I guessed to be a rather conservative posse, the upper-crust blondes and a few blue-haired ladies. I needed to find a scene that didn't take place in bed, that didn't rely on my heroine's graphic stream of conscience and all those four-letter words. Funny, isn't it? I found it easy enough to write them, hard to read them out loud.

I started to read. I was pleased at a laugh and then another. But my eye, darting ahead, could see on the next page, just a few paragraphs away, the word *pussy* . . . oh dear. What could I do? I lightly slipped it right into my reading. They gasped. I went on. Oh dear. One woman held her head in her hands. Another giggled nervously. I felt myself flush. Thank heaven I was almost finished. I saw the chapter ending just ahead.

I closed the book and looked up with a silly grin on my face. They cheered. And the bluest of the blue-haired ladies toasted me with the dregs of her Chardonnay.

I was actually grateful that Jean's English was limited. He smiled and toasted, too. That evening, one of the staff brought in a trunk of Moroccan jewelry for sale. Everyone gathered around. Naomi Linden found a necklace she loved. I tried on a silver necklace with coral beads set around a medallion.

"C'est un cadeau pour toi," said Jean. "A gift for you."

I was touched by his sweetness, the romantic gesture. By that time, I guess anyone who cared enough to notice knew something was going on. Indeed, the Mondavi winery was full of unresolved romantic intrigue that fall. Margrit Biever, Mondavi's gracious Belgian public-relations woman, had apparently not yet left her husband. I remember meeting him at one of our dinners. But not long after, she would become Mrs. Robert Mondavi.

I don't think I articulated it at the time even in my own thoughts, but what drew me to Jean was that he was a man, a grown-up man. He was the manliest man I'd known—straight, basic, seemingly uncomplicated. He cooked. He loved to cook. He loved that Michelin admired the Troisgros cooking. He played between meals. The other men in my life, wonderful, maddening men, had been overgrown boys, babies, neurotic, wounded, driven, uncertain. Not Jean. Not the Jean he showed to me.

When his son Georges married a daughter of the Poujol restaurant family in New York, Jean's American friends were invited to the wedding, but I was not. His Roanne woman, officially now his fiancée, had asked him not to invite me.

"But how can he give in to her?" I wailed to Naomi. "And the least he could do is call and tell me himself," I said. "I would forgive him if he called."

"But he can't call," Naomi said. "He wouldn't know what to say to you. He's a simple person. He can't do it any other way."

I knew Naomi was right. He wouldn't know what to say. And he couldn't handle my tears. It was easier just to pretend everything was all right. But I was hurt. I never saw Jean again. I did not visit Roanne in the years before he died from a heart attack on the tennis court at just fifty-six.

I think of him often, that playful athletic man, dead so young. Whenever I read something about the tradition of the Troisgros restaurant that neglects to mention him, deliberately I believe, as if he never existed, I am furious, and then sad. It seems as if the surviving brother, Pierre, or his wife, Olympe, fear that to credit Jean might dilute the triumph of their son Michel, who, on his own now, has kept the family's three stars.

Sometimes I try to re-create the fig dish Jean invented in the Mondavi kitchen. He squeezed the juice of grapefruits, oranges, and lemons into a pot, added cabernet—reduced, reduced, reduced—spilled in some sugar, and cooked the figs just a little. Spooning the tart syrup over the fruit, he ladled it into a big tureen. "These are figs Candy Blue," he said.

Jean Troisgros's Figs
Candy Blue

2 medium-size lemons
½ bottle full-bodied red wine (Jean used a Mondavi cabernet sauvignon; I use a
    Côtes du Rhone)
¾ cup freshly squeezed orange juice
Scant ½ cup sugar
8 or 10 cloves tied in cheesecloth
¼ tsp. cinnamon, plus an extra pinch
¾ cup (100% fruit) apricot preserves
12–16 fresh figs (3 or 4 per person, depending on fig size)

Remove and julienne the peel from the lemons. Cut away the white skin, then cut lemons into thin slices, discarding any seeds.

Combine wine, orange juice, sugar, cloves, and cinnamon in a nonreactive pan, bring to a gentle boil, uncovered, and continue to simmer till volume is reduced to half (about 30 minutes). After the first 15 minutes, add half the julienned peel and apricot preserves. Stir well and continue gentle boiling.

Remove pan from stove and let contents cool for 5 minutes. Add rest of peel.

Place the figs in a wide, shallow pan that will hold fruit in one layer and then place pan on burner. Pour cooled syrup over figs until figs are three-quarters covered. Roll the figs to coat them with syrup. Add sliced lemon. Simmer 5 to 6 minutes uncovered, till figs are just cooked. Add a few drops of balsamic vinegar if the sauce seems too sweet.

Spoon figs and lemon slices into small compote dishes and spoon sauce on top.

Serves 4.

Store any extra syrup in the refrigerator to use another day on sliced raw peaches or nectarines.

39

IT'S NOT EASY BEING GREENE

IT WAS THE FALL OF 1977. I WAS LIVING MY LIFE OF SUBLIME EXCESS, DATing a new man for a while and then another, sleeping with old faithfuls, dining out with friends, straining to find new metaphors for the same old adjectives in my reviews. "I saw your name written on the wall of a john in a ladies' room at a restaurant," my editor told me. "It said, 'Gael Greene uses a thesaurus.'" She insisted the story was not a joke.

I devoted summer at the beach to jump-start the new novel. William Morrow, fired up by their score on *Blue Skies, No Candy*, leaped to buy my new book at a celebration lunch at Le Cirque. All I had was a title, *Doctor Love,* and a two-sentence description. "It's about a man, a doctor of emergency medicine, who is a wonderful lover but has never been in love. A sudden serious illness inspires him to revisit all the women who've ever loved him." I smiled. My agent nodded sagely. Morrow's boss shook his head, as if to say, Whatever. Whatever. We drank a warming, complex, expense-be-damned Lafite and clinked glasses all around.

My life bubbled with pleasures. I'd finally made it. I had become a B-list celebrity. I got quoted. My recipes made entertainment roundups in what insiders called "the bungalow magazines." I got invited everywhere—to first nights, screenings, restaurant and club openings—and since I went only to discos where I was known, I was greeted with the quick dropping of velvet ropes. New Yorkers were deeply into food. Our readers wanted to know where to go, to be the first . . . to discover greatness. And they looked to me to tell them. Indeed, food-world professionals read *New York* to find out what they were up to. I was busy exploring exotic tastes from the city's newest immigrants, discovering the renaissance of Columbus Avenue, heralding chefs with potential, damning supersonic cuisine aboard the new *Concorde*. When I didn't stop to think about what was missing—love, loving, being loved—I was too busy to miss it. A life of the senses was pleasantly distracting.

And then Jamey was back. It was like a blur. It happened so fast. What could I have been thinking? I must have felt I was so emotionally together, I could take him or leave him. He was shocked that his "real girl-friend," Andrea, was not at the pier to meet his boat. But there I was, trim in a tight blue denim jumpsuit. And then I was washing the dishes that had been moldering in the sink as he threw down his suitcase and unpacked. "Don't you look cute?" he said, pinching my cheek, grabbing me from behind in a hug.

"I'm just clearing the sink and that's it," I said. "I'll send my house-man over to do something with this kitchen, if you promise not to fuck him or sign him up to make dirty movies." Bernard, my house cleaner, was the loving and sensitive son of a mother who had insisted he learn how to clean while his brothers became, respectively, a doctor and a lawyer. Well, that was his story. People were always propositioning him on the subway, he said, and giving him things—most recently, a piano. He was going to take lessons, and he could use the extra money.

I convinced myself I could play with Jamey, enjoy him in small doses, liberated from the desperation that had clouded my mind in Paris, the perversity of wanting what I couldn't have. He was broke and needed help getting back on track toward the career he now insisted he really wanted. And I knew he was too passive to do it without me. One day, he announced he would do a Sylvester Stallone with our book: produce it, direct it, star in it.

"I better finish it soon and sell it, or you'll be too old to play yourself," I said.

He must have thought he could handle me, too. He was loving and affectionate. And charming. His enthusiasm for whatever was happening at that moment was disarming. He was welcomed back by restaurateurs, who found his joy in eating endearing, by friends who were bemused by us as a couple. Sex clubs flourished all over town, and ordinary people with libidos juiced up by the new sexual openness were curious. Everyday middle-class civilians and the celebrated might be spotted dancing fully dressed among the towel-wrapped players at Plato's Retreat, which fate planted in the former gay baths below the Ansonia apartment house, steps from my door.

I paid Jamey fifty dollars a week to keep taping his diary for our book. Conversation never dragged at our reviewing dinners à deux, since nothing interested him more than himself. I found his memories of childhood neglect touching and his tales of porn life fascinating. His needs were bizarre, the rationale simply weird. It was not that I bought into his delusions; I just accepted that they were part of the package. He was affectionate and relaxed. If the foreplay tended to be solipsistic, I was definitely there when it got to fucking. I loved it. In just a few months, I'd become addicted to contending for his company again, the alternating torture and triumph.

Nearly broke, he threw himself back into the porn-film life and the sex-world parties. "Why can't I go?" I asked.

"You won't like what happens."

"But I'm your Boswell."

He was right. Though his X-rated comrades were friendly and he agreed I looked "pretty hot" in a shiny black satin tunic, an elastic mini, and high-heeled suede boots with chains, I felt awkward and out of my element at a party for *Cheri* magazine.

I suggested he call the agent, lie to her, tell her he'd stayed in Sweden for a couple of small movie jobs and that now he was back, eager to work. He stared at me as if I were a creature from another world (as I suppose I was). I had forgotten how proud he was that he never lied.

"Maybe I don't really want to work," he said. "My father never worked. I'm more sophisticated and aware, but in many ways, I'm like him. Maybe you and I should buy a Kentucky Colonel franchise in Stockholm. I only need to have a young girl once a day, and we could be happy."

I sent him yellow roses for his birthday, April 20—Hitler's birthday, as he pointed out.

When I came by to pick him up the next day, the roses were dying.

"I don't know what's wrong," he said. "I put them in the window to get the sun."

He hadn't realized cut flowers need water, not sun.

When the agent didn't return his calls and the Actors Studio auditions she'd pushed him to pursue were already overbooked, he grew angry with me. "There's no point in running after the Actors Studio. I already did acting school. I'm an actor. I'm not in the mood for disappointments these days." He couldn't handle rejection. He'd told me that clearly. I refused to listen. He was sliding back, taking even the sleaziest sex-reel jobs to pay the rent.

I nagged and tugged and cajoled. Why wouldn't anyone just accept him the way he was? he cried. What could I say? I did it for you, Jamey? I did it for me. I was trying to make him into the man who would be right for me. Surely he could never leave me—the string-puller of his fame, the godmother of the sweet life.

The tapes, which I had once thought would help me keep my perspective, seemed to get me more involved. He'd met a stunning Vassar girl, he confided to his journal. She invited him to spend the night in her dorm. He'd canceled a dinner with me to go, he said on tape. I suddenly wasn't so cool anymore. I was angry and hurt.

I backed off, but I couldn't let go. When I called with a dinner I thought he couldn't refuse, he offered me Clarissa, the Vassar girl.

"We'll all go to dinner and spend the night at my place."

Clarissa was taller than I, taller than Jamey, with thick dark hair in a boy cut and a classic Mediterranean face. I tried to imagine what she could possibly be thinking as she silently pulled off her sweater and stood there in a copper silk teddy.

"Come to bed," Jamey said.

Clarissa made love to me. She was a wonderful lover. She knew everything she needed to know. I lay there, wrapped in the sensation, heightened by the idea that it was a woman, the fantasy I'd wanted for a long time. Just as I felt myself going over the edge, I remembered the etiquette (all those porn-film threesomes I'd seen were ménage à trois for dummies). I wasn't supposed to just lie there reveling in her skilled lovemaking. So I roused myself and kissed her small, high breasts. Her eighteen-year-old skin was magical, her body long and tight and rounded. No wonder they all love young girls.

Jamey seemed barely engaged, though he fucked us both in turn.

"I thought you'd be wildly hot and more into it," I said a few nights later. "What was wrong?" I wondered if we'd made him feel redundant.

"I didn't expect it to be so much flesh," he admitted. "The two of you. So much woman. I did it just to amuse you."

There were no bidders for *The Prince of Porn Is a Happy Man* as nonfiction. Editors told my agent I should write the story as a novel. Everyone wanted the next novel by the best-selling author of *Blue Skies,* it seemed. Except William Morrow, that is, the eager publisher-to-be of *Doctor Love*. After accepting the first hundred pages, they'd read the second big chunk of the manuscript and then told me, "We could not be happy publishing this book." I was frantic. I had two-thirds of a novel and no publisher.

Don Congdon, my wonderful old-world agent, with his gracious ways and wild Pucci ties, sent the rejected *Doctor Love* manuscript out for auction. Richard Marek and Joyce Engelson, who had their own imprint at St. Martin's Press, bid almost three times what Morrow had committed to pay and submitted a proposal for major promotion. I promised Jamey our life as a novel would be my next project, once *Doctor Love* was finished.

Jamey was frantic, falling in love every other week. He was wild about Annabelle—she was the sound technician on a film set. He loved her integrity, her contempt, that she had no respect for his work.

"Are you kidding?" I asked. "As compared to whose . . . my contempt isn't good enough?" He could see only Annabelle, till her contempt got overwhelming.

Jamey was depressed. He hadn't known how much he wanted a straight acting life till I convinced him. He hadn't seen how meager his life was, what a prisoner he'd become, till I made him see it. He seemed furious, bitter that I had misled him into imagining it would all be so easy. He was losing faith that we would ever sell his book—or our book, or whatever it might be—or that he would ever make the impossible jump to stage or screen. Hopes for an adult-films crossover, which had looked so imminent—that a major director would use real sex in a conventional film—faded. "Even in *Last Tango in Paris,* it isn't actual sex," Jamey complained. "And Brando doesn't undress."

He was away for work, and then so was I. But we got together for an evening with friends from Paris, people Jamey liked. The two of them were kissing, nuzzling, happy together. I was wildly jealous. Jamey read my mind. We didn't say much. He took my hand as we wandered back toward his place. He settled into his new Barcalounger, my Christmas gift—maybe the ugliest thing I ever did for love.

I stood there thinking, Why am I standing here?

It wasn't fun anymore. I had found a man who was as happy as a pig in shit and then turned him into an unhappy pig in shit.

"We shouldn't see each other for a while," I said. "We're both unhappy." It was the best I could come up with. "We'll go to the Four Seasons wine tasting together and that's it."

"Is there someone else?" he asked. For a minute, I didn't know what he was talking about. Should I lie and say yes? I wondered. I hinted there might be someone special. All those guides to romance that say you should play hard to get . . . I was above all that. But Mom and Helen Gurley Brown were right. The sex was particularly intense; it felt like he was fucking *me* that night and not his fantasy behind tight-shut eyelids.

Jackhammers outside woke us both the next morning. I whispered, "Bye-bye, Jamey." He put his arm around me, silent, not letting me get up. "You have to make me your duck with figs. You promised. And you said we would go to the Barolo tasting."

"There will always be Barolo tastings," I said.

He was silent.

I dressed, walked to the door, turned the knob.

"Gael."

I turned to him.

"I love you," he said.

I went back to the edge of the bed. He kissed me. I was pleased by the stale cigarette taste of his mouth. Reality: He was human.

*   *   *

A friend called to tell me that Jamey was living with the porn actress Serena. I remembered her from the movies: alabaster skin, a platinum blonde, very Marilyn Monroe, very beautiful.

Jamey called, complaining that he couldn't find his shoes because Serena had rearranged everything. And she'd had the audacity to refuse to have sex with a couple he'd invited home. Who did she think she was to refuse? he demanded.

"It would help if you don't call me anymore, Jamey," I said.

How quickly he had healed. I was hoping to do the same.

40

CUISINES FROM
THREE MARRIAGES

Tooling along the bicarbonate blacktop, crisscrossing this land of mythic bounty, once meant (and still often does mean) risking gastrointestinal insult and betrayal even in an item as casual as a grilled cheese sandwich. So it was quite a joy in the summer of 1977 to find a restaurant as ambitious as the Quilted Giraffe in a near-bucolic corner of Ulster County.

Nestled into a Victorian clapboard house on a quiet path in New Paltz, about ninety miles north of Manhattan, the Quilted Giraffe was, I wrote in "A Celebration of Amateurs," "vivid testimony that amateur in its sense of 'loving' can infuse the mere act of nutrition with sensory adventure." Neither Barry nor Susan Wine was a trained cook. Neither spoke much French. Midwesterners both, he was a Wall Street lawyer who loved to cook; she enjoyed baking. In a not unusual sixties dropout mode, they had escaped Manhattan. He would be a country lawyer. She would open a gallery and a shop selling children's clothes. The restaurant was an afterthought, a lunchtime mecca, "like the big shopping centers do" to keep customers from straying too far. The baby shop explained the gibberish of giraffes. They came in patchwork on the window shades, frolicked across banquettes, hung in quilted portraits, and made irresistible plastic swizzle sticks. (Am I giving away too much if I confess I still have one in my collection of swizzle sticks?) It was a shock and a giggle to find a giant inflated giraffe nested in the bathtub in the ladies' room.

Like most of the self-taught American cooks of that time, Alice Waters among them, the Wines tried to be French. I remember ordering *canard aux navets* and being disappointed when the lusciously roasted duck arrived surrounded with olives instead of turnips. "There must be a mistake," I told the waiter.

He summoned the tall redheaded Irish headwaiter, whom he described as "our house expert in French." The headwaiter smiled indulgently and assured us that olives were correct.

When I insisted that *navets* meant turnips, not olives, he turned on his heel and disappeared, returning with a butter-stained volume of Julia Child's *Mastering the Art of French Cooking,* riffling the pages till he found the recipe. "Ohhhh . . . I guess you're right."

But beyond the occasional mistranslation, and early culinary gaffes like duck with bananas, the Quilted Giraffe was remarkable for its sensitive lighting, fresh daisies, giant goblets, the sophistication of its wine list, Chopin by a pianist—live—upstairs, and deft service by graceful young men who took obvious pride in the venture.

After each serious rave, Barry and Susan Wine became more ambitious, finally giving up lunch to concentrate on dinner. After a few courses down the road at the Culinary Institute of America in Hyde Park, Barry decided he could do as well as any chef. And his passion ratcheted up the ambition. There were Susan's crusty baguettes hot from the oven, a kidney-studded sweetbread terrine, a lemon-ice intermezzo, a classic veal Oscar, and fresh arugula in the salad. You could follow your New Paltz kir (cassis and white wine) aperitif with the Menu Gourmand (twenty dollars) or Le Menu Nouvelle Cuisine (twenty-one dollars) or what may have been the first tasting menu in America—Le Grand Menu Servi en Petites Portions (thirty dollars), a "degustation chosen by the chef," with a *grand assortiment of desserts,* including a soufflé at just $7.50 extra.

Given all those *grand*s, and an inspirational two weeks in Paris, the Wines were clearly primed to take on New York. They rented a building on Second Avenue, not at all daunted by the fact that it was just around the corner from Lutèce. ("We knew we had to live over the store," Susan Wine said. "This is not a job; it's a lifestyle.") In that, of course, they were clamoring up the stairwell after the lead of André and Simone Soltner, who lived above Lutèce. A narrow Greek luncheonette was transformed into cozy elegance, all pink and spicy, an embrace of booths, dark wood, inlaid mirrors, café au lait ultrasuede (ah, seventies luxe). On Memorial Day in 1979, they locked the doors in New Paltz, shipped the convection oven south, and one week later opened the citified Quilted Giraffe.

The hungry nomads who'd loved them in their adolescence upstate followed. And new friends proved loyal. Barry, wide-eyed and usually smiling, remained sweetly obsessed, a perfectionist with a passion for quality, the urge to experiment, and the gene for high risk. He delighted in circling the room, introducing guests to a two-foot rod of Japanese radish.

"It's so hairy," women squealed.

"It tastes like potato," Barry would announce proudly.

He would not let a customer eat an entrée garnished the same way twice. And no table ever received the same vegetable twice in the same night. He would be out back, juggling thirteen possibilities, driving the sous-chef crazy. He did shoestrings of vegetables long as spaghetti . . . was he the first? One day, I stopped by and found him experimenting with mustard ice cream to go with the brain salad.

"Must you?" I said.

"Only if it's wonderful," he promised.

Decades later, when maniacally creative chefs had made mustard ice cream seem no more bizarre than rum raisin, Wine reminded me.

"But it was awful, Barry," I said. "It's still awful."

"Awful? What do you mean? Really. It was delicious."

The Wines were a succès fou in any language. They were so successful, they could afford to close both Saturday and Sunday and drive to New Paltz for the weekend in their navy blue Rolls. Susan, trim and tiny and pretty, was famous for being cranky and snapping at any customer who complained of real or imagined abuse. Even now, Barry marvels at her almost supernatural knack for booking tables with a minimum of customer overlap. The restaurant was small and they were turning away hundreds of supplicants every day. There was no bar for customers to wait in, and the vestibule was minuscule. When Bill Paley came in, he needed to be seated without undue delay. "Tables were never empty for more than sixty seconds," Wine recalls.

A parade of gifted chefs moved through the kitchen of the Quilted Giraffe and its later sophisticated high-tech steel and black lacquer sibling, the Casual Quilted Giraffe, in what is now the lobby and retail bazaar of the Sony Building on Madison Avenue at Fifty-fifth Street. Noel Comess (who went off to found TomCat Bakery) ran the range when the Quilted Giraffe won its four stars from the *Times*. At that point, there wasn't a cutesy giraffe in sight except for the giraffe swizzle stick in your cocktail glass. Barry Wine's beluga caviar and crème fraîche–stuffed beggar's purses (a borrowing from France that became his signature) carried a twenty-dollar surcharge. Heavy monogrammed silver, expensive china, and goblets with twisted stems spelled opulence.

Giraffe alumni Tom Collichio (Mondrian, Gramercy Tavern, Craft), Troy Dupuy (Lespinasse-Washington, La Caravelle), and Wayne Nish (March) speak of Barry with fondness and admiration for his innovation and passion. "I learned everything I know about running a luxury restaurant from Barry," says Wayne Nish. "As for creativity, he would come up with ideas. Not everything was brilliant. Gefilte fish with blueberries did not amuse the critics. We would cook Mexican for six months, or Japanese for six months. I did things you just couldn't do then, like mixing olive oil with soy and sesame—it came from an idea I had."

In the mid-eighties, a sake dealer invited Barry to see Japan, and he fell under its spell. His food at the Casual Quilted Giraffe (which soon became the only Giraffe when business could not support two) became more and more Japanese—small dribbles and dots of food arranged asymmetrically on exquisite imported hand-thrown ceramics. Barry wore a Japanese chef's coat and practiced calligraphy. He perfected his iconic tuna wasabi pizza (still offered in homage to him at the Mercer Kitchen). Not all his Japanese fusion scored. "That was the same week we did mashed potato sushi rolls," he later confessed. "Ehhh." He made a face. "Who needed it?"

When Sony—coveting the Giraffe space on the street for retail use—made the Wines an offer they couldn't resist, they took the money and, much to the surprise of many, including me, did not go off to open a still grander Giraffe. Instead, they split and went off in search of themselves. So much for cuisine from one marriage.

"How innocently it begins," I once wrote. "He does exotic omelets. She is celebrated for her blueberry pie. He moves on to meltingly tender veal shanks in polenta. She turns out a shimmering salmon in aspic and does all her own pasta—by hand.

" 'You two are so good you ought to open a restaurant,' their friends say. Thank heaven, most of us resist the temptation. And thank Julia Child and her butcher, Bob and Karen Pritsker did not," I wrote in the fall of 1979. "The fruit of their ambition and their passionate gastromania is Dodin-Bouffant, a cloister of highly personal and creative culinary wizardry on East 58th Street."

Like the Wines, the Pritskers had prepped their act out of town. That was in Boston. Born in Pawtucket, Rhode Island, he had a law degree but never practiced. She came from Westchester, daughter of a Broadway impresario, and worked in advertising. They taught themselves to cook from books. Cooking was a hobby.

"Then one day, we went to Julia Child's butcher," Bob told me. "There was a lot of fanaticism at that counter, a lot of intensity. I'd never seen anything like it." Stlll calling it a hobby, they began to cater dinners for the Newton/Wellesley crowd. Then having listened to the wily snake and tasted the forbidden apple, they opened Dodin-Bouffant, dedicated to the awesome perfection pursued by the gourmand hero of *The Passionate Epicure* (the book whose pot-au-feu I had used to challenge the chef of the S.S. *France*). Bob went to market every day. From noon to midnight, they cooked together.

In the summer of 1976, they drove through France, fueling imagination (on the same route I followed, though we never met), falling out of Alain Chapel's stunned by sublime excess, mesmerized by the bravura of Troisgros. Home again, the Pritskers fired the maître d' and installed Karen in the dining room, but then something shook up the business plan. There was a separation. "If the restaurant hadn't destroyed the marriage, the marriage would have destroyed the restaurant," *Boston* magazine commented. Feeling cruelly exposed, Karen wanted out.

The Pritskers reconciled, then sold the Boston place and moved to New York, planning to import New England oysters. But that restaurant virus still raged. It took a year to find the narrow Eastside town house east of First Avenue, seven scarring months of renovation. Dodin-Bouffant finally opened in mid-January 1979. Stalkers of cuisinary bulletins, first to sniff the rumors of greatness, were quick to trip down the icy stairs to the stylish vestiary with a door open to the kitchen, where Bob might look up from a casserole with his ingenuous smile. And then they were led upstairs to a striking, unusual den of cool. Pale blue banquettes, a chill of chromed chairs, sedately papered walls quite bare, an arched tulip or two reflected in an oval mirror. The voluptuous display of Karen's desserts was the only relief from pale blue and beige, leaving the spotlight for gently illuminated faces and the exquisite food.

Boston's Dodin-Bouffant was textbook classic—boringly classic, some critics complained. Now there was never a boring moment. Nouvelle cuisine and their own confidence had liberated the Pritskers. What they did was original, strikingly personal, even eccentric at times: *Lotte* in a fragile batter with scallion. Calf's brain fritters with cherries Karen pickled herself. Or brains poached in a peppery bouillon that was reduced, enhanced with mustard and cream, then garnished with a crunch of carrot. Lamb salad, rose pink and tender, served still warm on arugula in a subtle vinaigrette, beside a tiny hill of baby beans, and purees of celery root and, at first unrecognizable, radish. I savored and delighted in the mystery and the rush of discovery. Every day, the menu changed. Expensive for the time, of course, I noted (one hundred dollars for two with wine).

Karen's desserts were a happy vacation from New York's French restaurant cliché. They were mood-elevators for neophiliacs: Pineapple-lime soufflé, smartly tart. The still thrilling kiwi and orange in sabayon. Ricotta pepper tart with nutmeg ice cream. And a stunning bread and butter pudding with caramelized apricots and a splash of crème anglaise. (I don't believe anyone, except Le Cirque, did bread and butter pudding, certainly not so elegantly embellished, but soon everyone would.)

Some people found Karen haughty. It was true she could be a bit stern, tightly coiled. As stern as her pale, unmade-up oval face, as tightly coiled as her dark hair. I thought it was shyness or a certain discomfort that provoked a defensive irony in her delivery that could seem arrogant. Caught off guard, relaxed, at play, she was a charmer. And Bob, so amiable, jokey, and adorable in his spattered whites—I thought he looked

like a street urchin—had a tyrannical temper when crossed. Dishwash-
ers rarely lasted more than two weeks. "All this is to say they are not Bar-
bie and Ken playing restaurant," I wrote. "As the menu notes, 'Being
Dodin-Bouffant is not easy.' "

"Centuries from now Venusian archaeologists digging in the rubble
of Manhattan will find shards of old Cuisinarts and rusted truffle tins and
the melted, twisted hulks of electric pasta machines—relics of a civiliza-
tion that prattled endlessly about what to feed its stomach . . . and
how . . . and where . . ." I wrote in a March 1980 issue of *New York,* confessing that I envied my most food-obsessed playmates because they got
to eat in their favorite restaurants again and again and again, while the Insatiable Critic was doomed by profession to move on relentlessly in
search of new wunderkinder. "If I were free to go anywhere I pleased
tonight, I would choose . . ." And then I described eight wonderful dinners.* It was another of many roundups of bests and favorites I would
persuade the editors I must do to justify yet another delicious spree at
Lutèce or the Four Seasons on the magazine's dollar.

Just six months after my first review, Dodin-Bouffant had become
the most exciting French restaurant in town. "Every day they play with
cuisinary fireworks," I wrote. "And once in a while they get burned. But
cooking is like love. Great adventure is worth any risk. Sometimes you
just have to leap off the cliff not knowing if there's a feather bed or a
rocky gorge below." Of course, I was writing more about my own life—
that love was always worth the risk—than I was about the Pritskers in
the years when I could not seem to make a sensible romantic commitment. I was writing of my philosophy at a time when the men I chose
were more dessert than sustenance. When the one sure joy and the only
certainties in my life were work and dinner.

The irony of my metaphor for the Pritskers became apparent a year
later when rave reviews and the clamor for tables were not enough to
distract them from the unhappiness of their marriage. They separated
again and Dodin-Bouffant closed the next summer. Friends begged them
to try at least working together. It reopened in the fall—he in the

---

*The wondrous eight, in order of cuisinary astonishment, were Dodin-Bouffant,
the Palace, Lutèce, Le Plasir, the Four Seasons, Shun Lee Palace, Trattoria da Alfredo,
the Palm.

kitchen, she in the dining room, each keeping different hours. But there was too much anger and pain. He offered to buy or sell. She did not want to buy. She had fallen in love and planned to move to California. He says now that she would never agree to a selling price that made sense for him. On August 10, 1982, Dodin-Bouffant closed forever.

David Waltuck studied marine biology "just long enough" to know it wasn't what he wanted to do. He had always cooked. Six months wandering Europe, eating, exploring the markets, brought him to La Pyramide in Vienne. For him, as for me many years earlier, it was a career epiphany. Back in New York with no experience at all, he got a job as a cook at the Empire Diner, then did a year at the Culinary Institute of America in Hyde Park and became night *saucier* at Tavern on the Green. A second year at the CIA was "too stultifying," so he quit, got a job as sous-chef at La Petite Ferme in the Village. All winter, in long johns, he and his wife, Karen (an émigrée from the fashion world), hunted for affordable space. They sold shares to raise the $110,000 it took to transform the funky bodega and *cuchifritos* stand on Grand Street and open the doors of Chanterelle, with just David and a dishwasher alone in the kitchen.

It was like a mirage, a stage set . . . a teasing dream. Black streets so desolate at night, threatening and littered against the shadowy cast-iron facades on the outer edge of early SoHo. Suddenly, there was a cube of light: a tall storefront, magnetically aglow: Chanterelle. Inside, I found a studied elegance—soaring columns and wooden wainscoting, a blizzard of white linen against gray carpet, a great fan of exaggerated flowers, birds-of-paradise, so stately that they seemed wondrously silly.

Karen—a stylish Sally Bowles with her zany trill, a big smile, arched brows, dark hair in a modish boy cut—hung your coat in an armoire and danced you to a table. There, deliberately casual waiters in white shirts and long white aprons demonstrated proper French manners and American agreeableness.

The high French style of the Waltucks' dream was impressive, especially in this no-man's-land: big balloon glasses, sweet butter in a ramekin, the astonishingly superior bread, so rich and chewy—from Hoboken, I learned, at a time before great bread became an obsession in New York restaurants. The menu was dated for the week, with its drawing by the artist Marisol, both à la carte and a thirty-five-dollar eight-course prix fixe. Among the offerings: a fricassée of seafood in sea urchin cream, a delicate layered pastry of oysters, salmis of duck with scalloped turnips, perfect greens, exquisite cheese from Dean & DeLuca— vacherin, Pont l'Eveque, crottin de Chavignol, and a froth of fresh goat. Tart grapefruit sorbet cleared dizzied senses, followed by a tray of goodies: crisp palmier cookies, candied grapefruit peel, chocolate truffles, bitter and dark.

By the time I made my third visit, a fussy avant-garde of affluent food-obsessed citizens had found Chanterelle. David Waltuck could afford a sous-chef. But he was only twenty-four years old, really still learning. He continued to experiment as he went along, and his work was uneven. Two weeks earlier, he had tasted a vegetable sausage at the Pritskers' Dodin-Bouffant and it had inspired his own oyster sausage with a sublime watercress cream. He could turn out a lobster *navarin* in a haunting sauce perfumed with cream and then send out a wine sauce reduced to an unpleasant aftertaste or serve a gritty frozen slab of something called hazelnut ice cream.

The Waltucks were disappointed by the litany of flaws I listed in that first review—"The Daring Young Man on Grand Street"— that was so close to a rave. "David Waltuck is not yet as brilliant as he intends to be, but when he is good, Chanterelle, in SoHo, is astonishing," the opening line read.

At that moment, unqualified praise for Chanterelle would have brought savvy eaters down to SoHo with impossible expectations. It was safer for the Waltucks (and my reputation) if readers came expecting less than perfection. Many were likely to be less demanding than I. There was always the chance they might be dazzled. And ultimately, they were. First there were three stars, and then four.

I'm not sure what the moral is or even where the wisdom lies in the story of "Cuisines from Three Marriages." But Chanterelle survives and thrives twenty-five years later, and so, it seems, does the Waltuck marriage. I wrote this chapter to see if there was a lesson here for me, but I have not found it.

41

BONFIRE OF THE FOODIES

IT WAS JANUARY 1980. THE LID HAD BLOWN OFF MOUNT SAINT HELENS IN Washington. China sent its first Olympic team to the winter games in New York. Gold soared to $802 an ounce. New York's kitchen all-stars were warming up, too, obsessed with game, legally farmed or outright booty, inspired by new ingredients from adventurous farmers and food brokers. "Now comes winter to celebrate the cuisine of astonishment," I wrote in "Great Chefs, Inspired Feasts" that January. "Wild pheasants appear, an unexplained miracle. Remarkable venison, wild ducks, five perfect squabs. Don't ask where they came from. Fresh chanterelles are being flown in from Oregon," I marveled. "Someone has bootleg raw foie gras." Suddenly, we would discover the *lotte* had a liver. Chanterelle had persuaded its Cape Cod scallop supplier to bring in *lotte* liver. At the Palace, chef Michel Fitoussi's mousselike lobes of *lotte* liver floated in a piquant sea with slivers of snow peas for crunch. Snow peas were the pea of choice now. Radicchio, crunchy and costly red lettuce from Italy, colored aristocratic salads. Perfectionist chefs paid five dollars a pound for twig-thin French string beans.

In the eighties, certain hoity-toity snobs liked to say they had never been south of Fifty-seventh Street. For some, Saks Fifth Avenue was the Maginot Line. But budgets pinched by financial hard times in the late seventies had inspired pioneers to explore desolate corners ripe for re-vision. Raoul, Chanterelle, and Greene Street were the pioneers in SoHo and now in TriBeCa, wherever that was—the cabdriver would find it, we hoped. We ventured downtown to J. S. Vandam and Capsuto Frères. Giant red neon letters spelling out Odeon became a beacon for the eclectic chic in 1980. During the transit strike, it seems, the McNally brothers—Brian and Keith (veterans of Cafe Un Deux Trois, One Fifth, and Mr. Chow)—and Keith's wife-to-be, Lynn Wagenknecht, happened to walk by an old luncheonette on a nowhere block way west. They could afford it, especially if they kept the tacky metal chairs, the homely ban-quettes, the Takacheck machine. With Regine's alumnus Patrick Clark at the stove, the Odeon's draw would be good food and laid-back atti-tude—Frank and Ella and confit of duck. Bachelor rogues of showbiz, fashion's precious babies of every sexual persuasion, suburban squares, punksters with tufts of apricot hair, refugees from Elaine's, and John Belushi, Richard Gere, Milos Forman, David Bowie, Warren Beatty, and Mary Tyler Moore, blissfully unnudged by a crowd determined not to betray the pulse throb of the thrill, all showed up. We were getting a taste of the McNally magnestism. By August, Odeon would be the hottest contender for bistro of the year.

W chronicled leveraged buyouts, Le Cirque hair, and glitz, glitz, glitz. The Reagans were poised to move Hollywood into the White House. The Carters' almost endearing just plain folksism was finished. What a per-fect time it must have seemed for Jean-Jacques Rachou, restless in the confines of his tiny and wildly successful Lavandou, to sink his savings into restoring the frumpy La Côte Basque. In the fourteen years since his death, Henri Soulé's beloved "playpen for the poor," run by his persnick-ety longtime companion, Mme. Henriette, had faded. And so had she. Bernard Lamotte, painter of the sunny murals radiant with light that gave Soulé's pampered ménage the illusion of dining alfresco at the port of Saint-Jean-de-Luz, dropped by that March to pay his respects. As the new carpet was being tacked into place, the artist, intoxicated by the re-newal, ran out for tubes of color and, using a plate as a palette, began to brush new figures into his murals, people and mules, chimney smoke and swirling wind. He summoned Rachou to see. On a building where Lam-otte had long ago lettered "Restaurant Côte Basque—Henri Soulé," it now read "Jean Jacques Rachou." "I was not planning to do it," he confessed to Rachou. "A hand was guiding my hand." Côte Basque did become Rachou's arena, free of the old snobbery, with its brand-new state-of-the-art kitchen and the giant plates of the nouvelle cuisine style, just like Michel Guérard's. Rachou always was a weekend painter. Now using beurre blanc and glace de viand as his media, he sketched astonishing flowers and feathers in the sauce. Very more is more, as I wrote. A parade of young American chefs would rotate through that kitchen, acquiring a Gallic discipline that the next generation of chefs might never know.

It was the era of the grand café, of everyone wanting to get into the feeding game, of big budgets and drop-dead design, of American chefs cooking American. Joanna's, a late-night brasserie on East Eighteenth Street, signaled that the vast, soaring, slightly roguish grand café was about to trump the town. I spotted Mayor Ed Koch in the hodgepodge of darlings from every niche our town celebrates assembled there, among the polyestered sycophants devouring the scene and an unfocused American menu. Sure enough, a lot of ambitious entrepreneurs with venture capital went stalking for warehouses, garages, abandoned factories. The Flatiron District was prime.

Just when we'd stopped being amused by the nouvelle cuisine, food snobs began to rediscover Americana. Paul Prudhomme's blackened redfish led imitators to blacken everything. And soon every Zip code would have its Cajun canteen—Memphis, Cajun, Gulf Coast. Abe de la Houssaye and his wife, Alene, decked out Texarkana at 64 West 10th Street like a western saloon, with a rotisserie turning out the hot and smoky feasts of the Gulf Coast and Southwest. We flocked there for spicy crayfish stews, delicate fried catfish, pungent barbecues, and homemade catsup.

At Vanessa on Bleecker, Anne Rosenzweig calf's liver was an American classic with caramelized onions and bacon bits. Warner LeRoy's circus fantasy of stained glass and animals at Maxwell's Plum was amusing, but we loved him more for the house's lavish ways with black bean chile and the marvelous pecan pie. Some critics made fun of Larry Forgione for cluttering his River Café menu with a geography of credentials, but it was a forgivable quirk in his bold campaign to single out the newly rich harvest of buying American. Homey American desserts—cobblers, brown Betty, shortcake—fried Ipswich clams with fat little bellies and Portland hot slaw, and Chesapeake Bay crab cakes were revisited when Forgione opened his An American Place in 1983. Rosenzweig was also off on her own with Ken Aretsky to open the jewel-like Arcadia, with its bucolic mural wrapping the small room and a seasonally changing menu. Soon Rosenzweig's lobster club sandwich would be the talk of the lunch scene (inspiring the couturier sandwiches everywhere). I loved the flattering filtered daylight of Alan Stillman's Manhattan Ocean Club, along with his collection of Picasso ceramics in illuminated niches, Kumamoto oysters from the Pacific, perfect crab cakes, and Hawaiian wahoo (a new fish in town) served with another new arrival, grilled pineapple. Restaurant Associates marked its own rebirth and the rebirth of Rockefeller Center by spending a reported $22 million to create the Sea Grill and the American Festival Café.

A onetime Wall Street broker turned caterer, Martha Stewart, was hustling a book called *Entertaining*. As the fount of increasingly in-demand, rigorously drilled American chefs, the Culinary Institute in Hyde Park felt driven to vamp its Escoffier Room into the American Bounty Restaurant in 1982. By 1985, there would be a waiting list of jobs for every graduate.

Not that the French and Italians didn't fight back. At Le Cirque, Sirio resurrected crème brûlée, inspired by a crema catalana he'd fallen for in Spain. Like the tiramisú brought from Venice by the chefs at Castellano, it soon would be tweaked and twisted and, more often than not, fatally compromised. Roman film producer Dino de Laurentiis got into the food business on Columbus Avenue with DDL Foodshow (though not for long). Roger Vergé, the charming three-star chef of Le Moulin de Mougins on the Côte d'Azur, lent his sunny menu to the Polo Lounge at the Westbury Hotel in 1983. Bloomingdale's, in its endlessly creative golden era, gave Michel Guérard a kitchen for carryout, calling it Comptoir Gourmand. There, Guérard's right-hand man from Eugénie-les-Bains worked alongside a onetime jewelry designer named Alfred Portale and Troisgros scion Michel, creating classic charcuterie, while the enterprising food department offered 100,000-year-old prepollution ice from the North Pole at seven dollars a pound. At Il Cantinori, an art-world hangout, Pino Luongo prepped for his own eventual moguldom at Le Madri and Coco Pazzo. Olive oil, we learned, had to be Italian. We had to have it, even though some of us rarely cooked anymore, now that boutique carryout shops bloomed in every neighborhood.

In China, with a coven of food-world adventurers, I asked our scout master, David Keh, why no one in New York did pork in the variety we'd tasted. "You can't just sell pork," he protested. "It's the Jewish people who support the Chinese restaurants." Give them noodles, too, we suggested. He called it Pig Heaven (delivery was dubbed Pig-Out) and quickly drew his celebrity pets to the wondrously silly space with yellow vinyl and dancing pigs by designer Sam Lopata. Keh, glamorous in his mink and Rolls-Royce, had become a legend by the eighties. He recruited a quartet of graces from Taipei to tend the woks in the shiny black-lacquered sophistication of Auntie Yuan, another Lopata drama: matte black banquettes and pin spots casting pools of light on a giant clutch of white orchids, the luxurious details of Wedgwood, mock ivory flatware, and real linen. Two could share a tasting dinner of lobster or peking duck with serious wines, even a Château d'Yquem by the glass with the sorbet. To escape union demands, he downsized David K's, his proud flagship restaurant, and gave Zarela Martinez her big break at Café Marimba. I thought its thrilling poetry of light and shadow was Sam Lopata's most gorgeous design.

Macy's and Zabar's staged a take-no-prisoner's caviar price war as well-heeled gourmands lined up before New Year's Eve to score sturgeon eggs at rock-bottom prices. To keep up with merger play, one had to check out the Power Breakfast scene at the Regency. Sensing the time was ripe for decadence and mink-covered banquettes in Manhattan, the Petrossian brothers imported their caviar and wild smoked salmon concept from Paris and discovered the American brunch tradition. They gave us foie gras on French toast.

In the first wave of immigration from the organically fixated California scene, where Alice Waters had found her mojo in market cooking, Jonathan Waxman landed on East Seventy-ninth Street in 1984, calculatedly cool. With the forever-boyish wine seller from Britain, Melvyn Master, he opened Jams (for Jonathan and Melvyn), producing food as pristine and minimalist as the duplex space, all white, with splashes of color in borrowed art on the walls. At a moment when sauce was catnip in our time, Waxman talked of throwing a perfect piece of fish on a plate, and burying the chicken under a hill of sublime fries. "Let great ingredients speak for themselves," he said, setting off a mass infanticide of baby vegetables and an upscale run on french fries. He had mesquite on his grill, of course, and sent forth many a California salad—warm game and greens, sweetbreads with wild mushrooms on endive. Lobster was served with a crunch of tossed salad and homemade potato chips. Salad and mesquite, fuel for the eighties. Mesquite now blackened the skies. Cilantro sprouted like wild grass.

In upstate New York, a transplant from Israel started raising a new breed of duck, supposedly torturing them benignly (was that possible?) by using light and music to wake them up so they'd eat and fatten their livers. Now we had American foie gras.

Paul Levy's *Offical Foodie Handbook* (Motto: Be Modern, Worship Food) may have been British, but it captured the transatlantic silliness of it all, defining a foodie as "all palate, with a vestigial person attached."

Restaurant madness had New York in a frenzy. "Never before have so many people spent so much money on eating out . . . and everybody is talking about food," Patricia Morrisroe wrote in a *New York* cover story (November 26, 1984). The line to get into Mezzaluna stretched down Third Avenue, she noted. That Florentine import, cleverly stuffed into a small Upper East Side storefront, had barely room for anyone over size two at the teensy tables and certainly no room for a coat check. Society darlings blithely threw their Fendi minks into the cellar and sipped peach-blushed champagne Bellinis, pretending it was *amusant* to wait forty-five minutes to sit with knees touching knees at a postage stamp–size table and linger over two ounces of carpaccio or a plate-size pizza. The waiters were dashing young Italians who flirted. Soon there would not be many Upper East Side blocks without a copycat cantina. Italian spots multiplied: Prima Donna, Ecco, Trastevere 83, Erminia, Orso, Paola's, La Sirena, Georgine Carmella. Pesto and sun-dried tomatoes became staples. Everyone sipped so much white wine, there was a grape crisis. Clever marketeers quickly invented white zinfandel. I blush to remember it.

Many New Yorkers ate out morning, noon, and night. We were so many two-career couples with money to burn, I wrote in June 1985. We were newly single, anxiously returning to the perpetually adolescent dating scene. After an hour on the Nautilus or two hours with Jane Fonda's workout, we had little time to thaw, much less cook. And we were Yuppies, well traveled, curious, self-indulgent, postponing children or entrusting them to the au pair we didn't report to the IRS. And, of course, no one wanted to wear a tie anymore. The fusty grand French restaurants seemed irrelevent. Hushed eating in a temple was giving way to grazing in a raucous gym.

Everyone wanted to be in the restaurant business. "It's like a dinner party every night," the Gotham Bar and Grill's Jerry Kretchmer liked to say. But the Gotham was foundering in 1985, too hot too soon and experiencing trouble in the kitchen. Jonathan Waxman recommended Alfred Portale to the desperate owners. Last seen at Bloomingdale's Comptoir Gourmand, Portale had cooked under the fiery star chef from Nice, Jacques Maximin, consultant at Tucano in Ricardo Amaral's upscale disco, Club A, far east on Sixtieth Street. A few months after Portale moved into the kitchen, I was urging readers to marvel with me at the chef's straightforward, beautifully mounted food. And very soon afterward, the *Times* agreed. The Gotham was seeing three stars, a halo to mark the height of the chef's seafood salad.

The stakes were awesome now. Where once an amateur could toss flea-market tables and chairs into the basement of a Village brownstone and create a restaurant, now design reigned. These real estate developers, advertising wizards, playboy garmentos were willing to spend a million or two for a dramatic setting that might not last five months. Trompe l'oeil, peach walls, murals, and open kitchens with wood-burning pizza ovens were epidemic. And it had to be noisy. "Noisy is cozy," an architect, proud of his shattering decibels, assured me. "Noise creates energy." And no one really missed the glitter of conversation, because mostly people just talked about how many sit-ups they'd done that morning and which California chefs were rumored to be moving to New York any day. Often it was not about eating at all—just San Pellegrino at five dollars a bottle and shared nibbles.

Lemminglike masses ran from one hot new grand café to the next, detouring to queue up patiently to infiltrate the intense trattoria scene. Yuppies do not eat, I reported in June 1985. "They socialize, they network, they graze or troll. Tapas at a bar or a pizza* to share make perfect grazing food because [they] give a yup time to check out the crowd and

---

*Boutique pizzas were half the size and twice the price of the old coal oven blistered pies of New York tradition and were likely to be layered with such oddities as smoked salmon, duck confit, and seafood in the shell on romaine lettuce.

make sure he or she is in the restaurant of the moment." *Moment* was the operative word. Never had chic been so cruelly fickle.

Architect Sam Lopata had turned an old box factory on a forlorn stretch of West Eighteenth Street into Café Seiyoken, an Art Deco–Japanese–Continental brasserie for 1983. It was hot, it was fun, and the food was not bad at all, I noted in a column headed "O Tempura, O Mores." Avant-gardists found it an ideal runway to show off oddly wonderful Japanese fashion. Everyone wore black. When Café Seiyoken cooled, all that applied gorgeousness got tossed out to make way for the flying drapes and pillars architect David Rockwell dreamed up for La Colonna. It minted money, then faded, too. There were so many swan dives. *Bon Appétit* magazine got it right: The eighties witnessed the bonfire of the foodies.

Even before the doors swung open for the first time, there were crowds lined up outside America, Positano, and Canastel's. These vast, intensely torrid watering holes, all huddled near the Flatiron Building, might cool inexplicably overnight. How to keep up? "Look for a lurkage of limos," I suggested.

The renaissance in American cooking was unquenchable, inspiring a demand for free-range chickens, meatier ducks with silken livers, and exquisite miniature vegetables. It was amazing to realize how strongly the chefs of remote Gascony, a region of France not many Americans reached, influenced what we ate. Duck confit (simmered in fat), foie gras, even their fiery Armagnac infiltrated American menus. Then Ariane Daguin, daughter of the energetic Gascon booster chef-hôtelier André Daguin, set up d'Artagnan wth her partner George Faisan, supplying Hudson Valley foie gras and fresh game of a quality local chefs trusted, yet another factor in the dining revolution. Fresh herbs were now available all year round. It felt like a new winery was born every week. If upscale New Yorkers could not finance a million-dollar apartment, at least they could afford a $150 dinner. Was there ever a greater time to be alive and hungry in New York? Drew Nieporent, familiar from the maître d' stand at Maxwell's, had found his way to a dismal block of undiscovered TriBeCa to open Montrachet, with David Bouley in the kitchen. Montrachet had scored three stars in record time. By the time I got there, it looked like a foodie convention. Nieporent and his jacketless black-clad staff had to take the phone off the hook most of the day just to function.

Heating up as a countertrend was the craze for dormitory food—

macaroni and cheese, meat loaf, mashed potatoes with lumps, chocolate pudding complete with the skin. A few serious restaurants took notice of calorie counters and diet fads. Beans were big and getting bigger.

Restaurant consultant Barbara Kafka divined red meat as ripe for a revival. She also had the vision midway through the eighties to imagine that some women might stay home with their babies and cook again. Cookbook writer and teacher Paula Wolfert thought home entertaining was poised for a comeback. "We just bought a refectory table," she told me. "I'm tired of eating out."

"Dessert used to proceed sex," I wrote. "Now dessert is sex. Some say the waning of our national obsession with sex fuels this insane pre-occupation with food." (Indeed, Morrisroe had written that "the new indulgences were not one-night stands, but 'Sinful Chocolate Cake' and 'Tipsy Trifle.' ") "Others seem to think the increase in anorexia is a sign the food madness is fading," I went on. "If so, serious food lovers will be left sharing coq au vin in the dozens of little bistros that have opened this year without limousine fanfare—an alternative that's not to be sneezed at."

In 1985, Batons lured Richard Krause to Manhattan from Wolfgang Puck's Asian Chinoise on Main, and suddenly there was a blizzard of cornmeal replacing bread crumbs, a sea of farm-raised catfish. Tuna seared on the edge but rare in the middle was the rage. Other Puck-prepped stars ushered us into China Grill in CBS's Black Rock. Bronx cowboy Brendan Walsh branded Arizona 206 with his fantasy of southwestern cooking (surely more splendid than anything authentic). A dentist named Joe Santo and his family expanded their franchise a skip from Bloomingdale's to include Sign of the Dove, Yellowfingers, and Contrapunto, where American riffs on pasta were the theme.

Struck by Jonathan Waxman's southwestern moves at Buds on Columbus Avenue, a young cook named Bobby Flay, who'd never been west of New Jersey, reinvented southwestern cooking at Miracle Grill. The Balducci family splintered and Grace landed uptown. Animal activists convinced some tenderhearted New Yorkers to give up veal. Mob boss Paul Castellano was eighty-sixed outside Spark's Steak House that December. (I hoped it was after dinner.) Though speedsters on wheels were poised to deliver food to our homes and offices as never before, favorite old Shanghai and Szechuan haunts were vanishing as the Hong

Kongization of Chinatown made Cantonese prime. The growing community's ambitions spilled over into Little Italy, revising the calligraphy, even on Mulberry Street.

All the while, evil forces were gathering to terrorize our uninhibited gourmandism. Not just animal activists but also Jane Brody in the *Times,* with her disease of the week, who forced us to recognize cholesterol. The salt bogeyman conspired against us, too. Salt and fat were official enemies now, especially when Craig Claiborne's doctor took him off salt and he published *Craig Claiborne's Gourmet Diet. Gourmet* magazine printed a recipe for a meatless Thanksgiving.

Equitable bravely chose a tacky West Side address for its splashy, art-filled new headquarters and gave it cachet by luring Maguy and Gilbert LeCoze from Paris to open an American outpost of their two-star monument to the minimalism of fish, Le Bernardin. In the rotunda bar next door, Equitable installed a 128-foot mural in sunset reds and oranges, commissioned from Sandro Chia, of Siena's Piazza del Campo in the full throes of its annual Palio, the thundering horse race for which Tony May's smart, Josef Hoffmannesque restaurant above was named. "You may feel tramped or menaced by Chia's heroics. Or you may be cheered by what restaurants have come to in the Drop Dead division," I wrote.

One might become ironic, but it was impossible to be jaded.

42

ON MOUNTAIN TIME

I LIVED MY LIFE IN THE EIGHTIES BETWEEN MEALS. EACH SUMMER WAS A long parentheses focused on my writing somewhere in the Hamptons— in whatever rented cottage I could afford that year. Americans were infinitely less shocked by explicit sex when my second novel, *Doctor Love,* came out in 1981.

I went on the road to promote *Doctor Love,* leaving a trail of newspaper clippings, boosting it briefly onto the best-seller lists. Then I moved to the beach for the summer for another try at writing Jamey's story as fiction. Twenty-two publishers had already turned it down. They didn't seem to like either the Prince of Porn or the Junk-Food Queen. "Nobody cares about your two characters," my agent told me. Of course I took that personally. I knew some people found it hard to see beyond Jamie Gillis the porn star. Repugnance for porn colored their response to Jamey. As a writer, I had failed to capture the charm that had captivated me, perhaps because I was too angry with him for not letting my Henry Higgins turn him into My Fair Laddie. But had I made the fictional Upper East Side older woman who falls for him shallow and uninteresting, too?

"Most of the editors are women," my agent pointed out. "I think the book upsets them, that a woman like you could fall for this guy. It's too threatening." I was determined to make my protagonists more compelling. After all, if people were fascinated by Hannibal Lecter, why not us?

Waking one Sunday morning in 1981, I was not exactly hungover, but I was ruing a dismal reviewing dinner the night before. I brought myself breakfast in bed on a tray—espresso and a too-generous chunk of my favorite Russian coffee cake from Zabar's—and the Sunday *Times*. I could not get past one headline: CITY SCRIMPS TO FEED THE AGED. There was a photograph of a sad-faced old woman sitting in front of a partitioned plastic tray with food and some Styrofoam cups. It seemed there were 350 homebound elderly New Yorkers who got a hot lunch delivered every weekday, but government funds were inadequate to cover weekends and holidays. If Monday happened to be a holiday, some of these shut-ins—many of whom lived alone—would go without a meal for seventy-two hours. And the woman pictured was disabled, unable to get out of her third-floor walk-up except when her meal-delivery man carried her down on clinic day. She might save a banana or a slice of bread from Friday's lunch for Saturday. Just $340 per person would buy weekend meals for a year, a social worker was quoted as saying.

My Russian coffee cake sat like a lump in my stomach. It wasn't right that I lived a life of such delicious excess when aging, ailing people across town were so deprived—on the Upper East Side, no less. I called James Beard, knowing he was a spokesman for Vermont maple syrup and, I'd heard, all sorts of products. He'd seen the same story.

"Let's fill Christmas baskets for these people," I said.

"What about weekend meals?"

"Well, we'll take care of that, too," I responded without really thinking. It didn't sound like much money. "Call everyone you can think of and I will, too." I felt no one I knew could say no to helping the hungry. I started calling food-world pals: restaurant consultant George Lang, Sugar Foods executive Donald Tober, restaurant publicists Ed and Michael Gifford, Roger Yaseen (top gun of the Chaîne des Rôtisseurs—in my articles I referred to him as the "Wall Street voluptuary"). Some of them called their friends, too. Beard enlisted restaurant consultant and cookbook writer Barbara Kafka, who called Joe Baum and went through her Rolodex. We asked everyone to give $340. By Monday morning, our friends had pledged $35,000 and a truckload of Cookin' Good chickens.

At the NYC Department for the Aging, Commissioner Janet Sainer came on the line. "Friends in the food world have pledged thirty-five thousand dollars and some chickens," I said. "We want to pay for weekend and holiday meals for these homebound people, but you must promise not a dime will go for office expenses." I'd heard stories of charity funds that spent more than they raised.

She jumped right on it, gambling that we were not delusional. "No problem," she said. "We're a city agency with funds for administrative needs. Your money will go only for meals."

It turned out there were actually 6,500 homebound elderly New Yorkers getting weekday meal deliveries but nothing at all on weekends and holidays. Our modest funds bought Christmas dinner for thirteen thousand elderly neighbors who would otherwise have gone without. Throughout the city—in Harlem and Chinatown, in Bay Ridge, on Staten Island, on the Upper East Side (where there were thousands of impoverished elderly), voluntary centers opened their doors to cook the meals we'd bought.

I remember how thrilled we were at what we'd managed to do over a weekend. Now restaurateurs vowed to do more. Bloomingdale's found a Harlem community center to pick up everything left in its bakery at the end of each day. Shun Lee's owners, Michael Tong and T. T. Wang, initiated a campaign to get Chinese restaurateurs throughout the city to deliver meals to Chinatown community centers. We realized we had to organize. Janet Sainer asked her assistant Marcia Stein to channel our energy and keep us legal. We called ourselves Citymeals-on-Wheels. I reminded Marcia I could not solicit restaurateurs and cautioned her never to tell me who said yes and who declined. We would do a fund-raiser at Club A. We would have an auction of gourmand adventures money could not buy.

In Paris, Yanou Collart rallied the greatest chefs of France, hôteliers, the famous wine and champagne houses. She created priceless gourmand adventures for our first auction at Le Périgord. Our guests, smashed on their own rare bottles of wine, couldn't resist a market trip with Paul Bocuse, lunch with the Troisgros family, a Sunday at home with Frédy Girardet. I auctioned a manila envelope stuffed with menus and memorabilia from the late Pavillon. It went to Ed Victor, the late Henri Soulé's lawyer, for eight hundred dollars. *New York*'s editor, Ed Kosner, let me write a column about Citymeals, and checks poured in. "But money cannot buy family," I wrote. "For some, loneliness is starvation too." I dreamed that every family, every Cub Scout troop, every grade-school class or PTA—even banks and restaurants, grocery stores and canasta groups—would adopt a neighborhood shut-in. I felt a shiver of delight imagining the old woman lucky enough to be adopted by the employees of Zabar's.

My adoption fantasy was never realized, although the ranks of volunteers who visit homebound seniors keeps growing. I soon became as obsessed with raising money for Citymeals as I had been with dancing or sex or seared foie gras. It was an incredible rush when I asked for ten thousand dollars and someone said yes.

The 1980s were a strange time, aptly dubbed the "Me Decade" by *New York*. Some of us were dancing on the edge of the bonfire. Some of us were dying. The growing AIDS plague, seemingly confined to gay men and IV-drug users, had not yet terrorized me and my free-loving friends, but we were growing nervous and more careful.

I wrote my reviews. I tried to keep up with the ecstatic flights and shocking tumbles, rushing to be first in print with the newest sizzle before it fizzed out. I usually danced after dinner. Night-world gatekeepers at the Sanctuary, the Roxy, and the Palladium seemed to have my name on the list. My faithful agent sent the revised version of my novel around again. I tried calling it *Hard Candy.* Still no takers. Jamey had long ago lost faith that there would be a book. Now I was beginning to lose mine. It had taken four years to write *Blue Skies,* five years to finish *Doctor Love.* Now I had nothing to show for all the years of living, transcribing, and writing this novel.

I knew I needed to publish another book. Joyce Carol Oates had probably published a dozen novels in the time I'd spent struggling to make my characters appealing. Since I had not surrendered to the computer age yet, it would take a year to redo the Jamey book yet again on my Royal standard. And if anyone bought it, another year would pass before it would be published. Maybe the Prince of Porn and the Junk-Food Queen were hopelessly unsympathetic people, as the rejection letters said. Maybe there was nothing I could do to make a reader care. It was already 1984 and I had no contract. What could I write quickly? That was the summer of thirty-day-wonder books. *Thin Thighs in 30 Days. 30 Days to a Tighter Bottom. Thirty Days to a Flat Abdomen.* I created a proposal for *Better Sex in 30 Days.* The replies were maddening. Everyone wanted to keep a copy of the proposal, but no one wanted to publish my clever treatise.

"I don't think it's for us," one editorial director wrote. "Needless to say, I've Xeroxed the material and am keeping it beside my bed."

"Thanks for sending me Gael Greene's proposal. It has changed my life," the president of a small publishing house wrote. "Unfortunately, I'm surrounded by a group made up of feminists . . . and they won't let me do it."

"It is with great dismay that I must return the manuscript," a top executive wrote, promising to collect a five-dollar readership fee from anyone at his office who asked to see the manuscript and a twenty-five-dollar fee for onetime use of a single technique from "anyone actually using any of the suggested techniques to improve their intimate interpersonal relationships."

So much for a sure thing. Then someone pointed out to my agent that there was already a book called *Thirty Days to Better Sex.* I bought it and wept. It was so thin and serious and unimaginative compared to mine. I spent that summer fussing with the Jamey book again.

A year later, Prentice Hall, deciding its list needed some juice, bought the book. I dropped the thirty-day concept and rearranged my advice from anatomy for beginners to advanced sexual play for keeping a longtime relationship hot. I threw in a recipe for Chocolate Wickedness, designed a page of cards with sexual requests for shy people winning at strip poker to present to the loser, and outlined fantasy scenarios for those of limited imagination. Alas, *Delicious Sex,* a third of it devoted to "fork play" (foreplay at the table), was published just as news headlines were forecasting an imminent breakout of AIDS in heterosexuals. Prentice Hall didn't want to seem irresponsible by dropping a "recipe book" for joyous sex into the marketplace. *Discretion* was the byword. The full-page ad in the Sunday *Times Book Review* looked very medical, as if it were for mail-order liver pills. It saddens me that *Delicious Sex* never got the workout of the *8-Week Cholesterol Cure.* It was much more fun.

That winter, I read the ads for Hampton rentals with fading enthusiasm. Moving to the beach every summer with the hope of falling in love and writing my novels had reached a dead end. Every summer, there were the same parties, the same cast of characters—some I adored; some were amusing—the same men, along with their new wives or their new ex-wives or their newest playmates. A friend said she would join me and share the rent wherever I went as long as it was in the United States. Where should I go? I needed a place that was not too hot in August and stirringly beautiful, with a little bit of culture, a reasonable source of single men, and disco dancing. Many friends suggested Aspen. It had mountains and men, a famous music festival, and men, and discos and men to dance with.

Once we had moved out of our first rental, a Woody Creek house with bats that swooped into our hair, my friend and I settled into an overpriced hovel on a not-yet-gentrified street, eager to get into an Aspen groove. We had decided the summer was an ideal time to get thin. Every night, we took turns broiling skinless chicken breasts and tossing a salad with just lemon or wine vinegar. Then, cranky and craving sugar, we headed for the bars, where there were, in fact, a wealth of great-looking gray wolves, really fit from mountain life, single guys our age or not that much older. Susan, my roommate, was great at bar talk. I was not. I tried to pretend I was a reporter writing a story on life in Aspen, but it didn't work. I was at a loss on a bar stool. I would wander home alone. Once, I found the oven still on and a chicken breast turned to charcoal.

One day, the two of us were in town, trying not to think about lunch, when Susan spotted a man she knew from college seated at a table on the deck of a restaurant called the Weinerstube. The two of them chatted. I talked to his friend, a tall, tan, dramatic-looking woman named Darlene. "Have you been hiking yet?" she asked.

Hiking. Oh yes, that was why everyone was clunking around in those high-top boots with tank treads. "Not yet," I admitted.

Darlene took me hiking up Hunter Creek trail. Susan begged off on the grounds of having bad feet. Up was easy enough even for me, a city creature who had worked out with a trainer every day for a decade. Down was scary, with rubble that moved when you stepped on it. Still, I was thrilled I could do it. I felt like an athlete.

"I have a friend who says he knows you from New York," Darlene told me the next day. "You went to a party at his loft once with your husband."

She introduced him at the bar that night. Steven Richter. I didn't remember the party or the face, but he looked good—tan, with a hippie mustache and a fabulous smile, the top of his brown hair lightened by the sun. He seemed very Western in an old tweed jacket and baggy worn jeans, drinking Mexican beer from a bottle held low at the crotch between swigs. I figured that was western, an old mining town thing. Darlene invited him to hike with us the next day.

Steven wore frayed cutoffs and had great legs. He taught me a few downhill tricks. You needed to lean back so you would fall on your ass and not on your knees. Funny how we both expected I would fall.

I invited him to dinner that evening. I can't imagine what I was thinking, but I served him a skinless breast of chicken. At least it wasn't carbonized. In his honor, we dressed the salad and opened a bottle of red wine. That helped. I discovered he was a Bronx-born cowboy, very smart. He didn't say much, but when he spoke, his comments were pointed and witty.

He spent the night. Next morning, he was still there. He liked my coffee. I thawed a bagel from the freezer. He didn't seem to be in a hurry. Eventually, he went off to his job at the Aspen Art Museum.

I was wowed. How lucky can you be? He was not a foreigner I would have to adjust to. He was a homeboy. We shared big-city paranoia and a love of pizza. In New York, men are always leaving. Sometimes they have to get home to their wives or their dogs, or to their special pillows for their asthma, or because they can't wear the same shirt two days in a row. Once, I dallied with a guy who had to go home to walk his parrot. Another date had claustrophobia in anything smaller than a king-size bed. Another's mother would be upset if she called and he did not answer. Steven Richter was not in a hurry to leave. And he returned for dinner the next night. I was ready with a big sirloin, a baked potato, and garlic bread. I think he went home seven or eight days later to do the laundry. I went along. By that time, we were an item.

He lived down valley, in affordable Basalt, as many Aspen workers do. His zucchini had taken over the vegetable garden in his absence. I said I could do all kinds of things with zucchini—pancakes, frittata, crisps, grated zucchini cakes. We were an odd couple, and I think that was part of the attraction. I was decidedly, incurably an indoors person. Steven had become a mountain man in the twenty-five years he'd been in Aspen. He'd gone there to ski, worked as a busboy at the Red Onion, then as a bartender, and spent two summers fighting fires in Alaska. He would go back to New York just to make enough money as a graphics designer to spend the winter skiing. Finally, he had settled in Aspen, working as a carpenter and contractor, remodeling old Victorian houses. He specialized in kitchens. Ah, Fate. By the time we met, he was working at the Aspen Art Museum, designing and installing shows. I thought it was not too late to get a little outdoorsy myself. Soon it was my feet in those lace-up tank-treads boots. At one point, I even signed up for cross-country ski lessons—I thought strength from years of aerobics would make up for lack of grace and balance. The instructor was discouraging. "I've never seen anyone less flexible," he said. (I'll admit I'd heard this before, though not in an Achilles-tendon context.)

Steven was surprised to hear I'd never gone camping. "It's not because I don't want to go camping," I said. "It's just that people seem to think I'm not the type." He borrowed a four-wheel-drive truck so we could climb right up the pass to Lincoln Gulch, his favorite camping site. He pulled off the trail near a hidden knoll beside a stream and began to unload the tent, a roll-up mattress, down pillows, patchwork quilts, and a bottle of red wine. He handed me potatoes to peel and slice, while he built the fire to grill our steaks in a huge black iron skillet. It grew dark and the smell of potatoes frying in butter was dizzying. There were more stars than sky above—millions of stars, a few of them streaking across the sky. Undearneath my jeans and sweater, I wore a red satin teddy.

I began to commute back and forth to Aspen as often as I could, arriving with enough eating research to write four or five columns for *New York*. His friends turned out at the Explore bookstore for an autograph signing of *Delicious Sex* and bought copies by the half dozen.

I noticed Steven had not read the copy I autographed for him. When I mentioned this, he said, "I don't have to. I live with the original."

I could not decide if that line revealed something wonderful about me or something unknowable about him. But I forgot to worry about it as I headed back to New York table games.

Juliette's Grandma's Fruit Crumble

In summer, I use blueberries, plums, or nectarines; peaches are okay, too, except you have to peel them. In the fall, I use tart apples like Granny Smiths, unpeeled and sliced thin. I sometimes mix the apples with half a cup of slivered dried apricots. This is the low-fat version. Needless to say, it's better with butter.

3 pints blueberries or 5 cups sliced plums, nectarines, or Granny Smith apples
½ cup sugar (plus 4 tbsp. more if the plums are very sour)
3 tbsp. freshly squeezed orange juice
1 tbsp. quick-cooking tapioca
¾ cup all-purpose flour
½ cup brown sugar
1 tbsp. canola oil
½ cup uncooked oatmeal or Grape-Nuts
Low-fat cooking spray

Preheat oven to 350° F.

Spray an 8-by-8-inch glass baking dish with cooking spray. Wash berries or fruit. Slice if you're using nectarines, plums, or apples (⅓-inch slices for nectarines and plums, thinner for apples).

Put fruit in a bowl, add sugar, 1 tablespoon of the orange juice, and tapioca, then mix it up well with a wooden spoon. Spoon into baking dish.

Mix flour and brown sugar by hand in another bowl or in the food processor. Add the canola oil and 2 tablespoons of orange juice and mix again with the wooden spoon or pulse in the food processor till it makes lumps. Stir in oatmeal or Grape-Nuts. Spoon this topping over the fruit, covering it as much as you can. Bake in oven for 25 to 30 minutes, till fruit feels soft to your fork and the top is golden brown. If fruit cooks before the top colors, brown under broiler. Let cool.

Serves 8 to 10.

This dish can be garnished with a sweet yogurt cream or you can pass the cream in a separate dish at the table.

Sweet yogurt cream:
⅔ cup no-fat plain yogurt
¼ cup brown sugar
1 tsp. vanilla
2 tsp. dark rum

Stir brown sugar, vanilla, and rum into yogurt and pour into a pretty pitcher or a small bowl. Cover with plastic wrap and let it sit in the fridge at least 20 minutes to dissolve any sugar bumps. Stir again before serving.

43

DINING ON THE LIP
OF THE VOLCANO

DISPATCHED TO RUN LAFAYETTE IN THE DRAKE HOTEL TWO YEARS EARlier, Jean-Georges Vongerichten did his master Louis Outhier's fancy French bidding. But he knew something was wrong. By the time he'd thrown out the bone-rich stocks and finished playing with the menu, its divisions into "perfumed oils," "vegetable extracts," "bouillons" and "les vinaigrettes" was a call to revolution. Wild herb and morel salads covered with hot mushroom broth and the New Jersey tomato tart served with clear tomato water were flavor revelations, freeing chefs across the country to copy and improvise. "Startlingly gifted,"*Times* critic Brian Miller wrote (April 22, 1988) in awarding Vongerichten four stars at the age of thirty.

The old "21" had plastic surgery and (as sometimes happens) emerged with a frozen smile. Not everyone appreciated Anne Rosenzweig's revised "21" burger with its herbose green ooze and the reformulated chicken hash. "When old customers complain about the hash, I tell them we decided to put some chicken in it," she said. Still, we were grateful that a fiercely aggressive businessman named Marshall Cogan was willing to spend thirty million or more to keep the landmark saloon alive.

He'd lured Ken Aretsky and Rosenzweig from Arcadia to juice up the crowd. There was a decade of legend to live up to. Taking note of the prices, Groucho Marx once ordered a lima bean, then sent it back to be peeled. Le Cirque's most recent ex, Alain Sailhac, seemed surprised to find himself running the "21" kitchen. "What do you think is American food?" he kept asking. And how did Rosenzweig run a kitchen run by Sailhac? "With great respect," she said, biting her lip. "I bought him James Beard's book *American Cookery*. 'Just so you'll know what a Lady Baltimore cake is,' I told him." Union pickets protesting the job loss paraded outside.

At that first lunch, I knew something dramatic was happening when I saw Eli Zabar's wonderously chewy onion-etched baguette in the bread dish. The saloon, with its hanging toys, was properly peppered with certifiable stars. Mary Martin was Peter Pan in pink, seated two derrieres to my right.

"Does snapping my fingers disturb you?" she asked my companion.

"Nothing you do could disturb me," he replied. Lingering to say good-bye, speaking of grandchildren and great-grandchildren, Martin exited, kissing most everyone in sight. It was exactly the New York theater that made prices moot, especially for the "21" crowd. I only worried that the old-timers would be unsettled by the food actually being good, at times even brilliant.

Rents were soaring. Liquor sales had slowed. Expense-account meals were now only 50 percent deductible. There was a surge in what industry overseers called "substantial" restaurants filing for Chapter 11, the *Times* reported. Burnout was epidemic. "About 75 per cent of restaurants close or change hands within five years of opening," the *Times* quoted a representative of the State Restaurant Association as saying. That was July. Then came Black Monday. On October 19, 1987, the Dow dropped 508 points. A glut of hotels were in the works. Christian Lacroix arrived in town a week after the crash with clothes—his fifteen-thousand-dollar poufs—of "a luxury and defiance" that hadn't been seen, *New York* magazine's Julie Baumgold wrote, "since eighteenth-century French aristocrats rattled in carts over cobblestones on their way to the guillotine." The cover line read "Crash Chic." Food-world entrepreneurs got caught mid-step, too. The Reagan years were over. Now it had to be bistro, intimate, neighborhood. Small seemed cozy; laid-back was reassuring. A trio of Frenchmen at Park Bistro carved out a small empire of informal spots on Lower Park Avenue, opening Les Halles, a bistro-cum-butcher shop.

Red meat was in and out and in again. Pork, touting itself as "the other white meat," enjoyed an amazing renaissance. We were lured downtown by Provence, Barocco, Arqua. The potato was back, mashed, smashed, fried in ribbons, matchsticks, shoestrings. Snapple put iced tea in a bottle.

We worked one-on-one with our trainers, vacationed at spas, discovered AA, put the *8-Week Cholesterol Cure* on the best-seller list, and caused a run on oat bran. Fruits and vegetables had designer labels. Barbara Kafka's *Microwave Gourmet* (1987) made us take another look at a tool serious foodniks sneered at.

Joe Baum signed on to make the old Rainbow Room atop Rockefeller Center look newly Art Deco again, spiffier than the first time around, with silver lamé–skirted tables and cigarette girls in Broadway costumes selling teddy bears. Twenty million dollars? Twenty-five? "We don't know yet," Baum admitted. Like a great born-again beauty reliving a glamorous youth at the age of fifty-three, Rainbow had been rescued from dowdy neglect by the century's master restaurant creator. By raising the floor, architect Hugh Hardy had engineered a stunning new skyscape. Everyone who knew and loved Joe Baum was thrilled he had found a landlord who could afford him. "In the Renaissance, the popes hired Michelangelo," observed labor lawyer Ted Kheel. "Today the Rockefellers have Joe Baum. And this is his masterwork." An opening night gala, just before Christmas in 1987, drew the high and the mighty and a few ringers. Leona Helmsley wore a white strapless gown and gazed up into the face of her Harry as if he were her prom date. Eager young people who had never danced together before, possibly hearing an unamplified live band for the first time, improvised the mambo and merengue.

Success played the tramp on the night crawlers' circuit, never faithful for long to the hot spot of the week. I made the rounds downtown in the rainy spring of 1988. Caffe Roma, torrid for one season, was shuttered. Il Palazzo, having obliterated Café Seiyoken, was nearly deserted. The action had cooled at America. Joanna's was abandoned and forlorn. The savvy had pretty much written off Studio 54. Steve Rubell and Ian

Schrager had left the Palladium behind. Savants of the night snubbed Nell's, where wistful whippersnappers leaped out of prom-night limousines to bounce off the velvet ropes. Canastel's, the radiator of Park Avenue South, with Marc Packer's following of mannequins and the guys who paid their bills, still steamed along. Mezzogiorno, in SoHo, and Karen Jean's dollhouse, Bistro du Nord, were jumping.

Café Iguana looked as if it had been slapped together with scissors and paste—fake wisteria, tinseled stars, a couple of stuffed iguanas. The warehouse stretched endlessly, full of promise, and still there wasn't room to pack everyone in. And it was not about the food, though after a few margaritas (these were actually made with tequila), the sleaziest enchilada seemed wonderful. Mama Iguana herself, as the endlessly affectionate Joyce Steins liked to call herself, slithered through the crowd, using a linebacker to clear the way, kissing, reaching out, stepping into the hugs of her loyal brood. It was a place to feel loved and wanted even if you had to wait an hour outside in the rain.

I didn't need a thermometer to get the drift at Canal Bar. There was already a hint of divine smugness in the air. Everyone was wearing black, minis and turtles and tribal kimonos, granny shoes and bootees, bikini tops and elastic bands. It was that era when Brian McNally—after Odeon and Indochine—could do no wrong. A decade earlier, Bianca Jagger would have celebrated her birthday at Studio 54. This year, her bash drew even Sly Stallone to Canal Bar.

McNally could take a tacky joint on the edge of nowhere, splatter a bit of paint about, and open. No need even to hang the name outside. Canal Bar—nowhere near Canal Street, to be provocatively perverse— was as improvisational as the wait crew.

Keith Haring, Tina Chow, and Lauren Hutton dropped in to celebrate Julian Schnabel's Whitney retrospective. You could spot architect Philip Johnson, designer Carolina Herrera, or restaurateur Ken Aretsky (almost nightly) in the see-and-be-seen booth of honor. "I don't understand it quite," McNally would say in his disarming way. "I'm astonished people come."

Eric Goode got his badge for spookiness as a partner at Area, with its bizarre dioramas. So no one was surprised that a pair of stuffed Dobermans guarded the fake Miró and coats got checked in the vault of a lounge and disco called M.K. in what once had been a bank. There was usually a modest match at the pool table in the library, with its high school lab cases of dusty skulls and bones. The decorous posed while chatting on the pink velvet–canopied bed. "You have time to explore, practicing scream suppression, waiting 90 minutes for your 10:30 reservation," I observed. "Soon you, yes, Mouseburger you, will be inches away from Mick Jagger, Fred Hughes, Steve Rubell, the nocturnal rogues of the literary brat pack—Jay McInerney and Bret Easton Ellis. Count on getting in to M.K. summer weekends," I suggested, "when anyone with a shred of dignity who doesn't have a house in the Hamptons will stay home pretending he does."

The door torture at Au Bar on East Fifty-eighth Street, located in a basement tarted up with books bought by the yard to look vaguely English library, made me defensive. "Amazing that a nation so indifferent to bondage could be so hungry for humiliation," I wrote. "What is a doorman anyway? Just someone who isn't smart enough to get a real job. Are you going to grovel? Why, he's spent more time on the street than the trash trucks." I watched families torn apart by the doorman's waiting list. Two would get the nod. The rest, dashed by rejection, waved good-bye. The elected two hesitated, dazed by the horror of the moment . . . and then they entered. After all, they were the chosen.

And for what? The place was empty. Even so, we were led to the worst table in the house without a murmur. Night chroniclers thought Howard Stein was smart to escape Xenon when disco mania succumbed to restaurant madness. And he'd made a fortune across the street at Prima Donna till it tumbled into Chapter 11. Now this. "He must know our secret terrors," I wrote. "Our unspeakable desires."

It had taken forever and a year after his abrupt departure from Montrachet for David Bouley, his brothers, and a kitchen crew with nothing else to do to fashion the graceful vaulted ceiling arches and the distinctly Provençal facade of Bouley, a mirage of France in a quirky corner of TriBeCa. Nothing but Limoges and handmade linens would do for David. It was no trick at all to get drunk waiting for a table and drunker still waiting for dinner that fall of 1988. It felt as if the budding diva was out there at the range doing it all himself, reluctant to surrender your terrine to a hapless waiter. By the time you'd mopped up a silver tray of pistachio *tuiles,* blueberry *financières,* and truffles, lemon tartlets might arrive, still warm from the oven. You'd aged a few months and gained a pound, and now you had to find a taxi in the midnight gloom.

Given his nimbus of fame from triumph at the River Café, Charles Palmer's debut at Aureole in an expensively redone duplex at 34 East 61st Street in 1988 was closely watched. Quite frankly, I didn't get the charm of swans, turtles, frogs, and one baleful cow staring right at me in plaster relief on the wall. But Palmer's satiny sea scallops sandwiched in crunchy potato crusts on a puddle of citrus-scented olive oil was a dish for the century. And the flying buttresses of architectural desserts by Richard Leach would have made Howard Roark jealous. Certainly they inspired looming architecture in sugar from pastry wizards across town.

In 1988, Ian Schrager proved you didn't need spacious bedrooms to launch a hotel à la mode by hiring Philippe Starck to design the Royalton. Lounge lizards soon claimed all of Starck's futuristic pastel velvet chaises and settees and then the furniture had to be trussed up in ill-fitting protective white sailcloth muumuus. Exempted from camouflage were the chartreuse banquettes of the lobby restaurant "44," where the last chef of the late, lamented Maxwell's, Geoffrey Zakarian, was running the range. One Friday night, I noticed that everyone at dinner looked like a rock star. I felt redundant.

As the rising stars of American cooking got all the press, ossified French monuments struggled to stay relevant. But Italian feederies just kept on spawning—from the ultimate in truffled opulence, San Domenico, to Pino Luongo's celebration of mother's cooking, Le Madri, where we swooned over the truffle oil–scented cheese-stuffed foccacio in May 1989. Sette Mezzo charmed uptown's masters of the universe. The Sindonis and their cousins, the Lattanzi clan, blossomed on the Upper East Side and then everywhere, even going kosher.

Sonny Bono was elected mayor of Palm Springs. Bertolucci's *The Last Emperor* swept the Oscars. Harvard scored a patent for a genetically altered mouse. If our shoulder pads got any wider, we could never get into the ark two by two. Food-world seers charted East meets West, dubbing it "Pacific Rim" cooking (later it would be Asian fusion and ultimately global confusion). Carmine's family-style platters were cheap. The ballet world found a hangout—Punsch—and then cruelly abandoned it.

Prepared-food sections in supermarkets continued to grow. No one was about to give up sushi, fajitas, or gravlax; we were just more likely to take them home as we cut back on eating out. Restaurants in New York had always come and gone. But now shocking losses mounted. In the darkness of the stumbling economy, you could actually book a table for lunch at Le Bernardin, even dinner at Lutèce, without calling more than a few hours ahead. Terrance Brennan was in the kitchen of Prix Fixe, preparing marvelous gourmand dinners for just twenty-one dollars. But all those bankruptcies led to cheap leases that enabled established restaurateurs to spawn. It was, and is, the New York religion. Where someone else has failed, I will survive.

44

Le Cirque: Having My Cake and Eating It, Too

STAR CROWNED CHEFS COME AND GO BUT LE CIRQUE'S MENAGERIE STILL swings from the rafters, jostling for position," I wrote in the late winter of 1987. It was a time when Sirio Maccioni's closely crowded tables turned three times at lunch, the ultrachic Europeans arriving tousled from bed at 2:30 PM, even 3:00. Oh how Sirio relished his role as the table juggler, the courtly hand smoocher, the ego massager to generations of the high and the flighty. He feigned humility and affected pain as he flaunted the reservation book for lunch to me one day. "Look. Look," he said, as if scarcely able to bear the torture. "VIP" it said next to a famous name. "Very VIP." "Very VIP." The lineup was one man's Red Alert. He studied the blizzard of gleaming white tablecloths, adjusting the seating plan. He would put Governor Hugh Carey's eight at that VIP table. Jerome Zipkin, First Lady Nancy Reagan's walker, could have President Nixon's usual corner post, across the way from Bendel's Gerry Stutz. That left a conspicuous side by side on the coveted banquette for sable-swathed Ann Getty and her publishing partner, Lord Weidenfeld. Oh such rarefied bodies affirming the status of his banquettes. There were often times when someone congenitally unrefusable arrived, and then hyperventilating waiters would wrestle a table into the breezy few spare inches that permitted entrance at the front door. Sirio seemed quite pleased with himself, I thought.

That this impoverished orphan farm boy from Tuscany would be passing Parmesan toast to the ex-president. That so many swells had come to consider Le Cirque their own private canteen. That Sirio, freshly arrived in 1956 as an accomplished captain from transatlantic steamship luxury—scorned and rejected as Italian by the New York haughty French feeding establishment—now ruled the podium of the hottest French restaurant in town. These were the consummate cavalier's golden days.

He charm was so slick, that dimpled smile so quick, it was impossible to imagine the anger inside. Years later, when we became confidants, Sirio began spinning tales of the rocky road that had led him to East Sixty-fifth Street. Fresh out of Tuscan hotel school, he had won a coveted apprentice spot at the Plaza Athénée in Paris. When it became clear he didn't speak French, he was kicked out, penniless, not to return till he spoke French. He looked up the one person he knew from home in Paris, Ivo Levi, known then as Yves Montand. The dashing actor got Sirio a job in the chorus line of the Follies Bergères, where the nudity of the showgirls left Sirio perpetually aroused, and he was subsequently fired. It wasn't till I read his autobiography* that I felt the full force of the rage that he still carries: the early death of his mother, his father killed by the retreating Nazis, his grandmother sending him off to hotel school in his father's shoes painted black, the poor country bumpkin his classmates laughed at and girls would not date, the doors closed to Italians.

I'd loved being nobody, unnoticed, at the Colony at the dawning of *New York*. There, Sirio quickly learned who was who in the discreet, nonchattering upper crust. Maccioni apparently thought my critique of the Colony in 1969 unnecessarily cruel because it mentioned shutting down part of the pastry room because of rats in the cellar. He was an obsesser. He never forgave me for mentioning the rats. In the oblige of his new noblesse, he insisted he was amused at my take on Le Cirque as "soup kitchen for the anguished orphans of the late Colony," though I ranked it thirteenth in my 1975 ratings of the best French restaurants. It didn't

---

Sirio: The Story of My Life and Le Cirque, with Peter Elliot (Wiley, 2004).

make sense to complain anymore about my stingy praise, he decided. He relished his spot as a power player in the pages of our magazine.

Once I could no longer remain anonymous, Sirio simply set out to seduce me as he tried to seduce all journalists (as he felt he had seduced Craig Claiborne) with his free-flowing ooze of charm—the irresistible blizzards of white truffle that would fall onto the risotto, the pasta primavera that was not on the menu but appeared as if by magic, the dance of unordered sweets. I called it "doing the Sirio."

It was not about sex, although, dimpled and lean at fifty in his thousand-dollar custom-made Italian suits, Sirio was a looker. There were beauties who offered, pressing telephone numbers into his hand. "If only I had the time," he would moan. All restaurateurs have that break between three and six o'clock, time for a nap, time to skip a nap. But no, there was not even a whisper of gossip about Sirio.

I even fell for the outrageous concept that I, in my no-name line-blocker shoulder pads off the final, final sale rack at Bendel's, had an unassailable claim to a "Very VIP" banquette west of Barbara Walters and east of Liz Smith. Did I resist? Of course not. Though I always warned anonymous readers they might wither and waste away in the gulag behind the bar, where Sirio, caught in the gravity pull of his pets, rarely wandered. "Le Cirque without Sirio hovering is not Le Cirque at all," I wrote.

One day, my guest and I were nibbling, savoring, oohing and aahing, trembling in response to a fusillade of enticements from the new chef, Daniel Boulud, a name that meant nothing then. I couldn't help noticing that while we were sharing a daunting feast, most everyone else was simply having lunch. I spied an omelette across the room and a chef's salad not far away. I surveyed the regulars, the bouffant blondes, small women with large jewels, and svelte beauties who made a career of marrying better each time. Well, too bad, I thought. Let them eat sole.

There were flaws in the early Boulud kitchen (my critical faculties were never truly blinded by Sirio's fawning). But a melting flan of porcini and foie gras beside lobster in a spinach nest made me shiver. And I was enraptured by what would become Boulud classics: the barely cooked rouget wrapped in bands of crisped potato on a butter-slicked red wine sauce, and the layering of scallop slices with rounds of black truffle in heady truffle butter. (Boulud has disarmingly shared the credit for both

with Sottha Khunn, the alter ego he'd brought along with him to Le
Cirque from the kitchen of Le Régence at the Plaza Athénée.)

Every fall after his annual holiday in Italy, Sirio would return to Le
Cirque with boxes of the first white truffles and, every year, another Italian notion. As his confidence grew, Sirio began diluting Le Cirque's
French cast with the food of his own Italian reveries: ravioli, risotto, the
Parmesan toast, focaccia, *crostini al lardo,* sheer white pig fat—"less cholesterol than butter," he assured me. Sirio was worried that the Lyon-
born Boulud would not be up to the house's traditional Thursday lunch
masterwork—the *bollito misto*—the classic boiled meats, Italian-style,
with its aromatic boiled calf's head, tongue, brains, brisket, and capon.
It came with a constantly multipying platter of condiments: assorted
salts, a trio of mustards, green sauce, red sauce, *mostarda di frutta* (candied fruit spiked with mustard). The solution was to alternate Sirio's
classic *bollito* with Daniel's French boiled dinner, the pot-au-feu. Thursday was my favorite day for lunch.

Heads would turn. All eyes were riveted with shock, if not revulsion,
to my right, where two captains lowered a mammoth platter to a hastily
planted service table beside me. I felt like Henry VIII in a room full of
panicked anorexics. Happily, one or two small tidbits of filet, rib,
haunch, foie, cabbage, turnip, parsnip, celery root, and carrot were
quickly arranged clockwise on my plate and the platter was trundled off
to tempt Henry Kissinger.

I thought that Sirio seemed almost happy in that golden era when Ag-
nellis and Rothschilds got off the plane at JFK and rushed to Le Cirque,
baggage and all, when *Town & Country* photographed Sirio's best-dressed
blondes all in a row on the front banquette, with the dashing host draped
across their tables. Le Cirque was home base for visiting French chefs.
Paul Bocuse, Roger Vergé, Gaston Lenôtre, and their camp followers
would fill a big round for late lunch and then return for dinner. Le
Cirque's crème brûlée—its unique gossamer finish credited to a pastry
sous-chef named Francesco Gutierrez—was already legendary. It would
appear even on Paul Bocuse's menu as crème brûlée Sirio. For me, the
voluptuous bread and butter pudding was easily its equal. I was never
forced to choose between them. Sirio always sent out both.

And then would come the silver compote of sugared-glacéd fruit,
candied peel, coconut macaroons, tartlets with berries gleaming like

jewels from Bulgari, and killer cookies. And chocolate truffles, of course, discreet in their own covered crystal box. Driven as always, Sirio had recently sprung for new $125 service plates. "The pastry chefs are insisting I must buy big plates for the dessert specials, every one a different color," he confided, sighing like a man hopelessly in love with a profligate wife. "I think I will let them persuade me."

One afternoon some years later, I let William Reilly, my big boss from Primedia, the new owner of *New York*, arrive before I did and found him sitting in purdah. It was a few minutes before Sirio dashed by and caught sight of me in his peripheral vision.

"Why are you sitting here?" he cried in alarm. "Let me move you to another table."

I could feel Bill Reilly shift in his seat, ready to make the move. He was the new media power in town, and it would do nothing for his image to be seen in Siberia.

"But I like this table, Sirio," I insisted. "Now I can see what it's like to be nobody at Le Cirque."

Sirio lowered his head in exasperation. "You know everyone is the same here," he said. He always said that. I think he actually believed it.

As teenagers, Sirio's sons began to appear. He loved showing them off. When they were children, his wife, Egi, would often take the three boys along for dinner at six o'clock so they could have a chance to see their father. Sirio began sending them out on the floor when they were about twelve. Marco, the sociable middle son, used to go up to Sirio and say, "Don't you want me to bring the people champagne?" Later, Sirio shook his head, remembering. "It seems the people were giving him five-dollar tips. I never found out, or I would have killed him. Then I discovered the secret."

As one son or another won compliments for finding prime tables for the demanding masters of the universe in the usually overbooked Le Cirque, Sirio Maccioni defended himself: "It's not my fault they want to be in this business. I pushed them to be doctors, lawyers, architects, anything but this. Maybe I pushed too hard." He would brood.

Egi Maccioni gave him credit. "Sirio, he didn't push. We never encouraged them to take on this difficult life. Still, you know, they started to breathe this atmosphere when they were very little. We took them every summer all over to the restaurants of the great chefs. And you know Sirio, how he is. He has only one subject."

The oldest, Mario, according to brother Marco, never went along with Sirio's idea of saving the best tables for special friends. Mario would seat Kissinger in the far corner. "A table is a table," he would say—a line guaranteed to ignite a tirade from Papa.

Marco was innocent and eager for initiation his first Saturday officially on the job at Le Cirque. He recalled that day: "My dad was eating a late lunch at the bar. Definitely you didn't want to go near him then. He told me to answer the phone and tell everyone it was full, full, full. But people were so insistent. They wouldn't take no. They insisted on talking to Sirio. I handed him the phone. He was furious. 'You take care of it. I don't care if it's the president or the pope.' Then I discovered he was testing me. . . . He had Felix the bookkeeper calling and asking for a reservation. One day, the president's office did call, and I said, 'No. We're full.' And my father grabbed the phone. 'You idiot,' he was shouting. 'That *is* the president.' "

Marco had a nose for wines. Sirio instructed him, "When it's a table of good people, people that you know, offer a good bottle of wine." One day, Sirio caught the youth giving away a three-thousand-dollar Petrus.

Marco defended himself: "But Papa, you told me to offer a good bottle of wine."

My Aspen Mountain man, Steven, and I were spending the summer in Pietrasanta, less than an hour from Montecatini. It was 1995, the year Sirio spent trying to open Circo. "The little trattoria for my wife and sons," he called it. Every summer, Maccioni would close for August and the family would retreat to Montecatini. There, they lived in what had been the mayor's home, where Sirio, as a boy, would peer into the windows and marvel at the luxury.

Invited for dinner, we met the Maccionis in the market one afternoon, where Egi was buying a crate of bright yellow zucchini blossoms and fruit so ripe, you could smell the peaches a block away. In the early evening, Egi and Sirio's sister began flouring and deep-frying a forest of zucchini flowers as their friend Franca, the gifted chef of Romano's in nearby Viareggio, on her night off, seasoned a huge *branzino*. Sirio's new assistant, Elizabeth Blau, and a young woman hired to cook at Circo had been invited for the week, the better to absorb the Tuscan spirit and re-produce it on West Fifty-fifth Street once Circo opened. As usual, Sirio was ranting about the abuses he suffered from Adam Tihany, the architect he loved to berate but wouldn't put down a floor without.

We were to be fourteen at the table for dinner, but every few minutes the phone rang and Sirio invited someone else. The dining room table grew and grew, till finally it stretched into the kitchen, now set for twenty-three. I was adding flatware and glasses when Sirio came downstairs, flushed and triumphant.

"My son Marco. He is so smart," he said proudly. "He sends a fax." Sirio waved a sheet of paper. "There are so many VIPs at Le Cirque tonight that I must assign the tables and fax him back." He sat down happily to solve the crucial geometry.

Sirio had fed the cardinal and the pope, presidents, and everyone else. No one thought to ask him, but how fitting that there he was at the top of the steps, breasting the crowd at St. Bartholomew's Church on Park Avenue for the funeral of Malcolm Forbes, hissing sotto voce instructions to the ushers—who should sit where because, well, who else would know?

Sirio was deeply wounded when Daniel Boulud left to go off on his own at Café Boulud after almost six years. He was livid when I wrote "A Petit Pan," criticizing Sylvain Portay, the Ducasse hand he'd imported to share the kitchen with Sottha Khunn after Daniel bowed out. A favorite of Sirio's took me to dinner several months later. Sirio looked through me. Finally, he could stand it no more. He swerved toward our table. "We don't need people like you," he sputtered. Two courses later, the dessert seduction commenced.

He only stopped ranting about my ingratitude and betrayal to anyone too polite to beg off when, not long after, Ruth Reichl cleverly gave Le Cirque a double ranking: one star for unknowns, three stars for regulars. Now in his anguish and rage at Reichl, my complaints seemed almost forgivable.

I can't recall ever seeing Sirio happy at Le Cirque 2000. When he didn't like the renewal lease terms on Sixty-fifth Street, he let himself be courted by the sultan of Brunei's brother at the Palace Hotel. They offered him the moon and he accepted. Perhaps he let himself bask in affection at the preview opening on his birthday, when his world paid court. And certainly his spirits must have soared the evening he knew that Sottha Khunn's kitchen had won back its wandering fourth star from the *Times*. I could see he was thrilled the night of his book launch in 2004, with a meteor shower of stars and heavenly bodies gathered at the best book party ever. "It's nothing special," he insisted. "Just old friends."

But he was bruised and astonished by the reaction to Le Cirque 2000. "Either we are a genius or we are completely crazy," he liked to say. Did he think *he* owned Le Cirque 2000? I wrote. I guess he didn't imagine we would take it so personally. "The Park Avenue blondes, waspish trust fund babies and Jewish American princesses, we gourmand priests and food-world flapsters, we jet-stream migrants and Euro transplants, we owned Le Cirque." And we went into a tizzy the day Sirio threw open the doors.

" 'If I brought this chair home and said it was for my new restaurant, you'd say I was out of my mind,' cried one regular, craning her neck from behind the tall, one armed velvet chair with its amusing clown buttons. 'You can't see who's here.'

" 'It's chaos, but it's so early. Give them time,' a loyalist countered. 'The chairs will go. Sirio and his sons will saw them down themselves.' "

The majority of regulars seemed shocked at the neon and plastic contempo that architect Adam Tihany had installed in the landmark rooms. "It's like putting a Ferrari in a palazzo," Tihany kept insisting, as if that were a trick we'd all like credited in our obituary.

"How could they desecrate these beautiful historic rooms?" moaned an anguished and expensively preserved preservationist. "Neon and schmutz," one fan summed it up after a $160 lunch. Alas, the million-dollar kitchen—Sottha's dream—was forty-six seconds away from our table, on a flight path blocked by casual amblers and clustered arrivals at the maître d's stand. No wonder the focaccia—too long out of the oven—was ossified in its slick of embalming oil. Without the familiar royal banquette up front, how could you know if you counted? No one was sure which room was Siberia. That could unsettle your tummy even before lunch.

Sure enough, by my sixth visit, they'd shrunk the chairs. Jacques Torres, the Fabergé of pâtissiers, was sending out his cunning chocolate stove, the cassis topiary, and a wintry tree made of chocolate, with branches nuzzling bonbons. Many of the ladies who munch chopped *salade* for lunch were claiming their tables. But it would soon be obvious that certain "Very, Very VIPs" had already fled for the kindergarten tables at Harry Cipriani's.

Though Le Cirque and Circo at the Bellagio in Las Vegas, and celebrations rotated at great expense through party rooms upstairs at Le Cirque 2000, would make him rich, Sirio seemed restless and unfulfilled. His tirades against real and imagined injustices became legendary. He would move Le Cirque yet again. He would open another canteen for his sons at the new Bloomberg building. And they wanted him in Paris, he confided, warning not to tell a soul. The great chef André Soltner tried to persuade him to let go. Soltner, the workhorse patron of Lutèce, had surprised everyone by reveling in retirement after selling out to Michael Weinstein of publically held Ark. But he could not persuade Sirio to slow down.

This time, Sirio would show us all once again. There would be a reincarnation of Le Cirque, he insisted. The orphan farm boy who went off to the nearby hotel school wearing his dead father's shoes walks in his own shoes now, and his moneyed pets—the faithful and the strayed—will follow him wherever he decides to venture next.

45

AND TO THINK THAT I SAW
IT ON WOOSTER STREET

IT SEEMS TO ME IT'S ENDEARING—THOUGH SOME MIGHT THINK IT'S PITI-
ful—that New Yorkers (both those to the manner born and those imported)
are never quite sure they count until they get *that* table. Think of the street-
smart peasants and derniers arrivistes we have wooed in our hunger and insecurity over the decades to get *that* table: Henri Soulé at Le Pavillon; his
ex-cashier, Mme. Henriette at La Côte Basque; the impoverished orphan
from a Tuscan farm, Sirio Maccioni; the neighborhood saloon keeper,
Elaine Kaufman; the custom-shirt vender, Glenn Birnbaum at Mortimer's.
For a few thrill-racked fortnights in 1989, we looked for affirmation to
Brian McNally, self-taught son of a stevedore from London's South End.
Grown-ups, powers who decide what news is fit to print, billionaires,
princelings, proper little Junior Leaguers with their velvet headbands, we
vie for *that* table. But then so many of us are street-smart, too, peasants and
newly hatched rich. And for a short, happy moment in 1989, we were
nourished by Brian's nod to a reserved niche at 150 Wooster Street.

It had no name at all, just an address. A former body shop faintly
aglow on a desolate strip of nighttime SoHo. Drive by and you'd think
someone had left a light burning in a garage. Still, a body shop, in its
Brian body-worshiping way. And overnight. Boffo.

Yes, you needed a reservation. No, you couldn't get one unless you were desperate enough to settle for a table at 6:30. You joined the meek at the bar, waiting to inherit, hoping someone would invite you to join their booth in the continuous house party, watching pals darting about the room, lobbing kisses and innuendo. The youthquake, the shock troops of fashion. Women with saucers on their heads. Men with pleated paper fans and green plastic bangles. Lots of Eurolings and South Americanos and Japanese, a Zen master, all his minions carrying cameras. Beauties with bared thighs, bared backs, bared shoulders. People you recognized at once, even though you didn't know who they were. "And did you see? It's Bianca."

"If only we could bottle Brian McNally," I gushed in my early review. "If only some Harvard MBA could reduce McNally's seemingly improvisational fumblings to a formula. Dazed entrepreneurs of feeding, riding the equilibrium-defying roller coaster toward Chapter 11, would love to plump the secret of his knack. How he chooses the most remote outburb and makes it 'in.' How he spruces things up so subtly the room looks evolved or almost undone. That even the food counts. Do not forget that Patrick Clark came of age at the stove of Odeon. The Canal Bar's Matthew Tivy is no slouch. And Ali Barker, who pleased folks at the Union Square Cafe despite a drift toward excess, has calmed down here."

Even the serving crew was beautiful. Young women from exotic cultures in garments that fit like wet suits. Our waiter, who looked like James Dean and was young enough to say, "James who?" offering club soda after bathing my sleeve in beurre blanc. Everyone was smiling and pretending not to stare.

So why did Brian look so sad? "This isn't what I wanted," he lamented. "I wanted a quiet, mellow, serious restaurant with good food. This is horrifying. Horrifying. I'll never open another restaurant." He gazed across the room, spying Ron Darling. "Now that's impressive." He smiled and left to greet the Mets ace pitching star.

And oh yes, Bianca was there.

The hole in the ozone was growing. Alaska sued Exxon and a few other oil firms for the massive March spill. Hungary allowed sixty thousand East Germans into Austria to seek freedom. "Why They Kill to Get into 150 Wooster" was the news flash from Manhattan.

All day, the phone lights would flash at the SoHo hot spot. The reservationist would listen to the outpourings of emotion, jotting notes but making no commitments. The struggle to be in the right place before Calvin and Bianca moved seemed a never-ending one. No table would get leased for the evening until Brian McNally came in midafternoon, studied the candidates, and designed the room for the evening. "Look who we didn't accommodate yesterday because I had to be away at a wedding," he said, brooding. "Paul Simon. Bret Easton Ellis. Jay McInerney." Dear me, I thought. Mercury. Apollo. Pan.

Never mind cops narrowing the street to guard the Italian foreign minister. Never mind financier Al Taubman introducing his daughter to designer Mary McFadden (chalk pale, all in black) beside her new baby cupcake husband. Never mind the scattering of Gwathmeys, filmmaker Joan Micklin Silver, Ian Schrager with his niece and Steve Rubell's nephew, plus the usual art-world suspects, the assorted Lady Gotrocks. "The evening was lost as far as I was concerned," McNally told me.

Friday night. There was art darling Mary Boone, tanned and wearing white. Behind me, I heard *Time*'s art guru Robert Hughes explaining the house's barley dish: "It's halfway between a risotto and a couscous."

"But that's impossible," Brian was saying into the phone. "Your secretary couldn't have reserved two weeks ago, because we never book more than three days in advance." He studied the Saturday-night lineup: Zubin Mehta, Charlie Sheen, Rusty Staub. "Rusty Staub?" he said, startled to see the Mets player among such predictables as actor Griffin Dunne and his fiancée, Carey Lowell. "It says here, 'the new Bond girl,' he snorted, "in case I didn't know." There were the inevitables of the era: Prince Michael of Greece, art dealer Tony Shafrazi with a party of twenty. McNally granted investor Stephen Swid his requested table for seven. "What shall I do about John Clavini?" he mused. "He's so nice. He's just a real nice guy, another one of those you have to resent because he comes with such wonderful girls. Tell him yes," he instructed the reservationist, then turned to me and said, "Don't think we just book by whim."

Whim, savvy, loyalty, witchcraft, hormones. "Brian's heaven is a room criss-crossed by dazzling women, long-haired wraiths in clingy bits of cloth, saucy, pouty, buds of ancient civilizations," I wrote. From afar, or even close-up, you could say Brian McNally had rubbed a few sticks together, scattered a few tiles, planted a palm tree, and for now he had the hottest destination in town. "I caw't think wot to caw it," he said in his down-London way. "We'll name it later."

It had been a quiet week—Jewish holidays, a Rolling Stones concert—but the place did fine. There was sudden intake of breath and silence at the entrance of the tabloid's toy of the moment, onetime Miss American Bess Myerson, six feet in heels. The *Times*'s Abe Rosenthal, his wife, novelist Shirley Lord, and the Arthur Gelbs (he being Abe's right hand, they the biographers of Eugene O'Neill) in the power booth on the right looked stunned and rose to a greeting. And then in the late show, A&M Records cofounder Jerry Moss and Jellybean Benitez; Diane Von Furstenberg; a contingent from the hot retailer Barneys; boss Gene Pressman with his house restaurateur, Pino Luongo. Between flicks: Brian De Palma, Bob Rafelson (*Five Easy Pieces*), Don Simpson and Jerry Bruckheimer (*Flashdance, Top Gun*), the L.A. inseparables, David Geffen, Barry Diller, Sandy Gallin. Michael Douglas, off the plane from Japan, checked in at 150. Everyone's eyes were blinking as if in a supermarket-induced trance. Heads swiveled out of control. Model Beverly Johnson was just one flash of beauty you might recognize from *Vogue*. Tom and Meredith Brokaw. Carl Bernstein working the room. The department store zillionaires from San Francisco, Prentis and Denise Hale. Calvin and Kelly with filmmaker Howard Rosenman. A swirl of orange as Bianca was embraced. At our table, we sat tingling and giggling while our butter sauce congealed.

"That's Prince Michael of Greece in a booth with five women," I told my friends, who did not track dynasties that came before *Dynasty*. "Actually, one of those women is a man."

My friend corrected me. "Two of those women are men."

Well, of course Brian was wowed. That's one of his charms. And he could be as starstruck as anyone, making sure I heard about the night he had Robin Williams, Bruce Willis, Paul Simon, and Steve Martin at one station, with Madonna across the room. Or the time Robert De Niro was in the first right-hand booth, Isabella Rossellini at the adjoining post, Arnold Schwarzenegger and Maria Shriver in the left-corner booth, and Claudia Cohen with Ronald Perelman and Carolina Herrera front and center. Or the night there was a communal intake of breath and utter silence . . . for Elizabeth Taylor. And the vroom outside that had the girls squealing, expecting a certain notorious cycling Don Juan, and in walked

Malcolm Forbes in a gleaming white motorcycle helmet, unzipping leather to reveal the pinstripes underneath.

"People used to drink and drug," pointed out my pal Hal Rubenstein, restaurant critic of the hipper-than-thou *Details* and editor-to-be of Malcolm Forbes's ill-fated *Egg* magazine. "Now they're sober and sane. Their septums have been fixed. They go to their AA meetings and they want to go out to eat. It's a slightly different crowd here, older, more sure of themselves. At Canal Bar, they table-hopped. Here, they walk. And we're all such media junkies. We hate to miss anything."

Anthony Haden-Guest, nightlife hipster and my colleague at *New York,* introduced his date: a born-yesterday beauty with a skimpily bandeaued shelf above an expanse of perfect midriff. "Lisa Gaye stars in *Toxic Avenger 2* and *Toxic Avenger 3,* but that's not why I brought her here," he told Brian.

"It's about a monster evolved from garbage," said Lisa, lending me her glasses so I could case the room again. The crowd was giving way to late-late look-alikes. That's either Nell Campbell's sister or Anna Wintour's cousin, we decided, focusing on a red Dutch-bob helmet of hair.

Haden-Guest was expanding as a British observer on the appeal of 150 Wooster's unfinished state. "Americans reject perfection. They like things unfinished. All those fancy done-up postmodern restaurants closed because they were too finished. You felt like an extra. Here, you feel you're part of the action. That's why people prefer the sketch to the painting."

"Do you think that's why men prefer young girls?" I asked.

Anthony clutched Lisa Gaye's hand. "Perhaps. Perhaps."

Brian stopped by again. He had the distinct advantage of not being remarkably tall. He didn't have to lean so far, double over, or crouch as he cruised the room, chatting up friends, poking fun, laughing, deliciously amused, happy. "I just came from a table where everyone was talking Yiddish," he marveled.

"You know what they say," muttered Haden-Guest. "Talk British. Think Yiddish. A Brian place is like an Eagles song," said Haden-Guest, babbling on. "Brand-new, it sounds like a standard."

"You're so lyrical," cried Brian. "You should be a writer. You should stop typing and start writing."

I returned a week later. Just days from his fortieth birthday, McNally seemed ambivalent, a bit weary, I thought. Though he often gazed around the brightish (for best visibility) unfinished room and marveled to see every seat taken by someone he knew. " 'Tiz sort of amaaaazing. It's a lot of fawning," he told me. "Lots of groveling. Lots of pulling on the forelock. I'm buying the time to do nothing one day."

Alas, McNally's backers at Canal Bar took one look at the 150 Wooster revelers and sued him for luring their crowd to SoHo. One day we arrived and found the door padlocked. It was a slam to the excess and the delicious superficiality of the eighties. Given fifteen minutes of fame, 150 Wooster rode the wave for less than five. Brian never had a comeback to equal it. Brother Keith would be the McNally with a genius for the nineties.

46

Memories of Maguy and Gilbert LeCoze

Maguy LeCoze was a saucy, flirtatious sylph in a futuristic jumpsuit, with a shiny Dutch bob and thick black bangs drifting into dark-kohled eyes above a turned-up nose, and Cupid's bow lips so red and perfect, they might have been painted on with enamel. (Years later, after she and her brother Gilbert had captured New York, she confided to a fashion magazine that it took her twenty minutes every day to paint those lips.)

But this was the first time I saw her, fussing playfully over the Parisian regulars who'd brought me to the original little cubby (yes, cubby) Le Bernardin on the Left Bank in the spring of 1977, a few years after its launch. So she might have been just thirty-two, and Gilbert, the handsome swashbuckler in blue jeans and a fishmonger's apron, too shy to come out of the kitchen at first, was just thirty-one. He had a thick shock of shiny brown hair, significant sideburns, and mustache below his straight pointed nose, which he would twitch like a truffle dog in the heat of the hunt. For me, it was instant infatuation. I had a crush on them both, and on the stunning simplicity of the seafood, as well. Tiny gray shrimp nesting in a crock, delicate and sweet. Saint Pierre set raw on a plate, then bathed in a coriander-spiked broth before reaching the table opaque and sublime. The baby *bar,* sautéed in butter with cèpes along-side, was a contrasting punctuation in scent and taste and, ever so subtly, in texture. It was refreshingly more naturelle than nouvelle and free of nouvelle pretension.

The two of them as children, born eighteen months apart in Port Navalo, Brittany, were often left in their own small cosmos while Papa and Mama worked. Maguy remembers feeding the infant Gilbert, hold-ing him, once dropping him on his head, tormenting herself, convinced that if he died, she would die, too. A reluctant student, Gilbert did not mind at all rising at 5:00 AM to join his grandfather and papa on the fish-ing boat. As soon as they were old enough, Maguy and Gilbert were drafted for chores, long, exhausting hours scouring, scrubbing, destring-ling haricots verts at the Hôtel du Rhuys, the small inn and restaurant where the family lived upstairs.

With their parents focused on survival, Maguy and Gilbert moth-ered each other. They became inseparable. "Between us there was no space," Maguy has written. At eighteen, already a local homme fatal in his skintight jeans, Gilbert went off to military duty in Tahiti. And Maguy left for Monaco and then Paris. Liberated from the military, Gilbert joined her there in 1966, picking up odd jobs as a bartender and in a beauty salon, in clubs and discos. She worked in restaurants and hotels. They danced till dawn. "We were happy," Maguy recalls. "We had the best life."

Then at twenty-six, Gilbert seemed driven to find a focus, some-thing of their own. A restaurant seemed to be the only answer. It was all they really knew. They borrowed from everyone to turn a small antiques shop on the Left Bank into Le Bernardin in 1972. The first raves from the Paris critics filled the house. But they were ingenues, over their heads, really, and a couple of scathing notices soon emptied the place. It took three years to find their groove, Gilbert haunting the fish market to learn all he could, Maguy conquering her own shyness. Dancing on the bar in discos surrounded by pals was easy for her, but she always had to steel herself to walk up to a table of strangers in the restaurant. Then one day, the critic from *L'Express* rhapsodized about the turnaround, and suddenly they were pop stars—she dimpled and flirty in her miniskirts and pointy-toed boots, he with his mod mustache, smoldering good looks, and passion for fish and fun.

For me, it was a delicious package, a find for *New York* readers who were discovering in the early seventies the joys of eating their way across France—this adorable brother-and-sister act in an out-of-the-way spot on the quai, and Gilbert's brilliantly minimalist fricassée of coquillage, the barely cooked salmon with truffles, and his riff on raw fish lightly slicked with olive oil. By 1976, even Michelin had noticed and awarded a star.

Because Gilbert was untutored and raw, with no exposure to great kitchens, he had no choice but simplicity, Maguy has written. The idea of raw fish, she says, came from Uncle Corentin, at sea off Brittany, who would take a fresh-caught cod, skin it, and eat it on bread. It was her own obsession for raw tuna that inspired Gilbert's tuna carpaccio, she suggests. Of course the restaurateur brothers Jean and Paul Minchelli, lauded by the gourmand cognoscenti for their bravado, had been astonishing us at Le Duc with the exquisite raw coquillage, minimally poached langoustines, and oil-slicked raw fish I'd first tasted in 1973. And Maguy's special friendship with Jean must have given inspiration, and certainly sources, to the novices from Brittany.

But that's a small historical hiccup. The telling fact, after all, is that ten years after I'd first been so taken with the purity of his food, Gilbert LeCoze's carpaccios and tartares and smoked salmon rillettes and his daringly just-cooked halibut and rosy salmon with mint at Le Bernardin in New York would forever change the way Americans cooked and ate fish.

Maguy and Gilbert had moved in 1981 to a bigger space on rue Troyon near l'Etoile (where Guy Savoy is now) by the time I returned. Gilbert was infinitely less shy and cooking more confidently than ever. How lucky I was that our publisher, Clay Felker, keeper of the money bags at *New York,* understood that what I ate in France was a predictor of what we'd all be eating very soon in New York. The yearly swing through France was still essential, crucial research.

Now at dinner in the Brittany sky blue nook off the Champs Elysées, I was that writer who had followed the LeCoze star for *New York*'s impressionable readers, the properly smitten Pied Piper whose lyrical waxings had prompted a flow of impressionable mouths from America. Small saucers of new dishes I must taste punctuated the meal. Gilbert urged me to join him after the kitchen closed that night at Castel, the late-night restaurant and disco hangout for chefs and food-world habitués, Gilbert's usual haunt, where he smoked relentlessly and downed cognac after cognac. And we danced—disco but tight—rubbing into each other, provocative vertical seduction. I remember his lean, muscled body in the skintight polyester print shirt, one button opened, then two, then three, the hair on his chest slightly damp. Suddenly, we were in a taxi, kissing, caressing, zipping, unzipping. The same hand that so nimbly filleted a monkfish undid my bra with a single snap. I hugged myself together to get through the lobby of my hotel.

Inside my room, I had time only to drop my handbag on a chair. He was kissing me, tugging at my clothes, the room so dark that my filmy black underwear was barely perceptible against white skin, the bikini panties a puddle of lace around one ankle. He backed me against the door and fucked me standing up. I sank to the floor. We lay there kissing on a pile of pillows and covers he'd pulled from the bed. I stood up and opened the curtains a few inches so I could look at him in the light from the street and the sky . . . enough light to see that face, that wonderful profile.

We got into bed and shared a slow, romantic, movingly connected making of love. "I need to sleep a little," he said in French. He had me set my alarm for 4:00 AM. I was deep in sleep when it woke us. He pulled me close and kissed me, and just when it seemed like we might be leaping off a cliff again, he jumped out of bed. "I can't be late for the market," he said.

Gilbert was a wonderful lover. He loved to kiss. Endless wonderful kisses, sexy, teasing, demanding, romantic. When I was with him, he made me feel no other woman existed. He loved skin and breasts and everything two people could do in bed (at least everything that I knew about). He loved women. At the time, I don't think I imagined the intensity of that lust. I never let myself become jealous at rumors of his womanizing because I never thought of Gilbert as a serious man in my life. He was younger, of course, and clearly needed to run free. (I can hear my beloved therapist say, "You never took him seriously, so of course he didn't take you seriously.")

In most of the years when we were opportunistic lovers, I had one or two difficult men in my life back home—funny how I managed so often to fall for men who loved women with such passion that they found it impossible to settle for just one. Anyway, Gilbert was in Paris and our times together were clearly all about heat and lust. Heat, lust, and dancing, my favorite after-dinner pastimes, my only drugs.

At one point, I was forced to acknowledge Gilbert had a steady woman. She would arrive at the restaurant on rue Troyon in the evening and wait for him. And I liked her, too. She worked in a lingerie shop. I remember Maguy taking me there to pick out a shocking pink satin garter belt edged in black lace, a birthday gift from her and Gilbert. (My rigid policy of returning all gifts from food-industry friends or acquaintances did not, in my mind, include lovers.) Gilbert and his woman did not live together. I don't think Maguy or Gilbert ever actually lived with any of their lovers, at least not in France.

It seemed to me they were too attached to each other and devoted to the restaurant to accommodate the intimacy and demands of living with anyone else. We, their fans and friends, knew this. And Maguy has described that closeness: two French halves of a whole that made a life together. "Gilbert was the most important person in my life, and I in his. We had a bond that was blood . . . and more than blood."

I mused on the possibility that they were lovers, too, incest being the last taboo in the emancipating seventies. The thought was thrilling. And from the way Maguy embraced me each time we met, rubbing and wiggling against me breasts to breasts, I wondered if one day we might be a threesome. We Americans can be so literal. The French are more artful, sensual, and such flirts. Maguy was clearly shocked when I finally spoke of it. Her hug was just a hug, not an invitation.

On one of my research trips to France, Gilbert agreed I could go to the market at Rungis with him in the early morning. As Maguy tended the last clients, we fled to his place, made love, and dozed off, but not for very long. Instantly, he was awake and we were driving into the blackness of the night. If he was thrilling in bed, I have to say he was almost as sexy in the market. I tried to keep up with him in high heels on the slobbering floor as he stalked the best sea critters, crisscrossing the vast expanse of the chilly market, poking the fish with his finger, sticking his hook into their gills to look them in the eye, challenging each fishmonger to find something even better. We speed-walked by Jean Minchelli, who was shopping for Le Duc, and I waved hello. In that instant, I lost Gilbert. I stopped in a puddle, trying to spot him, leaping aside as carts trundled past, threatening to roll over my toes.

Suddenly, he was back, grinning in triumph. "I was waiting for the *oursins* from Brittany," he said. The best sea urchins were a prize. "What is here is the shit. Voilà. It's done." He'd beaten Le Duc to the best haul by hunting down the truck just as it arrived from Brittany and claiming an entire shipment of sea urchins. What joy. Would we go back to his room to celebrate? I wondered. No. Now he really did need a two-hour sleep before hitting the kitchen.

During late nights at Castel's or on their globe-trotting tours, many French chefs talked about storming New York. And they would warn one another that New York is quicksand, that the critics are crocodiles, and that American gourmands are piranhas, waiting to devour unwary invaders alive. Gaston Lenôtre, the powerhouse caterer and master pâtissier of Paris, had braved Manhattan but, ultimately, retreated. ("He didn't do his homework," one vulture observed, "or he would have known many New Yorkers get married on Sunday.") New York, not on your life. Japan, surely, said Paul Bocuse. And Disneyland was a pushover. Michelin two-star Michel Rostang and his gang of five chef chums figured Los Angeles would be less thorny than New York, more welcoming. And it was true. Le Colisée limped away from early success on East Fifty-ninth Street, after a dazzling publicity launch, with fish flown in from France and bread FedExed from the masterly baker Lionel Poilâne. Each day, they cut that precious bread thinner. And sometimes it was stale. Le Colisée soon faded away. With Joe Baum running the show at Aurora, the Parisian chef Gérard Pangaud did well, but not for long. Only Antoine Bouterin, a young talent of disarming sweetness from Saint Rémy in Provence, tucked under veteran Georges Briguet's wing at Le Périgord, took root and bloomed.*

But cozy as they were with their two stars on rue Troyon, Maguy and Gilbert wanted New York. The city was throbbing with excitement over emerging American chefs when the two of them arrived to case the state of our piscatory world in 1978. It was a time when most Americans knew only knew frozen fish and shrimp cocktail. Sea scallops got doc-

---

*Ultimately, he opened Bouterin, a place of his own that looks like a Provençal granny's front parlor, far east on Fifty-ninth Street, where once the Palace reigned.

tored on the boat for survival and the roe was tossed overboard. Tuna was canned. Sea creatures arrived at the Fulton Fish Market already postadolescent. All we had to boast of were our clams, oysters, bay scallops, soft-shell crabs, and Maine lobster. The latter, alas, almost always overcooked to cardboard.

Friends took Maguy and Gilbert to the Oyster Bar, Seafare of the Aegean, the Gloucester House. They ordered fish from André Soltner's Lutèce supplier and then experimented with cooking it in the kitchen of Andre Sfez's Pizza Pino restaurant (now defunct). There, the Italian chef, a twenty-year veteran of the local scene, assured them that parsley was the only fresh herb they would find in winter New York. And that was almost true. I brought them twenty-dollar pots of thyme and tarragon, basil and mint from Eli Zabar's E.A.T. The dearth of herbs was real unless you were eager to send Eli's kids to college or grow your own in a greenhouse. Gilbert experimented with the fish. We tasted. He didn't look happy.

One night, I took the two of them to Xenon, the pulsating disco in an old theater, which I favored over Studio 54 (for the simple and painful reason that I couldn't get by the doorman at Studio 54 but was persona grata at Xenon). We danced, the three of us. And then without even a word, Gilbert and I disappeared, leaving Maguy sipping champagne at a small VIP table. She tells me that at first she was surprised when she realized we were gone, but then, being used to Gilbert running off with a woman, she was not really surprised.

Well, our fresh fish wasn't good enough for them at that moment. Gilbert found the best specimens shabby, the supply severely limited. The deal they were seeking never gelled. They came back again. Twice, perfect deals in midtown soured and they went home to Paris demoralized. But a few years later, Ben Holloway, eager to give cachet to Equitable's new corporate home, offered to pave the sidewalk at 151 West 51st Street with greenbacks for Le Bernardin. It was a sweetheart deal.

I was anxious about reviewing a chef I was sleeping with. They were wary too, worried, they said, that I would review them too soon. "I always wait a minimum of three weeks," I promised Maguy. "I'll come later, without warning, once you get going. A new place needs time to shake down." Every foodie in New York had reserved at Le Bernardin that first week in January of 1986. I started getting calls: "It's so French. It's so perfect. The food is amazing." "Eli Zabar arrived for dinner carrying his own bread," one source reported. "They were fainting over the halibut." *Halibut? Lowly supermarket fodder.* "We rated the desserts fifteen out of a possible ten," one piranha told me. "It couldn't be smoother if they'd been open two months," a notoriously demanding foodnik insisted. I was feeling like an orphan, abandoned and deprived not to be there at the dawning. And so I went that first week, reserving anonymously, of course, but I was greeted with an angry glare by Maguy.

And it was wonderful, very French, very proper, the waiters drilled daily, to the point where many were protesting the extra hour required for the daily training session. The lazier ones left. The survivors got their rough edges sanded. Halibut (at two dollars a pound), never before seen on an upscale restaurant's menu, was suddenly an aristocrat—the Eliza Doolittle of the sea. And more sophisticated New Yorkers—already disciples of the sushi faith—were primed to ooh and aah over raw black sea bass slivers with cracked coriander seed and thin ribbons of salmon "cooked" in an essence of tomato scented with olive oil, cracked coriander, and grains of cumin seed. So simple, so lush, so seductive, and right here on West Fifty-first Street. How wonderful to have a mouth. What a time to be a restaurant critic.

Dessert had never been especially tempting on rue Troyon. But while waiting for the liquor license to be approved, Gilbert and his pastry chef, François Payard, dreamed up a soul-stirring brûléed passion fruit mousse with raspberries inside, and the celestial variations on a caramel theme that would become a rage. There were all sorts of cookies, too, and searingly bitter chocolate truffles. I wrote a rave. The *Times* followed with highly un*Times*ean speed, dropping a four-star benediction.

I assumed Gilbert's woman would soon arrive from Paris. I think she did, too. But Gilbert was on to a new life, rich with caboodles of blondes and restless wives slipping him telephone numbers, drinking late and dancing at Au Bar. He didn't speak much English, but he didn't have to. His smile, his kisses, and his hands spoke for him. He seemed to thrive on a few hours of sleep. Half a dozen of my women friends, women he'd met through me, had comments to make about Gilbert's behavior in bed. Now that we were both always in the same town, the lust seemed to be less compelling. I guess we were always friends, but bed does confuse friendship. Anyway, now he seemed farther away on West Fifty-first Street than he had in Paris. Once every few months, we went out to dinner and sometimes danced after. It was a time when the fear of AIDS had transformed the city's most wanton free spirits into neopuritans.

By 1993 Gilbert had met Amy Sacco, a young woman who ruled in the night world of restaurants and clubs.* He surprised even himself by falling in love with her and sharing his space. Maguy was living in Miami, running the LeCoze Brasserie there and the Brasserie that still exists in Atlanta. Perhaps that made living with Amy possible.

We continued to have late dinners once in awhile, gossiping, debating politics—he was endlessly curious, opininated, a delicious gossip, and interested in everything. Settled into my own predictable domesticity with Steven, sometimes in Aspen, sometimes in New York, I felt glamorous and sexy just walking into a room with Gilbert or feeling him soften and grow sensuous with the second or third cognac. I remember one evening at the now-defunct Sign of the Dove. He asked for a window seat so he could smoke (illegally) and exhale his cigarette smoke toward the street. The last thing he ever wanted to eat was someone else's seafood. At night, when Le Bernardin's service ended, he and Maguy could be found at a table near the kitchen, eating filet mignon. But this night, he let me order Andy D'Amico's luscious rare tuna loin in a broth, even agreeing to taste it. I was pleased that he liked it, too. He had a Town Car waiting outside. He pulled up my skirt and put his hand between my thighs. I was wearing the shocking pink garter belt. He laughed. My bedroom was conveniently unoccupied that evening.

"How do you make love to just one person, the same one woman all the time?" he said quietly, very thoughtful.

We were lying in my bed on the balcony.

"You act out fantasies together," I suggested, self-styled expert. After all, I was the author of *Delicious Sex*. "Or," I went on, "you sleep with other women once in awhile and are extremely discreet, so that no one can ever know."

He was just forty-eight when he died. It was impossible to believe that he could fall asleep in the gym and never wake. I was out of the

---

*Owner of popular lounges Lot 61 and Bungalow 8, and, more recently, the restaurant Bette.

country at the time. That made it seem even more unreal, though I managed to write a brief tribute for the magazine. He was not just a lover and my friend; he was the great god of fish. Everywhere, American menus acknowledge the fish he discovered and his minimal hand with raw slivers and fillets, and even the variations of caramel. Chefs who had never met Gilbert came to say farewell. It seemed especially cruel that a man who had so fiercely embraced life could simply stop breathing. "I'm not a domesticated animal," he used to say to his chef de cuisine, Eric Ripert. "I'm a wild animal. I want to be a panther."

I worried, of course, that Maguy might not survive, as did everyone who knew them well. But she threw herself into making Le Bernardin warmer and better and different in homage to Gilbert. Yet even now, her voice breaks and her eyes mist whenever she speaks of him, speaks of feeling him near.

And with the art and soul and passion of Eric Ripert, Le Bernardin is astonishingly more wonderful than ever. Except that Gilbert is not in the kitchen or flirting at the bar in his whites. I am never there without feeling his presence. I think of him when I walk down the narrow corridor where there used to be a window into the kitchen. I remember always stopping to watch the amazing ballet of dinner service, throwing a kiss to Gilbert. I wonder if he is furious for the cruelty of dying so young. I embrace Maguy—she still wiggles seductively. If I feel his presence, what must she feel every day in that room where they plotted together? There is always something unspoken between us, and I feel we are bound together forever.

47

My Dinners with André

He is the John Wayne of *beurre blanc*, defending the fort long after the rebels have hoisted the flag of radicchio," I wrote in September 1993. André Soltner, ruler of a tiny world on East Fiftieth Street, in a dollhouse castle eighteen feet wide by one hundred feet long, shepherd of America's most celebrated restaurant for decades, struck me in the hebephrenic nineties as our town's one pure chef—fearless in his conviction, immune to flash and fad, dedicated to his idea of perfection, endearingly modest. "I'm just a cook," he liked to say. His streak of naïveté was refreshing, though one might also see it as stubbornness (like refusing to upgrade the house's bland French roll when the city was rich with young American baking talent). "He is simply what he is, no apology, no pretension, proud of his faith," I wrote.

Sirio Maccioni might phone a dozen strayed customers every morning to woo them back for lunch. André had never called one. It would never have occurred to him. Unlike the gallivanting playboys of the American range and the Bocuse mileage-plus gang, he famously never strayed from the kitchen. "We are cooks, not ambassadors," he liked to say. "I missed just four nights in thirty years," he told me proudly. Knee surgery forced two of his absences from the kitchen. Asked to join his confreres in a splashy tasting dinner to benefit Citymeals-on-Wheels,

André agreed to send dessert. That way, he could rush over to take his bow after his Lutèce clients had been sufficiently cozened and fed.

There were no Technicolor drawings in his sauces, no layered pyramids, none of the flying buttresses on the plate, technical tics of the nineties. "*Cook* means what it means—to cook the food, not to architect it." Unlike Sirio, who could always create a table at Le Cirque if an unexpected VIP suddenly materialized, André rationed out his tables judiciously but never had one left for the last-minute big cheese or friend of the house. One night, he had to send his onetime boss and partner, the creator of Lutèce, André Surmain, to Le Cirque for dinner. "I will call Sirio myself," Soltner offered. "He will have a table for you."

In 1975, I took a look at Manhattan's top French restaurants—rating them not with stars or Michelin boutonnieres but with mouths signifying "culinary excellence" and hearts for "total pleasure" quotient. Lutèce led what I described as "the frozen-in-amber crowd" with five mouths and four hearts. "Lucullan appetites have one extraordinary hero," I wrote. "André Soltner never stops inventing, perfecting, rethinking, improvising.

"In a world of so few eternal verities, there is Lutèce. The neighbors change. New gaudy awnings confuse. But there it is, two steps down to the narrow town house with its unassuming beige door, circa February 16, 1961." That was the day André Surmain opened what he brashly promised would be "the best restaurant in the world." He would be the first to serve on bone china and Baccarat crystal, he insisted, first to bring in Christofle silver, first to use Irish linen napery. ("We gave that up when we couldn't find anyone to iron it properly," he said later.) Everything would be fresh, a radical concept at the time. "Dover sole and freshly smoked Scottish salmon was flown in from England daily," he told me. And it was he who tasted the filet mignon Wellington at a Parisian restaurant named Hansi and persuaded the twenty-seven-year-old chef, André Soltner, to bring himself and that pastry-wrapped hunk of meat to New York and run the tiny kitchen of Lutèce. "A miracle on Fiftieth Street," as Surmain billed it, thrilled when his young chef returned home to compete and win France's coveted Meilleur Ouvrier award a few years later. I loved it with an ingenue's exuberance from my earliest review in 1970, though I knew that Craig had dissed it crankily in the *Times.*

Claiborne, swayed by his admiration for Henri Soulé as the arbiter of fancy French dining—red velour banquettes, sketchy murals, cold striped bass with sauce gribiche in tempting display—found Lutèce sorely lacking. Surmain, in his country squire tweeds and suede Hush Puppies, was slammed as both rude and rudely dressed. And the pen in his pocket. To the ever-proper Craig, that was unforgiveably barbaric. Later, Craig admitted to me that he'd let Souléism blind him to André Soltner's grace, and he bowed and threw in a few more stars in a later assessment.

Dizzy and genuinely thrilled by the high-wire acts of younger chefs, I would go often to Lutèce in the early nineties for a calming déjà vu. I would nod to Madame Soltner, the unsmiling Simone, tucked into her cloistered crib, tracking the bills. I'd walk past the scrawny Pullman kitchen with its pass-through eye on traffic, then into the parlor with its luxury of space, and sometimes into the trellised garden, where affection and expectation refracted the daylight. Always the same. There would be roses in a silver pitcher, the famous Redouté print of the rose on the menu, a museum piece with its retro foie gras en brioche, the venerable mousse of pigeon with juniper berries, that *ancien* relic of the sixties, *mignon de boeuf en feuilletée*—the signature beef Wellington by any other name. Habitués, of course, never saw the menu. We ate the plats du jour. Those who ordered "whatever André feels like cooking" ate best of all.

It was only after the day in 1972 when André Surmain, in a fitful midlife crisis, packed up his wife and four children and sailed his own boat across the Atlantic to Majorca, leaving the chef behind to buy him out, that Soltner was forced to emerge from the kitchen to do the dining room rotation that had been Surmain's routine. "Smiling, eyes tilted up at the corners, Soltner stood, one hand on his hip in his laundry-issue whites—no custom embroidery here," I wrote, in 1993. "There are chefs working six weeks and they must wear their name. Not me. I don't need it. People know me anyway," he said.

He would take the order. "What do you suggest?" we would say.

"Meat, fish . . . chicken?" he would ask. Not altogether graceful in this verbal rap, but never mind. How they loved him. Newcomers were thrilled by his attention. The devout (regulars) fairly gushed: "It's like eating at home. He does dishes for us he wouldn't cook for just anyone."

His Alsatian mother's *baekoffe*—layering lamb shoulder with onions and potatoes—was a rustic nostalgia prepared only for special friends. With that famous Soltner grin, he would deliver a portion of calf testicles—*"amorettes,"* he called them when we asked. Once I requested something lemony for dessert. Not to seem too sycophantic, I suspect, he ignored the lemon part and created a complex masterwork—what I came to call "the Sunshine Tart"—with fresh orange segments caramelized on top, a thin layer of genoise underneath to capture runaway juices, so as not to dilute celestial Grand Marnier–spiked crème pâtissière below in its buttery crust. "This is the best I could do," he offered. "I spent the day with the tax man." I begged him to put the Sunshine Tart on his menu, but he just laughed. Indeed, he never made it exactly that way again.

But witnessing the kitchen revolution abroad during his August *vacance,* he began to experiment. When Lutèce regulars raved about the specifics of a thrush mousse they had tasted at Troisgros, he nodded with interest. One week later, he served them tiny egg-shaped ovals of creamy pigeon mousse spiked with juniper berries gathered at his upstate retreat near the ski trails of Hunter. He had clearly succumbed to a taste epiphany at Frédy Girardet in 1979 and began to do what seemed like daring tricks for Lutèce. Just barely cooked *rouget* flown in fresh from the market of Rungis, outside Paris, appeared as the plat du jour. And French scallops with bright blushing coral still attached thrilled house loyalists. His new vegetable terrine was held together with its own juices, and there was a shocking presence of cilantro. But he was proud of thrifty improvisation, too. Every day at lunch, there was a different soup. "Try my chicken soup," he urged. And when I complimented him, he confided triumphantly, "For this, the ingredients, it costs me ten cents to make it."

André started offering tasting dinners—a forty-five-dollar parade of hors d'oeuvre and entrées with a Gewurztraminer marc–doused lemon ice in between and then two desserts. He began cooking fish noticeably less, though he still nursed old-fashioned notions. I begged him to do my venison rare. Just the thought of it made him screw up his face in distaste. Even now he likes to tell people how misguided I was to demand my chicken "pink" when I am sure what I said was, "Less cooked, André." It was the squab I wanted rare. He acquiesced, and it was the best squab

I'd eaten to date (in 1980), faintly gamy, with threads of celery root and rather punky spatzle. He came by to watch my reaction and was skeptical: "It's not too bloody?"

He was almost sixty-one and complaining about his cartilage-ravaged knees the day in 1993 when I asked if he could do two tasting dinners for the four of us—a challenge for the finale of what I didn't know would be my final review of André Soltner's Lutèce. That evening's new dishes were surprising in their complexity. And the simplicity of his mellow signature tarte flambé was stunning in its perfection. There were flaws and I listed them, too, of course.

"My affair with Lutèce mirrors scenes from a long marriage," I wrote at the end. "The first storm of passion. The deepening of love. Affectionate familiarity. A certain ennui. The seven-year-itch. Irritation at the other's inability to be anything but what he is. And now, admiration and tenderness for exactly that."

How long could he fly down those stairs to the prep kitchen? I wondered. Who would take over? The Soltners were childless. He had told friends that Simone longed to go home to France. The staff was family (with pensions), and even the busboys had been there for twenty years. He could not simply leave them, he said. He'd brought in chef Pierre Schutz and a maître d' for a six-month trial marriage, hoping they'd decide to buy the place. But Schutz found it an impossible dream. "Lutèce is André Soltner," he told me. "No one can replace him."

The choice was painful. To let Lutèce survive without its soul or to sell the town house minus its name . . . and see the legend disappear forever. A year later, Michael Weinstein was thrilled to add Lutèce to the mostly pop-feeding ventures of Ark, and the Lutèce family of regulars went into mourning. André's kitchen staff scattered. Eberhard Müller, the first chef de cuisine of Le Bernardin, took up the fallen whisk. André and Simone bought a retreat on the Riviera but decided to stay in New York, living above the store as always.

"I always check the kitchen before we go to bed at night, to be sure the oven is off," André reported. I thought that the compulsive workaholic would pine away in retirement. But he surprised us by joining the faculty at the French Culinary Institute and becoming a celebrity regular on the luxury-cruise circuit . . . seeing the world gratis in exchange for a few demonstrations. He would disappear for weeks at a time with the constantly radiant Simone smiling . . . yes, always smiling now. I like to think they float on gentle seas in a buttery pool on an endless honeymoon.

48

THE DAY THE MUSIC DIED

Dancing stopped. Discos lost their edge. People still went to clubs and there was music, a beat for stomping, but it didn't seem to be about dancing. Sometimes preppy kids got up and swayed. Mostly, it seemed to me that people drank and stood around in aimless clots, staring at one another, just checking it out. Hanging out in the ladies' room of the Tunnel one evening, watching the flirtatious moves of an adorable blond club kid who looked almost female on eight-inch platform sandals, I felt like an obsolete appendage. Not that graceful at just hanging loose. Alpha woman, A-type personality. Does anyone still dance? I wondered. AIDS had chilled the exuberance, certainly mine. When Steven was in Aspen, I found myself going to bed earlier and more prudently—alone.

Just when Americans had every right to be celebrating the end of the Cold War, the fall of the Berlin Wall, and Poland, then Czechoslovakia tossing aside Communist regimes, the joy was dimmed by a plague that wouldn't go away. "That cutting edge of insanity and creativity has just lost its steam," the *Times* quoted a major disco entrepreneur of the eighties as saying, explaining why he'd decamped to Los Angeles in 1991. With the first George Bush in the White House, recession compounded by war in the Gulf made entrepreneurs nervous, and yet, as *Food Arts* reported in December 1990, "People are eating out in numbers that would have paralyzed our ancestors with disbelief."

Eating out had become a habit that no amount of upscale carryout could cure. Indeed, the perversity of dining trends in the nineties conspired to make New York dining more glorious than ever. Health issues, discoveries about transfats, ever-evolving slimming regimes—low-fat, Dr. Atkins, low-carb diets—inspired a rush of new products onto the supermarket shelves, little stars signifying low-fat selections on a few menus, a small bubble of vegetarian sanctuaries, and a new respect for seafood.

Could anyone claim they didn't know the bad news about fat and cholesterol? Defying the odds was just another high-risk sport. Bistros and new American cooks thrived by selling Grandma's fat-oozing short ribs, greasy pork shanks, and potatoes in every permutation. After a pious breakfast of non-fat yogurt and high-bran kibbles and bits, and a penitent lunch of undressed vegetables and salad greens, I blithely confronted the caramelized fatty crust of duck confit or the myriad sausages of a nicely crumbed cassoulet. Did I imagine my blood thickening just from inhaling the fumes? It's my job, I told myself; someone had to do it.

Steak houses multiplied in this town of celebrated sirloin. Ambitious chains from out of town invaded the city, to chauvinist jeers. Where once fifteen ounces of prime sirloin satisfied the raging carnivore, now unabashed meat lovers, in innocence or denial, favored the fattier rib eye or porterhouse, even a giant Fiorentina slicked with olive oil, or an outsize fifty-six ounce haunch for two. Gallagher's touted the General Schwarzkopf steak—a filet mignon stuffed with Roquefort. By the time Laurent Tourondel dreamed up BLT Steak in 2004, even health-savvy affluents would line up to rebel against dietary sanctions, seduced by the chef's giveaway prologue of chicken liver mousse, imported charcuterie, and buttery popovers as big as a toddler's head, before even getting to the beef, with a side of creamy truffled gnocchi—"for the table to share." Armored with cholesterol blockers, it was arteries be damned.

Just when most of us knew enough about wine to impress one another, even to the extent of being boring, cocktails came back, classics revisited, creations ever wilder and more exotic: martinis in every flavor—watermelon, green apple, passion fruit—mojitos and margaritas to lubricate the new Latino fusion craze. The very French cheese course before dessert that we early foodies adopted in the seventies, when we were trying to seem more French, had almost vanished as desserts got more ambitious and imperative. Stocking cheese for a dwindling few and watching it age was costly. But then Terrance Brennan at Picholine proved that a cheese sommelier pushing a trolley paved with manna of goat, cow, and sheep could lure us back to butterfat. Ambitious cheese wagons reappeared. *Bon Appétit* attributed this denial of cardio-reality to a backlash against conflicting, confusing, and restrictive notions about health.

I lived my life in two time zones. In New York, I kept up with the endlessly evolving restaurant scene, with its strange liaisons, its swift triumphs, the cruel washouts. I tracked the openings, waited for the buzz, gathered friends from a vast Rolodex of willing tasters to share my reviewing meals while my main man toiled in Aspen. The grandiose dreams of the eighties grand cafés had left a wake of wounded amateurs, but the survivors never seemed to stop scrambling. Once again, *bistro, trattoria, rustic,* and *homey* were the buzzwords. Each year, the culinary schools mustered a new crop of ambitious pups, along with eager grown-ups changing careers midlife. I kept my little spiral notebook tucked under the table—I can't even guess how many hundreds I've filled with nearly unintelligible scratchings I would struggle to decipher and transcribe the next morning. I was swept along, thrilled by the richness and constant change. Each evening, I picked up the menu, full of the hope that I was about to discover the next wonder.

Every few weeks, I'd fly out to the house Steven and I had rented in Aspen Meadows for a modest sum from the ready-to-wear manufacturer turned art collector Larry Aldrich—in exchange for Steven keeping watch all winter, shoveling, and, if necessary, repairing. I loved being with a man who could fix things and build stuff, steer a car calmly in a blizzard, walk up hills on cross-country skis, and do handsome graphics, too. It felt healthy to dip into outdoor life. Awkward, cogenitally unathletic, and full of unexpressed fears, I acted as if I weren't the spoiled après-ski sybarite I certainly was. As a Bronx-born mountain man, Steven seemed to be a perfect blend of street smarts, intellect, and artistry. I was impressed that he did the *Times* crossword every day in ink. His friends—artists, museum people, and moneyed supporters—

became part of my world. I introduced them to the potluck dinner concept I'd picked up in the Hamptons—just prepare one dish and be free to swim, ski, or work all day. We were hosts to wildly eclectic feasts of spicy tamales, scallops and shitake salads, bacon-topped meat loaf, a tofu-cashew-bean toss, and German chocolate cake.

The writers among us read from our works in progress. I couldn't look at Steven when I came to the erotic scenes in my porn-star novel. I didn't have the courage to see if he felt exposed. But our time together was cozy. I loved his face, especially his sunny dimpled smile, and the fact that, with his mustache and broken nose, he looked like my father—although not enough to be spooky. It was clear then that we liked the same people, and agreed on those we could live without. We both had a passion for travel, and when we were home, the silence was pleasant, even soothing as he watched television and I cooked or read or clicked the typewriter keys.

When I finally realized that the Prince of Porn novel needed a drastic makeover, I retreated from the challenge by writing a children's book about a little girl named after Julia Child, who had to eat out every night because her mother was a restaurant critic. The first chapter, set at the Four Seasons, had the Aspen potluck crowd roaring. I had hoped it would be fun for grown-ups to read, too. I guess I'll never know. No one was buying *Juliette Noodles,* either.

Did my obsession with Citymeals stall my novel? Certainly it drained my energy as our annual budgets grew and we stretched to raise more money to feed the city's fastest-growing population. There were constant crises, people to be wooed or offended, feelings to be soothed. I was not born to run a million-dollar enterprise. To say I was not exactly a diplomat was a mild way to put it. I was a bulldozer, a diva, as my friends on the board let me know. But New Yorkers who liked what we were doing jumped in.

Our auction items were priceless (thanks to the persuasive power of my Parisian ami Yanou and her loyal French cronies, who seemed willing to donate whatever she asked). We never started the bidding till the crowd was tipsy. I was irreverent and outspoken at our board meetings, not at all boardlike, sharing the lead with renowned community leaders Lew Rudin and Bob Tisch after Jim Beard died.

I was especially obsessed with our special events. If the staff didn't follow up on my suggestions immediately, I did so myself. I drove them crazy, I was told. But what could they say? I was like a machine fueling public awareness. I started reading the "Business" section of the *Times,* tearing out the names of who was up and who was down and who might want to rehabilitate their name by becoming our benefactor. I documented our mission in *New York* and readers sent checks. I wrote fundraising letters that conveyed the tragic reality of the ailing homebound elderly. I went on talk shows. I got friends in the press to tell our story.

But the truth is, it wasn't a tough sell. New Yorkers were deeply moved by the specter of the austere lives of our elderly homebound neighbors. Supporters liked knowing that every dollar they gave went only to deliver meals. They were generous, realizing that we were not asking them to finance a dream, for the dream was already a reality: Meals were going out every day, including weekends and holidays, on the street where they lived or just minutes away. I could say I didn't write another novel because Citymeals chewed up so much time, creativity, and passion. But maybe it was plain old procrastination—that I lost myself in Citymeals to avoid rejection and the work of finding a way to tell a story no one seemed willing to publish.

My mother had surgery for breast cancer, and I flew to Detroit to see her, though never often enough not to feel guilty. We spoke on the phone twice a day. "When you have some time between feeding all those old ladies in New York, you could come to see me," she said, not that she wasn't proud of what I'd done with Citymeals. Our executive director, Marcia Stein, flew her and my late sister's oldest daughter, Dana, to New York as a surprise on the night I was honored at a CMOW benefit in the Rainbow Room—the dinner itself was a gift from Joe Baum and his partners at Rainbow. Robin Leach auctioned five minutes on *Lifestyles of the Rich and Famous.* We sold it for $55,000—twice. By the time Robin came to a reviewing dinner and breakfast in bed, served by Gael Greene, Joe Baum was so mellow, he kept his paddle in the air till the bid reached eleven thousand dollars.

Saralee's cancer had spread to her bones. She could no longer drive. In the suburbs outside Detroit, that was a major deprivation. She hated being dependent on everyone. What bothered her most, she admitted, was not being a redhead anymore. As a young woman, her hair had been a rich silken auburn. She covered the gray with henna, and as her hair grew white, the colorist gave it an *I Love Lucy* orange glow. Even as her hair thinned, she kept that teased copper halo. But the chemotherapy had left strange lesions on her face and scalp and she could no longer tolerate the dye.

"I look in the mirror," she said, "and I wonder, Who is that little old white-haired lady?"

I realized in the middle of an evening call one day that my mother was coughing a lot.

"Mom, you're coughing," I said. "You were coughing yesterday, too. And clearing your throat."

"It's nothing," she said.

I knew she saw her oncologist every few weeks. "What does the doctor say?"

"He says it's okay for me to buy green bananas." It was her way to ask the terrible question without really demanding to know. On each visit, she would ask the doctor that same question and look into his eyes as he responded without cracking a smile.

I worried about that cough. The next day, she boasted that she was losing weight.

"But why are you losing weight?"

She admitted she was having trouble swallowing. "Even lettuce. It makes me gag. I can't seem to swallow it."

I called my brother, the doctor, in Chicago. "Something is wrong, Jim," I said. "She's coughing all the time, and now she says she has problems swallowing. Do you mind calling the oncologist? How could he have missed that cough? I'm too angry to call him. He'll take your call before he'll take mine."

She had cancer of the esophagus. No one was sure if it was a new cancer or metastasis from the breast cancer. But it didn't really matter. There it was. The hospital put her first on one drug, then on another. When the disease reached her kidneys, she went into a coma. She died in the early hours of the morning in the king-size bed she'd shared with Daddy, surrounded by my sister's children—one on the pillow sleeping beside her, the other two sleeping on the floor. My niece Dana came to tell me in the room next door, where I was sleeping. A hospice nurse had suggested not calling anyone right away when my mother stopped breathing, fearing the police might rush her to an emergency room, where they would try to revive her.

"Do you think you could go back to sleep for a while?" I asked. My niece, her face streaked with tears, looked at me as if I were out of my mind. I was not crying. That surprised me, too. But I was grateful death had come quickly. I thought of all the pain, her terror, the terrible indignities. She had been peaceful, pale but pink-cheeked, as she lay there the night before. A few days earlier, she had frightened her caretaker by saying she saw people at the window.

"Don't you see those three people?" my mother had asked. "They're waiting for us. They're waiting to take us away." I felt comforted thinking my mother believed she was just going away and would see Margie again. I thought about family reunions in a heaven I don't believe in, wondering how old everyone would be. And I fell asleep. Two hours later, I woke and we called 911.

At noon, men from the funeral home wheeled her body away through the hall outside my room. I saw them pass. There was a woman sitting at my portable typewriter, finishing the restaurant review that was due by fax at *New York* that very minute. I am not sure I know that woman.

49

KISS KISS BEFORE DINNER

I T'S BREAD AND CIRCUSES AS THE ENTIRE EASTERN SEABOARD PILES INTO Keith McNally's faux French Balthazar Brasserie and bakery on the frumpy heel of Spring Street." That was the lead-in for my review that May in 1997. Keith McNally was claiming his crown, or his crown of thorns (as he might have seen it in his dark psyche), as the restaurateur for the nineties. "Any success to me is postponed failure," he once remarked with his characteristic doomsday glower. "Once you know this, you can begin to enjoy things," Keith told *New York*'s Beth Landman in a profile that captured the somber brother back from Paris and London a year earlier, on the eve of launching Pravda, with its ersatz-aged Eastern European speakeasy look. "Keith, the dour one who looks as if he didn't sleep last night. Next to Brian's hail fellow eager-to-please, he seems painfully shy, perpetually embarrassed," the profile went on.

Home from self-exile and filmmaking abroad, Keith had gauged Manhattan nightlife and conceived Pravda, with a soft golden glow, hammer and sickle patterns embedded into the tile floor, and languid Slavic waitresses, who delivered caviar and infused vodkas in laboratory tubes. Who could have guessed that was just what the nomadic night owls needed? Even after charting decades of the town's flighty migrations, particularly the chic squalls descending wherever the McNally brothers beckoned, I was amazed to see how quickly Pravda—not that easy to spot under a furniture store on Lafayette—ignited.

Keith, like Brian, had a way of settling off the beaten path and turning it into easy street. Balthazar on the lonely, untraveled edge of SoHo. Pastis on desolate Gansevoort, long before clubs and couturier chic started chasing cows out of the Meatpacking District. Lucky Strike had opened in 1989 with an affectation of indifference: No name beckoned outside. Just a yellow nicotine aura in the evening drear of SoHo and a small decal on the Grand Street door. A feeding frenzy quickly evolved. It was noisy, smoky, young—striplings with lots of hair, myopia behind dark-rimmed specs, thrift-shop duds. The "look like you fell off a truck" style was hot. "Anyone over 30 looks old," I wrote. "Is the name a hypnotic? Most everyone is smoking. They haven't been alive long enough to feel mortal."

Bag-lady rags and washwoman topknots went with the calculated seediness—walls that look yellowed by a century of exhalation, pressed tin, the menu lettered in gold on a moldering mirror, tables of patched-together wine-crate ends, hints of the applied wrecking-yard chic we would go nuts about later.

"Eli [Zabar] was here earlier," McNally told our table. "He's taught me about baking bread. But ours is not as crusty or as brown as it should be. The ovens aren't hot enough."

By the time we got to Balthazar, the crusty country bread looked positively Poilâne. Artful water stains splotched the walls for the look of aging by a million smoldering Gauloise. And Keith's golden glow of clever lighting that works like a cosmetic had been perfected.

"It's hard to believe Keith McNally didn't dig up a corner of Montparnasse and ship it directly to Spring Street, bringing a jolt of life to a moribund block and swiftly extending SoHo eastward. Voilà," I marveled. Balthazar was an incurable Francophile's nostalgia: the scarred mirrors (tilted for optimum tittle-tattling), the scuffed tile floor, the vintage wooden bar with its pewter top and custom-carved caryatids, the crusty dark rounds of bread incised with a giant *B,* the fruity scent of yeast in the adjacent bakery with its romantic painted ceiling from Burgundy. Lobsters, giant shrimp, and oysters spilled over the raw bar.

"Aggggh," cried Le Bernardin's Maguy LeCoze with a charactcristic wiggle of excitement. "I am in France." Balthazar's one-week-old kitchen struggled to keep up with the frenzy of table turns, but the food, with a duo of Daniel veterans—Riad Nasr and Lee Hanson bossing the range— was already better than what you could eat in most Paris brasseries. The crush was barbaric. And Keith, clearing a table himself, looked rumpled and bleary-eyed.

I recorded the players: art-world and Seventh Avenue swashbuck-lers, media grandees, and the restless, ragtag, night-smart kibitzers. The air fairly crackled with insecurities. Rotating in and out of the power seats, certain trendetti seemed to be in virtual residence. Bob Colacello and Ross Bleckner suffered worshipful table hoppers while waiting for Bianca. Susan Sontag was but a bolster away. Ian Schrager and his wife, Rita, with Peter Morton and Elizabeth Salzman, ignored the stares. Restaurateurs' pet Steven Greenberg (you could be a pet, too, if you drank Petrus and paid in cash). Anna Wintour. Amy Spindler. Gotham Bar and Grill's Alfred Portale. Jean-Georges Vongerichten with Kerry Simon, the chef he had signed to take Vong global. Dean and DeLuca at separate tables. Calvin and Kelly in opposite corners, too. Calvin stopped by to greet her. The room drew a breath. What theater.

I admit all this *Sturm* and slapstick meant nothing beside famine and disease and the world's perpetual mayhem, but it certainly worked like caffeine for me. How could I complain that my work meant missing the-ater and dinner parties when so often I got to watch such compelling soap opera? Gossip was a ubiquitous preoccupation, the narcotic of the nineties. I often saw it live the night before.

Keith finished out the century conjuring Pastis, a blue-collar hangout with artfully rusted tin ceilings and greasy finger smudges on the walls, that same golden nimbus, wine by the carafe poured into small tumblers, homey crocks of onion soup sealed with Gruyère, and fabulous frites standing up in a paper-lined tin scoop. The place looked like someone had dusted off a slatternly old bar and hash house in the grunge of the undeveloped meatpacking zone. "Long live Les Halles on Little West 12th Street," I wrote. "As if Manolo Blahnik stilettos and pony skin totes had not already corrupted the warehouse iconography of this remote dis-trict." Again, as at Lucky Strike, there was a snootily elastic "no reserva-tion" policy. All animals were equal, except that some animals were more equal than others. That's why you would wait, toes curling with anger, while Calvin was seated. As much as I needed to be unrecognized to do my best reconnaissance, I couldn't help but be thrilled to be rushed by the seething supplicants to a table, as if I were a royal or a rap star.

By the time the meat market became riddled with luxury—four-hundred-dollar panties and nine-hundred-dollar Jimmy Choo stilettos, Keith could be found opening Schiller's Liquor Bar, distinctly not French, with his usual instant antique stage set and a wine list divided into Cheap, Decent, and Good. It straddled a corner in the next remote microquadrant of the Lower East Side poised for the mad lemming rush.

Perhaps being a worrier has its rewards. Most of the restaurants Keith McNally has had a hand in are still around: Odeon, Cafe Luxembourg, the esoteric Pravda, and, yes, even Lucky Strike. I've not been there myself for twenty years, nor have I heard anyone mention it. But I looked in a recent Zagat, shocked and rather pleased to find it. Is there a crowd smoking on the sidewalk now? Even the lady from Kalamazoo could probably score a table.

50

EATING HUMBLE PIE

TRADING DOWN WAS THE MANTRA OF THE NINETIES. DOWNTOWN—FROM the Flatiron teens and the Village on down—with its cheaper rents, a lingering aura of clubs come and gone, and reveries of Wooster Street migrations, was the place to be. A one-block street no one had ever heard of was all Alison Becker could afford when she wrapped the room in blue velvet and opened Alison on Dominick. There, Tom Valenti buffed his rustic touch with lamb shank on a garlicky pile of white beans, favas, and Swiss chard. There was no stinting in Terrance Brennan's sensuous complexity in the twenty-one-dollar dinner at Prix Fixe. "The kinder and gentler feedery has dimmed the glitz, shaved the tab, unstarched the hauteur," I wrote in February 1990. "Welcome to the morning after."

Underappreciated at Rakel, Thomas Keller had already taken his froths and the mushroom cappuccino acquired in a stint abroad at Alain Chapel and gone west. I partly blame myself. Perhaps my basic rave had been pocked with too many whining cavils to lure gourmands to remote Varick Street. The greater the chefs were, the more I wanted to rescue them from their flubs and overreaches. I never doubted that I knew when they strayed. Hadn't I developed my taste buds at the tables of the masters? I knew the unctuous silk of a great sweetbread, the buttery fragility of *pâté brisée,* and how gossamer the ultimate puff pastry could be. I didn't give them an inch of slack. Well, maybe I was a bit full of myself.

It was a time for master chefs to exploit Asian flavors. Gray Kunz's Asian palate and Girardet lineage had won fans to Adrienne at the Peninsula Hotel, but he couldn't resist moving to a one-million-dollar makeover at the St. Regis, where his four-star fusion at Lespinasse would distract us from the banal faux French decor. Alsatian-born and classically trained Jean-Georges was already in love with tamarind, galangal (a gingerlike root), and the citric combavas leaf from his days in Bangkok, Singapore, and Hong Kong when he landed in New York at Lafayette. He'd left to stage something really grand on his own, but given recession woes, a modest bistro like JoJo, with its telephone booth–size kitchen, seemed a smart first move. Jean-Georges did the desserts himself in a small closet behind a love seat.

Television discovered chefs. Publishers bankrolled chef-driven cookbooks. Did anyone actually cook from them? The Internet was a minefield of recipes. Cod was the big fish. Garlic, soothed into cream, crisped into chips, blitzed into *aioli,* was the food ingredient of the year, *Food Arts* reported.

"When times are mean and you can't pay your mortgage, a good meal is a luxury you can afford," I wrote in May 1991. The Hudson River Club celebrated local products and helped us find the Battery. I sent readers to Serendipity for the Tuesday blue plate special—a hulking chunk of caramelized meat loaf with buttery mashed potatoes and a big red-white-and-blue sundae topped with an American flag.

Tiny greens were getting tinier. Sprouts sprouted everywhere. Nothing but sashimi grade tuna would do. Scallops were likely to be diver-harvested or even alive and still in the shell. Boutique farmers cropped up to supply demanding chefs. Desserts were more important, more beautiful, more complex, more architectural. At some point, panna cotta became the new tiramisú.

With Tom Collichio at the stove, plush and tranquil Mondrian could show the most pampered French chauvinist what American chefs were up to. Cherubs, menacing bats in a Miss Havisham setting by architect David Rockwell, and fruity chillers like the Harvey Cave Hanger and the Volcanic Bat Bite made Bar Bat standing room only (filled with nobody we knew or wanted to know). Chiam introduced a cultural mishmash with a sorbet intermezzo between hacked chicken and Chinese roast duck. Wolfgang Puck's pan-Asian Chinois on Main inspired China Grill in what had been the Ground Floor (focus of my first ever restaurant review) at the CBS building.

Planet Hollywood's Fifty-seventh Street opening had traffic paralyzed. Even Esther Williams was there. Hard Rock Cafe veteran Robert Earl walked me to the dress Judy wore in *The Wizard of Oz,* now housed in a glass vitrine. "We paid two hundred and fifty thousand dollars for that," he confided. The stars arrived, preceded not by trumpets but by frantic bruisers hyperventilating into cellular telephones—the smaller the star, the bigger the entourage.

Bobby Flay, a rough-cut, restless redheaded teenager who just sort of fell into the business, left Miracle Grill to expand his peppery persuasion at Mesa Grill on a strip of newly gentrified Fifth Avenue.

"I don't want it to be too Thai," Jean-Georges said, launching Vong, an East-West collision in a David Rockwell Thai fantasy that drew the town's whole toot and scramble in its first few minutes. "I just want people to leave with a mouth full of spices and pleasure."

A posse of piranhas from the press vied with Dr. Kissinger, Barbara Walters, Woody and Soon-Yi, Wolfgang Puck and Barbara Lazaroff, and socialite Nan Kempner for tables at the long-delayed Daniel. Anna Murdoch didn't mind a two o'clock lunch at one of the better tables. Yes, already there were better tables. Limoges custom-design china had misspelled it Bulud on the bottom of the plate. I looked. "It would be less expensive to change his name than to redo the plates," I wrote.

On a scale of how many new ideas per square foot, Alan Stillman's new Park Avenue Cafe with chef David Burke's countless whimsies won the solid gold whisk with mizumi-leaf clusters. Especially cute was the laminated ticket that came with the swordfish chop he had his fishmonger sculpt from a giant collarbone. It was numbered like the pressed duck at the Tour d'Argent.

Built as a safe house for the chronically chic (jet-set division), Baraonda seemed to inspire exhibitionism. I'd never have guessed the crowds would still be trooping in ten years later, still dancing on the tables. But then, *baraonda* means "crazy fun." Banana Café with Matthew Kenny was so hot, it couldn't possibly cool down, but, of course, it did. The Chinatown we felt we owned twenty years earlier had become inscrutable, a miniature Hong Kong, with tanks of live fish everywhere, bazaars of affordable fakery, and neon shopping malls with escalators rising to twelve-hundred-seat restaurants, where my guests and I were the only non-Chinese eating dim sum for lunch.

Many empires were seeded. Many grew. The Bromberg brothers found a mojo at Blue Ribbon. Pino Luongo's empire surged and ebbed (remember Mad 61 at Barneys?). For some mouths, Mortimer's was the center of the earth. Or Le Cirque. Or the Grill at the Four Seasons. Limousines with darkened windows ventured to a remote TriBeCa for the beatified food of David Bouley. Surely the woman knitting between courses had to be a regular, since the rest of us went crazy during the painfully long in-betweens.

By 1994, the economy was sizzling again. People were spending money. Christian Delouvrier in the kitchen of the fiercely stylized Les Célébrités had whipped himself into a creative frenzy. "The sweet smell of excess," I called it. Steak wars were back. Jet-streaking chefs out peddling their books and whisking away on the telly were becoming the new rock stars. Bobby Flay went to Spain for two weeks of research and opened Bolo, where his own deeply flavored take on Spanish food struck me as better than the real thing. Doug Rodriguez came north from Miami to thrill us with his pan-Am games at Patria.

Asian fusion got more playful, as in hot fudge dim sum at JUdson Grill and Gary Robins's chili-detonated mango sundae with coconut ice cream, macadamia praline, tamarind, and lime at Aja. Early in his Gotham charge, Alfred Portale watched his seafood salad just grow and grow, like Pinocchio's nose. In his briefcase, Portale carried a tape measure, "the same way some people carry a pocketknife." All over town, chefs started to build towers, too. Pastry chef Richard Leach unleashed became the Michael Graves of sugar with his neomoderne columns, undulating chocolate walls, and pecan brittle pediments.

"In tuna belly circles, the landfall in Manhattan of Nobu Matsuhisa was hailed as if it were the Second Coming, if not the First. The wisdom of the chef's wit, honed on a path from Japan to Alaska, to Peru and Argentina, had lured the crème de la crème and the skim milk of Hollywood to his cramped temple of vinyl on La Cienaga," I wrote. Now, in league with Robert De Niro and Drew Nieporent, Nobu got a cobalt blue horizon behind gauze and winter twigs, a copper-leaf ceiling, real birches with fake branches, tall sushi bar stools with chopstick feet, and a curving wall of black river stones—David Rockwell's most lyrical design yet.

Danny Meyer was setting a new style of service at Gramercy Tavern. "Redefining luxury dining in New York" was how Ruth Reichl put it in the Sunday *Times* in December 1994. Wayne Nish was finding his niche at the luxurious March. La Goulue was packed wall to wall. Steven Hanson's Park Avenue Cafe drew the leggy noctambulists.

Almost twenty years after it had first opened, Windows on the World reopened with a $25 million redo, having recovered from the first World Trade Center bombing in 1993. With typical Joe Baum exuberance, the new bar was called the Greatest Bar in the World. Theme restaurants had their day: Along with Hard Rock there was the Harley-Davidson Café, Motown, and the Official All-Star Café. Drag queen waiters (even in a ruffled pinafore, the server's Adam's apple was a dead giveaway) lured the curious to Lucky Cheng's. No one was all that shocked at the appeal of the S&M café La Nouvelle Justine in 1997, where clients had a choice of having their boots licked by a slave or being humiliated by a whip-flicking dominatrix.

A wunderkind named Rocco DiSpirito at Union Pacific (we'd discovered him at Dava) had gourmands buzzing about his brilliant Taylor Bay scallops in the shell with sea urchin and mustard oil. Less talented chefs struggled to make news. Foie gras with lemongrass was a desperate cry. Blue Water Grill, Circo, Harry Cirpriani, Butterfield 81, Naples, the Crab House, Cascabel, Granville, the Monkey Bar, the Cub Room, Arizona 206, Redeye Grill, the Screening Room, Angelo & Maxie's, Quilty's, Ping's, Churrascaria Plataforma: "Why are all those guys running around with skewers?" Eli Zabar's Across the Street, Drover's Tap Room, Clementine, Fred's Beauty, the Park. Dozens arrived every month in Manhattan alone. Some closed before I got there to say goodbye. Others survived the heat waves that cooled and found an audience in the neighborhood. A few just never cooled down.

Malcolm Forbes was often his own restaurant critic, publishing his picks and pans in *Forbes*. He was an early Citymeals supporter, too. At lunch one day in the *Forbes* formal dining room, Malcolm invited me to join him, two of his sons, and a small covey of motorcycle aficionados on his private jet, the *Capitalist Tool,* for a Forbes Friendship Tour of Spain. Malcolm's genius for mixing marketing and his expensive hobbies was legendary. His hot-air balloon team would meet us in Spain with a giant balloon in the shape of Christopher Columbus's ship, the *Santa Maria.* With the Barcelona Olympics not far off, *New York*'s editor, Ed Kosner, agreed that a guide to eating in Spain would be timely.

The sleek gold-and-green *Tool* took off from Teterboro, a gift motorcycle for the King of Spain stashed in the hold, stewards smoothly refilling the luncheon buffet, and Malcolm bending down to pick fuzz balls from the freshly laid carpet. Assured that all his guests were eating too much, he went off to nap in his king-size bed.

Once we landed in Spain, we learned the routine. At 6:00 AM that first morning in Seville, the current lifted the *Santa Maria* up, up, up. Steven and I jumped into the chasers' van as it tried to follow the ship's path on the ground to help when it descended. Early-morning Sevillians seemed delighted by the clipper ship floating overhead. Suddenly, the balloon slowed, hovering over Seville's revered bullring.

"The city refused us permission to land there," someone said. Never mind. The balloon was clearly descending. We raced to the ring. The gate was locked. All of us ran in different directions, looking for someone with the key. A passerby directed me to the apartment of the live-in concierge. I rang the bell, and knocked.

"I am Mrs. Malcolm Forbes," I said in my approximation of Spanish. "I must be inside the bullring when my husband lands." Madame led the way. We ran after, the chasers leaping down the stairs to the floor of the ring, where the balloon was already collapsing. It had been a very tight fit in the tiny jewel of a stadium. Steven was the only photographer there. His photos would appear that evening and the next morning in the Spanish papers and later in *Forbes.* As Malcolm strode from the ring like a conquerer, an official charged in, snapped his feet together, and presented him with a certificate: Seville's official permission to land in the bullring.

That night, Forbes entertained the king and Seville society at dinner. All the men were in black tie with dazzling formal shirts except for Malcolm, King Juan Carlos, and Steven—they wore business shirts with bow ties. Noblesse oblige.

*   *   *

When I confided to Malcolm that I could see myself arriving at Citymeals' garden party in Rockefeller Center that June on the back of his motorcycle, he agreed to be my date. There he was, posed astride his machine, a gladiator in black tie and a black-and-white helmet, parked at the fire hydrant on my corner. We rode like the wind through midtown Manhattan, with me in periwinkle blue chiffon. I felt a frisson of danger, remembering the trailing scarf that caught in the Bugatti wheels and broke Isadora Duncan's neck. Malcolm agreed to a pit stop at Le Bernardin, two blocks from Rockefeller Plaza. I dashed inside, helmet intact, as mouths dropped and waiters stared, racing to the powder room so I could undo my hot curlers and arrive on Fifth Avenue with my hairdo more or less salvaged. I'll remember that triumphant ride forever, but my most vivid image is still Malcolm on the *Capitalist Tool,* picking up fuzz balls. That fall, he launched *Egg* with Hal Rubenstein as editor and died not long after.

Corn Soup with Sautéed Scallops and Bacon

On a writing retreat at the cabin of screenwriter Vicki Polon, we put together this fragrant soup.

6 ears corn
4 cups water (reserve water after the corn has cooked)
2 tsp. olive oil for vegetables
2 medium yellow onions, chopped
3 cloves garlic, minced
1 jalapeño pepper, seeded and minced
Juice of half a lime
Clam broth, to taste
2 slices bacon
6 large sea scallops, quartered
Salt and freshly ground black pepper
1 tbsp. chopped cilantro or basil

Cook corn in four cups of water. Remove corn, strain water of corn silk, and reserve cooking water.

Cut kernels from cobs and reserve the corn. Return cobs to cooking water, simmer till water reduces to half. Then remove cobs and reserve water.

Scrape cobs with dull knife to extract all the corn milk and reserve this liquid.

Sauté onions, garlic, and jalapeño in olive oil in nonstick skillet. Don't let them brown.

Add reserved corn kernels and corn milk to vegetables, then toss and cook on low heat for 2 minutes. Puree half of this mix in a blender or food processor.

Add puree and remaining corn-vegetable mix to reduced corn water. Then add lime juice and clam broth, to taste.

Cook bacon until crisp, drain, and cut into ribbons.

Sauté scallop quarters quickly in bacon fat till slightly browned. Don't overcook.

Reheat soup. Add scallops and bacon to mixture in the corn water. Season with ground pepper and salt, to taste. Add more lime or clam juice if necessary.

Serve in bowls with minced cilantro or basil sprinkled on top.

Serves 4.

51

AFTERMATH:
NO MERE TRUFFLE

I LOVED BEING FORTY-TWO. SURELY IT IS THE BEST AGE FOR A WOMAN. ONE is fully ripe and much wiser than at twenty-two, or even thirty. I was forty-two for such a long time—thirty-nine felt too Jack Benny and forty seemed rudely transparent—that I forgot how old I really was. When someone asked how long I'd been the restaurant critic at *New York,* I would say, "Oh, forever," and if they persisted, I'd reply, "At least twenty years." But then, in 1998, the magazine celebrated its thirtieth anniversary, and as I was singled out for being there at the dawning, I got trapped by the klieg lights. Even surrounded by younger friends, as I often am, it became more difficult to hide in their aura. When my thirty-five-year-old pals suddenly started turning fifty, I couldn't even be fifty anymore. Forced to consult a mirror when penciling on turquoise eyeliner, I rarely looked very hard. But occasionally I caught a glimpse of my face through eyes that felt young and was surprised to see me. Scary.

I was starting to feel enslaved by too many Monday-morning dawn wake-ups, required by my bad working habits, to deliver a review due at 10:00 AM. I loved the eating. I loved the thrill of discovery. I didn't mind the evenings at the mercy of misguided toques or ungifted journeymen all that much. But the increasingly rushed and often arbitrary editing of my copy was making me cranky. I missed the brilliant word wrangling from the days before computers, when an editor would go through a story line by line, forcing me to find a better word or sexier metaphor.

At one point, I'd asked to share the weekly reviewing job with a second. "You mean like Pauline Kael and Penelope Gilliatt at *The New Yorker*?" the editor asked. "Six months on. Six months off." I hadn't meant that, but why not? I lived in this vital, vibrant city. Each week, I would tear out pieces of paper announcing exhibits, walking tours, lunch-hour theater, auctions, showroom sales, but I never got to any of them. After eight or nine hours in the office, I rarely had the energy for cocktails, book parties, wine tastings, or screenings before dinner, even the few that I accepted. Surrounded by the feast of New York life, I was sentenced to tuna tartare and foie gras. Work, work, work. Work came first and seemed to preclude play. But with six months off, I could rediscover ballet, go to dinner parties, go shopping for a loft. And I would be free to travel the way Steven and I liked to—settling into an apartment steps from the Deux Magots on boulevard Saint-Germain, or in Hong Kong's Happy Valley, or surrounded by the street hubbub of old Hanoi for a month or more.

Three months on and three months off was the only way to do it and not lose touch with the drama of New York in its full-blown love affair with food. Steven and I decided to spend that first winter in Italy: two months in Rome in a duplex near the Piazza Navona, a month in Venice in a charming walk-up above a Chinese restaurant. Drugged by the mysterious shift of light in mist and cold winter sun in Venice, Steven forgot he had rusty knees. He spent hours walking to the farthest edge of neighborhoods rarely seen by tourists on a three-day jaunt, capturing moments—Venice in the snow, a thousand cherubs—that would become his most collected photographic work. Mornings, I trailed after him or strolled ahead so he could work as invisibly as possible. Afternoons, I tapped away on the laptop.

Rich friends were jealous. They could afford any trip but not the time we devoted. That summer, we spent July on the Côte Basque, August in the Alpes Maritime above Nice, and September in Paris. Then home again, back in the office, with its fresh piles of accumulated paper—reams of press-agent quackery, Citymeals reports, domestic and financial obligations, and professional journals. I am not going to whine

about this idyllic existence except to note that coming home meant stepping off the plane and rushing to the newest restaurant. We never got to
the ballet. And the price of the sprawling loft we fancied doubled while
we were in India and doubled again during our second winter in Venice.
And then we were off for three months in Southeast Asia and Beijing.

Half my life, I couldn't tap-dance fast enough. I left the house every
morning before Steven awakened. The first time we had together all day
was in the taxi on the way to dinner. But every three months, I trudged
onto a plane behind Steven, heart pounding with the effort of getting
away. And even before the stewardess brought the hot mixed nuts, my
pulse was beginning to slow. Distance brought languor and constant to-
getherness. At lunch, we would eat a giant bowl of salad—arugula,
puntarelle, wild greens, and cherry tomatoes from the Campo di Fiori
market or the Rialto or the Sunday organic market on the boulevard Ra-
spail—usually with great cheese and bread when slimming resolve
faded, as it did when Steven walked in with a huge round of olive bread
rich as pound cake. We ate silently. I would wade through *New Yorker*s
from the past three months or a novel set in the city we were in. Steven
would read the *Herald Tribune*. Sometimes our knives would bump over
the aged Parmigiano.

For a man who subsisted so many years on Stouffer's frozen lasagna
and cheap steaks, Steven quickly adjusted to my reviewing life. Today he
is often more critical than I am. Something must be working because
we've been together now since 1986 and we've negotiated a civilized
truce in the inadequate-closet conflict.

The American food world swept into the zeros on a riptide of exuberance. Supermarkets stocked exotica and the organic. Dozens of restaurants opened every week in New York. Uncounted others faded out,
some creaking with age, others newly-hatched, their hopes quickly
dashed. Across the country, restaurant food got better and better. And
worse, too, I'm afraid. Save us from the mindless pretensions of chest-
nut-leaf baked organic burdock root with air-dried duck and black plum
oil, or chocolate-braised bison short ribs with black huckleberries.

Now everyone I knew, indeed, New Yorkers of every tribe and class
and bankroll, was a restaurant critic, a chef groupie, a discerning palate,
or on the Internet getting the latest bark from Chowhound.com and

sending me E-mail reports of the spanking newest Thai hovel on a street somewhere near Yonah Schimmel's mythic knishes.

If you eat out in almost any major city, you don't need me to tell you what was on the menu at the dawn of the new millennium. You know about small plates "meant to be shared," teeny and tangy tastes served in Chinese soup spoons, surprises from the chef in a demitasse cup (often good for a laugh), tuna burgers and foie gras sliders, the sweeping advance of the short rib and the pork cheek, crème brûlée and panna cotta in multiples of exotic flavors, the persistent creep of bitter herbs into sorbets and bonbons. Asparagus *bavarois* with candied asparagus anyone? But then who could have dreamed dermatologists would discover a benign use for botulism or that the romance of a casual fling, a brief affair, or even a one-night stand would evolve into the harsh imagery of the contemporary "hooking up."

The generation that watched the Food Network while nibbling baby food or supposedly doing homework knows all the players, the stars, the overreaching divas who tripped the iron chefs. From invisibility, varicose veins, and stained whites, chefs have leaped into spiffy custom jackets, *People*'s "Fifty Most Beautiful" roundups, and *Fortune*'s Entertainment 500. What the French mock as foodism has long been an established ism here.

New York was frosty to Alain Ducasse, who arrived in 2000, self-styled missionary of the three-star Michelin faith. Our warm and bumptious city, which has welcomed millions of immigrants—the hungry, the persecuted, outcasts and dreamers, Cuban baseball players, Italian tenors, and Indian novelists on the run—found the high-flying Robochef a tad too confident and condescending. He insulted us with pretentions designed to astonish the bougeoisie, such as sending the waiter with a choice of knives for the pigeon. "How do I know what knife to choose, Alain? You tell me, please." And then asking us to select a couturier pen from the dozen swathed in a velvet sheath to sign the staggering check. A few days after opening, he vanished, off to launch a restaurant in Tokyo, unwilling even to pretend he was running the kitchen, leaving us with a bill that hit a new high for conspicuous extravagance—at least till Masa settled in the Time Warner mall.

In 1999, I had asked the editor of *New York* to find someone to take my place as the weekly critic. I wanted time to write long features, and

I would keep in touch by doing a two-hundred-word "Ask Gael" column every week. The search began. Just before Christmas 2000, I put together my farewell: "Where to Eat in 2001." "New York's entrepreneurial marathon to maximize, market, brand, expand, and reinvent the bistro, café, canteen, tapas stand, and chop house is torrential," I wrote. "So many openings. So many threatened launches to come. In retrospect, the restaurant madness of the eighties seems almost tame. So here it is: mad-cow stampede, saucier's apprentice run amok, lamb's tongue vinaigrette, wasabi sorbet, foie gras–stuffed chicken wings. And yes, peanut butter-bacon-and banana means Elvis is in the house."

It's 2005. Supposedly, chefs as matinee idols have been so overexposed that nobody cares anymore who they sue or marry, but watching the adoring masses devouring Bobby Flay with longing eyes in the kitchen at Bar American, I rather doubt it. The price of an average unremarkable meal is rising, but that doesn't seem to discourage the ranks of bonus babies. No way could I have predicted people would pay for something called vitamin water or dumplings made purple by the stamen of a Thai iris. Or that the pastry chef would shower my melting chocolate cake with a glitter of salt and cognoscenti would boldly tote their favorite crystals from distant seas in small snuffboxes. That dinner might start with salmon tartare in a tiny cone and the wine would come from Austria or Connecticut, or that anyone would be all that interested in tuna-coconut-lime cake at the Petrossian café. Actually, I don't think many were.

Freed from the relentless deadlines of being the weekly critic, I miss taking my friends to dinner every night and having the last word on what's great and what's not. But I'm still eating out seven nights a week, often on my own dollar (that was a shock). The first time I asked for a table for two and got a table for two, I panicked. Chefs were running wild. Foie gras with anchovy and cocoa nibs? I was stunned that some critics lapped it up. Taste is subjective, Thomas Keller insists. But I disagree. There are tastes that are gorgeous, heavenly, textures and combinations that sophisticated mouths will love and eager ingenues can learn to savor.

So I'm still eating and celebrating discoveries in New York. No other city in the world is better for eating out. New York's first star chefs—those that survived cocaine, shabby business advisers, aggressive landlords, overreaching expansion, the inability to be as good as the critics said they were, those in comeback, those who never went away—are graying now, many still on the cookbook circuit, some still wrestling the range. Larry Forgione's An American Place found a niche at Lord & Taylor and both of his sons followed him into the trade. Brought back to earth by ventures in Napa Valley, Charles Palmer decided he could comfortably track his bi-coastal empire by jet, and he resettled with his wife and brood of boys out West near his Healdsburg inn venture in Sonama County. Jonathan Waxman pleased old Jams fans with a market-minimalism revival at Washington Square, then abruptly retreated to a simpler gig at the wood-burning oven of Barbuto. Alfred Portale, a full partner now, kept Gotham Bar and Grill humming with a polished perfection as he went off to consult at Striped Bass in Philadelphia. David Bouley, as maddeningly secretive and elusive and seductive as always, running hot and cold on his constantly revised corner of TriBeCa, shifted into expansion mode with his new Bouley Bakery and Market—café, food emporium, cooking school, sushi bar. I found him there in late summer 2005, as handsome as ever in granny glasses, flipping burgers behind the counter in Upstairs at Bouley Market. One taste of his ambrosial scallops, caramelized and just barely gelled, with wild mushrooms, coconut juice and ginger, said it all. The transcendent cook is back.

A triumvirate of gifted immigrants from France continued to dazzle—Daniel Boulud, Jean-Georges Vongerichten, and Eric Ripert at Le Bernardin. Alas, Jean-Georges's avid global sprawl has already cast a few cracks in his luster. Daniel had vowed he would never open an annex anywhere he could not peddle to by bike, then joined the carpetbaggers a jet away in Palm Beach and Las Vegas. Eric Ripert has so far not let a handful of consulting stints distract him from passionate and brilliant hands-on direction at Le Bernardin. And the shimmer and shock of Japanese purity embracing Peruvian and Italian flavors dared by Nobu Matsuhisa in TriBeCa seemed undimished as Nobu seeded itself in midtown, though the chef himself perpetually rides the jet stream to global riches. After seven years in limbo, Gray Kunz himself seemed relieved to rediscover his elegant and complex cooking mojo at Café Gray, as did his fans. The all-star team of the Time Warner collection—Gray, Masa, and

Thomas Keller at Per Se—was still testing whether their combined wattage could melt our congenital urban aversion to fine dining in a shopping mall.

Citymeals-on-Wheels still consumes much time and energy. But our longtime executive director, Marcia Stein, is as obsessed and dedicated as I, so it no longer feels I am carrying it all. The staff brings in sleeping bags when special events dictate late-nighters. The board is more activist than ever. In our twenty-fourth year, we would deliver more than two million meals to seventeen thousand homebound New Yorkers. Feeding invisible neighbors who might otherwise go without has been richly rewarding to me. I don't often stop to think of it that way, but I do feel it in my soul. For those who thought writing about food for rich people to eat was too frivolous, it gives my work meaning. Many food-world professionals and New Yorkers I'll never meet like the idea of feeding frail and needy neighbors. Restaurateurs who used to think I was a bitch, or a diva, now seem to see me as a near saint.

Some restaurants and chefs still treat me as a power. I am amazed and I wallow in it. I remember what Julia said: We must enjoy it now, because who knows how long it will last. As soon as I finish this memoir, I will go back to writing a novel. I feel my children's book just needs a rewrite. I've not yet been to Africa or South America or the Antarctic, which seems to be melting faster than my favorite birthday cake with pralines and cream from Baskin-Robbins.

I suppose I will always be carrying inside me that little girl who wasn't pretty enough and would have to be a star one day to astonish her daddy. I try as determinedly as I am able not to be the controlling woman, the aggressive arranger scheming to make life work for my man so he can't imagine life without me and will never abandon me. (Another delusion. They did live without me.) But Steven is stubborn and resists my meddling. That may be what saves us.

I miss the extravagant love notes, the demented poems, the endearingly worshipful boy toys, the unexpected breakfasts in bed, champagne and peanut butter sandwiches in the park. I miss dancing all night and not needing to diet. I miss falling in love, being obsessed with sex. I miss fucking into oblivion and coming back. I was going through letters I saved that had been stashed upstate in a warehouse after I finally sold the little church on the hill. I found one written in impressive calligraphy from a rough-cut Romeo I'd known in the seventies who had moved away.

"I miss your happiness," he wrote. That line stopped me, and for a moment I was indeed sad.

I did have that happiness. It was that gift of living in the moment. So many moments in the mouth trade were ecstatic. Even the pain of not getting what you wanted could be ecstatic, though the withdrawal of love was shattering. In wanting to give directions to the joy—recipes for sensuous adventure—I don't think I ever let sadness or doubt creep into my column. I still feel flashes, even hours of that kind of happiness when I catch myself in the middle of intense pleasure. But mostly what I have now is calm, purpose, a certain predictability, and, in Steven, a loving, protective companion.

I can't wait to taste the food of the third generation of great American chefs. I can't wait to see what new madness young rebels are cooking up in Spain. I'm ready to explore the rustic backlash in France. I fully expect to go on eating and critiquing forever and that on my deathbed my last words will echo those of Brillat-Savarin's sister, who cried, "Bring on dessert. I'm about to die."

INDEX

Reading Group
Guide

Discussion Questions

1. Ultimately, *Insatiable* is about more than food, restaurant reviews, and sexual encounters. It is about a woman who reinvents herself. What are Gael Greene's strengths and weaknesses, and how does she use both in creating her *persona*?

2. If a major theme of *Insatiable* is passion, what is Gael Greene passionate about? Can you contrast the characteristics of a person who lives with passion with one who doesn't? Do you think that having a passion in one's life changes how one lives it or how it turns out? Overall, what are the consequences of a passionate life?

3. The story of Gael Greene's marriage to Don Forst is bittersweet. She reflects that "someone less myopic than I might have seen the small gray cloud floating over our marriage. Not me. I was too much in love" (p. 72). What do you think caused the relationship to fail? If you were a marriage counselor, would you say the marriage could have been saved . . . or not? Why?

4. In being unabashedly frank about her intimate relationships, Gael Greene left herself vulnerable to those who would criticize her morality and her lifestyle. Do you think she cares what others think of her? Do celebrities operate by a different set of rules?

5. Sexual behavior and sexual attitudes have dramatically changed since the 1950s. Women in the fifties wore girdles and white gloves, had no access to legal abortions, fewer methods of birth control, and an attitude that "nice girls don't." But can a case be made that premarital or extramarital sex in the 1950s and 1960s was actually more liberated than in the twenty-first century?

6. The supporting characters in *Insatiable* range from chefs to writers, celebrities to a porn star. Which characters did you find most interesting? Is there a man here you would find irresistible?

7. What qualities does Gael Greene value when she reviews a restaurant? Can you construct "guidelines" *á la Gael Greene*? If you chose one of your own favorite restaurants (or a popular national franchise) and reviewed it from a "Gael Greene" point of view, would it be a pick or a pan?

8. Gael Greene talks about being a "foodie" and about "foodism." What does she mean? What evidence can you point to that we have become a nation of "foodies"?

9. When you next dine out, will you view the experience any differently after reading *Insatiable?* If so, to what specifically will you be paying more attention?

10. Gael Greene covers the huge changes that have taken place in American culture regarding food and drink since the 1950s. For example, she notes that "fresh-turned pasta was a fetish of the seventies" (p. 185). She follows the growth in the popularity of drinking wine. What do you believe are some current trends in American tastes? What changes have you spotted in your local grocery store in the past decade? Have any specialty food stores or restaurants opened up in your community in the past few years? If so, what do you think they reflect?

11. For Gael Greene, food and sex are inextricably linked. What do both hungers have in common—for Gael or for anyone?

12. The young of each generation need to rebel. What were Gael Greene's forms of rebellion in the 1950s? What were the rebellions of the 1960s? How about the 1990s? What are those of today's teens? What does each form of rebellion reflect about the times . . . and perhaps about what we choose to eat?

13. What was the best meal you ever had? Why was it the best? Is a great meal only about the food? What else is involved?

14. Gael Greene has strong opinions about romance. She says of her own and her siblings' failed marriages, "Perhaps we all had exaggerated romantic expectations" (p. 13). She writes of her husband, Don Forst, "He was also brashly cynical, like all romantics" (p. 26). Can you explain the apparent paradox in these statements? What is the danger of believing too deeply in romance? Do you think Gael Greene is a romantic?

15. To have great success, a person has to take great risks. What risks did Gael Greene take in her life and her career? Which ones panned out? Which ones flopped, like a fallen soufflé?

16. Do *Insatiable* and Gael Greene deserve a place among the gastronomic classics? From the writing to the content, what puts this book a cut above the rest?

Questions We Asked Gael

Q. You took some great personal risks in revealing so much about yourself in this book. Did you hesitate about "naming names" in this memoir? What kind of feedback have you gotten?

A. A few friends are immensely relieved not to be included. Others are insulted. As for risk, I survived a similar risk in my erotic novels—*Blue Skies, No Candy* and *Doctor Love*—that it no longer seemed to me such a risk. Rather I hoped I could convey how it felt, what it meant, how caught up I was in the adventure and how much I need to feel true to myself. That the reader would understand. I was careful not to identify very private people, but I did not hesitate to name movie stars who are known for their romantic exploits.

Q. You have a hugely successful book. You have made some television appearances. What's next on your plate? Can we expect to see more of you on television . . . with or without your hat? Is another book in the works?

A. I got a kick out of being a judge on *Iron Chef* and would love to do more TV, but as long as I am reviewing restaurants, I'm stuck hiding under that hat. I am working on a book I hope children and adults will love, the story of a little girl whose mother is a restaurant critic. And an idea for a new novel is simmering in my head. I do my best writing when my guy and I travel and settle in one place for a month.

Q. Speaking of books, it seems natural that you would compile and/or create a cookbook. Are you planning one? Why haven't you written one in the past?

A. I was convinced I did not have enough recipes that weren't borrowed or unconsciously stolen. Fiction is my first love.

Q. You liberally spice your writing with humor and you prefer not to dwell on the most painful moments of your life—but you have lived through some difficult times. What advice can you offer other women who face divorce, disappointments, and the death of loved ones? Beyond a pint of premium ice cream, can food help?

A. Great friends, a loving psychotherapist, and loving my life got me going when I felt overwhelmed by loss. Rum raisen is a false friend because it makes you fat.

Q. You have traveled around the world in pursuit of good food. Where to next? What cuisines have endured as your favorites?

A. I need to go to France at least once a year. But mostly I travel for adventure and out of curiosity. South America, Africa, and Northern Asia are on my list.

Questions Gael Asked Herself

Q: Have you ever counted how many meals you've eaten in the line of duty?

A: 17,966 give or take a few thousand. Happily my brain tends to obliterate memories of the worst. I wake up every morning full of hope that this will be the day I discover a talented new chef or, at the very least, taste something astonishingly delicious.

Q: Forgive me for jumping to the obvious, but what in the world does Elvis Presley have to do with fine dining?

A: I feel my boldness in simply jumping into bed with the young beautiful Elvis fifty years ago signaled the passion for adventure and fearlessness a good food writer needs. And though I didn't realize it at the time, the fact that I don't remember how good the sex was, or who sat on top, as vividly as I remember Elvis ordering a fried egg sandwich, suggests I was destined for a career in food.

Q: Do you think your foodie readers will give a fig about your erotic hijinks?

A: As Wolfgang Puck always says whenever we meet, "The two essentials of life are food and sex." It doesn't hurt to give non-foodie readers something to savor. And besides—all that passion, all that disco dancing—that was what life was for some of us in the seventies when America was just beginning to fall in love with food. Before raddichio, before vinegars in twenty flavors, before sushi madness and crème brulée, before *Iron Chef*. It was a totally different world.

Q: It seems to me you didn't leave anyone out.

A: But I did. I am sure there will be some men who will be relieved I left them out and a few who will be disappointed.

Q: Won't readers, and some food writers too, think it's a pretty big stretch to link food and sex?

A: But in fact they are inextricably linked. We use the same senses at table to measure a great meal as we do to appreciate a fine time in bed—the eyes, the nose, the mouth. The skin that registers the heat of torrid spices or the thrill of a passionate caress. The ears that measure the crunch of a superior French fry or a murmur of love. I believe the sexual revolution prepared Americans for the food revolution . . . a whole nation began thinking of how it felt and how it tasted and how much pleasure indulgence could be.

Q: You're not suggesting everyone you knew was ready for sex orgies . . . even if you did live on the same street as Plato's Retreat.
A: No, not at all. Very few people I knew were ready for orgies. But through the sex revolution and through feminist writings, everyone became more sensually aware. We had been a nation where the upper-class, uptight notion of dinner was an overcooked lamb chop and tapioca pudding, and it wasn't proper to carry on about food. And look at us now—a nation of foodies, whole foodies obsessed with the organic, classic foodies just looking for cuisinary thrills, incurable trendies intent on the flavor of the month. Supermarkets everywhere are international food bazaars. And these days almost everyone is a restaurant critic.

Q: Besides jumping into bed with Elvis, what made you a candidate to be *New York* magazine's restaurant critic?
A: Nothing really. Compared to Craig Claiborne, then the powerful critic at the *New York Times*, I had no credentials at all. I was an amateur in the real sense of the word: I just loved to eat. And I told Clay Felker that when he called a few months after launching his new magazine. As a successful freelancer, I couldn't afford to work for the infant *New York*. "People are begging to be the restaurant critic so they can charge all their meals to us," he said. Fireworks exploded. It was my chance to order from the left side of the menu instead of the right. I couldn't refuse. I decided that as a newspaper reporter I could report the who, what, where, and why of Manhattan dining games. As for judging, I taught myself on the job. One day I noticed something was wrong with the quiche and I said so, and that was that. I was a critic.

Q: You dared to tell André Soltner of Lutèce the filling of his frozen soufflé was dry and boring?
A: Well, I cooked. I took cooking lessons. And I was an early foodie before the word existed. My friends and I went to France once or twice a
year for cuisinary epiphany. I had eaten the food of the greatest chefs of
that time. So I was actually somewhat equipped to brave humiliation in
the city's snobby French restaurants and at the imperious "21" to give the
reader courage. I wanted to convey to the puritanical or untraveled
reader the sensuality of a glorious meal. I think I gave New Yorkers a new
way to think about food. And Soltner later admitted I was right . . . the
filling was dry. Although he teases me that I was wrong about everything
else and I ordered my chicken pink.

Q: What do you miss most about not being *New York* magazine's weekly
critic anymore?
A: I loved taking friends to dinner every night on the magazine's expense
account. Given *New York* magazine's power and influence, I could invite a
total stranger to lunch—I remember a glorious picnic lunch with Mayor
Lindsay on the floor of his office at City Hall. And a total stranger offering to show me his cache of morels growing wild in Central Park. And
women begging me to have lunch with their husbands for their birthday.
Also I miss not having the last word . . . the best revenge for an unhappy
and expensive evening is knowing you can expose it and maybe even persuade a misguided restaurateur to shape up. There is always joy and gratification in being the first to discover new talent.

Q: What's next?
A: I'm a flop at calling trends. I never know what's happening till we are
wallowing in it. Like powdered sugar on dessert plates or herbs—I think
of them as hideous lawn clippings—in desserts. But I am worried now.
Star chefs are so busy branding themselves and becoming feeding
moguls, we are not allowed to expect to see them live in their restaurants anymore. A burst of new kitchen technology is liberating, letting a
dessert cook make instant sorbet in small batches. But I worry about
Frankenfoods and overly creative combinations by chefs with little talent
and no taste all trying to one-up the Spanish God of Food as Chemistry,
Ferran Adria at El Bulli. Ugly gels, powders that catch in the throat, a sea

of insipid foams. Who needs raisin paper on the plate when a raisin tastes so much better? Pouring melted chocolate over Gorgonzola isn't brilliant if it isn't edible.

Still the quality of product has never been better. Chefs demanding local produce and properly raised animals has led to better food in America's supermarkets and farmers' markets thriving. We're a nation of foodies now. Indeed, star chefs, the passion for fine products, the mission to find sustainable foods . . . that's global now.

Gael Greene on Gael Greene

My father told me I would be brilliant at whatever I decided to do and I guess I liked that idea. I never doubted him. So it wasn't merely a hope, it was a certainty, and once I realized art was not the path to fame and I wasn't beautiful enough to be a leading lady on stage or screen, it was clear that I would be a writer.

At seventeen I was ready to follow the Ernest Hemingway path to literary fame—I sat at a table at the Deux Magots on Paris's Left Bank and thought about what I would write when I was ready to write and concentrated most of the day on making the earth move.

Indeed, life and love and sensory adventure always seemed to come before actual work. As a newspaper reporter, I did have to pound the keys on deadline (torture) as well as report (a chance to socialize, compete, flirt), and a front page byline made it all worthwhile.

The truth is I hate to write. It is lonely and never stops being difficult. Writing was the price I had to pay for the glorious meals and the thrilling mingles in restaurants someone else was paying for, and the fun of defining the sociology of the beautiful people in the latest hot café. But when I began to receive praise from critics and readers, writing became even harder . . . there was no way I could ever be as brilliant again as I was last week.

Did I love writing? No, I loved having written. Did I love cooking? No, but I loved having cooked. The instant gratification of people laughing at a phrase or swooning over my dauphinoise potatoes and the mythic chocolate roll made a day's fevered chopping and mincing and whisking worthwhile. To write a book took forever. And then, what if no one liked it?

Even when my novel *Blue Skies, No Candy* became a bestseller and I needed to write another one fast, I chose la dolce vita; trying to write fiction summers between my increasingly glamorous life as *New York* magazine's restaurant critic and my increasingly astonishing sexual discoveries as a divorced woman in that wondrous moment between the pill and the plague.

Did I always choose the easy way? I cannot decide. Now that I've written my memoir and read it a few times, I realize I had vivid fantasies, and my strength was that I wasn't afraid to make them come true.